Nation and Narration

edited by

Homi K. Bhabha

Nation and Narration

London and New York

First published 1990
by Routledge
11 New Fetter Lane, London EC4P 4EE

Simultaneously published in the USA and Canada
by Routledge
29 West 35th Street, New York, NY 10001

Reprinted in 1993

Typeset in 10/11 Bem by Mayhew Typesetting, Bristol
Printed in England by
Clays Ltd, St Ives plc

British Library Cataloguing in Publication Data

Nation and narration.
1. English literature, critical studies
I. Bhabha, Homi
820.9

Library of Congress Cataloging in Publication Data

Nation and narration.
    Includes bibliographical references.
    1. Nationalism in literature.   2. Imperialism in
literature.   3. Politics and literature.   4. Literature,
Modern—History and criticism.   I. Bhabha, Homi K.

PN56.N19N38   1990   809′.93358   89–24051

ISBN 0–415–01483–2 pbk

ISBN 0–415–01482–4

Contents

Notes on contributors   vii

Acknowledgements   ix

1 **Introduction: narrating the nation**   1
Homi K. Bhabha

2 **What is a nation?**   8
Ernest Renan

3 **Tribes within nations: the ancient Germans and the history of modern France**   23
Martin Thom

4 **The national longing for form**   44
Timothy Brennan

5 **Irresistible romance: the foundational fictions of Latin America**   71
Doris Sommer

6 **Denaturalizing cultural nationalisms: multicultural readings of 'Australia'**   99
Sneja Gunew

7 **Postal politics and the institution of the nation**   121
Geoffrey Bennington

8 **Literature — Nationalism's other? The case for revision**   138
Simon During

9 **Sir Joshua Reynolds and the Englishness of English art**   154
John Barrell

10 **Destiny made manifest: the styles of Whitman's poetry**   177
David Simpson

11 **Breakfast in America — *Uncle Tom's* cultural histories**   197
Rachel Bowlby

12   Telescopic philanthropy: professionalism and
     responsibility in *Bleak House*   213
     Bruce Robbins

13   European pedigrees/African contagions: nationality,
     narrative, and communality in Tutuola, Achebe, and
     Reed   231
     James Snead

14   English reading   250
     Francis Mulhern

15   The island and the aeroplane: the case of Virginia Woolf   265
     Gillian Beer

16   DissemiNation: time, narrative, and the margins of the
     modern nation   291
     Homi K. Bhabha

     Index   323

Notes on contributors

John Barrell is Professor of English in the School of English and American Studies at the University of Sussex.

Gillian Beer is Professor of Literature and Narrative at the University of Cambridge and a Fellow of Girton College, Cambridge. Her publications include *Darwin's Plots* (1983), *George Eliot* (1986), and *Arguing with the Past* (1989).

Geoffrey Bennington is Senior Lecturer in French at Sussex University. He is author of *Sententiousness and the Novel* (1985), *Lyotard: Writing the Event* (1988), and of forthcoming books in French on Rousseau and Derrida.

Homi Bhabha is a lecturer in English at the University of Sussex. His collection of essays, *The Location of Culture*, is to be published by Routledge.

Rachel Bowlby teaches English at Sussex University. She is author of *Just Looking* (1985) on femininity, consumerism, and the novel, and *Virginia Woolf: Feminist Destinations* (1988).

Timothy Brennan currently teaches English and Comparative Literature at Purdue University and is a visiting professor at the University of Michigan. His publications include *Salman Rushdie and the Third World* (1989).

Simon During lectures in English at the University of Melbourne.

Sneja Gunew teaches in Literary Studies at Deakin University, Victoria, Australia. She has edited *Displacements: Migrant Storytellers*, *Displacements 2: Multicultural Storytellers*, and co-edited *Beyond the Echo: Multicultural Women's Writing* and *Telling Ways: Australian Women's Experimental Writing*.

Francis Mulhern teaches at Middlesex Polytechnic in north London. His publications include *The Moment of 'Scrutiny'*.

Bruce Robbins maintains a professional affiliation with the English Department of Rutgers University. He is the editor of *Intellectuals: Aesthetics, Politics, Academics* (forthcoming).

David Simpson is Professor of English at the University of Colorado, Boulder. His most recent books are *The Politics of American English, 1776–1850* (1986) and *Wordsworth's Historical Imagination: The Poetry of Displacement* (1987).

James Snead was, until his death in the spring of 1989, Associate Professor of English and Comparative Literature at the University of Pittsburgh. His publications include *Figures of Division: William Faulkner's Major Novels* (1987).

Doris Sommer, Professor of Romance Languages and Women's and Gender Studies at Amherst College, Massachusetts, has published on a variety of Latin American writers, and on Walt Whitman. She is also the author of *One Master for Another: Populism as Patriarchal Rhetoric in Dominican Novels* (1983).

Martin Thom is a translator and freelance writer, working at present on *Republics, Nations and Tribes: The Ancient City and the Modern World*, a study to be published by Verso.

Acknowledgements

My greatest debt is to my contributors whose response to an unusual idea was both creative and collaborative. There are others, less visible, who have made this book possible. The lively participation of students at Sussex University in my *Novel and Nation* seminar convinced me of the need for a volume of this nature. My colleagues at Sussex provide the kind of support and stimulation that is not easily found. Without the enthusiasm and advice of Janice Price at Routledge this project would never have got off the ground. On her own turf she combines the book-maker's racy instinct for what might be true but untried, with a rigorous determination to get it right. My editor Jane Armstrong was alive to the many possibilities of this volume and her opinion has been invaluable. Sarah Pearsall and Giuliana Baracco dealt with the production process in a way that was patient and forgiving. Above all I should like to thank James Donald, Stephen Feuchtwang and Robert Young for having listened and talked and read with such commitment that they turned my task into a common pursuit. James and Robert are editors' editors and they have generously contributed to 'cleaning up' the manuscript. Jacqueline Bhabha's work on immigration and refugee law emphasized the historical perspective of the diasporic and the homeless on the nation's story.

Amongst those of us who have shared in making this book, Jamie Snead has a special place that must now remain empty. At short notice, and in adverse circumstances, he agreed to write his essay. He sent it to me, shortly before he died of a long illness that he had kept private. It was then that I appreciated his true generosity. While honouring my deadline, Jamie was desperately involved in his own tragic race against time.

Homi K. Bhabha

Introduction: narrating the nation

Homi K. Bhabha

Nations, like narratives, lose their origins in the myths of time and only fully realize their horizons in the mind's eye. Such an image of the nation — or narration — might seem impossibly romantic and excessively meta-phorical, but it is from those traditions of political thought and literary language that the nation emerges as a powerful historical idea in the west. An idea whose cultural compulsion lies in the impossible unity of the nation as a symbolic force. This is not to deny the attempt by nationalist discourses persistently to produce the idea of the nation as a continuous narrative of national progress, the narcissism of self-generation, the primeval present of the *Volk*. Nor have such political ideas been definitively superseded by those new realities of internationalism, multi-nationalism, or even 'late capitalism', once we acknowledge that the rhetoric of these global terms is most often underwritten in that grim prose of power that each nation can wield within its own sphere of influence. What I want to emphasize in that large and liminal image of the nation with which I began is a particular ambivalence that haunts the idea of the nation, the language of those who write of it and the lives of those who live it. It is an ambivalence that emerges from a growing awareness that, despite the certainty with which historians speak of the 'origins' of nation as a sign of the 'modernity' of society, the cultural temporality of the nation inscribes a much more transitional social reality. Benedict Anderson, whose *Imagined Communities* significantly paved the way for this book, expresses the nation's ambivalent emergence with great clarity:

> The century of the Enlightenment, of rationalist secularism, brought with it its own modern darkness. . . . [Few] things were (are) suited to this end better than the idea of nation. If nation states are widely considered to be 'new' and 'historical', the nation states to which they give political expression always loom out of an immemorial past and . . . glide into a limitless future. What I am proposing is that Nationalism has to be understood, by aligning it not with self-consciously held political ideologies, but with large cultural systems that preceded it, out of which — as well as against which — it came into being. (19)

The nation's 'coming into being' as a system of cultural signification, as the representation of social *life* rather than the discipline of social *polity*, emphasizes this instability of knowledge. For instance, the most interesting accounts of the national idea, whether they come from the Tory Right, the Liberal high ground, or the New Left, seem to concur on the ambivalent tension that defines the 'society' of the nation. Michael Oakeshott's 'Character of a modern European state' is perhaps the most brilliant conservative account of the equivocal nature of the modern nation. The national space is, in his view, constituted from competing dispositions of human association as *societas* (the acknowledgement of moral rules and conventions of conduct) and *universitas* (the acknowledgement of common purpose and substantive end). In the absence of their merging into a new identity they have survived as competing dogmas — *societas cum universitate* — 'impos[ing] a particular ambivalence upon all the institutions of a modern state and a specific ambiguity upon its vocabulary of discourse'.[1] In Hannah Arendt's view, the society of the nation in the modern world is 'that curiously hybrid realm where private interests assume public significance' and the two realms flow unceasingly and uncertainly into each other 'like waves in the never-ending stream of the life-process itself'.[2] No less certain is Tom Nairn, in naming the nation 'the modern Janus', that the 'uneven development' of capitalism inscribes both progression and regression, political rationality and irrationality in the very genetic code of the nation. This is a structural fact to which there are no exceptions and 'in this sense, it is an exact (not a rhetorical) statement about nationalism to say that it is by nature ambivalent'.[3]

It is the cultural representation of this ambivalence of modern society that is explored in this book. If the ambivalent figure of the nation is a problem of its transitional history, its conceptual indeterminacy, its wavering between vocabularies, then what effect does this have on narratives and discourses that signify a sense of 'nationness': the *heimlich* pleasures of the hearth, the *unheimlich* terror of the space or race of the Other; the comfort of social belonging, the hidden injuries of class; the customs of taste, the powers of political affiliation; the sense of social order, the sensibility of sexuality; the blindness of bureaucracy, the strait insight of institutions; the quality of justice, the common sense of injustice; the *langue* of the law and the *parole* of the people.

The emergence of the political 'rationality' of the nation as a form of narrative — textual strategies, metaphoric displacements, sub-texts and figurative strategems — has its own history.[4] It is suggested in Benedict Anderson's view of the space and time of the modern nation as embodied in the narrative culture of the realist novel, and explored in Tom Nairn's reading of Enoch Powell's post-imperial racism which is based on the 'symbol-fetishism' that infests his febrile, neo-romantic poetry. To encounter the nation *as it is written* displays a temporality of culture and social consciousness more in tune with the partial, overdetermined process by which textual meaning is produced through the articulation of difference in language; more in keeping with the problem of closure which plays enigmatically in the discourse of the sign. Such an approach contests the traditional authority of those national objects of knowledge — Tradition, People, the Reason of State, High Culture, for instance — whose pedagogical value often relies on their representation as holistic concepts located within an evolutionary narrative of historical continuity. Traditional histories do not take the nation at its own word, but, for the most part, they do assume that the problem lies with the interpretation of 'events' that have a certain transparency or privileged visibility.

To study the nation through its narrative address does not merely draw attention to its language and rhetoric; it also attempts to alter the conceptual object itself. If the problematic 'closure' of textuality questions the 'totalization' of national culture, then its positive value lies in displaying the wide dissemination through which we construct the field of meanings and symbols associated with national life. This is a project that has a certain currency within those forms of critique associated with 'cultural studies'. Despite the considerable advance this represents, there is a tendency to read the Nation rather restrictively; either, as the ideological apparatus of state power, somewhat redefined by a hasty, functionalist reading of Foucault or Bakhtin; or, in a more utopian inversion, as the incipient or emergent expression of the 'national-popular' sentiment preserved in a radical memory. These approaches are valuable in drawing our attention to those easily obscured, but highly significant, recesses of the national culture from which alternative constituencies of peoples and oppositional analytic capacities may emerge — youth, the everyday, nostalgia, new 'ethnicities', new social movements, 'the politics of difference'. They assign new meanings and different directions to the process of historical change. The most progressive development from such positions take 'a *discursive* conception of ideology — ideology (like language) is conceptualised in terms of the articulation of elements. As Volosinov said, the ideological sign is always multi-accentual and Janus-faced'.[5] But in the heat of political argument the 'doubling' of the sign can often be stilled. The Janus face of ideology is taken at face value and its meaning fixed, in the last instance, on one side of the divide between ideology and 'material conditions'.

It is the project of *Nation and Narration* to explore the Janus-faced ambivalence of language itself in the construction of the Janus-faced discourse of the nation. This turns the familiar two-faced god into a figure of prodigious doubling that investigates the nation-space in the *process* of the articulation of elements: where meanings may be partial because they are *in medias res*; and history may be half-made because it is in the process of being made; and the image of cultural authority may be ambivalent because it is caught, uncertainly, in the act of 'composing' its powerful image. Without such an understanding of the performativity of language in the narratives of the nation, it would be difficult to understand why Edward Said prescribes a kind of 'analytic pluralism' as the *form* of critical attention appropriate to the cultural effects of the nation. For the nation, as a form of cultural *elaboration* (in the Gramscian sense), is an agency of *ambivalent* narration that holds culture at its most productive position, as a force for 'subordination, fracturing, diffusing, reproducing, as much as producing, creating, forcing, guiding'.[6]

I wrote to my contributors with a growing, if unfamiliar, sense of the nation as one of the major structures of ideological ambivalence within the cultural representations of 'modernity'. My intention was that we should develop, in a nice collaborative tension, a range of readings that engaged the insights of poststructuralist theories of narrative knowledge — textuality, discourse, enunciation, écriture, 'the unconscious as a language' to name only a few strategies — in order to evoke this ambivalent margin of the nation-space. To reveal such a margin is, in the first instance, to contest claims to cultural supremacy, whether these are made from the 'old' post-imperialist metropolitan nations, or on behalf of the 'new' independent nations of the periphery. The marginal or 'minority' is not the space of a celebratory, or utopian, self-marginalization. It is a much more substantial intervention into those justifications of modernity — progress, homogeneity, cultural organicism, the deep nation, the long past — that rationalize the authoritarian, 'normalizing' tendencies within cultures in the name of the national interest or the ethnic prerogative. In this sense, then, the ambivalent, antagonistic perspective of nation as narration will establish the cultural boundaries of the nation so that they may be acknowledged as 'containing' thresholds of meaning that must be crossed, erased, and translated in the process of cultural production.

The 'locality' of national culture is neither unified nor unitary in relation to itself, nor must it be seen simply as 'other' in relation to what is outside or beyond it. The boundary is Janus-faced and the problem of outside/inside must always itself be a process of hybridity, incorporating new 'people' in relation to the body politic, generating other sites of meaning and, inevitably, in the political process, producing unmanned sites of political antagonism and unpredictable forces for political representation. The address to nation as narration stresses the insistence of political power and cultural authority in what Derrida describes as the 'irreducible excess of the syntactic over the semantic'.[7] What emerges as an effect of such 'incomplete signification' is a turning of boundaries and limits into the *in-between* spaces through which the meanings of cultural and political authority are negotiated. It is from such narrative positions between cultures and nations, theories and texts, the political, the poetic and the painterly, the past and the present, that *Nation and Narration* seeks to affirm and extend Frantz Fanon's revolutionary credo: 'National consciousness, which is not nationalism, is the only thing that will give us an international dimension'.[8] It is this *inter*national dimension both within the margins of the nation-space and in the boundaries *in-between* nations and peoples that the authors of this book have sought to represent in their essays. The representative emblem of this book might be a chiasmatic 'figure' of cultural difference whereby the anti-nationalist, ambivalent nation-space becomes the crossroads to a new transnational culture. The 'other' is never outside or beyond us; it emerges forcefully, within cultural discourse, when we *think* we speak most intimately and indigenously 'between ourselves'.

Without attempting to précis individual essays, I would like briefly to elaborate this movement, within *Nation and Narration*, from the problematic unity of the nation to the articulation of cultural difference in the construction of an *inter*national perspective. The story could start in many places: with David Simpson's reading of the multiform 'body' of Whitman's American populism and his avoidance of metaphor which is also an avoidance of the problems of integration and cultural difference; or Doris Sommer's exploration of the language of love and productive sexuality that allegorizes and organizes the early historical narratives of Latin America which are disavowed by the later 'Boom' novelists; or John Barrell's exploration of the tensions between the civic humanist theory of painting and the 'discourse of custom' as they are drawn together in the ideology of the 'ornamental' in art, and its complex mediation of Englishness; or Sneja Gunew's portrayal of an Australian literature split between an Anglo-Celtic public sphere and a multiculturalist counter-public sphere. It is the excluded voices of migrants and the marginalized that Gunew represents, bringing them back to disturb and interrupt the writing of the Australian canon.

In each of these 'foundational fictions' the origins of national traditions turn out to be as much acts of affiliation and establishment as they are moments of disavowal, displacement, exclusion, and cultural contestation. In this function of national history as *Entstellung*, the forces of social antagonism or contradiction cannot be transcended or dialectically surmounted. There is a suggestion that the constitutive contradictions of the national text are discontinuous and 'interruptive'.[9] This is Geoff Bennington's starting point as he puns (with a certain postmodern prescience) on the '*post*al politics' of national frontiers to suggest that 'Frontiers are articulations, boundaries are, constitutively, crossed and transgressed'. It is across such boundaries, both historical and pedagogical, that Martin Thom places Renan's celebrated essay 'What is a nation?'. He provides a careful genealogy of the national idea as it emerges mythically from the Germanic tribes, and more recently in the interrelations between the struggle to consolidate the Third Republic and the emergence of Durkheimian sociology.

What kind of a cultural space is the nation with its transgressive boundaries and its 'interruptive' interiority? Each essay answers this question differently but there is a moment in Simon During's exposition of the 'civil imaginary' when he suggests that 'part of the modern domination of the life-world by style and civility . . . is a process of the *feminisation* of society'. This insight is explored in two very different contexts, Gillian Beer's reading of Virginia Woolf and Rachel Bowlby's study of *Uncle Tom's Cabin*. Gillian Beer takes the perspective of the aeroplane — war machine, dream symbol, icon of the 1930s poets — to emphasize Woolf's reflections on the island race, and space; its multiple marginal significations — 'land and water margins, home, body, individualism' — providing another inflection to her quarrels with patriarchy and imperialism. Rachel Bowlby writes the cultural history of readings of *Uncle Tom's Cabin*, that debate the feminization of American cultural values while producing a more complex interpretation of her own. The narrative of American freedom, she suggests, displays the same ambivalence that constructs the contradictory nature of femininity in the text. America itself becomes the dark continent, doubly echoing the 'image' of Africa and Freud's metaphor for feminine sexuality. George Harris, the former slave, leaves for the new African state of Liberia.

It is when the western nation comes to be seen, in Conrad's famous phrase, as one of the dark corners of the earth, that we can begin to explore new places from which to write histories of peoples and construct theories of narration. Each time the question of cultural difference emerges as a challenge to relativistic notions of the diversity of culture, it reveals the margins of modernity. As a result, most of these essays have ended up in another cultural location from where they started — often taking up a 'minority' position. Francis Mulhern's study of the 'English ethics' of Leavisian universalism pushes towards a reading of Q.D. Leavis's last public lecture in Cheltenham where she bemoans the imperilled state of that England which bore the classical English novel; an England, now, of council-house dwellers, unassimilated minorities, sexual emancipation without responsibility. Suddenly the paranoid system of 'English reading' stands revealed. James Snead ends his interrogation of the ethics and aesthetics of western 'nationalist' universalism with a reading of Ishmael Reed who 'is revising a prior co-optation of black culture, using a narrative principle that will undermine the very assumptions that brought the prior appropriation about'. Timothy Brennan produces a panoramic view of the western history of the national idea and its narrative forms, finally to take his stand with those hybridizing writers like Salman Rushdie whose glory and grotesquerie lie in their celebration of the fact that English is no longer an English language. This, as Brennan points out, leads to a more articulate awareness of the post-colonial and neo-colonial conditions as authoritative positions from which to speak Janus-faced to east and west. But these positions across the frontiers of history, culture, and language, which we have been exploring, are dangerous, if essential, political projects. Bruce Robbins' reading of Dickens balances the risks of departing from the 'ethical home truths' of humanistic experience with the advantages of developing a knowledge of acting in a dispersed global system. Our attention to 'aporia' he suggests, should be counterpointed with an intentionality that is inscribed in *poros* — practical, technical know-how that abjures the rationalism of universals, while maintaining the practicality, and political strategy, of dealing professionally with local situations that are themselves defined as liminal and borderline.

America leads to Africa; the nations of Europe and Asia meet in Australia; the margins of the nation displace the centre; the peoples of the periphery return to rewrite the history and fiction of the metropolis. The island story is told from the eye of the aeroplane which becomes that 'ornament' that holds the public and the private in suspense. The bastion of Englishness crumbles at the sight of immigrants and factory workers. The great Whitmanesque sensorium of America is exchanged for a

Warhol blowup, a Kruger installation, or Mapplethorpe's naked bodies. 'Magical realism' after the Latin American Boom, becomes the literary language of the emergent post-colonial world. Amidst these exorbitant images of the nation-space in its transnational dimension there are those who have not yet found their nation: amongst them the Palestinians and the Black South Africans. It is our loss that in making this book we were unable to add their voices to ours. Their persistent questions remain to remind us, in some form or measure, of what must be true for the rest of us too: 'When did we become "a people"? When did we stop being one? Or are we in the process of becoming one? What do these big questions have to do with our intimate relationships with each other and with others?'[10]

Notes

1 M. Oakeshott, *On Human Conduct* (Oxford: Oxford University Press, 1975), p. 201.
2 H. Arendt, *The Human Condition* (Chicago: Chicago University Press, 1958), pp. 33–5 and *passim*.
3 T. Nairn, *The Break-up of Britain* (London: Verso, 1981), p. 348.
4 Patrick Wright's *On Living in an Old Country* (London: Verso, 1985) and Paul Gilroy's *There Ain't No Black in the Union Jack* (London: Hutchinson, 1987) are significant recent contributions to such an approach.
5 S. Hall, *The Hard Road to Renewal* (London: Verso, 1988), p. 9.
6 E. Said, *The World, The Text and The Critic* (Cambridge, Mass.: Harvard University Press, 1983), p. 171.
7 J. Derrida, *Dissemination* (Chicago: Chicago University Press, 1981), p. 221.
8 F. Fanon, *The Wretched of the Earth* (Harmondsworth: Penguin, 1967), p. 199.
9 G. Spivak, *In Other Worlds* (London: Methuen, 1987), p. 251.
10 E. Said, *After the Last Sky* (London, Faber, 1986), p. 34.

2

What is a nation?[1]

Ernest Renan

(Translated and annotated by Martin Thom)

What I propose to do today is to analyse with you an idea which, though seemingly clear, lends itself to the most dangerous misunderstandings. [Consider] the vast agglomerations of men found in China, Egypt or ancient Babylonia, the tribes of the Hebrews and the Arabs, the city as it existed in Athens or Sparta, the assemblies of the various territories in the Carolingian Empire, those communities which are without a *patrie*[2] and are maintained by a religious bond alone, as is the case with the Israelites and the Parsees, nations, such as France, England and the majority of the modern European sovereign states, confederations, such as exist in Switzerland or in America, and ties, such as those that race, or rather language, establishes between the different branches of the German or Slav peoples. Each of these groupings exist, or have existed, and there would be the direst of consequences if one were to confuse any one of them with any other. At the time of the French Revolution, it was commonly believed that the institutions proper to small, independent cities, such as Sparta and Rome, might be applied to our large nations, which number some thirty or forty million souls. Nowadays, a far graver mistake is made: race is confused with nation and a sovereignty analogous to that of really existing peoples is attributed to ethnographic or, rather linguistic groups.

I want now to try and make these difficult questions somewhat more precise, for the slightest confusion regarding the meaning of words, at the start of an argument, may in the end lead to the most fatal of errors. It is a delicate thing that I propose to do here, somewhat akin to vivisection; I am going to treat the living much as one ordinarily treats the dead. I shall adopt an absolutely cool and impartial attitude.

I

Since the fall of the Roman Empire or, rather, since the disintegration of Charlemagne's empire, western Europe has seemed to us to be divided into nations, some of which, in certain epochs, have sought to wield a hegemony over the others, without ever enjoying any lasting success. It is hardly likely that anyone in the future will achieve what Charles V,

Louis XIV and Napoleon I failed to do. The founding of a new Roman Empire or of a new Carolingian empire would now be impossible. Europe is so divided that any bid for universal domination would very rapidly give rise to a coalition, which would drive any too ambitious nation back to its natural frontiers.[3] A kind of equilibrium has long been established. France, England, Germany and Russia will, for centuries to come, no matter what may befall them, continue to be individual historical units, the crucial pieces on a chequerboard whose squares will forever vary in importance and size but will never be wholly confused with each other.

Nations, in this sense of the term, are something fairly new in history. Antiquity was unfamiliar with them; Egypt, China and ancient Chaldea were in no way nations. They were flocks led by a Son of the Sun or by a Son of Heaven. Neither in Egypt nor in China were there citizens as such. Classical antiquity had republics, municipal kingdoms, confederations of local republics and empires, yet it can hardly be said to have had nations in our understanding of the term. Athens, Sparta, Tyre and Sidon were small centres imbued with the most admirable patriotism, but they were [simply] cities with a relatively restricted territory. Gaul, Spain and Italy, prior to their absorption by the Roman Empire, were collections of clans, which were often allied among themselves but had no central institutions and no dynasties. The Assyrian Empire, the Persian Empire and the empire of Alexander the Great were not *patries* either. There never were any Assyrian patriots, and the Persian Empire was nothing but a vast feudal structure. No nation traces its origins back to Alexander the Great's momentous adventure, fertile though it was in consequences for the general history of civilization.

The Roman Empire was much more nearly a *patrie*. Roman domination, although at first so harsh, was soon loved, for it had brought about the great benefit of putting an end to war. The empire was a huge association, and a synonym for order, peace and civilization. In its closing stages, lofty souls, enlightened bishops, and the educated classes had a real sense of the *Pax Romana*, which withstood the threatening chaos of barbarism. But an empire twelve times larger than present-day France cannot be said to be a state in the modern sense of the term. The split between the eastern and western [empires] was inevitable, and attempts at founding an empire in Gaul, in the third century AD, did not succeed either. It was in fact the Germanic invasions which introduced into the world the principle which, later, was to serve as a basis for the existence of nationalities.

What in fact did the German peoples accomplish, from their great invasions in the fifth century AD up until the final Norman conquests in the tenth century? They effected little change in the racial stock, but they imposed dynasties and a military aristocracy upon the more or less extensive parts of the old empire of the west, which assumed the names of their invaders. This was the origin of France, Burgundy, and Lombardy, and, subsequently, Normandy. The Frankish Empire so rapidly extended its sway that, for a period, it re-established the unity of the west, but it was irreparably shattered around the middle of the ninth century; the partition of Verdun[4] outlined divisions which were in principle immutable and, from then on, France, Germany, England, Italy, and Spain made their way, by often circuitous paths and through a thousand and one vicissitudes, to their full national existence, such as we see it blossoming today.

What in fact is the defining feature of these different states? It is the fusion of their component populations. In the above mentioned countries, there is nothing analogous to what you will find in Turkey, where Turks, Slavs, Greeks, Armenians, Arabs, Syrians, and Kurds are as distinct today as they were upon the day that they were conquered. Two crucial circumstances helped to bring about this result. First, the fact that the Germanic peoples adopted Christianity as soon as they underwent any prolonged contact with the Greek or Latin peoples. When conqueror or conquered have the same religion or, rather, when the conqueror adopts the religion of the conquered, the Turkish system — that is, the absolute distinction between men in terms of their religion — can no longer arise. The second circumstance was the forgetting, by the conquerors, of their own language. The grandsons of Clovis, Alaric, Gundebald, Alboin, and Roland were already speaking the Roman tongue. This fact was itself the consequence of another important feature, namely, the fact that the Franks, Burgundians, Goths, Lombards, and Normans had very few women of their own race with them. For several generations, the chiefs only married German women; but their concubines were Latin, as were the wet-nurses of their children; the tribe as a whole married Latin women; which meant that, from the time the Franks and the Goths established themselves on Roman territory, the *lingua francica* and the *lingua gothica* did not last too long.

This was not how it was in England, for the invading Saxons undoubtedly brought women with them; the Celtic population took flight, and, besides, Latin was no longer, or rather had never been, dominant in Britain. If Old French had been generally spoken in Gaul in the fifth century Clovis and his people would not have abandoned German for Old French.

The crucial result of all this was that, in spite of the extreme violence of the customs of the German invaders, the mould which they imposed became, with the passing centuries, the actual mould of the nation. 'France' became quite legitimately the name of a country to which only a virtually imperceptible minority of Franks had come. In the tenth century, in the first *chansons de geste*, which are such a perfect mirror of the spirit of the times, all the inhabitants of France are French. The idea, which had seemed so obvious to Gregory of Tours,[5] that the population of France was composed of different races, was in no way apparent to French writers and poets after Hugh Capet. The difference between noble and serf was as sharply drawn as possible, but it was in no sense presented as an ethnic difference; it was presented rather as a difference in courage, customs, and education, all of which were transmitted hereditarily; it did not occur to anyone that the origin of all this was a conquest. The spurious system according to which nobility owed its origin to a privilege conferred by the king for services rendered to the nation, so that every noble was an ennobled person, was established as a dogma as early as the thirteenth century. The same thing took place after almost all the Norman conquests. After one or two generations, the Norman invaders no longer distinguished themselves from the rest of the population, although their influence was not any less profound because of this fact; they had given the conquered country a nobility, military habits, and a patriotism that they had not known before.

Forgetting, I would even go so far as to say historical error, is a crucial factor in the creation of a nation, which is why progress in historical studies often constitutes a danger for [the principle of] nationality. Indeed, historical enquiry brings to light deeds of violence which took place at the origin of all political formations, even of those whose consequences have been altogether beneficial. Unity is always effected by means of brutality; the union of northern France with the Midi was the result of massacres and terror lasting for the best part of a century. Though the king of France was, if I may make so bold as to say, almost the perfect instance of an agent that crystallized [a nation] over a long period; though he established the most perfect national unity that there has ever been, too searching a scrutiny had destroyed his prestige. The nation which he had formed has cursed him, and, nowadays, it is only men of culture who know something of his former value and of his achievements.

It is [only] by contrast that these great laws of the history of western Europe become perceptible to us. Many countries failed to achieve what the King of France, partly through his tyranny, partly through his justice, so admirably brought to fruition. Under the Crown of Saint Stephen, the Magyars and the Slavs have remained as distinct as they were 800 years ago. Far from managing to fuse the diverse [ethnic] elements to be found in its domains, the House of Hapsburg has kept them distinct and often opposed the one to the other. In Bohemia [for instance], the Czech and German elements are superimposed, much like oil and water in a glass. The Turkish policy of separating nationalities according to their religion has had much graver consequences, for it brought about the downfall of the east. If you take a city such as Salonika or Smyrna, you will find there five or six communities each of which has its own memories and which have almost nothing in common. Yet the essence of a nation is that all individuals have many things in common, and also that they have forgotten many things. No French citizen knows whether he is a Burgundian, an Alan, a Taifale, or a Visigoth, yet every French citizen has to have forgotten the massacre of Saint Bartholomew,[6] or the massacres that took place in the Midi in the thirteenth century. There are not ten families in France that can supply proof of their Frankish origin, and any such proof would anyway be essentially flawed, as a consequence of countless unknown alliances which are liable to disrupt any genealogical system.

The modern nation is therefore a historical result brought about by a series of convergent facts. Sometimes unity has been effected by a dynasty, as was the case in France; sometimes it has been brought about by the direct will of provinces, as was the case with Holland, Switzerland, and Belgium; sometimes it has been the work of a general consciousness, belatedly victorious over the caprices of feudalism, as was the case in Italy and Germany. These formations always had a profound *raison d'être*. Principles, in such cases, always emerge through the most unexpected surprises. Thus, in our own day, we have seen Italy unified through its defeats and Turkey destroyed by its victories. Each defeat advanced the cause of Italy; each victory spelled doom for Turkey; for Italy is a nation, and Turkey, outside of Asia Minor, is not one. France can claim the glory for having, through the French Revolution, proclaimed that a nation exists of itself. We should not be displeased if others imitate us in this. It was we who founded the principle of nationality. But what is a nation? Why is Holland a nation, when Hanover, or the Grand Duchy of Parma, are not? How is it that France continues to be a nation, when the principle which created it has disappeared? How is it that Switzerland, which has three languages, two religions, and three or four races, is a nation, when Tuscany, which is so homogeneous, is not one? Why is Austria a state and not a nation? In what ways does the principle of nationality differ from that of races? These are points that a thoughtful person would wish to have settled, in order to put his mind at rest. The affairs of this world can hardly be said to be ruled by reasonings of this sort, yet diligent men are desirous of bringing some reason into these matters and of unravelling the confusions in which superficial intelligences are entangled.

II

If one were to believe some political theorists, a nation is above all a dynasty, representing an earlier conquest, one which was first of all accepted, and then forgotten by the mass of the people. According to the above-mentioned theorists, the grouping of provinces effected by a dynasty, by its wars, its marriages, and its treaties, ends with the dynasty which had established it. It is quite true that the majority of modern nations were made by a family of feudal origin, which had contracted a marriage with the soil and which was in some sense a nucleus of centralization. France's frontiers in 1789 had nothing either natural or necessary about them. The wide zone that the House of Capet had added to the narrow strip of land granted by the partition of Verdun was indeed the personal acquisition of this House. During the epoch when these acquisitions were made, there was no idea of natural frontiers, nor of the rights of nations, nor of the will of provinces. The union of England, Ireland, and Scotland was likewise a dynastic fact. Italy only tarried so long before becoming a nation because, among its numerous reigning houses, none, prior to the present century, constituted itself as the centre of [its] unity, Strangely enough, it was through the obscure island of Sardinia, a land that was scarcely Italian, that [the house of Savoy] assumed a royal title.[7] Holland, which — through an act of heroic resolution — created itself, has nevertheless contracted an intimate marriage with the House of Orange, and it will run real dangers the day this union is compromised.

Is such a law, however, absolute? It undoubtedly is not. Switzerland and the United States, which have formed themselves, like conglomerates, by successive additions, have no dynastic basis. I shall not discuss this question in relation to France, for I would need to be able to read the secrets of the future in order to do so. Let me simply say that so loftily national had this great French royal principle been that, on the morrow of its fall, the nation was able to stand without her. Furthermore, the eighteenth century had changed everything. Man had returned, after centuries of abasement, to the spirit of antiquity, to [a sense of] respect for himself, to the idea of his own rights. The words *patrie* and citizen had recovered their former meanings. Thus it was that the boldest operation ever yet put into effect in history was brought to completion, an operation which one might compare with the attempt, in physiology, to restore to its original identity a body from which one had removed the brain and the heart.

It must therefore be admitted that a nation can exist without a dynastic principle, and even that nations which have been formed by dynasties can be separated from them without therefore ceasing to exist. The old principle, which only takes account of the right of princes, could no longer be maintained; apart from dynastic right, there is also national right. Upon what criterion, however, should one base this national right? By what sign should one know it? From what tangible fact can one derive it?

Several confidently assert that it is derived from race. The artificial divisions, resulting from feudalism, from princely marriages, from diplomatic congresses are, [these authors assert], in a state of decay. It is a population's race which remains firm and fixed. This is what constitutes a right, a legitimacy. The Germanic family, according to the theory I am expounding here, has the right to reassemble the scattered limbs of the Germanic order, even when these limbs are not asking to be joined together again. The right of the Germanic order over such-and-such a province is stronger than the right of the inhabitants of that province over themselves. There is thus created a kind of primordial right analogous to the divine right of kings; an ethnographic principle is substituted for a national one. This is a very great error, which, if it were to become dominant, would destroy European civilization. The primordial right of races is as narrow and as perilous for genuine progress as the national principle is just and legitimate.

In the tribes and cities of antiquity, the fact of race was, I will allow, of very real importance. The tribe and the city were then merely extensions of the family. At Sparta and at Athens all the citizens were kin to a greater or lesser degree. The same was true of the Beni-Israelites; this is still the case with the Arab tribes. If we move now from Athens, Sparta, and the Israelite tribe to the Roman Empire the situation is a wholly different one. Established at first through violence but subsequently preserved through [common] interest, this great agglomeration of cities and provinces, wholly different from each other, dealt the gravest of blows to the idea of race. Christianity, with its universal and absolute character, worked still more effectively in the same direction; it formed an intimate alliance with the Roman Empire and, through the impact of these two incomparable unificatory agents, the ethnographic argument was debarred from the government of human affairs for centuries.

The barbarian invasions were, appearances notwithstanding, a further step along this same path. The carving out of the barbarian kingdoms had nothing ethnographic about them, their [shape] was determined by the might or whim of the invaders. They were utterly indifferent to the race of the populations which they had subdued. What Rome had fashioned, Charlemagne refashioned in his own way, namely, a single empire composed of the most diverse races; those responsible for the partition of Verdun, as they calmly drew their two long lines from north to south, were not in the slightest concerned with the race of the peoples to be found on the right or left of these lines. Frontier changes put into effect, as the Middle Ages wore on, likewise paid no heed to ethnographic divisions. If the policies pursued by the House of Capet by and large resulted in the grouping together, under the name of France, of the territories of ancient Gaul, this was only because these lands had a natural tendency to be joined together with their fellows. Dauphiné, Bresse, Provence, and Franche-Comté no longer recalled any common origin. All Gallic consciousness had perished by the second century AD, and it is only from a purely scholarly perspective that, in our own days, the individuality of the Gallic character has been retrospectively recovered.

Ethnographic considerations have therefore played no part in the constitution of modern nations. France is [at once] Celtic, Iberic, and Germanic. Germany is Germanic, Celtic and Slav. Italy is the country where the ethnographic argument is most confounded. Gauls, Etruscans, Pelasgians,[8] and Greeks, not to mention many other elements, intersect in an indecipherable mixture. The British isles, considered as a whole, present a mixture of Celtic and Germanic blood, the proportions of which are singularly difficult to define.

The truth is that there is no pure race and that to make politics depend upon ethnographic analysis is to surrender it to a chimera. The noblest countries, England, France, and Italy, are those where the blood is the most mixed. Is Germany an exception in this respect? Is it a purely Germanic country? This is a complete illusion. The whole of the south was once Gallic; the whole of the east, from the river Elbe on, is Slav. Even those parts which are claimed to be really pure, are they in fact so? We touch here on one of those problems in regard to which it is of the utmost importance that we equip ourselves with clear ideas and ward off misconceptions.

Discussions of race are interminable, because philologically-minded historians and physiologically-minded anthropologists interpret the term in two totally different ways.[9] For the anthropologists, race has the same meaning as in zoology; it serves to indicate real descent, a blood relation. However, the study of language and of history does not lead to the same divisions as does physiology. Words such as brachycephalic or dolichocephalic have no place in either history or philology. In the human group which created the Aryan languages and way of life, there were already [both] brachycephalics and dolichocephalics. The same is true of the primitive group which created the languages and institutions known as Semitic. In other words, the zoological origins of humanity are massively prior to the origins of culture, civilization, and language. The primitive Aryan, primitive Semitic, and primitive Touranian groups had no physiological unity. These groupings are historical facts, which took place in a particular epoch, perhaps 15,000 or 20,000 years ago, while the zoological origin of humanity is lost in impenetrable darkness. What is known philologically and historically as the Germanic race is no doubt a quite distinct family within the human species, but is it a family in the anthropological sense of the term? Certainly not. The emergence of an individual Germanic identity occurred only a few centuries prior to Jesus Christ. One may take it that the Germans did not emerge from the earth at this epoch. Prior to this, mingled with the Slavs in the huge indistinct mass of the Scythians, they did not have their own separate individuality. An Englishman is indeed a type within the whole of humanity. However, the type of what is quite improperly called the Anglo-Saxon race[10] is neither the Briton of Julius Caesar's time, nor the Anglo-Saxon of Hengist's time, nor the Dane of Canute's time, nor the Norman of William the Conqueror's time; it is rather the result of all these [elements]. A Frenchman is neither a Gaul, nor a Frank, nor a Burgundian. Rather, he is what has emerged out of the cauldron in which, presided over by the King of France, the most diverse elements have together been simmering. A native of Jersey or Guernsey differs in no way, as far as his origins are concerned, from the Norman population of the opposite coast. In the eleventh century, even the sharpest eye would have seen not the slightest difference in those living on either side of the Channel. Trifling circumstances meant that Philip Augustus did not seize these islands together with the rest of Normandy. Separated from each other for the best part of 700 years, the two populations have become not only strangers to each other but wholly dissimilar. Race, as we historians understand it, is therefore something which is made and unmade. The study of race is of crucial importance for the scholar concerned with the history of humanity. It has no applications, however, in politics. The instinctive consciousness which presided over the construction of the map of Europe took no account of race, and the leading nations of Europe are nations of essentially mixed blood.

The fact of race, which was originally crucial, thus becomes increasingly less important. Human history is essentially different from zoology, and race is not everything, as it is among the rodents or the felines, and one does not have the right to go through the world fingering people's skulls, and taking them by the throat saying: 'You are of our blood; you belong to us!' Aside from anthropological characteristics, there are such things as reason, justice, the true, and the beautiful, which are the same for all. Be on your guard, for this ethnographic politics is in no way a stable thing and, if today you use it against others, tomorrow you may see it turned against yourselves. Can you be sure that the Germans, who have raised the banner of ethnography so high, will not see the Slavs in their turn analyse the names of villages in Saxony and Lusatia, search for any traces of the Wiltzes or of the Obotrites, and demand recompense for the massacres and the wholesale enslavements that the Ottoss inflicted upon their ancestors? It is good for everyone to know how to forget.

I am very fond of ethnography, for it is a science of rare interest; but, in so far as I would wish it to be free, I wish it to be without political application. In ethnography, as in all forms of study, systems change; this is the condition of progress. States' frontiers would then follow the fluctuations of science. Patriotism would depend upon a more or less paradoxical dissertation. One would come up to a patriot and say: 'You were mistaken; you shed your blood for such-and-such a cause; you believed yourself to be a Celt; not at all, you are a German.' Then, ten years later, you will be told that you are a Slav. If we are not to distort science, we should exempt it from the need to give an opinion on these problems, in which so many interests are involved. You can be sure that, if one obliges science to furnish diplomacy with its first principles, one will surprise her many times in *flagrant délit*. She has better things to do; let us simply ask her to tell the truth.

What we have just said of race applies to language too. Language invites people to unite, but it does not force them to do so. The United States and England, Latin America and Spain, speak the same languages yet do not form single nations. Conversely, Switzerland, so well made, since she was made with the consent of her different parts, numbers three or four languages. There is something in man which is superior to language, namely, the will. The will of Switzerland to be united, in spite of the diversity of her dialects, is a fact of far greater importance than a similitude often obtained by various vexatious measures.

An honourable fact about France is that she has never sought to win unity of language by coercive measures. Can one not have the same sentiments and the same thoughts, and love the same things in different languages? I was speaking just now of the disadvantages of making international politics depend upon ethnography; they would be no less if one were to make it depend upon comparative philology. Let us allow these intriguing studies full freedom of discussion; let us not mix them up with matters which would undermine their serenity. The political importance attaching to languages derives from their being regarded as signs of race. Nothing could be more false. Prussia, where only German is now spoken, spoke Slav a few centuries ago; in Wales, English is spoken; Gaul and Spain speak the primitive dialects of Alba Longa; Egypt speaks Arabic; there are countless other examples one could quote. Even if you go back to origins, similarity of language did not presuppose similarity of race. Consider, for example the proto-Aryan or proto-Semitic tribe: there one found slaves speaking the same language as their masters, and yet the slave was often enough a different race to that of his master. Let me repeat that these divisions of the Indo-European, Semitic, or other languages, created with such admirable sagacity by comparative philology, do not coincide with the divisions established by anthropology. Languages are historical formations, which tell us very little about the blood of those who speak them and which, in any case, could not shackle human liberty when it is a matter of deciding the family with which one unites oneself for life or for death.

This exclusive concern with language, like an excessive preoccupation with race, has its dangers and its drawbacks. Such exaggerations enclose one within a specific culture, considered as national; one limits oneself, one hems oneself in. One leaves the heady air that one breathes in the vast field of humanity in order to enclose oneself in a conventicle with one's compatriots. Nothing could be worse for the mind; nothing could be more disturbing for civilization. Let us not abandon the fundamental principle that man is a reasonable and moral being, before he is cooped up in such and such a language, before he is a member of such and such a race, before he belongs to such and such a culture. Before French, German, or Italian culture there is human culture. Consider the great men of the Renaissance; they were neither French, nor Italian, nor German. They had rediscovered, through their dealings with antiquity, the secret of the genuine education of the human spirit, and they devoted themselves to it body and soul. What an achievement theirs was!

Religion cannot supply an adequate basis for the constitution of a modern nationality either. Originally, religion had to do with the very existence of the social group, which was itself an extension of the family. Religion and the rites were family rites. The religion of Athens was the cult of Athens itself, of its mythical founders, of its laws and its customs; it implied no theological dogma. This religion was, in the strongest sense of the term, a state religion. One was not an Athenian if one refused to practise it. This religion was, fundamentally, the cult of the Acropolis personified. To swear on the altar of Aglauros[11] was to swear that one would die for the *patrie*. This religion was the equivalent of what the act of drawing lots [for military service], or the cult of the flag, is for us. Refusing to take part in such a cult would be the equivalent, in our modern societies, of refusing military service. It would be like declaring that one was not Athenian. From another angle, it is clear that such a cult had no meaning for someone who was not from Athens; there was also no attempt made to proselytize foreigners and to force them to accept it; the slaves of Athens did not practise it. Things were much the same in a number of small medieval republics. One was not considered a good Venetian if one did not swear by Saint Mark; nor a good Amalfitan if one did not set Saint Andrew higher than all the other saints in paradise. In these small societies, what subsequently was regarded as persecution or tyranny was legitimate and was of no more consequence than our custom of wishing the father of a family happy birthday or a Happy New Year.

The state of affairs in Sparta and in Athens already no longer existed in the kingdoms which emerged from Alexander's conquest, still less in the Roman Empire. The persecutions unleashed by Antiochus Epiphanes in order win the east for the cult of Jupiter Olympus, those of the Roman Empire designed to maintain a supposed state religion were mistaken, criminal, and absurd. In our own time, the situation is perfectly clear. There are no longer masses that believe in a perfectly uniform manner. Each person believes and practises in his own fashion what he is able to and as he wishes. There is no longer a state religion; one can be French, English, or German, and be either Catholic, Protestant, or orthodox Jewish, or else practise no cult at all. Religion has become an individual matter; it concerns the conscience of each person. The division of nations into Catholics and Protestants no longer exists. Religion, which, fifty-two years ago, played so substantial a part in the formation of Belgium, preserves all of its [former] importance in the inner tribunal of each; but it has ceased almost entirely to be one of the elements which serve to define the frontiers of peoples.

A community of interest is assuredly a powerful bond between men. Do interests, however, suffice to make a nation? I do not think so. Community of interest brings about trade agreements, but nationality has a sentimental side to it; it is both soul and body at once; a Zollverein[12] is not a patrie.

Geography, or what are known as natural frontiers, undoubtedly plays a considerable part in the division of nations. Geography is one of the crucial factors in history. Rivers have led races on; mountains have brought them to a halt. The former have favoured movement in history, whereas the latter have restricted it. Can one say, however, that as some parties believe, a nation's frontiers are written on the map and that this nation has the right to judge what is necessary to round off certain contours, in order to reach such and such a mountain and such and such a river, which are thereby accorded a kind of a priori limiting faculty? I know of no doctrine which is more arbitrary or more fatal, for it allows one to justify any or every violence. First of all, is it the mountains or the rivers that we should regard as forming these so-called natural frontiers? It is indisputable that the mountains separate, but the rivers tend rather to unify. Moreover, all mountains cannot divide up states. Which serve to separate and which do not? From Biarritz to Tornea, there is no one estuary which is more suited than any other to serving as a boundary marker. Had history so decreed it, the Loire, the Seine, the Meuse, the Elbe, or the Oder could, just as easily as the Rhine, have had this quality of being a natural frontier, such as has caused so many infractions of the most fundamental right, which is men's will. People talk of strategic grounds. Nothing, however, is absolute; it is quite clear than many concessions should be made to necessity. But these concessions should not be taken too far. Otherwise, everybody would lay claim to their military conveniences, and one would have unceasing war. No, it is no more soil than it is race which makes a nation. The soil furnishes the substratum, the field of struggle and of labour; man furnishes the soul. Man is everything in the formation of this sacred thing which is called a people. Nothing [purely] material suffices for it. A nation is a spiritual principle, the outcome of the profound complications of history; it is a spiritual family not a group determined by the shape of the earth. We have now seen what things are not adequate for the creation of such a spiritual principle, namely, race, language, material interest, religious affinities, geography, and military necessity. What more then is required? As a consequence of what was said previously, I will not have to detain you very much longer.

III

A nation is a soul, a spiritual principle. Two things, which in truth are but one, constitute this soul or spiritual principle. One lies in the past, one in the present. One is the possession in common of a rich legacy of memories; the other is present-day consent, the desire to live together, the will to perpetuate the value of the heritage that one has received in an undivided form. Man, Gentlemen, does not improvise. The nation, like the individual, is the culmination of a long past of endeavours, sacrifice, and devotion. Of all cults, that of the ancestors is the most legitimate, for the ancestors have made us what we are. A heroic past, great men, glory (by which I understand genuine glory), this is the social capital upon which one bases a national idea. To have common glories in the past and to have a common will in the present; to have performed great deeds together, to wish to perform still more — these are the essential conditions for being a people. One loves in proportion to the sacrifices to which one has consented, and in proportion to the ills that one has suffered. One loves the house that one has built and that one has handed down. The Spartan song — 'We are what you were; we will be what you are'[13] — is, in its simplicity, the abridged hymn of every *patrie*.

More valuable by far than common customs posts and frontiers conforming to strategic ideas is the fact of sharing, in the past, a glorious heritage and regrets, and of having, in the future, [a shared] programme to put into effect, or the fact of having suffered, enjoyed, and hoped together. These are the kinds of things that can be understood in spite of differences of race and language. I spoke just now of 'having suffered together' and, indeed, suffering in common unifies more than joy does. Where national memories are concerned, griefs are of more value than triumphs, for they impose duties, and require a common effort.

A nation is therefore a large-scale solidarity, constituted by the feeling of the sacrifices that one has made in the past and of those that one is prepared to make in the future. It presupposes a past; it is summarized, however, in the present by a tangible fact, namely, consent, the clearly expressed desire to continue a common life. A nation's existence is, if you will pardon the metaphor, a daily plebiscite, just as an individual's existence is a perpetual affirmation of life. That, I know full well, is less metaphysical than divine right and less brutal than so-called historical right. According to the ideas that I am outlining to you, a nation has no more right than a king does to say to a province: 'You belong to me, I am seizing you.' A province, as far as I am concerned, is its inhabitants;

if anyone has the right to be consulted in such an affair, it is the inhabitant. A nation never has any real interest in annexing or holding on to a country against its will. The wish of nations is, all in all, the sole legitimate criterion, the one to which one must always return.

We have driven metaphysical and theological abstractions out of politics. What then remains? Man, with his desires and his needs. The secession, you will say to me, and, in the long term, the disintegration of nations will be the outcome of a system which places these old organisms at the mercy of wills which are often none too enlightened. It is clear that, in such matters, no principle must be pushed too far. Truths of this order are only applicable as a whole in a very general fashion. Human wills change, but what is there here below that does not change? The nations are not something eternal. They had their beginnings and they will end. A European confederation will very probably replace them. But such is not the law of the century in which we are living. At the present time, the existence of nations is a good thing, a necessity even. Their existence is the guarantee of liberty, which would be lost if the world had only one law and only one master.

Through their various and often opposed powers, nations participate in the common work of civilization; each sounds a note in the great concert of humanity, which, after all, is the highest ideal reality that we are capable of attaining. Isolated, each has its weak point. I often tell myself that an individual who had those faults which in nations are taken for good qualities, who fed off vainglory, who was to that degree jealous, egotistical, and quarrelsome, and who would draw his sword on the smallest pretext, would be the most intolerable of men. Yet all these discordant details disappear in the overall context. Poor humanity, how you have suffered! How many trials still await you! May the spirit of wisdom guide you, in order to preserve you from the countless dangers with which your path is strewn!

Let me sum up, Gentlemen. Man is a slave neither of his race nor his language, nor of his religion, nor of the course of rivers nor of the direction taken by mountain chains. A large aggregate of men, healthy in mind and warm of heart, creates the kind of moral conscience which we call a nation. So long as this moral consciousness gives proof of its strength by the sacrifices which demand the abdication of the individual to the advantage of the community, it is legitimate and has the right to exist. If doubts arise regarding its frontiers, consult the populations in the areas under dispute. They undoubtedly have the right to a say in the matter. This recommendation will bring a smile to the lips of the transcendants of politics, these infallible beings who spend their lives deceiving themselves and who, from the height of their superior principles, take pity upon our mundane concerns. 'Consult the populations, for heaven's sake! How naive! A fine example of those wretched French ideas which claim to replace diplomacy and war by childishly simple methods.' Wait a while, Gentlemen; let the reign of the transcendants pass; bear the scorn of the powerful with patience. It may be that, after many fruitless gropings, people will revert to our more modest empirical solutions. The best way of being right in the future is, in certain periods, to know how to resign oneself to being out of fashion.

Notes

(Notes followed by an asterisk are the translator's.)

1* A lecture delivered at the Sorbonne, 11 March 1882. 'Qu'est-ce qu'une nation?', *Oeuvres Complètes* (Paris, 1947—61), vol. I, pp. 887—907. An earlier translation, which I have consulted, is in A. Zimmern (ed.), *Modern Political Doctrines* (London, 1939), pp. 186—205.

2* I have left *patrie* in the original French because it seems to me that to translate it into another European (or, indeed, non-European) language would be to eliminate the kinds of association the term had, in a very large number of countries, throughout the epoch of liberal-democratic nationalism. *Patrie* draws with it a whole cluster of complex and interlocking references to the values of the *patria* of classical republicanism. For an observer like Marx, these values were destroyed forever in the black farce of 1848. In another sense, as Marx's arguments in *The Eighteenth Brumaire* allow, they continued to influence the leaders of liberal, nationalist revolutions throughout the nineteenth century — although, obviously, if one were to phrase it in Italian terms, the Cavourian moderate rather than the Mazzinian or Garibaldian radical wing. It may be worth noting that, in the domain of scholarship, Fustel de Coulanges' *The Ancient City* (1864), a study which profoundly influenced Emile Durkheim and which Renan himself had very probably read, shattered the vision of classical republicanism which men such as Robespierre and Saint-Just had entertained.

3* The doctrine of natural frontiers was given its definitive formulation in the course of the French Revolution, and was subsequently applied to other European countries, such as Germany or Italy; it was this doctrine that fuelled the irredentist movements of the second half of the nineteenth century. Justification of territorial claims often rested upon the interpretation of classical texts, such as Tacitus's *Germania* or Dante's *Commedia*.

4* The partition of Verdun (AD 843) ended a period of civil war within the Frankish Empire, during which the grandsons of Charlemagne had fought each other. Two of the newly created kingdoms, that of Charles the Bald (843—77) and that of Louis the German (843—76), bear some resemblance, in territorial terms, to modern France and modern Germany. Furthermore, much has been made of the linguistic qualities of the Oaths of Strasbourg, sworn by Louis and Charles to each other's armies, in Old French and Old High German respectively. This has often been regarded as the first text in a Romance language (as distinct from Latin) and, by extension, as the first symbolic appearance of the French (and German) nations.

5* Gregory of Tours (*c.* 539—94) was a Gallo-Roman and Bishop of Tours from 573 to 594. His *History of the Franks* is an account of life in Merovingian Gaul.

6* Upon the occasion of the massacre of Saint Bartholomew, in 1572, many thousands of Huguenots were killed. This was an event with momentous repercussions for the history of France in general, and for the development of political theory in particular.

7 The House of Savoy owes its royal title to its acquisition of Sardinia (1720).

8* The Pelasgians were believed, in the eighteenth and nineteenth centuries, to have been the original inhabitants of Italy.

9   I enlarged upon this point in a lecture, which is analysed in the Bulletin of the *Association scientifique de France*, 10 March 1878, 'Des services rendus aux Sciences historiques par la Philologie'.

10 Germanic elements are not more considerable in the United Kingdom than when they were in France, when she had possession of Alsace and Metz. If the Germanic language has dominated in the British isles, it was simply because Latin had not wholly replaced the Celtic languages, as it had done in Gaul.

11 Aglauros, who gave her life to save her *patrie*, represents the Acropolis itself.

12★ *Zollverein* is the German word for customs union. Both participants in bourgeois, national revolutions and later commentators emphasize the relation between the nationalist cause and free trade within a single territory. However, E.J. Hobsbawm's comments, on pp. 166—8 of *The Age of Revolution* (London, 1962), shed some light upon Renan's aphorism, in that the vanguard of European nationalism in the 1830s and 1840s was not so much the business class as 'the lower and middle professional, administrative and intellectual strata, in other words, the educated classes'. At another level, Renan's observation reflects his shock at the defeat of France by Prussia in the Franco-Prussian war, which is expressed in both major and occasional writings.

13★ Such epitaphs were part of the habitual repertoire of early-nineteenth-century nationalism, as Leopardi's 'patriotic' *canzoni* make plain.

3

Tribes within nations: the ancient Germans and the history of modern France

Martin Thom

The central argument of 'What is a nation?', a lecture delivered by Ernest Renan at the Sorbonne in 1882, is perfectly clear. 'His main purpose', Ernest Gellner has observed,

> is to deny any naturalistic determinism of the boundaries of nations: these are *not* dictated by language, geography, race, religion, or anything else. He clearly dislikes the spectacle of nineteenth-century ethnographers as advance guards of national claims and expansion. Nations are made by human will. . . .[1]

A deeper understanding of Renan's position in 1882 would require an analysis of the polemical debate between French, German, English, and Italian scholars and politicians, in the aftermath of the Franco-Prussian War, regarding the disputed title to Alsace and Lorraine, territories which Louis XIV had seized and which the Treaty of Frankfurt had returned to Germany in 1871.[2] I lack the space to develop this analysis here and wish merely to observe that Renan, as inspection of his earlier writings would show, was less committed to the 'voluntaristic' argument than his lecture suggests.[3]

My concern in the present essay is with his subsidiary argument, namely, that 'it was ... the Germanic invasions which introduced into the world the principle which, later, was to serve as a basis for the existence of nationalities' (Renan, 1882).

Countless studies of French history, from the sixteenth century onwards, rested their interpretation upon either a 'Germanist' or a 'Romanist' attitude to the early Middle Ages. Renan himself was deeply committed to a Germanist approach, as the title of a study by Georges Sorel, '[The] Germanism and historicism of Ernest Renan', makes clear.[4]

Those who are familiar with English history will know of the rhetoric regarding the Norman yoke, and will recall how often, across the centuries, the Anglo-Saxons have been depicted as the true English nation. It may help the reader to grasp how an early tribal people, such as the Franks, could have such symbolic importance in French politics, if it is borne in mind that they too, like the Angles and Saxons, invaded in the fifth century AD. The real or imaginary status of this invasion is in part the topic of the present essay.

Before I begin to investigate Renan's claims regarding the importance of the barbarian invasions of the fifth and sixth centuries AD, it may be worth noting that our information regarding the ancient Germans and their social and political identity is extremely scanty. There is the additional problem that the various sources extant cover the best part of a millennium. For the earlier period, there is Caesar's *On the Gallic Wars*, Tacitus's *Germania*, together with a number of passages in the works of Strabo and various other writers under the empire. For the later period, the key source is the *History of the Franks*, an account by Gregory of Tours (*c.* AD539–594), himself a Gallo-Roman and Bishop of Tours, of life in Merovingian Gaul. Yet Gregory had no knowledge of any German documents. What we do know of the German tribes after Tacitus is therefore largely culled from the later law codes (for example, the *Lex Salica*) of the barbarian peoples. Given this paucity of information, it is a little surprising to discover just how powerfully these tribes have, time and time again, captured the imagination of European thinkers. Tacitus, perhaps the greatest of all the Roman historians, was in large part responsible for this. Indeed, his *Germania* repeatedly served the purposes of those wishing to challenge the universalist claims of either the Pope or the Emperor. The discovery of a manuscript of Tacitus's work in fifteenth-century Italy was hailed with enthusiasm by German humanists, keen to defend the cause of the Protestant Reformation against Rome.[5] Subsequently, the *Germania* was turned in an anti-Napoleonic direction by French writers in the early nineteenth century, an interpretation that was to have some influence upon Renan's own views. Aspects of the picture Tacitus had painted of the ancient Germanic tribes were in fact claimed as present virtues, so that the war waged against Napoleon, in 1813–15, by the German states, was to become an emblem of martial heroism pitted against despotism. 'The war of 1813–15', wrote Renan, 'was the only one in our century to have an epic and lofty quality.'[6]

The fame of the *Germania* clearly derived from its apparent celebration of the unsullied moral virtues of the ancient Germans, for example, their disregard for precious metals (G,5), the chastity of their women (G,18), and their warrior spirit, qualities which earned the praise of almost all European publicists, from the time of its rediscovery in the fifteenth century. Yet for Fustel de Coulanges, the historian responsible for demolishing the myth of Germanism in the 1860s and 1870s, Tacitus's antinomies were merely analytic in intent, and not moralistic.

The presence, within French nationalism, of a Germanist current is therefore the main theme of the present essay. I wish also to consider the conflict in nineteenth-century thought between the values of the Enlightenment and those of Romanticism. More specifically, I wish to argue that the advocates of Enlightenment thought in Italy managed, during the Restoration (1814–30) and subsequently, to refuse the spiritualist, organicist, and hierarchical tenets of so much of Romantic thinking. Whereas the new comparative philology, of which Renan was so famed an exponent in France, often anchored the ancient Germanic tribes to a pure Aryan origin, Italian writers such as Carlo Cattaneo, unswerving in their belief in the values of the Mediterranean city, dismissed the notion that nomadism was a source of fresh values. I want, therefore, to contrast Renan's Germanism with an intellectual tradition which rejected Germanism in all its forms. This account will serve, I hope, to place in question the excessively monolithic sense one at times has, in major studies by writers such as Edward Said and Martin Bernal, of the characteristics of nineteenth-century scholarship regarding language, culture, and race.[7] Finally, I wish to show how the establishment by Durkheim and his pupils of a scientific ethnology in France can be better understood if the writings of his teacher, Fustel de Coulanges, on Merovingian and Carolingian Gaul, are explored more deeply.

Germanism and anti-Germanism, 1720—1830

Chateaubriand

The first, and most intemperate expression, in the nineteenth century, of the Germanist interpretation of French history was that of Chateaubriand. *The Martyrs*, a historical prose poem completed in 1810 but begun over seven years earlier, was one of the crucial influences upon the new Romanticism; it ranged across much of the Roman Empire, beginning with the persecutions of the Christians under the Emperor Diocletian, towards the end of the third century AD, and continuing into the fourth and fifth centuries. The Germanic invaders of Roman Gaul, the Franks, were depicted, through selective quotation from Tacitus, Caesar, and others, as a fierce, liberty-loving (but monarchical) Christian people, that had created a fresh civilisation in the midst of imperial decadence. The modern world was thus defined as beginning where the classical one ended and, if much was made of the contrast between the woods and mists of the North and the sunlit Mediterranean, it was in order to show that it was out of the former that Christian Europe had emerged in all its purity.[8]

One can perhaps grasp something of the impact Chateaubriand's extraordinary work had upon French culture by considering Augustin Thierry's first, enraptured response to it, when at college in 1810. In his preface to his *Considerations on the History of France*,[9] Thierry recalled how, in his school textbook, the unadorned account of Clovis's assumption of the Frankish throne, and of the creation of the French monarchy had enthralled him but nothing had prepared him for the magnificent passages in Chateaubriand describing the savage demeanour of the barbarians:

I had no notion of the Franks being as terrible as M. de Chateaubriand had described them, clad in hides of bears, seals, urochs and wild-boars, of this camp fortified with leather boats with chariots harnessed to huge oxen, of this army disposed in a triangle in which one could make out only a forest of javelins, animal hides and half-naked bodies.[10]

One might suppose from such reminiscences, and from the dedication of the *Considerations* to Chateaubriand, 'the writer of genius who inaugurated, and who still dominates the literature of the new century', that an uninterrupted intellectual lineage, from Chateaubriand through Thierry to Renan, might be constructed.[11] It is true that Thierry was one of Renan's mentors, but in certain crucial respects his interpretation of French history was opposed, as we shall see, to that of Chateaubriand and Renan. Thus, Thierry's earlier historical writings, the first series of letters on the history of France (1818—20), seek to justify the Third Estate through a staunchly 'Romanist' interpretation of early French history. I shall discuss his contribution below. First, however, we should look at one or two earlier interpretations, both Romanist and Germanist, of French history.

The Comte de Boulainvilliers and the Abbé Dubos

It is often believed that European scholars first became deeply interested in the medieval period in the early nineteenth century, and the enormous popularity of the writings of Chateaubriand and of Madame de Staël is invoked as proof of this.[12] Yet this is a misconception, for it disregards both the pioneering archival work of men such as Leibniz and Muratori, early in the eighteenth century, and the larger theoretical formulations of Vico, Montesquieu, and many others. More specifically, much of the most crucial speculation regarding the Germanic invasions is contained in works written in the years that run from Vico's *First New Science* (1725) to Montesquieu's *The Spirit of the Laws* (1748). It was, for example, in the Comte de Boulainvilliers' *History of the Ancient Government of France, with Fourteen Historical Letters on the Parlements or Estates-General* (1727) that the terms 'feudal government' and 'feudality' were first used to describe the nature of a social order.[13]

If one locates the crucial advances in European scholarship regarding the Middle Ages in the first half of the eighteenth century rather than in the period when Romanticism prevailed, it quickly becomes plain that many of the scholars in question — whose intellectual formation, being juristic, was tilted towards a Romanism, either absolutist or republican in emphasis — wished to condemn rather than to celebrate the medieval order. Still heavily indebted to Roman historians rather than to contemporary Jesuit missionaries for their conception of a primitive society,[14] these thinkers often regarded the ancient German tribes, on the other side of the Rhine, not just as a threat to the Rome of Tacitus's day but as an emblem of the nomadic hordes that threatened the settlements, agriculture, lawcourts and assemblies of all civil orders. Vico, for example, whose alignment was very plainly with the *ceto civile* of Naples against the baronial class of the unpoliced rural areas, employed the *Germania* as a source for both his account of the original barbarism of human societies and for his description of the 'returned' barbarism of the Middle Ages, which, he believed, had lasted up until his own time.[15] It was in part because they were considered to be nomadic (although, in fact, as Fustel de Coulanges was to demonstrate in the 1870s and 1880s, they were not wholly so) that the barbarians were seen by the Romantics as bearers of fresh values that the cities, in their decadence, had lost, but Vico was far too Roman in his sympathies to share this enthusiasm for nomadism. Indeed, he was saddened by the *ricorsi* to which polities of his day were vulnerable.

Whereas theorists such as Edward Said and Martin Bernal have tended to view 'Orientalism' or 'Indo-Germanism' as a virtually all-pervasive quality of mid-nineteenth-century scholarship, the Enlightenment inter-pretation of Vico that was sustained by thinkers such as Carlo Cattaneo raised a high barrier between his thought and that of the Romantics. Thus, while Renan, Burnouf, and Max Müller, for example, celebrated the contribution of the Aryan nomadic tribes to European culture, Carlo Cattaneo, using the *Germania* itself as his source, argued that it was the urban traditions of Egypt, Phoenicia, and Asia Minor that had created a basis for civilization in the Mediterranean.[16] To the 'walled encamp-ments' of the great leaders of pastoral peoples, such as Cyrus, Ghenghis Khan, Attila, and so on, Cattaneo counterposed the more intensive forms of Mediterranean agriculture which, he declared, in terms that are Vichian in texture, was 'prudent and thoughtful, because dwellings were stationary and ownership was certain'.[17]

However, in the aftermath of Louis XIV's reign, a number of aristo-cratic interpretations of French history were advanced, which, against the 'Romanist' emphases of absolutism, sought to provide a Germanic genealogy for the *noblesse d'épée*. It was from such writers, foremost among them Boulainvilliers, that Renan's perspective on the history of France derives. As the leading spokesman of the old aristocracy, Boulain-villiers attacked the re-Romanization of the state under the Capetian monarchy, and lamented the destruction of the free society founded by the Franks, with its elective kingship and its annual, aristocratic assemblies.[18]

In an attempt to refute Boulainvilliers, the Abbé Dubos published a *Critical History of the Founding of the French Monarchy* (1734), which claimed that the Franks had not in fact entered Gaul as military conquerors, but rather as close allies of the Romans. This argument, reiterated in the 1860s and 1870s by Fustel de Coulanges, meant that the rise of the French monarchy could not be regarded — as, for example, Renan was later to regard it — as 'a Romanist aberration from sound German begin-nings'.[19] Clovis's pre-eminence among the Franks could then be seen to derive from the fact that he was a Roman officer, and Justinian's cession of the crown, around AD 540, had made the Frankish kings the direct heirs of the Caesars. The Abbé Dubos also insisted that the Champs de Mars, which had been claimed by the old French aristocracy as the precursor of the Estates General and by the *noblesse de robe* as the precursor of the *parlements*, had been nothing more than a rallying place for troops for the spring campaign.

The Romanist thesis not only served to bolster the cause of absolutism; it also could be used to justify the claims of the Third Estate. This, indeed, was precisely what historians such as Augustin Thierry and Guizot were to do during the Restoration, when the historical gains of the French Revolution were threatened by the *ultras*. One such ultra-royalist was Montlosier.

Montlosier and Thierry

Montlosier, who had been an aristocratic representative on the Estates General, and who had returned to France, profoundly embittered, after the Terror, was commissioned by Napoleon, when First Consul, to write an account of his country's institutions that would in effect ratify the imminent establishment of the empire. As Thierry observed, a wholly different kind of document was eventually produced, one which unleashed all of his present bitterness upon the past.[20]

What was to prove influential in Montlosier's polemic, although Thierry defended what Montlosier had condemned, was the claim that the history of France could be understood as a struggle of two enemy peoples on the same soil, a Frankish nobility against a Gallo-Roman third estate.[21] Thierry, a scrupulous and brilliant historian, therefore employed Montlosier's notion of a conquest (the enduring relation between conquerors and conquered), to research into the infancy of the Third Estate.

Whereas, for Montlosier, as for other ultra-royalists, the French 'nation' had consisted of the free, warrior nobilities that had invaded Roman Gaul, for Thierry it was the original inhabitants, the Gallo-Romans, who had preserved the arts, industries, and political traditions of ancient Rome, in spite of the destruction wrought by the barbarians.[22]

In order to sustain so absolute a dichotomy between the two 'races', a historian would have to suppose that the conquered people was itself, in all its pathos, a unity. This assumption, much criticized by Romagnosi, in his contributions to the Milanese journal, *Il Conciliatore*,[23] and by Cattaneo, in his review in *Il Politecnico* of Thierry's book on the Norman Conquest,[24] led to a consolidation of the concept of race, so that the mid-century physiological 'ethnography' of de Gobineau had the ground prepared for it in advance by certain tendencies within Romantic historiography. Thierry, Cattaneo observed, regarded the indigenous peoples of England as an amalgam of Angles, Saxons, and Danes, and forgot that they had themselves earlier been the conquerors of the Gaels and the Britons.[25] Thus, the Norman Conquest had not been a struggle between nation and nation, but 'the continuous increase of a religious and patrician confraternity that was bit by bit woven out of mixed fragments of the roman, celtic, germanic and slav peoples'.[26] So Machiavellian a view of the nature of culture contact and social change militates against the organicism of Romantic Indo-Europeanism (or Indo-Germanism, as it was also called) and is quite at odds with the account of the Germanic invasions given by Renan in his earlier writings.[27] 'The Gallic race', Renan observes, 'would seem to need, if it is to produce all that is in it, to be from time to time fertilised by the Germanic race.'[28]

Thierry, Guizot, and Cattaneo all believed fervently in the civilization of the communes. As Guizot remarked in a letter to Fauriel in 1820, 'Monsieur Thierry would seem to wish to do for the communes what Boulainvilliers and Montlosier had done for the nobility'.[29] Indeed, Thierry's reading of Sismondi's *History of the Italian Republics* encouraged him in the belief that all that had been said of the Italian communes of the eleventh and twelfth centuries applied to France also. 'It seemed to me', Thierry recalled in 1834,

> that in searching carefully our history, in looking over chronicles and archives, we should find something similar to what the historians of the thirteenth century tell us of the Communes of Milan, Pisa and Florence. It was then that there arose in me the first regrets that France was deficient in a truly national history.[30]

By 'national' Thierry still meant, as Sieyès had done in 1789, that pertaining to the Third Estate. This emphasis is missing in Renan's 1882 lecture.

Renan: revolution and restoration

References to the French Revolution abound in Renan's writings, but they are of a puzzlingly diverse nature. First, there are the rhetorical flourishes. The Revolution, we are told, was 'great, heroic, rash'; it was 'the French epic';[31] Renan also wrote of 'the great sacred intoxication of its first days'.[32] Assertions of this order clearly attribute everything and nothing to the Revolution. Renan was always unstinting in his appreciation of the power of glory, a military virtue, in the social world; for him it was akin to myth, in Sorel's sense of the term — pledged to infinity, coruscating with symbol and short on dialectic, it drove humanity, like a herd, onwards.[33]

Secondly, Renan never denied that it was the particular contribution of the French Revolution to have proclaimed that a nation exists of itself (Renan, 1882). Yet Renan's fundamental belief was that the principle of nationality was the creation of both a more recent period (1813—15) and of a more distant one (the period of the Germanic invasions).

Renan's pairing of the wars of 1813—15 with the Germanic invasions of the fifth and sixth centuries AD is only truly comprehensible if one grasps that the struggle of the German states against the armies of imperial France seemed to him, as to Chateaubriand and de Staël, a vindication of Germanic liberty. What, though, was meant by opposing Germanic (or modern) to Roman (or classical) liberty?

Classical liberty, which had found expression in the political writings of Jean-Jacques Rousseau and in the Jacobinism of Year II, was held to favour the rights of the state over those of the individual; modern liberty, which derived from the Germanic invasions, was based upon the new principles of absolute individualism and 'fealty' which flowered in feudal Europe.[34] The social orders established by the ancient Germanic tribes were regarded as exemplary.[35] Bismarck's Germany, in particular, after the Franco-Prussian War, stood in Renan's *La Réforme Intellectuelle et Morale* as an incarnation of the military spirit which France had lost:

> Medieval France was a Germanic construction, built by a Germanic military aristocracy with Gallo-Roman materials. France has striven long and hard to drive out from its breast all the elements deposited by the Germanic invasions, up until the time of the Revolution, which represented the last convulsive attempt.[36]

The execution of Louis XVI was, for Renan, the great crime of the Revolution; had it been halted at the aristocratic stage, all would have been well. All the difficulties experienced in the course of the nineteenth century in establishing or re-establishing a dynasty, whether Bourbon, Orleanist, or Bonapartist, were so many proofs of the terrible errors that the regicides had made. However, the French, unlike the English, whose history was glossed in a more Burkean manner than Thierry, for example, would have allowed, lost their way long before the French Revolution. Indeed, in criticizing, much as the Comte de Boulainvilliers had done in the 1720s, the centralizing and absolutist measures taken by the early Capetian kings, it is as if Renan was attacking their legal advisers, trained in the newly revived law schools of Bologna and Paris, the precursors in spirit of the Girondin and Jacobin lawyers who dominated the revolutionary assemblies. 'The beginnings of the Revolution were assuredly admirable', Renan observed in 1871, 'and if it had limited itself to convoking the Estates General, to making them annual, the truth would have been entirely on its side'.[37] It was almost as if Renan, as Boulainvilliers before him, had the annual aristocratic assemblies of the Franks in mind here.

If, therefore, Renan's concept of a constitutional monarchy seems at first to be a moderate one, and if the reader might suppose, from a cursory reading of the 1882 lecture, that he was sceptical about the moral value of dynasties, one should note that he differs from historians such as Thierry to the degree that his interpretation of French history is Germanist, and therefore irrationalist. The experience of the revolutionary period had made almost all theorists question the abstract nature of Jacobinism, but there is a great difference between the relatively mild Vichian historicism of Vincenzo Cuoco, for example, and the irrationalism of Renan's pronouncements regarding royal dynasties in Europe.[38] 'Such dynasties', Renan observed, 'were only founded through the particular harshness and arrogance of the Germanic race in barbaric and unconscious epochs, in which forgetting is possible and in which humanity lives in those mysterious shadows which found respect.'[39] When, therefore, Renan emphasizes how important forgetting is for the principle of nationality (Renan, 1882), he is not simply alluding to the necessarily inventive aspect of nation-building, as Ernest Gellner and Benedict Anderson have supposed.[40] There is in fact an additional, irrationalist, anti-Jacobin aspect to this term, for, like de Maistre, Renan observes and — for all his fervently expressed belief in science — sets his heart against, the unmasking of power by reason. In this respect, the 1882 lecture presents a remarkably muted version of Renan's monarchist beliefs, the true nature of which can be gleaned from earlier polemics, such as *La Monarchie Constitutionelle* or *La Réforme Intellectuelle et Morale*. Indeed, the Germanism of Renan, reliant as it is upon the figure of the nomad and the barbaric invader, celebrates what, to a jurisconsult of the early eighteenth century such as Vico — or, indeed, Maffei[41] — would have been feudal residues, and turns his back upon reason itself, in the name of rite, symbol, mystery, and brute force. Georges Sorel observed that Renan belonged to the Restoration and that, by 1871, his moment had passed.[42] However, in another sense, as Sorel's own use of Renan's writings proves, his moment had not yet come. The crisis of values of the late nineteenth and early twentieth century was clearly anticipated in Renan, for he celebrated, against socialism, the solidarities that ancient symbolisms and legends can assure.[43]

Fustel de Coulanges, Durkheim, Renan: The Third Republic and the origins of French sociology

Fustel de Coulanges, Renan, and Germanism

In 1864, a remarkable study of classical antiquity appeared in Strasbourg, *The Ancient City, A Study of the Religion, Laws and Institutions of Greece and Rome*. Before analysing the central tenets of *The Ancient City*, a work which was much acclaimed, and which was reprinted twelve times between 1864 and 1888, it may be worth considering the qualities which earned Fustel de Coulanges the admiration of so many readers, both in his own time and since. His work was, first of all, in sharp contrast to that of Romantic historians such as Thierry and Guizot and, it must be said, to that of Renan. There is nothing highly coloured or melodramatic about his writing, and he urged his students to eschew all metaphors. Lucid and austere in style, his histories rest upon the documents and the documents alone, so that he seems almost to share the reverential attitude of Renaissance humanists, as revived by Mabillon and the Benedictines of St Maur, to the written word. It has been argued that Fustel was trying to construct a historical semantics, and this seems to me an accurate description, as if he were the creator of the kind of enquiry that Marcel Mauss and Émile Benveniste subsequently favoured.[44] This is also in part why he has been revered by anthropologists within at least three different national traditions.[45]

If one were to draw, for the sake of argument, a contrast between two traditions of European philology, an earlier, humanist approach to the study of text and context, and a later, comparative philology, associated in most cases with Romanticism,[46] the temptation would be to range

Fustel de Coulanges in the former category rather than in the latter, but in fact his work runs awkwardly across both of them. Indeed, he was deeply influenced by the comparative philology and the comparative mythology of his own time — that of Max Müller, Ernest Renan, and Émile Burnouf — and tended to round off his references in *The Ancient City* to Greek, Roman, Sabine, and Etruscan civilization with accounts of similar beliefs, practices, and institutions recorded in the *Rigveda* and in the Laws of Manu. Yet there is no good reason to suppose that Fustel had read deeply in such areas. He quotes extensively from Burnouf's *Essai sur le Vêda*, published in Paris during the previous year, and from the above-mentioned Indian texts. In 1883, Salomon Reinach remarked of Fustel that he wrote 'as an Aryan to Aryans',[47] and it is plain that he, like the other scholars mentioned above, refused to admit that there was any similarity between the institutions, customs, and beliefs of the Aryan peoples and those of the Semitic peoples.[48]

Fustel's account of the early religion of the ancient city therefore posits a primordial Aryan civilization as source.[49] Emile Durkheim, who was taught by Fustel at the *Ecole Normale*, had a deep respect for his austere and scholarly approach, but subsequently came to question the limitations of his comparative method. It is my belief that his criticism of the limited use Fustel made of the comparative method rested in part upon his teacher's Aryanism.

In spite of Fustel's insistence upon the absolute neutrality of his scholarship, there is, both in his work on classical antiquity and in his studies of the early history of France, a hidden political programme. Yet is is unclear what the precise function of his Indo-Europeanism was. There would seem, for instance, to be a contradiction between the profoundly anti-Germanist nature of his studies of the early history of France and the Aryanist groundswell of *The Ancient City*. The first point to note is that Fustel's *declared* purpose in writing *The Ancient City* was to counter the use, in all of post-revolutionary French politics, of the values of classical republicanism. The trust that the Girondins and Jacobins had placed in Ciceronian oratory was destroyed forever by 1848 and by the *coup d'état* of Louis Bonaparte; the scorn of a young communist such as Karl Marx is matched by that of a basically conservative scholar such as Fustel de Coulanges, who wished, as Momigliano has noted, to dig a trench between himself and the Terror.[50]

Secondly, the introduction of references to classical India may have served to demolish Jacobinism as an ideal but, by the same token, it constructed a prehistory that rested upon religion, the family, and private property. Ancestor worship, in which the dead became divinities for the *gens*, with religion being located at first in house and tomb rather than in temple, was in some respects a perfect founding myth for a conservative French nationalism. At any rate, *Action Française*, in spite of the protests of Fustel's own pupils, believed it to be so. It is always hard to arrive at a final judgement in these matters, yet it is clearly the case that Fustel was forever 'squinting at France' in *The Ancient City*.[51] Indeed, as Gellner has pointed out, his account of the rise to power of the *plebs* is informed by the very confusion between ancient and modern history which he had himself castigated, as is his manifest opposition to agrarian communism (a doctrine which, curiously enough, had also been justified by reference to Tacitus's *Germania*).[52]

Fustel gradually shifted his attention from ancient history to that of the institutions of early France, some of his lectures at the University of Strasbourg in the 1860s being devoted to the subject. Gabriel Monod, who taught with Fustel in later years at the *Ecole Normale*, denied that his attack on the Germanist interpretation of French history was simply motivated by hostility towards Germany itself, and insisted that his 1861–8 lectures at Strasbourg had been equally emphatic about the Roman nature of the government of Clovis and his sons.[53] This may be true, and yet Fustel's first version of his *Histoire des Institutions Politiques de l'Ancienne France: L'Invasion Germanique et la Fin de L'Empire* (1875) appeared only five years after the Prussians had themselves invaded France and brought the Second Empire to a close, and in this, his second great work after *The Ancient City*, Fustel quite simply demolished the Germanist interpretation of French history.

Because the 1875 study proved so controversial, Fustel spent his remaining years redrafting it. He had hoped originally to compose a four-volume work, with volume II on feudalism in France, volume III on the French monarchy when its power was limited by the Estates General, and volume IV on absolutist monarchy, but the need to prove his point regarding the Germanic invasions meant that the six-volume work that was eventually published — two volumes completed in his own lifetime, four drafts reworked posthumously by his colleague, Camille Jullian — never got beyond Carolingian France.

If Renan's Germanism is more muted in his 1882 lecture than it had been in a number of his earlier writings, it is very probably because he had read the 1875 version of Fustel's history and incorporated some of its basic points into his own argument. This, as I have already pointed out, is a little surprising, for he was clearly the most prominent representative in France of the Germanist historiography that Fustel had attacked in 1872. If we look in more detail at the 1882 lecture, we find that, by contrast with Augustin Thierry, who had argued for an enduring opposition between whole peoples, as conquerors and conquered, Renan observed that the Germanic tribes:

(i)   'effected little change in the racial stock';
(ii)   'imposed dynasties and a military aristocracy upon the more or less extensive parts of the Old Empire of the West, which assumed the names of their invaders';
(iii) thereby founded France, Burgundy, Lombardy and Normandy;
(iv)   and, with the break-up of the Frankish Empire, through the Partition of Verdun (AD 842–3), established the conditions for the eventual creation of France, Germany, England, Italy, and Spain;
(v)   through the *fusion* of the component populations.

In short, whereas in Turkey, Slavs, Greeks, Armenians, Arabs, Syrians, and Kurds 'are as distinct today as they were upon the day they were conquered', the western European nations enjoy a unity both racial and cultural. Renan invoked two factors to account for this:

(i) the fact that the Germanic peoples had adopted Christianity as soon as they underwent any prolonged contact with Greek or Latin peoples;

(ii) the fact that they forgot their own language — the grandsons of Clovis, Alaric, Gundebald, Alboin, and Roland were already speaking Roman.

Much of what Renan has to say here accords with Fustel de Coulanges' remarkable contributions to the early history of France. For example, in the later version of his history, Fustel emphasizes — just as Romagnosi and Cattaneo had done — that the invasions were not the work of a huge mass of tribesmen, but a gradual introduction of a relatively small number, themselves to a significant degree already Romanized (as auxiliaries, mercenaries, and so forth). It was not, Fustel insists, 'a great conquest effected by one race at the expense of another'.[54] Likewise, by 1882, even Renan was prepared to allow that 'France became quite legitimately the name of a country to which only a virtually imperceptible minority of Franks had come.'

Fustel's avowed purpose in writing his history was to inspect the documentary evidence for the Germanist hypothesis, in all its variants. He stressed the lack of any documents actually by ancient Germans, whether annals, poetry, or law codes (although fragments survive in the accounts of the Roman historians and in the *Lex Salica* and in other, later barbarian law codes). Even Gregory of Tours lacked any first-hand knowledge of such documents. 'It is difficult', observed Fustel, 'to explain to oneself how the national memories of the ancient Germans can have disappeared so completely.'[55]

Whereas *The Ancient City* had been designed to break the hold of republican virtue upon the European imagination by replacing one key notion (civic republicanism) with another (ancestor worship), Fustel's later studies were aimed at a whole series of Germanist myths and he was therefore not able to identify a single guiding principle for ancient German society. In the introduction to the second version of his history, volume II, Fustel wrote: 'I have not spoken here of the spirit of liberty of the Frankish warriors, nor of an elective monarchy, nor of national assemblies, nor of popular juries, nor of the confiscation of the lands of the conquered, nor of allods distributed to the conquerors.'[56] These features, derived from passing remarks in Caesar, Tacitus, or Strabo, had been celebrated in varying combinations down the centuries by writers as diverse as Hotman, Boulainvilliers, the Abbé Dubos, Chateaubriand, Montlosier, Renan, and even by Marx and Engels. Yet, Fustel insisted, the Germanic peoples had not been without social distinctions — they had had slaves and a hereditary nobility — nor were they exactly primitive tribes. Indeed, they formed what Caesar, Tacitus, and Strabo and others called *civitates*, some of which were able to muster 60,000 warriors. Fustel doubted very much if the Germanic monarchies were in any sense elective, and his sceptical approach to the textual evidence scaled down the importance of the public assemblies (seen in an aristocratic light by Boulainvilliers and Renan, but more democratically by von Maurer and Engels and, it must be said, by certain students of English common law). If the Germans seemed to Tacitus to enjoy a freedom which Rome had lost centuries before, it was because, in his day, 'the Germans were still in that social condition through which the ancient Greeks had passed before their cities had become highly organised.'[57] Moreover, Fustel had no hesitation in stating that there were in fact ties of subjection among these liberty-loving peoples, but to persons rather than to the state, so that it was not liberty but subordination that prevailed in Germany. Three centuries of corruption by Rome had meant that the Germanic invasions were not the work of a young and vital people but rather of a decadent one.

Fustel de Coulanges, Durkheim, and Renan: The Third Republic, the nation, and the origins of French sociology

Emile Durkheim was 12 years old at the time of the Franco-Prussian War. We know from the recollection of others that the defeat of France was a severe blow to him, and that he had determined very early in his life to be 'a teacher and a scholar, but also an apostle, so vital did it seem to him to raise up the public spirit cast down by defeat'.[58] I wish, in this final section, to consider how Durkheim, the founder of French scientific sociology, understood the question of the nation, and how his understanding differed from that of Renan, for the emergence of sociology is intrinsically connected to the struggle to consolidate the Third Republic; and how, within sociology itself, the special emphasis upon ethnology expressed a need, on the part of lay, republican intellectuals such as Durkheim and his pupils, to counter polemical celebrations of the martial and monarchical values of the ancient German tribes within France's national boundaries with the distant, purely human, universal values of tribes from without, from Australia, from Polynesia, and so on. The birth of sociology is therefore closely linked to the debates within the historiography of France with which the present essay has been concerned.

During Durkheim's first year at the *Ecole Normale*, Jules Ferry was appointed Minister of Education. Since universal suffrage had always resulted in a massive royalist or Bonapartist vote, the republic's central task was to counter the priesthood's influence upon the French peasantry by establishing universal, free, lay, primary education. In addition, Prussia had already introduced just such a system; many believed that it was the Prussian schoolteachers who had won the Battle of Sedan.[59] The last years of Gambetta's ministry, 1879—82, were therefore marked by a ferocious struggle between the forces of radicalism and republicanism and those of the Church and clericalism, of monarchism, Bonapartism and that parody of Bonapartism, Boulangism, which culminated in the passing of a bill making primary education free, compulsory, and secular. From Holleaux's testimony we know that 'at the *Ecole* the great reforms of Jules Ferry were the subject of incessant discussions. Durkheim sought out these discussions, often starting them and throwing himself into them with true passion'.[60] The moral and intellectual reform of France was, he believed, in large part to be achieved through education, as his many writings and lectures on this subject show. Indeed, his more popular, pedagogical writings share the same tone as letters addressed by Jules Ferry, while Minister of Education, to the nation's schoolteachers.[61] By contrast, Renan's silence on such a topic, in a lecture delivered at the Sorbonne in, of all years, 1882, proves that he was not authentically a republican and that, in the early twentieth century, anti-Dreyfusards such as Maurice Barrès were to a degree justified in claiming him as an ancestor of *Action Française*.[62]

Although Durkheim was subsequently, in *The Elementary Forms of the Religious Life* (1912), to allow a greater autonomy to religious categories, his first struggle had been to establish the theoretical foundations for a lay morality. He therefore rejected Fustel's account of the relation between religion and social being, and was likewise scornful of Renan's belief that science was the fulfilment of religion. In these years of social and political chaos, he saw morality, somewhat anxiously, as a matter of social discipline, and it was not until the mid-1890s that he began to formulate an axiological approach to ethics.

As Durkheim made his preparations, in October 1885, for a visit to Germany, the Right was gaining in strength in France. In March 1884, Ferry had been forced to resign and, more ominous still, General Boulanger was becoming increasingly popular (he was to be appointed Minister of War in January 1886). The defeat of 1870, and the trauma of civil war, were very much on Durkheim's mind, and a brief look at two of the reviews which he wrote in 1885–6, of Schaeffle's *Bau und Leben des sozialen Körpers* and of Gumplowitz's *Grundriss der Soziologie*, will make it clear just how much he was preoccupied with the question which Renan had posed in 1882.[63]

Schaeffle had observed that a nation consisted of individuals, families, and institutions, linked by various kinds of social 'tissue'. Durkheim's summary ran as follows:

> Schaeffle has set out to subject present-day nations to an analysis and to resolve them into their principal elements. The author is frankly realist [in his approach]. Society is not a simple collection of individuals, it is a being which has preceded those of whom it is composed and which will survive them, which acts upon them more than they act upon it, which has its own life, its own consciousness and its own destiny. But what is its nature?[64]

This paragraph could as easily have been written by Thierry, Renan, or Fustel as by Durkheim, but the argument gains in precision as it proceeds. The reader is warned, first of all, that any use of the organic analogy should be regarded as strictly metaphorical, for 'the members of human societies are bound one to the other, not by a material contact, but by ideal ties'.[65] This observation would seem to align Durkheim with a 'voluntarist' rather than a 'determinist' view of the nation, and therefore with the perspective adopted by Renan in 1882, in the lecture at the Sorbonne, to which Durkheim in fact refers in a note.[66] Subsequently, these ideal ties would be, in Durkheim's relativist neo-Kantianism,[67] the collective representations upon which social solidarity was held to depend.

What Schaeffle was challenging in the thought of Espinas (author of Les Sociétés Animales, and the representative of one strand within French 'sociology' of the 1870s) was his adherence to a form of 'historical mysticism', which led him to posit an obscure consciousness reaching down into the smallest cells of the body, and to limit the parts played by a clear consciousness, and by reflection, in social life. For Schaeffle, Durkheim observed, 'the collective consciousness is above all composed of clear ideas. Undoubtedly, societies arise spontaneously, but this spontaneity is reflected upon'.[68] There is thus, in Durkheim's approving review of Schaeffle's book, as in his more negative appraisal of Gumplowitz, a stern refusal of every form of irrationalism. This was to become quite plain in his essay 'Individualism and the intellectuals', written at the time of the Dreyfus affair, but it was already clear in 1885–6 that he wished to settle accounts with the more obscurantist aspects of the Restoration tradition.

How then does Durkheim stand with regard to Renan? There is documentary evidence for his intellectual distrust of the high priest (with Taine) of French positivism, and this, I think, justifies my reading of the 1882 lecture against the grain.[69] While some critics, therefore, believe Renan's influence upon Durkheim was strong, I would merely acknowledge that both of them were appalled by the lack of national solidarity in the France of the 1870s and the 1880s and that both were concerned to propose a moral and intellectual reform.[70]

In his review of Schaeffle's work, Durkheim was less concerned with specific institutions that constitute a nation, its 'organs', as it were (Church, the universities, the state), than with the 'tissues' out of which such anatomical elements were formed. Histology, in the natural sciences, would therefore find its equivalent in a social science's concern with the ideal links — the values — which do or do not bind together the members of a community.[71] Durkheim listed those (social) 'tissues' or 'social bonds' which, in Schaeffle's view, held a nation together, and which derived from shared origin, territory, interests, opinions, religious beliefs, instincts of sociability, and historical traditions and language.[72] His paraphrase of the German professor's argument continued as follows:

> These different bonds do not traverse society in parallel. Yet they are interwoven in a thousand different ways. They cross in the heart of each individual. Thus, if one of them happens to break, the others suffice to maintain the mass which tends to detach itself from the organism. This is why a people presenting, uncontaminated by any

mixture, these eight characteristics, which had a national language, its own history as cult, an exclusive patriotism, a perfect ethnographic, geographical, economic, political and religious unity would form a solid, unshakeable whole that no hostile force, whether domestic or foreign, could ever succeed in broaching.[73]

Durkheim did not, I think, endorse this list of eight characteristics (which are, indeed, a little reminiscent of those five or six criteria rejected by Renan in 1882), but he does defend Schaeffle, who had defined national unity as the consequence of a complicated mesh of internal relations, against Gumplowitz, who had argued that, without invading armies and *Der ewige Kampf um Herrschaft* (the eternal struggle for mastery), societies would be wholly stagnant.[74] Durkheim therefore rejected all theories based upon enduring relations between conquerors and conquered, or upon what one might call a metaphysics of invasion. In short, he had learned from his teacher, Fustel de Coulanges, to reject the Romantic view of early European history and the populism which it fostered. Society was not a metaphysical whole; rather, it was composed of individuals, and it was they and they alone who '[were] the factors in social life'.[75]

If, in the aftermath of the Franco-Prussian War, Durkheim was preoccupied with the problem of creating a social science that might investigate the conditions for (national) solidarity, by the time of the Dreyfus affair, when one individual (Dreyfus) was being sacrificed to save France's national institutions (more especially, the army), Durkheim fought hard against the narrow and obscurantist celebration of the national legacy of memories to which writers such as Thierry, Fustel, and Renan had all referred, in order to defend individualism as a positive cult of human personality as such. Against notions of ancestor worship (cf. Renan, 1882), generally Burkean in texture if not in direct inspiration, Durkheim used Kant's categorical imperative in order to found a theory of the sacredness of the individual as abstracted from his particular race or class:

> According to Kant, I am only certain of acting well if the motives that influence me relate, not to the particular circumstances in which I am placed, but to my quality as a man *in abstracto*. Conversely, my action is wicked when it cannot be justified logically except by reference to the situation I happen to be in and my social condition, my class or caste interests, my passions etc.[76]

One can understand this position a little better if one contrasts it with that of an anti-Dreyfusard such as Maurice Barrès, who, in 1902, defined the *patrie* as *La Terre et les Morts* (a definition that accords well with Fustel's account in *The Ancient City* of early Indo-European religion). Furthermore, his scathing attacks upon intellectuals, or 'logicians of the absolute' is aimed at Durkheim and his colleagues:

> There is in France a state morality. One can perhaps put it that this official doctrine is Kantianism. . . . This Kantianism claims to regulate

universal man, abstract man, without taking individual differences into account. It tends to form our young persons from Lorraine, Provence, Brittany and Paris in terms of an abstract, ideal man, who is everywhere the same, whereas our need will be for men rooted solidly in our soil, in our history, in our national consciousness. ... We should shun a verbalism which distances the child from every reality, a Kantianism which uproots him from the land of his dead.[77]

Where these were the terms of the debate, one can readily understand how Durkheim had to take his distance from Fustel, a writer who, like Renan, was admired by Barrès and by other members of *Action Française*. Thus, in spite of the dedication of his Latin thesis to Fustel in 1892, he was to question the view, in *The Division of Labour in Society* [1893], that religion was the cause of social forms rather than the effect of them.[78] Speaking in very general terms, one can argue that Durkheim was mistrustful of Fustel's too restricted notion of the primitive family, to which he had also, in *The Ancient City*, ascribed a form of land ownership (familial property) which was precisely midway between individual smallholdings and agrarian communism. A few years later, in the preface to the first volume of the *Année Sociologique*, where Durkheim had of necessity to impose a division between history and sociology, he returned to his criticism of Fustel. The gist of his criticism was, again, that Fustel 'came to erroneous conclusions regarding the nature of the *gens*, in which he saw nothing but a large agnatic family: he was not acquainted with ethnographic analogies to this type of family'.[79] Durkheim then went on to insist that the true meaning of the Latin term *sacer* could only be understood in relation to the Polynesian term *taboo*, a bold claim, and one which would have been unthinkable to either Renan or Fustel. Barriers between families of languages were raised so high by orthodox Indo-Europeanists that no good reason was seen to compare categories used by the speakers of Aryan and Semitic languages, not to speak of more distant cultures. Even Durkheim himself had once been chary of using such exotic materials in his work.[80] By 1912, however, Durkheim and his pupils had, as Lévi-Strauss observes, 'rallied' to ethnography and spoke of the observation of phenomena as being at the same time 'historical and ethnographic'.[81] Cultures were eventually described as being either 'archaic' or 'primitive', and there was no implication that the former category was, as it had so often been for Indo-Europeanists, superior to the latter.[82]

This dramatic change in Durkheim's approach has been attributed by Lévi-Strauss to the effect that his editorial duties at the *Année Sociologique* had upon his reading habits. Among the sociological monographs that piled up on his desk were a number written by ethnographers working in the field, studies based on first-hand knowledge of tribal peoples by writers such as Boas, Swanton and Roth, Cushing, Strehlow, and Spencer and Gillen. Whereas, in the 1870s and 1880s, a French student of society had little detailed knowledge of any cultures more distant than those of the Maghreb, suddenly the social existence of Plains Indians or of Australian Aborigines was as vividly present as was that of the ancient Greeks or Romans.[83] Durkheim had been scornful of the ethnographic materials in the past because anthropology in the 1880s was still dominated by armchair anthropologists, compilers such as Wundt, Frazer, or Tylor, in whose work beliefs and practices were abstracted from their social context (as they had not been by his teacher, Fustel),[84] but he was full of respect for the fieldworkers, and used studies on Australian aboriginal society massively in his *The Elementary Forms of the Religious Life*.

It will, I hope, be apparent that I regard this explanation by Lévi-Strauss as of limited truth only, and that the history of ethnology must be seen in the context of a larger history, in which tribes outside the narrow circle of Aryanism were used to challenge intellectual orthodoxies attaching to Indo-Germanist doctrine. The Germanism of Marx and Engels (or, indeed, of Ruskin and Morris) proves that this is not an easy matter to judge.[85] Yet a finer-grained study of Durkheim and of the *Année Sociologique* would, I think, show just how urgent a task it was for republican or socialist intellectuals, especially if Jewish, to respond to the anti-Semitism of *fin-de-siècle* Europe by locating an elementary form of the religious life (totemism) beyond, or prior to that of Roman, Greek, or ancient Indian society (ancestor worship).[86] In these notes I have therefore sought to place Renan's thought in its historical context, and to bring it into polemical relation to two traditions — the 'classicism' of Carlo Cattaneo and the *Année Sociologique* school — which, though quite distinct from each other, were opposed to the Indo-Europeanism so prevalent in nineteenth-century scholarship.

Notes

1 E. Gellner, 'Nationalism and cohesion in complex societies', in *Culture, Identity and Politics* (Cambridge: Cambridge University Press, 1987), p. 8.
2 See Theodor Mommsen's letters to the Italian press, *Agli Italiani* (Berlin: E. Dentu, 1870), Numa-Denis Fustel de Coulanges' response, 'L'Alsace est-elle Allemande ou Française? Reponse à M. Mommsen' (Paris, 1870), letters by Max Müller and Thomas Carlyle to *The Times* during 1870, and Fustel de Coulanges' 'De la manière d'écrire l'histoire en France et en Allemagne', in *Revue des deux Mondes*, CI², pp. 241—51. Works by Renan that belong to this debate include his letters to the German scholar, Strauss (16 September 1870, 15 September 1871), his *La Réforme Intellectuelle et Morale* (Paris, 1871), and a number of other occasional writings of the 1870s.
3 See F. Chabod, *Storia della politica estera italiana, 1870–1896* (Bari: Laterza, 1951), vol. I.
4 G. Sorel, 'Germanesimo e storicismo di Ernesto Renan', in *La Critica*, 1931, vol. XXIX, pp. 110—14, 199—207, 358—67, 430—44, which was an introduction, completed in May 1915, to a never completed Italian translation of Renan's *La Réforme Intellectuelle et Morale*.
5 K.C. Schellhase, *Tacitus in Renaissance Political Thought* (Chicago: University of Chicago Press, 1976), p. 30 and ch. 2.
6 Quoted in Sorel, op. cit., p. 363.
7 E. Said, 'Islam, philology and French culture: Renan and Massignon', in *The*

World, The Text and The Critic (London: Faber, 1984), pp. 268–90; M. Bernal, *Black Athena: The Afroasiatic Roots of Classical Civilization*, vol. 1, *The Fabrication of Ancient Greece* (London: Free Association Books, 1987).

8 See also Mme de Staël's *De L'Allemagne* (London: John Murray, 1813).

9 This was a historiographical introduction, published in Paris in 1840 to the *Récit des Temps Mérovingiens* (Paris: Furne, 1840), which had originally been published as *Nouvelles Lettres sur l'Histoire de France* (1833–7).

10 A. Thierry, *Considerations on the History of France*, p. 12.

11 ibid., p. 13; J.E. Renan, 'Augustin Thierry', *Oeuvres Complètes* (Paris: Calmann Lévy, 1946–61), vol. II, pp. 86–108.

12 A. Omodeo, *La Cultura Francese nell'età della Restaurazione* (Milan, 1946).

13 As M. Bloch observed in *Feudal Society* (London: Routledge & Kegan Paul, 1965), vol. I, p. xvii.

14 In spite of the fact that this was the period in which the ethnographic work of Jesuit missionaries first attained standards which were subsequently to win the respect of social anthropologists, as, for example, J.-F. Lafitau, *Moeurs des Sauvages Amériquains comparées aux moeurs des premiers temps*, 2 vols (Paris, 1724).

15 See the entries 'Germany' and 'Tacitus' in the index to T.G. Bergin and M.H. Fisch's translation of *The New Science* [1744] (Ithaca: Cornell University Press, 1984).

16 C. Cattaneo, 'La Città considerata come principio ideale delle istorie italiane' [1858], in *Notizie sulla Lombardia* (Milan: Garzanti, 1979), pp. 118–19.

17 ibid., p. 119.

18 F.L. Ford, *Robe and Sword: The Regrouping of the French Aristocracy after Louis XIV* (Boston: Harvard University Press, 1953), *passim*.

19 ibid., p. 231.

20 Thierry, op. cit., pp. 130–3, 145–60; M. le Comte de Montlosier, *De La Monarchie Française depuis son établissement jusqu'à nos jours*, 4 vols (Paris, 1814).

21 Thierry, op. cit., pp. 153–4.

22 A. Thierry, *Historical Essays* [1818–1820] (Philadelphia: Carey & Hart, 1845), pp. 101–3.

23 G.D. Romagnosi, 'Della poesia considerata rispetta alle diverse età delle nazioni' *Il Conciliatore*, 10 September 1818, now in *Discussioni e Polemiche sul Romanticismo (1816–1826)*, ed. E. Bellorini (Bari: Laterza, 1943), pp. 416–26.

24 C. Cattaneo, 'Della conquista d'Inghilterra pei Normanni' [1839], *Scritti Storici e Geografici* (Bari: Laterza, 1957), vol. II, pp. 64–125.

25 ibid., p. 64.

26 ibid., p. 65.

27 See N. Machiavelli, *Discorso o dialogo intorno alla nostra lingua* [1515].

28 Quoted by Sorel, op. cit., p. 199.

29 Quoted in C. De Lollis, *Manzoni e gli storici liberali francesi della restaurazione* (Bari: Laterza, 1926), p. 7.

30 Thierry, *Historical Essays*, p. x.

31 J.E. Renan, *La Monarchie Constitutionelle, Oeuvres Complètes*, vol. I. pp. 478–9.

32 Renan, *La Monarchie Constitutionelle*, p. 486.

33 Renan influenced Sorel deeply, not only in his first books (published in the 1880s), but in *Reflections on Violence* also.

34 J.E. Renan, 'Philosophie de l'histoire contemporaine', *Oeuvres Complètes*, vol. I, pp. 34–5.

35 And medieval England, since it was believed to have been almost wholly untouched by Roman law, was regarded by some German scholars (and so by some French scholars also), as the purest of them all, as F.W. Maitland

observed in *The Constitutional History of England* [1887–8] (Cambridge: Cambridge University Press, 1908), p. 5.

36 J.E. Renan, *La Réforme Intellectuelle et Morale, Oeuvres Complètes*, vol. I, pp. 347–8.
37 ibid., pp. 336–7, 339.
38 V. Cuoco, *Saggio storico sulla rivoluzione napoletana del 1799* (Milan, 1800).
39 Quoted in Sorel, op. cit., p. 439.
40 B. Anderson, *Imagined Communities: Reflections on the Origin and Spread of Nationalism* (London: Verso, 1983), p. 15.
41 See appendix II to S. Timpanaro, *Classicismo e illuminismo nell' Ottocento italiano* (Pisa: Nistri-Lischi, 1965).
42 Sorel, op. cit., p. 437.
43 See M. Bloch's definition of feudalism in *Feudal Society*, vol. 2, p. 446, for it reads like Renan's programme for the intellectual and moral reform of France.
44 M. Bloch, 'Fustel de Coulanges: Historien des Origines Françaises', *Revue Internationale de l'Enseignement*, vol. 84, July 1930, p. 171.
45 By Durkheim, by Robert Lowie (USA), and by Edward Evans-Pritchard (in England).
46 Here I would refer the reader to Timpanaro's monograph (see note 41), which has strongly influenced the present essay.
47 S. Reinach, *Manuel de Philologie Classique* (Paris, 1880), p. 222 n.l.
48 N.D. Fustel de Coulanges, *The Ancient City*, translated by Willard Small (London: Lee and Shepherd, 1874); E. Burnouf, *Essai sur le Vêda* (Paris: Dezobry and Tandon, 1863), p. 13.
49 N.D. Fustel de Coulanges, *The Ancient City*, pp. 15, 22–4.
50 A. Momigliano, 'La Città Antica di Fustel de Coulanges', *Rivista Storica Italiana*, vol. 82, 1970, p. 89.
51 E. Gellner, 'The roots of cohesion', in *Culture, Identity and Politics* (Cambridge, 1987), p. 41.
52 For Fustel's critique of the work of L. von Maurer (among others) on the land tenure of the ancient Germans, see 'Recherches sur cette question: Les Germains connaissaient-ils la propriété des Terres?', in *Séances et Travaux de L'Académie des Sciences Morales et Politiques*, vol. 23, 1885, pp. 705–76, vol, 24, pp. 5–162. For Marx's enthusiastic endorsement of von Maurer, see his letters to Engels, 14 March and 25 March 1868, in K. Marx, *Pre-Capitalist Economic Formations*, ed. E. J. Hobsbawm (London: Lawrence & Wishart, 1964), pp. 139–42.
53 G. Monod, *Portraits et Souvenirs* (Paris, 1897), p. 148–9.
54 N.D. Fustel de Coulanges, *Histoires des Institutions Politiques de l'Ancienne France*, vol. 2, *L'Invasion Germanique et la Fin de l'Empire* (Introduction drafted in 1877), p. xi.
55 ibid., (1895), vol. 2, p. 234.
56 ibid., (1895), vol. 2, p. xi.
57 ibid., (1875), p. 304.
58 G. Davy, quoted in S. Lukes, *Emile Durkheim: His Life and Work* (Harmondsworth: Penguin, 1973), p. 45. I have relied heavily on B. Lacroix, 'La vocation originelle d'Émile Durkheim', *Revue Française de Sociologie*, vol. 17, April–June 1976, pp. 213–47, in this section.
59 Most notably, Renan, in *La Réforme*.
60 Lukes, op. cit., p. 47.
61 As quoted in J.P.T. Bury, *A History of France, 1814–1940* (London: Methuen, 1985), p. 159.

62 For a more sympathetic view of Renan's political stance, see G. Monod, *Les Maîtres de l'Histoire: Renan, Taine, Michelet* (Paris: Calmann Lévy, 1984).

63 E. Durkheim, 'La Sociologie selon Gumplowitz' [1885], in *Textes*, vol. 1 (Paris: Editions de Minuit, 1975), pp. 344—54; 'Organisation et vie du corps social selon Schaeffle' [1885], in *Textes*, vol. 1, pp. 355—77.

64 Durkheim, 'Organisation et vie', p. 355.

65 ibid., p. 356.

66 ibid., p. 374 n. 13.

67 See Lukes, op. cit., pp. 54—8.

68 Durkheim, 'Organisation et vie', p. 357.

69 Lukes, op. cit., p. 71.

70 Lacroix, op. cit., pp. 219—20 n.26.

71 Durkheim, 'Organisation et vie', p. 361—2.

72 ibid., p. 362.

73 ibid.

74 Durkheim, 'La sociologie selon Gumplowitz', pp. 348—9.

75 ibid., p. 351.

76 E. Durkheim, 'Individualism and the intellectuals' [1898], trans. S. and J. Lukes, *Political Studies*, vol. 17, no. 1, 1969, p. 21.

77 M. Barrès, *Scènes et Doctrines du Nationalisme* (Paris: Emile-Paul, 1902), pp. 56—7.

78 E. Durkheim, *The Division of Labour in Society*, trans. W.D. Halls (London: Macmillan, 1984), p. 130.

79 E. Durkheim, Preface to *Année Sociologique*, vol. 1, [1898] 1896—7, pp. i—vii, reprinted in K.H. Wolf (ed.), *Émile Durkheim, 1858-1917* (Ohio, 1960), pp. 342—3.

80 E. Durkheim, *The Rules of Sociological Method*, trans. W.D. Halls (London Macmillan, 1982), pp. 153—4.

81 C. Lévi-Strauss, 'What ethnology owes to Durkheim', *Structural Anthropology*, vol. 2, trans. M. Layton (Harmondsworth, Penguin, 1977), pp. 44—8.

82 See, for example, essays by Marcel Mauss or by Robert Hertz.

83 On Masqueray's monograph [1886] on the Berbers in Algeria, see Gellner, 'The roots of cohesion'.

84 R. Lowie, *The History of Ethnological Theory* (New York: Holt, Rinehart & Winston, 1937), pp. 36, 41 43, 54, 142.

85 See Ruskin's famous chapter, 'The nature of Gothic'.

86 See Momigliano, op. cit., p. 97.

4

The national longing for form

Timothy Brennan

Yo quiero mar y montaña
hablando mi propia lengua
Y a nadie pedir permiso
pa' construir la patria nueva
      (Cueca de la Confederación Unida de los Trabajadores (Chile))

For the beauty revealed to him was the soul beauty of a race which his larger audience despised, and he could not articulate the message of another people.

                              (W. E. B. du Bois)

We live in a world obsessed with national pride, and rampant with boundary wars, with nationalism on the banner of countless parties, no matter how conflicting their place or destination. At the same time, we study literature in a discipline with roots in a philological tradition first formulated with the idea of nations in mind, in the very period when modern nation-states were first being formed. The interplay of these factors is everywhere behind contemporary criticism, but rarely expressed openly.

In Europe and the United States, for the most part, the triumphant literary depiction of nationalism is Romantic. It is part of an earlier period when the forming of nations was a European concern, and before the experience of colonialism, world war, and fascism had soured people on what Edward Said has called nationalism's 'heroic narratives'. But the nationalist mood is, aesthetically as socially, more strongly felt in the emergent societies of the world today, including those ethnic or regional breakaways on the European continent itself (Basque, Irish, Albanian, and so forth).

My subject is 'myths of the nation'. The terms of this phrase are confusing because of their multiple meanings, which multiply still further when considered together: myth as distortion or lie; myth as mythology, legend, or oral tradition; myth as literature *per se*; myth as shibboleth — all of these meanings are present at different times in the writing of modern political culture. If one inclusive sense can be given, it is Malinowski's, where myth acts as a charter for the present-day social order; it supplies a retrospective pattern of moral values, sociological order, and magical belief, the function of which is to strengthen tradition and endow it with a greater value and prestige by tracing it back to a higher, better, more supernatural reality of initial events.[1]

As for the 'nation', it is both historically determined and general. As a term, it refers both to the modern nation-state and to something more ancient and nebulous — the '*natio*' — a local community, domicile, family, condition of belonging. The distinction is often obscured by nationalists who seek to place their own country in an 'immemorial past' where it's arbitrariness cannot be questioned. The British cultural historian, Raymond Williams, has commented on the need to distinguish between these senses:

'Nation' as a term is radically connected with 'native'. We are *born* into relationships which are typically settled in a place. This form of primary and 'placeable' bonding is of quite fundamental human and natural importance. Yet the jump from that to anything like the modern nation-state is entirely artificial.[2]

This impatience with the apparently divisive and warlike character of 'nation-statism' is very common among European critics in the postwar period, who work either within a Marxist tradition of 'internationalism' or a liberal tradition of sensible 'patriotism', perhaps most of all in England and the United States where even Left social critics (until very recently) have ritually denounced 'imperialism' while withdrawing their support from the oppositional forces that imperial legacy has inevitably unleashed.

For we often hear that nationalism is dead. Despite explosive independence struggles in the Philippines, El Salvador, Sri Lanka, and dozens of other places, many seem convinced of this. Some point to global developments that cast nationalism in the refractory light of heroic memory, where the invariable goals of creating an administrative economy, a repressive apparatus capable of waging war, and a sense of belonging that glosses over class conflicts, are being passed over in favor of local affiliations and loyalties on the one hand, and on the other, are being rendered obsolete by the international realities of multinational corporations and the telecommunications industry.

With a puzzling insensitivity to the emotional response to empire, Tom Nairn in *The Break-up of Britain* was an early and eloquent proponent of these views. He stresses what he calls nationalism's 'Janus-face' — the fact that it is both communal and authoritarian, friendly and bellicose, all at the same time. He insists that the most vital thing about it is its chameleon content: its ability to rouse unlike peoples in dramatically unlike conditions in an impassioned chorus of voluntary co-operation and sacrifice, in which nationalism's unviability is less an impersonal fact of neocolonialism-plus-technics than a political wish, since it is a reactionary throwback that impedes the solidarities of 'internationalism'.

On the other hand, operating as an analyst of what he calls 'cultural apparatuses', the Belgian communications scholar Armand Mattelart revises this view somewhat by supporting the one-world thesis without ignoring the value of the independence movements (he has, for example, actively endorsed the national-political strategies of Allende's Chile and post-1979 Nicaragua). He recognizes that the utopian projections of Marx and Engels in the *Manifesto*, which looked forward to the withering away of 'national one-sidedness and narrowmindedness' and the transformation of 'national and local literatures' into a single 'world literature' has grown, dialectically, into its opposite.

> The idea that it is necessary to smash the nation-state, the last obstacle to the new phase of the world-wide expansion of transnational capital, and transform it into a simple management state in an 'interdependent' world, is becoming naturalized . . . . [T]he transnationalization process creates an appeal for increasingly similar, ecumenical and universal values, or, to use the terms of Brzezinski, 'a new planetary consciousness,' a new 'harmony,' a 'new world unity' and a new 'consensus.'[3]

The value of these words is that Mattelart clearly states here an important ideological tendency that is often only implicit — namely, that on one level the 'nationalism is passé' school of thought is as unable to account for the positive necessity of defensive nationalism as imperial ideologues like former United States National Security advisor, Zbigniew Brzezinski, a member of the notoriously interventionist Trilateral Commission.

In another and more sensitive version, it was Paul Ricoeur who already in 1965 spoke of the tension — characteristic of the postwar period — between 'universal civilization' and 'national culture', between the involuntary mutual awareness and dependency of every people and region made possible (and inevitable) by 'civilization', as well as the dogged persistence of defensive movements helping subject peoples carve out a bit of space on the earth's economic turf:

> Everywhere throughout the world one finds the same bad movies, the same slot machines, the same plastic or aluminium atrocities, the same twisting of language by propaganda, etc . . . . [O]n the one hand, [the developing world] has to root itself in the soil of its past, forge a national spirit, and unfurl this spiritual and cultural revendication before the colonialists's personality. But in order to take part in modern civilization, it is necessary at the same time to take part in scientific, technical, and political rationality, something which very often requires the pure and simple abandonment of a whole cultural past.[4]

In fact, it is especially in Third World fiction after the Second World War that the fictional uses of 'nation' and 'nationalism' are most pronounced. The 'nation' is precisely what Foucault has called a 'discursive formation' — not simply an allegory or imaginative vision, but a gestative political

structure which the Third World artist is consciously building or suffering the lack of. 'Uses' here should be understood both in a personal,
craftsmanlike sense, where nationalism is a trope for such things as
'belonging', 'bordering', and 'commitment'. But it should also be
understood as the *institutional* uses of fiction in nationalist movements
themselves. At the present time, it is often impossible to separate these
senses.

The phrase 'myths of the nation' is ambiguous in a calculated way. It
does not refer only to the more or less unsurprising idea that nations are
mythical, that — as Hugh Seton-Watson wrote in his massive study of
nations and states as recently as 1976 — there is no 'scientific' means of
establishing what all nations have in common.[5] The phrase is also not
limited to the consequences of this artificiality in contemporary political
life — namely, the way that various governments invent traditions to give
permanence and solidity to a transient political form.

While the study of nationalism has been a minor industry in the
disciplines of sociology and history since the Second World War, the
premise here is that *cultural* study, and specifically the study of
imaginative literature, is in many ways a profitable one for understanding
the nation-centredness of the post-colonial world, as has begun to be
seen in some recent studies.[6] From the point of view of cultural studies,
this approach in some ways traverses uncharted ground. With the exception of some recent sociological works which use literary theories, it is
rare in English to see 'nation-ness' talked about as an imaginative vision
— as a topic worthy of full fictional realization.[7] Also, it should be said
that this neglect is not true of other literatures with a close and obvious
relationship to the subject — for example those of Latin America and
(because of the experience of the war) Germany and Italy. Even in the
underrepresented branch of Third World English studies, one is likely to
find discussions of race and colonialism, but not the 'nation' as such.

Only a handful of critics (often themselves tied to the colonized by
background or birth) have seen English fiction about the colonies as
growing out of a comprehensive imperial system.[8] The universality of
this system, and its effects on the imaginative life, are much clearer —
even inescapable — in the literature not of the 'colonies' but of the
'colonized'. The recent interest in Third World literature reflected in
special issues of mainstream journals and new publishers' series, as well
as new university programs, is itself a mark of the recognition that
imperialism is, culturally speaking, a two-way flow.

For, in the period following the Second World War, English society
was transformed by its earlier imperial encounters. The wave of postwar
immigration to the imperial 'centers' — including in England the influx
of large numbers of non-white people from Africa and the Caribbean,
and in America, from Asia and Latin America — amounted to what
Gordon Lewis calls 'a colonialism in reverse' — a new sense of what it
means to be 'English'. To a lesser extent, the same has happened in
France.[9]

The wave of successful anti-colonial struggles from China to

Zimbabwe has contributed to the forced attention now being given in the English-speaking world to the point of view of the colonized — and yet, it is a point of view that must increasingly be seen as a part of English-speaking culture. It is a situation, as the Indo-English author Salman Rushdie points out, in which English, 'no longer an English language, now grows from many roots; and those whom it once colonized are carving out large territories within the language for themselves'.[10] The polycultural forces in domestic English life have given weight to the claims of the novelists and essayists abroad who speak more articulately and in larger crowds about neocolonialism. And, in turn, such voices from afar give attention to the volatile cultural pluralism at home. The Chilean expatriate, Ariel Dorfman, has written that 'there may be no better way for a country to know itself than to examine the myths and popular symbols that it exports to its economic and military dominions'.[11] And this would be even truer when the myths come home. One of the most durable myths has certainly been the 'nation'.

Not the colonies, but the colonized. The 'novel of empire' in its classic modernist versions (*Heart of Darkness*, *Passage to India*, *The Plumed Serpent*) has been blind to the impact of a world system largely directed by Anglo-American interests, however much it involved itself passionately, unevenly, and contradictorily in some of the human realities of world domination. For English criticism — even among politically minded critics after the war — has refused to place the fact of domination in a comprehensive approach to its literary material, and that becomes impossible when facing the work of those who have not merely visited but lived it.

The rising number of studies on nationalism in the past three decades reflects its lingering, almost atmospheric, insistence in our thinking.[12] In cultural studies, the 'nation' has often lurked behind terms like 'tradition', 'folklore', or 'community', obscuring their origins in what Benedict Anderson has called 'the most universally legitimate value in the political life of our time'.[13]

The rise of the modern nation-state in Europe in the late eighteenth and early nineteenth centuries is inseparable from the forms and subjects of imaginative literature. On the one hand, the political tasks of modern nationalism directed the course of literature, leading through the Romantic concepts of 'folk character' and 'national language' to the (largely illusory) divisions of literature into distinct 'national literatures'.[14] On the other hand, and just as fundamentally, literature participated in the formation of nations through the creation of 'national print media' — the newspaper and the novel.[15] Flourishing alongside what Francesco de Sanctis has called 'the cult of nationality in the European nineteenth century', it was especially the novel as a composite but clearly bordered work of art that was crucial in defining the nation as an 'imagined community'.[16]

In tracing these ties between literature and nation, some have evoked the fictive quality of the political concept itself. For example, José Carlos

Mariátegui, a publicist and organizer of Peru's Quechua-speaking minority in the 1920s, outlined the claims of fiction on national thought, saying simply that 'The nation . . . is an abstraction, an allegory, a myth that does not correspond to a reality that can be scientifically defined.'[17] Race, geography, tradition, language, size, or some combination of these seem finally insufficient for determining national essence, and yet people die for nations, fight wars for them, and write fictions on their behalf. Others have emphasized the *creative* side of nation-forming, suggesting the cultural importance of what has often been treated as a dry, rancorous political fact: 'Nationalism is not the awakening of nations to self-consciousness; it *invents* nations where they do not exist.'[18]

The idea that nations are invented has become more widely recognized in the rush of research following the war.[19] To take only one recent example, the idea circuitously finds its way into Eric Hobsbawm's and Terence Ranger's recent work on 'the invention of tradition', which is really a synonym in their writing for the animus of any successful nation-state:

> It is clear that plenty of political institutions, ideological movements and groups — not least in nationalism — were so unprecedented that even historic continuity had to be invented, for example by creating an ancient past beyond effective historical continuity either by semi-fiction (Boadicea, Vercingetorix, Arminius the Cheruscan) or by forgery (Ossian, the Czech medieval manuscripts). It is also clear that entirely new symbols and devices came into existence . . . such as the national anthem, . . . the national flag, . . . or the personification of 'the nation' in symbol or image.[20]

Corresponding to Hobsbawm's and Ranger's examples, literary myth too has been complicit in the creation of nations — above all, through the genre that accompanied the rise of the European vernaculars, their institution as languages of state after 1820, and the separation of literature into various 'national' literatures by the German Romantics at the end of the eighteenth and the beginning of the nineteenth centuries. Nations, then, are imaginary constructs that depend for their existence on an apparatus of cultural fictions in which imaginative literature plays a decisive role. And the rise of European nationalism coincides especially with one form of literature — the novel.

Nation and novel

It was the *novel* that historically accompanied the rise of nations by objectifying the 'one, yet many' of national life, and by mimicking the structure of the nation, a clearly bordered jumble of languages and styles. Socially, the novel joined the newspaper as the major vehicle of the national print media, helping to standardize language, encourage literacy, and remove mutual incomprehensibility. But it did much more than that. Its manner of presentation allowed people to imagine the special community that was the nation. In the words of Benedict Anderson, the novel depicts:

> [T]he movement of a solitary hero through a sociological landscape of a fixity that fuses the world inside the novel with the world outside. The picaresque *tour d'horizon* — hospitals, prisons, remote villages, monasteries, Indians, Negroes — is nonetheless not a *tour du monde*. The horizon is clearly bounded.[21]

It was in the novel that previously foreign languages met each other on the same terrain, forming an unsettled mixture of ideas and styles, themselves representing previously distinct peoples now forced to create the rationale for a common life. Mikhail Bakhtin's work on the novel — usually discussed in terms of a purely textual understanding of his key terms 'heteroglossia' and 'dialogism' — describes this aspect of the novel more clearly than anyone.[22] But Bakhtin meant 'heteroglossia' to have basis in actual social life. The period of the novel's rise is that in which:

> the world becomes polyglot, once and for all and irreversibly. The period of national languages, coexisting but closed and deaf to each other, comes to an end . . . . The naive and stubborn co-existence of 'languages' within a given national language also comes to an end — that is, there is no more peaceful co-existence between territorial dialects, social and professional dialects and jargons, literary languages, generic languages within literary languages, epochs in language, and so on.[23]

If the novel for Bakhtin tended to parody other genres, the epic was that genre the novel parodied in its nation-forming role. Hobsbawm's description of the rhetoric of nationhood can be found also in Bakhtin's description of epic, where '"beginning", "first", "founder", "ancestor", "that which occurred earlier", and so on, are . . . valorized temporal categories' corresponding to the 'reverent point of view of a descendent'.[24] But, whereas it was a feature of epic never to be addressed to or for one's contemporaries, the novel (on the contrary) directed itself to an 'open-ended present'. In its hands, 'tradition' became what Hobsbawm calls a 'useable past',[25] and the evocation of deep, sacred origins — instead of furthering unquestioning, ritualistic reaffirmations of a people (as in epic) — becomes a contemporary, practical means of *creating* a people.

If the epic's 'ritual' view gives way to the novel's political one, the change is mirrored in the linguistic basis for the novel itself. The separation of literature into 'national literatures' at the outset of the novel's rise to prominence reflected the earlier victory of the European vernaculars over the sacred imperial 'truth-language' of Latin — only one instance that seems to justify Benedict Anderson's claim that the 'dawn of nationalism at the end of the eighteenth century coincide[d] with the dusk of religious modes of thought',[26] or, as he puts it in another place, that nationalism largely extended and modernized (although did not replace) 'religious imaginings', taking on religion's concern with death, continuity, and the desire for origins.

The religious answers to questions of continuity and origins were not specific enough to deal with the fragmentation of papal empire and monarchical realm. If languages imply nations, how many nations would eventually sprout from the hopeless polyglot entities following the decline of the medieval empires within Europe? If new collectivities are formed on a basis other than papal or dynastic authority, on what basis? How is a continual chaotic splintering to be prevented? The novel implicitly answers these questions in its very form by objectifying the nation's *composite* nature: a hotch potch of the ostensibly separate 'levels of style' corresponding to class; a jumble of poetry, drama, newspaper report, memoir, and speech; a mixture of the jargons of race and ethnicity.

One of the advantages of a broadly cultural approach to the dilemma of nationalist politics has been its illumination of nationalism's reliance on religious modes of thought. Regis Debray, for example, has assaulted the view that the nation, because historically specific in its late-eighteenth-century form, was also transient. He chose to take up the other half of Williams's dichotomy:

[L]ike language, the nation is an invariable which cuts across modes of production .... We should not become obsessed by the determinate historical form of the nation-state but try to see what that form is made out of. It is created from a natural organization proper to *homo sapiens*, one *through which life itself is rendered untouchable or sacred. This sacred character constitutes the real national question.*[27]

Debray's focus is relevant here as an explanation in *literary* terms of the nation's universal appeal, and so locates the symbolic background of national fiction. The nation is not only a recent and transitory political form, but also responds to the 'twin threats of disorder and death' confronting all societies. Against these, the nation sets two 'anti-death processes':

These are, first of all, a delimitation in time, or the assignation of origins, in the sense of an *Ark*. This means that society does not derive from an infinite regression of cause and effect. A point of origin is fixed, the mythic birth of the *Polis*, the birth of Civilization or of the Christian era, the Muslim Hegira, and so on. This zero point or starting point is what allows ritual repetition, the ritualization of memory, celebration, commemoration — in short, all those forms of magical behaviour signifying defeat of the irreversibility of time.

The second founding gesture of any human society is its delimitation within an enclosed space. Here also there takes place an encounter with the sacred, in the sense of the *Temple*. What is the Temple, etymologically? It was what the ancient priest or diviner traced out, raising his wand heavenwards, the outline of a sacred space within which divination could be undertaken. This fundamental gesture is found at the birth of all societies, in their mythology at least. But the myth presence is an indication of something real.[28]

Debray, of course, witnessed the vitality of nationalism as a younger

man in revolutionary Cuba, an experience (like that of Algeria and Viet-
nam for the generations of the 1950s and the 1960s) that sharply
modified Marxist and liberal theories of nationalism, and gave way to
what has been called 'Third Worldism': an endorsement of anti-
imperialist liberation movements that amounted to a panacea.[29]

This background of spirituality and permanence is never lost, even in
the historically specific cultural expressions of the national form. The
Marxist mystic, Walter Benjamin, has pointed out that the novel is
dependent upon the book, and was historically unique among literary
genres by being developed in its modern form after the invention of
printing. 'Print-capitalism', according to Anderson, meant ideological
insemination on a large scale, and created the conditions where people
could begin to think of themselves as a nation. The novel's created world
allowed for multitudinous actions occurring simultaneously within a
single, definable community, filled with 'calendrical coincidences' and
what Anderson calls (after Benjamin) 'traverse, cross-time'. Read in isolation, the novel was nevertheless a mass ceremony; one could read alone
with the conviction that millions of others were doing the same, at the
same time.

The *composite* quality of the novel cannot be understood only ethnically
or regionally. The novel's rise accompanied a changing concept of
'realism' itself, which acquired its present association with the lower
classes only after the Enlightenment when, as Auerbach describes, realism
came to involve: 'the serious treatment of everyday reality, the rise of
more extensive and socially inferior human groups to the position of
subject matter for problematic-existential representation'.[30] In other
words, the novel brought together the 'high' and the 'low' within a
national framework — not fortuitously, but for specific national reasons.

The first appearance of incipient nationalist consciousness, according to
Kohn, took place in the Cromwellian forces of the English Civil War.
The ideas here were so tightly bound up with the aspirations of the
middle classes for 'free expression', 'self-assertion', and freedom from the
authority of a wilful and tyrannical monarchy, that 'individual liberty'
became inseparable from the nationalist ethos. The incipient liberal
nationalism of Milton and, later, Locke found its way through the French
philosophes to North America, where it raised its head in the form of
attacks on authoritarianism, censorship, and the strangling of free trade.

On this North American terrain, the 'nationalistic' idea of oppression
from *afar* appeared, although it was not exactly the 'foreign' oppression
that would become so common in the period after the Second World
War. In this case, the same religion, language, and history were common
to England and its North American colony. But the very tenuousness of
the stated need for independence pushed the grounds for separation from
specific middle-class 'liberties' to the much broader *inalienable rights* — the
universality of which applied in principle also to the lower classes. All
this gave expression to Rousseau's concept of the collective personality
of the 'people', the unity and common destiny of a 'community' whose
cohesiveness relied upon forces emanating from the ground up, and

which, being natural, encompassed all. In Germany, Herder transformed Rousseau's 'people' into the *Volk*. The significance of this latter concept is its shift from Rousseau's Enlightenment emphasis on civic virtue to a woollier Romantic insistence on the primordial and ineluctable roots of nationhood as a *distinguishing feature* from other communities. Each people was now set off by the 'natural' characteristics of language, and the intangible quality of a specific *Volksgeist*.

It was, in fact, the urge to give solidity to this particular and differentiating 'spirit of the people' that led in Germany to the first serious collections of folktales and folksongs, which according to Bakhtin are the prototypes of the novel form: 'The novel's roots must ultimately be sought in folklore.'[31] These collections provided an impetus to the study of modern philology, which separated the study of literature into various 'national' literatures on the basis of linguistic distinctions considered to be inviolable and absolute. Contemporary literary study is still based on these distinctions first made in the period of incipient European nation-forming. In short, nationalism is enmeshed in the particular history of Europe and its ideology of 'democracy'; it necessarily invokes the 'people', although this people becomes, increasingly after the late nineteenth century, inseparable from the modern working class, both in the Marxist sense, and in that hybrid of Marxism and Third World populism made famous by figures like Ho Chi Minh, Amilcar Cabral, Kwame Nkrumah, Frantz Fanon, and many others.

The 'folk', the 'plebeians', the 'people', the 'working class' were now important components for any inclusive treatment of the nation in fiction, as Bruce King has pointed out:

> Nationalism is an urban movement which identifies with the rural areas as a source of authenticity, finding in the 'folk' the attitudes, beliefs, customs and language to create a sense of national unity among people who have other loyalties. Nationalism aims at . . . rejection of cosmopolitan upper classes, intellectuals and others likely to be influenced by foreign ideas.[32]

Without this sense of rejection of the 'cosmopolitan upper classes', plebeian authenticity has been a feature of English literature throughout the rise of modern nationalism in Europe. In the English nineteenth century, for example, authors adopted the concepts of German Romanticism, expressing them most often in debates over the 'literary language' and its debt to a 'common language' — the poor people's idiom, sometimes referred to as 'native speech'. In Wordsworth's 'Preface to the Lyrical Ballads', or Hazlitt's 'On familiar style', the issue of common speech had even gone beyond a defense of the writer's departure from the proprieties of style, and was associated with peasant virtue — an abstraction and an idealization of the democratic ideology necessary for the rise of market capitalism. This association is even more pronounced and even less concerned with style *per se* in Morris's 'Art of the people'. In *Marius the Epicurean*, Pater attempted to define a 'proletariate of speech' in the stylistic concept of 'Euphuism' — a fertile mixture of high and low idioms. There are, of course, many other examples.

The populist undercurrents of national thought have been put forth clearly by the novel's better known theorists, although not in the form of a 'national' concept *per se*. Both Lukács and (as we have said) Bakhtin, despite their differences in many other respects, explain the novel in terms of epic. In both, the two are inverted images of the other — the former supplanting the latter in a period of transition from one ruling class to another. In the early Lukács, this rupture is traced to the disintegration of organic community in antiquity, the breakdown of its naively authoritarian and religious hierarchies. When the bourgeois individual became the dominant myth, the external became the internal, the worldly became the textual.

In Bakhtin, as we will see, the issues are discussed less as content analysis than as an attempt to explain the evolution (and breakdown) of generic distinctions as such, where literary forms are shown to carry the weight of new perceptions made possible by changes in society. The epic is for him 'preserved and revealed only in the form of national tradition', which he describes as 'a commonly held evaluation and point of view'.[33] For Bakhtin, the upheaval is less between elements within a given society than between societies, and although (unlike Lukács) he takes his examples of the novel from Hellenistic Romance, Latin mock-epic, and medieval satire, like Lukács he concentrates on those periods when large, incorporating dynastic realms are in the process of decline. For the modern novel, this means precisely the period of market capitalism and the age of exploration, which was also the period of the transformation of the vernaculars into languages of state, the creation of national economies, and the subsequent recognition of nationalism as the dominant political ideology of the bourgeoisie.

Thus, for the late Lukács, the key event in the development of the modern, or (as he calls it) 'historical' novel, is the French Revolution; for Bakhtin, that period when 'the world becomes polyglot once and for all and irreversibly'.

It is striking to realize that these still pivotal theorists of the novel exhaust their analyses at their starting points — the era of the still revolutionary middle classes. Not only are the national-political implications of their work on fiction left merely implicit, but the contemporary consequences of their findings have remained completely submerged. According to Bakhtin:

> The embryos of novelistic prose appear in the heteroglottic and heterological world of the Hellenistic era, in imperial Rome, in the process of disintegration and decadence of the verbal and ideological centralism of the medieval Church. Similarly, in modern times the flourishing of the novel is always connected with the decomposition of stable verbal and ideological systems, and, on the other hand, to the reinforcement of linguistic heterology and to its impregnation by intentions, within the literary dialect as well as outside of it.[34]

Is it not natural to assume that the novel itself would assume new forms following the institution of another closed system with its accompanying universal language, whose disintegration (the system and the language) we are now witnessing? For of course the triumph of European nationalism co-existed with the consolidation of empire, and the world became Europe's 'little circle' — just as beleaguered and constrained as the ethnic and linguistic sub-communities had been under the rule of the imperial church, and the monarchies of the late Middle Ages and Renaissance. What then of the period following the Second World War?

Another pivotal critic, who is not normally thought of as an analyst of the novel, realizes much more than Lukács and Bakhtin the parameters of the contemporary novel. In 'The storyteller', Walter Benjamin provides the most useful leads for understanding the form of the novel in the postmodern period, because he evokes the conflict between originally oral literature and that (like the novel) which has from the beginning been dependent on the book. This conflict of the oral and the written, of course, suggest the conflicts now occurring between developed and emergent societies, a conflict that begins more and more to characterize the postwar political scene, as we will see below. But in Benjamin it leads to a more fundamental conflict between communal and individual experience — something which we saw above was contained contradictorily in nationalist ideology from the start:

> What differentiates the novel from all other forms of prose literature — the fairy tale, the legend, even the novella — is that it neither comes from oral tradition nor goes into it. This distinguishes it from storytelling in particular. The storyteller takes what he tells from experience — his own or that reported by others ... the novelist has isolated himself.[35]

Benjamin's thesis is that, in our time, 'experience has fallen in value' as a result of the cultural development of printing, especially in the form of the newspaper; and so (although he comes at it from a different angle), he joins Anderson in coupling novel and newspaper as the decisive print media of bourgeois society.

> [W]ith the full control of the middle class, which has the press as one of its most important instruments in fully developed capitalism, there emerges a form of communication which, no matter how far back its origins may lie, never before influenced the epic form in a decisive way. But now it does exert such an influence. And it turns out that it confronts storytelling as no less of a stranger than did the novel, but in a more menacing way, and that it also brings about a crisis in the novel. This new form of communication is *information*.[36]

Although Benjamin has been more prescient in isolating the relevant components of social communication, he is intriguing above all as a failed questioner. To counterpose information to epic (or folkloric) 'experience' is, as I hope to show below, a deep misunderstanding of what the novel has become in at least one trend of Third World fiction. Nevertheless, writing as a European between the wars, Benjamin instinctively predicted where the developments would occur. Benjamin belongs to that strain of nostalgic modernism, which revolts against the 'ready-made' quality of modern life made possible by the uprooting of communal, village life. In this sense he is very similar to the early Lukács. For Benjamin, information is contrasted to 'intelligence' or 'epic wisdom'.

> The intelligence that came from afar — whether the spatial kind from foreign countries or the temporal kind of tradition — possessed an authority which gave it validity, even when it was not subject to verification. Information, however, lays claim to prompt verifiability. The prime requirement is that it appear 'understandable in itself.'[37]

Clearly, as Benjamin uses it, information is inseparable from propaganda — it is that news which we receive from all parts of the globe that is already 'shot through with explanations'. There are three major areas where Benjamin's account seems contradicted by many novels of the contemporary Third World. As a negation of epic, he supposed the novel to stand against 'memory' — the 'epic faculty par excellence', whereas 'memory' — for example in the quasi-journalistic banana massacre episode of García Márquez's *One Hundred Years of Solitude* — is what many of these novels insist on preserving.[38] The novel was supposed to tend to substitute the story's moral with an abstract, philosophical investigation into the meaning of life, whereas novels as various as Khushwant Singh's *Train to Pakistan* or Vic Reid's *The Leopard* deliberately moralize recent local history sketching out known political positions. And, finally, because information must always sound plausible, the novel was thought to oppose the inclination of the storyteller to borrow from the miraculous, which the wholesale success of so-called 'magical realism' (not only in Latin America) has shown to be wrong. The fact is that 'news', precisely because it has become the nemesis of national fiction by originating in the imperial centers (which largely control the images projected to and about the Third World), is thematically and formally incorporated into the postwar novel. A large body of postwar fiction is in this sense 'neocolonial', composed of various novels of 'information', voices from the Third World seeking to project themselves into a European setting.

And yet it is precisely here that the greatest paradox of the new novel can be seen. For under conditions of illiteracy and shortages, and given simply the leisure-time necessary for reading one, the novel has been an elitist and minority form in developing countries when compared to poem, song, television, and film. Almost inevitably it has been the form through which a thin, foreign-educated stratum (however sensitive or committed to domestic political interests) has communicated to metropolitan reading publics, often in translation. It has been, in short, a naturally cosmopolitan form that empire has allowed to play a national role, as it were, only in an international arena.

Phases of the nation

Writers as various as Hans Kohn, Hugh Seton-Watson, Tom Nairn, and Horace Davis have combined to point out the internal inconsistencies, poses, and historical absurdities of nationalist thought.[39] Elie Kedourie has read the phenomenon entirely through the development of German idealistic philosophy, noting ominously, for example, Fichte's retrospectively shocking view that 'conflict between strata promotes indirectly to the self-realization of the whole human race'.[40]

Indeed, since the Second World War, in a conveniently European lapse of memory, studies of nationalism have not only increased; they have for the most part condemned the thing they studied. Kohn and Kedourie, for example, both define nationalism by suggesting it has a totalitarian edge: 'Nationalism is a state of mind in which the supreme loyalty of the individual is felt to be due to the nation-state.'[41] Both the interest and the negative judgment are the result of events directly bearing on the war — the rise of various 'imperial' nationalisms among those latecomers to empire in the developed west: Italy, Germany, and Japan. Here the witnessing of extreme group loyalties, manipulated by the repressive regimes of European fascism, led to a search for the nationalist roots of a western tradition previously thought to be civilized.[42]

The terms of nationalism have from the European perspective apparently reversed. Not freedom from tyranny, but the embodiment of tyranny. The question is: how much is this new perspective a result of owning, rather than suffering, an empire? That is, can't it be said that the recoiling from nationalism is also partly due to the challenge of the rising national movements of the developing world? Herbert Schiller, for example, has pointed out that since 1948, over ninety new nations have been formed out of the rubble of the European empires destroyed by the war — formed, that is, at our expense.[43]

A good deal of depression surrounding the term cannot, however, be explained by European prejudice alone. For one of its sources is the wholesale exporting of authoritarian military regimes to the fledgling countries of the Third World, although the observation is usually made without sufficiently noting the part played in this by the imperial legacies of differentiating administrative structures, unequal development, and 'foreign aid'. Lamenting the savagery of many states in what should have been the Third World's 'springtime' of nationalist idealism is not an activity limited to European sociologists. It forms a major sub-category of Third World fiction itself, featured in such representative works as García Márquez's *Autumn of the Patriarch*, Miguel Asturias's *El Señor Presidente*, Salman Rushdie's *Shame*, and many others — novels that are really a necessary adjunct to the insurgent and liberationist rhetoric of Fanon and his cultural descendents, although in an inverted form: a pointed exposure of the 'empire's old clothes' worn by a comprador elite who like Chile's Pinochet, Egypt's Mubarak, or Haiti's late Baby Doc Duvalier, take on the nationalist mantle only to cloak their people more fully with the old dependency.

Because the states which must transform the postcolonial territories into 'nations' are (unlike those in the creole nineteenth century), already bequeathed, and sitting upon seething disparities of class and background, the problem for the neocolonial writer has not only been to create the aura of national community eroded by the 'monopolization of the forms of cultural expression' in dominant culture, but to expose the excesses which the *a priori* state, chasing a national identity after the fact, has created at home. If, as Horace Davis argues, 'any reasonable consideration tells us that state and nation build each other' then the problem of nation is also the problem of the influence of state policy on national literary production; the conflict between anti-colonial inspiration, on the one hand, and on the other, the commercial and governmental preforming of the imagination. And what we really have now is merely a confusion of terms and a false and merely nominal continuity. For it is the first period of nationalism where the state predates or precedes nationalist sentiments, which are then called in after the fact, so to speak.

If European nationalism was a project of *unity* on the basis of conquest and economic expediency, insurgent or popular nationalism (not, that is, of the Pinochet variety) is for the most part a project of consolidation following an act of *separation* from Europe.[44] It is a task of reclaiming community from within boundaries defined by the very power whose presence denied community. Sometimes supporting, sometimes rejecting the political states in which they find themselves, the writers must have a goal that can only be a collective political identity still capable of being realized — despite multinational corporations and regional alliances like Contadora, OPEC, and the Pan African Congress — in any other form than the nation-state. It is not that people, or the artists who speak for them, can imagine no other affiliations, but that the solutions to dependency are only collective, and the territorial legacies of the last 200 years provide the collectivity no other basis upon which to fight dependency.

The crippling subaltern status implied by having to follow an imaginative form of another and oppressing culture is not fact, however, but myth. The constraints are real, but not their purported origins. As elsewhere, the myth thrives on a selective and ethnocentric history. We imagine that the advanced countries of Europe, under the pressures of Enlightenment ideals and the commercial needs of the rising industrial classes, *invented* the nation-state, and then exported it into Europe's dominions, where it would play a ridiculously unsuitable role, postdating the arbitrary division of the world into administrative and economic zones of influence, already with their own state apparatuses, and therefore having to project independence on the terms set down by the former rules.

This scenario is accurate except where it assigns origins. The nation-state is not only the by-product of the conditions created by European exploration; it was, more or less from the start, forged in acts of separation from the European centers of Madrid and London. If one discounts the civil wars of England and France, the first nationalists are not Frenchmen, Spaniards, or Englishmen, but the creole middle classes of the New World — people like Simon Bolívar, Toussaint L'Ouverture, and

Ben Franklin. From these clearest practical expressions, the age of European nationalism takes off following the French Revolution, combining the rise of the vernaculars, populist revery, and (on the other hand) the skillful transformation of the European dynasties (Romanov's, Hapsburgs, Hanoverians, and so forth) into national lookalikes in populist dress.[45]

For nationalism is an ideology that, even in its earliest forms in the nineteenth century, implied unequal development.[46] Even though as an ideology it came out of the imperialist countries, these countries were not able to formulate their own national aspirations until the age of exploration. The markets made possible by European imperial penetration motivated the construction of the nation-state at home. European nationalism itself was motivated by what Europe was doing in its farflung dominions.

The 'national idea', in other words, flourished in the soil of foreign conquest. Imperial conquest created the conditions for the fall of Europe's universal Christian community, but resupplied Europe with a religious sense of mission and self-identity that becomes *universal* (both within and outside Europe) after the war — a universalizing that today has led, dialectically to a break-up and a splintering. 'The twentieth century since 1945 has become the first period in history in which the whole of mankind has accepted one and the same political attitude, that of nationalism.'[47]

In a sense, then, nationalist doctrine takes over religion's social role, substituting for the imperial church; the most successful early European nationalist was Napoleon, who decried the regal centralization of power while marching across Europe in the name of France. In its European origins, nationalism was also messianic, modelled on patterns of Judeo-Christianity. According to Kohn, modern nationalism took three concepts from Old Testament mythology: 'the idea of a chosen people, the emphasis on a common stock of memory of the past and of hopes for the future, and finally national messianism'.[48] If the concept of superiority ('chosen people') characterizes the outlook of the European adventurer, it is the Hebraic underdog, the sense of being an outcast people, that characterizes the other:

> Not only oppressed nationalities took refuge in the hope of a messianic mission; . . . it expressed also the struggle of heretical sects and oppressed classes for the realization of their dreams and aspirations, and as the secular idea of historical progress it still retains today some of its religious force.[49]

The point here is how the earlier impulse towards *individuation* gave way through conquest to a universally shared outlook; the national becomes international in the postwar, to the point that it becomes possible to speak of such things as 'Islamic nationalism' or 'Latin American nationalism' in reference to entire continents or regions. There are two imperial legacies that have contributed to this internationalist feeling of solidarity against empire — the presence of vestigial 'world' languages (primarily Spanish, English, and Arabic) and international communications. Thus, a recurrent motif of contemporary fiction is the bridge that exists between imaginative literature and other forms of cultural information and communication: the place of literature within what C. Wright Mills called 'the cultural apparatus'. As with so much else, the imperial relationship has made this apparatus more visible.

A well-known UNESCO document of 1980 on world information imbalances (whose authors include García Márquez and the British cultural historian Richard Hoggart) suggests the special problem:

> It has become increasingly clear that the effects of intellectual and cultural dependence are as serious as those of political subjection or economic dependence. There can be no genuine, effective independence without the communication resources needed to safeguard it. The argument has been made that a nation whose mass media are under foreign domination cannot claim to be a nation.[50]

It is obvious how different this kind of cry is from 'no taxation without representation'. How does the Third World writer participate in national culture under the conditions of what Herbert Schiller calls 'the monopolization of culture' by ceaseless western commercial and informational outpourings?[51] What chance does the *natio* have against this constant reminder of dependency? How does one establish community on the grounds of an erstwhile imperial administrative sector, when the present rulers often perform like handpicked successors of the colonial regime? While, from an administrative and economic point of view, distinct nations are multiplying, the mutual awareness and interlocking influences of global culture begun by imperialism is still increasing, creating those conditions described by Bakhtin (but now applicable on a worldwide basis) in which 'languages cast light on one another' and 'the period of national languages coexisting but closed and deaf to one another, comes to an end'.

Exile vs. nationalism

How could the most universally legitimate political ideology of our time fail to become a *topos* in postwar fiction? And how could its existence be ignored, or replaced by the *topos* of 'exile', nationalism's opposite? In our thinking, 'exiles' have usually been those famous American and British artists seeking a change in creative surroundings. They have not referred usually to those displaced by world war and colonization, in the sense suggested by Edward Said when he says,

> [it] is necessary to set aside Joyce and Nabokov and even Conrad, who wrote of exile with such pathos, but of exile without cause or rationale. Think instead of the uncountable masses for whom UN agencies have been created, or refugees without urbanity, with only ration cards and agency numbers.[52]

Exile and nationalism are conflicting poles of feeling that correspond to more traditional aesthetic conflicts: artistic iconoclasm and communal assent, the unique vision and the collective truth. In fact, many words in the exile family divide themselves between an archaic or literary sense and a modern, political one: for example, banishment vs. deportation; émigré vs. immigrant; wanderer vs. refugee; exodus vs. flight. The division between exile and nationalism, therefore, presents itself as one not only between individual and group, but between loser and winner, between a mood of rejection and a mood of celebration. Literarily, the division is suggested by the tensions between lyric and epic, tragedy and comedy, monologue and dialogue, confession and proclamation, and has led in some recent Third World literature to what Barbara Harlow has called 'a full-scale counter-hegemonic aesthetics', with a striking absence of hostility toward 'modernity' and an attempt to preserve identity (if not traditional values) by acquiring the technologies, the diplomatic strategies, and the 'worldliness' of the former rulers.[53] Many of the novels often attempt to assemble the fragments of a national life and give them a final shape. They become documents designed to prove national consciousness, with multiple, myriad components that display an active communal life.

In this sense, it is important to see how contemporary nationalism has affected the English tradition *as a whole* — that is, not only the English-speaking former colonies, or in the fate of 'World English Literature's' reception into the academy, but in the writing of English cultural criticism itself. The nation-centered origins of literary studies distorts the coverage of that vast realm of experience arising from imperial contacts. Thus, for the most part, the English criticism of empire has been, until recently, almost all of one kind: the slightly ill-at-ease, slightly ashamed, but enormously forgiving recognition of imperial themes in writers from 'the center': Forster on the possibilities of intercultural communication, Conrad on the savagery of civilized man, Lawrence on the liberating chaos of primitive religion, Greene on the political intrigues of European governments in cultures they do not understand.

In *Fiction and the Colonial Experience*, Jeffrey Meyers illustrates the kind of criticism widely found in English studies of the 'colonial novel'. He recognizes liberally that 'Europe [has] impose[d] its manners, customs, religious beliefs and moral values on an indigenous way of life', and that the reverberations from centuries of foreign domination constitute 'one of the most significant historical developments in our century'.[54] But the spirit is past tense. He explains that 'the colonial novel runs parallel to the rise and fall of western colonialism', as if the colonial cycle had run its course. By doing so, he separates himself sharply from the discourse of critics from the former colonies who, despite their innumerable divisions and outlooks, are unified in identifying a postwar structure of neocolonial dependency.

In this framework of past transgression and present enlightenment, Meyers finds the pattern for his study of canonical 'colonial' literature. He sets the early Kipling short stories against the collective efforts of Conrad, Forster, and the Kipling of *Kim*, allowing him to complain of the stereotyping of the native in the earlier work, and, above all, its outlook in which 'all moral issues are seen from only one point of view'. On the other hand, the 'good' colonial novel offers what Meyers calls a 'humanistic' approach, which has the attraction of trading in firm moral conviction for 'a universal fascination with the savage and the incomprehensible'. This fascination is supposed to lead us to a point where we can mediate upon the 'human lessons of previous colonial entanglements'.

It is assumed that 'deracinated white men' who venture into hostile regions for the purpose of self-questioning are paying tribute to the native; their vision is purer than the early Kipling sort of white, because they understand that bestial nature is preferable to technological civilization. Modernism has redeemed white men from the modern world by teaching them (through the savage's mute example) that rationality, commitment, and technology are swindles. Myers' projection attributes to the 'savage' an incomprehensibility that conveniently obscures the inequality of the colonial relationship, while pretending to thank the 'native' for a quality that, under the conditions of a developing world, could only hinder him.

Similarly on the Left, Terry Eagleton's *Exiles and Emigrés* — a well-known work on the exile theme by a writer often sensitive to the undersides of English rule — is surprisingly reluctant to address the effects of colonialism on the concept of exile itself. He begins by referring to the absence of English writers among the century's best, and by pointing to 'certain central flaws and impoverishments in conventional English culture itself. That culture was unable, of its own impetus, to produce great literary art'.[55] Eagleton attributes these impoverishments to England's inwardness. On the contrary, the successful James and Conrad 'bring to bear on the culture a range of experience — of America, Europe, Africa, the East . . . . It was out of this tension that James and Conrad created their major work; and it was a tension notably absent in the work of their contemporaries'.[56]

Despite this suggestive way of putting things — finding in the transplanted English gentlemen, James and Conrad, a vital contact with the colonial world — Eagleton's book basically combats English insularity only by binding it more closely to European insularity. His efforts are unnecessarily modest. While Eagleton in other places attempts to revivify English culture with theories from Germany and France, he stops short of including in this work the thinking of colonial subjects, despite their screaming relevance to his theme. Once more the colonies are a passive fund of good writing material: Conrad brings back impressions from Africa and the east, whose noteworthiness lies in their contribution to the production of 'great literary art'.

Again, novels in the postwar period are unique because they operate in a world where the level of communications, the widespread politics of insurgent nationalism, and the existence of large international cultural organizations have made the topics of nationalism and exile unavoidably aware of one another. The idea of nationhood is not only a political plea, but a formal binding together of disparate elements. And out of the multiplicities of culture, race, and political structures, grows also a repeated dialectic of uniformity and specificity: of world culture and national culture, of family and of people. One of many clear formulations of this can be found in Fanon's statement that '[i]t is at the heart of national consciousness that international consciousness lives and grows'.[57] These universalist tendencies — already implicit in the concept of 'inalienable rights' — is accentuated by the break-up of the English and Spanish imperial systems, with their unities of language, their common enemies, and (in the case of Spanish America) their contiguous terrain. Examples of the persistence of this motif might be found, for instance, in the controversial role of the terms 'Africa' in the writing of the Nigerian author Chinua Achebe, or 'America' in the essays of the Cuban patriot José Marti.

Thus, of course, not all Third World novels about nations are 'nationalistic'. The variations range from outright attacks on independence, often mixed with nostalgia for the previous European *status quo* (as in the work of V. S. Naipaul, Manohar Malgonkar, and others), to vigorously anti-colonial works emphasizing native culture (Ngugi wa Thiong'o, Tayib Salih, Sipho Sepamla, and others), to cosmopolitan explanations of the 'lower depths', or the 'fantastic unknown' by writers acquainted with the tastes and interests of dominant culture (García Márquez, Wole Soyinka, Salman Rushdie, and others).

As we shall see, in one strain of Third World writing the contradictory topoi of exile and nation are fused in a lament for the necessary and regrettable insistence of nation-forming, in which the writer proclaims his identity with a country whose artificiality and exclusiveness have driven him into a kind of exile — a simultaneous recognition of nationhood and an alienation from it. As we have said, the cosmopolitan thrust of the novel form has tended to highlight this branch of well-publicized Third World fiction. One result has been a trend of cosmopolitan commentators on the Third World, who offer an *inside view* of formerly submerged peoples for target reading publics in Europe and North America in novels that comply with metropolitan literary tastes.

Some of its better known authors have been from Latin America: for example, García Márquez, Vargas Llosa, Alejo Carpentier, Miguel Asturias, and others. But there is also a related group of postwar satirists of nationalism and dependency — writers of encyclopedic national narratives that dismember a recent and particularized history in order to expose the political dogma surrounding and choking it. Here one thinks especially of the Indo-English author Salman Rushdie, of the Paraguayan novelist Augusto Roa Bastos, and the South African Nadine Gordimer, along with many others.

In the case of Salman Rushdie, for instance, the examples of India and Pakistan are, above all, an opportunity to explore postcolonial *respon-sibility*. The story he tells is of an entire region slowly coming to think of itself as one, but a corollary of his story is disappointment. So little improvement has been made. In fact, the central irony of his novels is that independence has damaged Indian spirits by proving that 'India' can act as abominably as the British did. In a kind of metafictional extravaganza, he treats the heroism of nationalism bitterly and comically because it always seems to him to evolve into the nationalist demagogy of a caste of domestic sellouts and powerbrokers.

This message is very familiar to us because it has been easier to embrace in our metropolitan circles than the explicit challenges of, say, the Salvadoran protest-author Manlio Argueta, or the sparse and caustic satires of the Nigerian author, Obi Egbuna. However, it is perhaps the trend's overt cosmopolitanism — its Third World thematics as seen through the elaborate fictional architecture of European high art — that perfectly imagines the novel's obsessive nation-centeredness and its imperial (that is, universalizing) origins. Distanced from the sacrifices and organizational drudgery of actual resistance movements, and yet horrified by the obliviousness of the west towards their own cultures, writers like Rushdie and Vargas Llosa have been well poised to thematize the centrality of nation-forming while at the same time demythifying it from a European perch. Although Vargas Llosa's erudite and stylistically sumptuous *The War of the End of the World*, for example is not at all characteristic of the 'counter-hegemonic aesthetics' of much Third World writing, its very disengagement frees him to treat the ambivalence of the independence process as a totality, and, although negatively, reassert its fundamental importance to the postcolonial imagination. His treatment may be neither the most representative nor the most fair, but its very rootlessness brilliantly articulates the emotional life of decolonization's various political contestants. It is 'in-between'.

Based on the historical classic, *Rebellion in the Backlands* (1902) by Euclides da Cunha, the novel immortalizes that notoriously elusive movement in the history of post-independence when, having declared itself a democratic republic, the country erupts into civil war, and all factions scramble for power. With the same cosmic pessimism as his earlier treatment of failed republicanism in *Conversation in the Cathedral* (1969), which dealt with the sadism and corruption of the Odría dictatorship in his native Peru as seen through the conversations of two characters in a seedy Lima bar, *The War of the End of the World* is in a sense a companion piece to that earlier novel. In a much less experimental prose and with a straight chronological structure recalling the Lukácsian high bourgeois 'historical' novel, it dissects the failures not of Peru, but of neighboring Brazil, whose epic dimensions amount in Vargas Llosa's view to a kind of Latin American model of disappointed promise, self-serving domestic machinations, and foreign interventions, which combine to ensure the continuity of military dictatorship.

If *Conversation in the Cathedral* followed the logic of his epigraph there from Balzac, that 'the novel is the private history of nations', and was filled with Vargas Llosa's own personal reminiscences of Peruvian life under Odría in the 1950s, *The War of the End of the World*, precisely because of Brazil's relative cultural distance within a common Latin American reality, allowed for a more reportorial stance, the country separated from him not only by language and geography, but by time, since the story's events take place in 1896–7. In a sense, its setting in Latin America, which (unlike Africa, Asia, and the Caribbean) achieved formal independence in the nineteenth century, captures with extraordinary clarity the ongoing link between the era of European nation-forming and the quite different process of contemporary decolonization, since the novel, published in 1981, can only be read backwards through those well-known events. An angry opponent of Latin American guerrilla movements, Vargas Llosa here chooses a setting that allows him to mull over the components of a domestic liberal democracy that has eluded his own land, and that is characteristic (in his view) of the nation-forming of a Europe that he emulates artistically, and knows and loves personally from several decades of travel.

The story deals with an actual history: the turn-of-the-century rise of a commune of religious fanatics in the Canudos backlands region of Bahía in north-eastern Brazil. They thrive under the direction of an apocalyptic visionary named Antonio Conselheiro (Anthony the Counsellor), whose devoted followers are drawn from Brazil's *jagunços* — an underclass of reformed criminals, landless peasants, and lumpen outcasts. Speaking in parables and working miracles, the 'Counsellor' wins an immense following dedicated to chasing the Devil from the land, and enraptured by his call to 'animate your collective memory in order to remember the future'. After a while, the rabble becomes a well-drilled, paramilitary cult defending the 'New Jerusalem' of Canudos, which has become, both in their own minds and in that of the government, a counter-base of power, fiercely Catholic (although they practice free love), and unwilling to recognize the new constitution, the national census, or the concept of using money as a unit of exchange. The millenarian promise of communal happiness enrages the local landowners after a series of raiding operations on the neighboring *haciendas* and the seizure of land.

As we watch the rise of Canudos and follow the dreams of its inhabitants the reaction of the outside world gets full play in the novel. In the on-the-spot reporting of a 'myopic journalist', the Brazilian public gradually learns of the cult but only through the distorting veil of the ruling party's newspapers. Eventually, the Bahian Progressive Republican Party tries to disgrace the ruling Conservatives by claiming that the cult is their creation, and by arguing that they have enrolled the aid of the English crown, which is supposedly running guns to the rebels through a certain Galileo Gall. A red-haired Scottish phrenologist, Gall is comically portrayed in the book as a libertarian anarchist and believer in scientific progress, who has fled imprisonment in Spain, writes political dispatches for a French journal, argues that Satan rather than God is the true rebellious prince of freedom, and who sets out for Canudos to find the living proof of his ideals. In fact, it is the Liberals who are arming Canudos. After three unsuccessful military expeditions, the army, by then thoroughly bedraggled and demoralized, finally crushes the commune in a genocidal fury in the novel's closing chapter.

In the unspeakable hopelessness and desolation of Vargas Llosa's vision of politics, the mythmaking necessary for mobilizing large social forces for change becomes nothing more than, on the one hand, the pitiful utopian dreams of what Fanon called in a different context the 'wretched of the earth', and, on the other, the quite deliberate lies of the old guard. Nevertheless, even if in a series of ironic reversals, it documents all the necessary components of nation-forming which is its real subject: the sense of religious mission with is attendant violence, the consolidating force of the national press, the treasonous impulses of a ruling clique relying on the aid of European intervention, the proto-socialist coloring of the guerrilla opposition, and the misplaced and naive solidarities of the fellow traveller. Particularly the attention Vargas Llosa gives to the political mythmaking of the 'word' — whether in the form of the prophetic utterances of the 'Counsellor' or the dispatches of the 'myopic journalist' (a central character of the novel) and those of Gall — is characteristic of the cosmopolitan writers of the Third World, who do not participate in the mythmaking, but comment on it metafictionally. This feature is especially pronounced here since Vargas Llosa's source is da Cunha's legendary 'non-fictional' *Rebellion in the Backlands.*

If political mythmaking is the novel's unifying theme, it is also important for Vargas Llosa to show its attractions to all contestants. In the end, not even the thorough obliteration of Canudos, in which tens of thousands die horribly, can destroy the persistent self-delusion of the dispossessed. Asked by an army colonel what happened to the commune leader Abbot João, an old peasant woman gleefully says in the novel's closing lines, 'Archangels took him up to heaven ... I saw them'. Similarly, in one of the many conversations between Galileo Gall and the stoical landowner, the Baron Canabrava, the image-making of the other side is discussed:

> 'As is the case with many idealists, [General Moreira Cesar] is implacable when it comes to realizing his dreams .... Just think what's going to happen when that idealist has the monarchists, Anglophile insurgents of Canudos at his mercy,' he said in a gloomy voice .... 'He knows that they're really neither one, but it's useful to the Jacobin cause if that's what they are, which amounts to the same thing. And why is he doing what he's doing? For the good of Brazil, naturally. And he believes with all his heart and soul that that's so.'[58]

It would be wrong, however, to think that Vargas Llosa was merely anatomizing a general process — that his cosmopolitanism freed him from the same national obsession found in the writerly milieu he was implicitly critiquing. How can one miss his scornful caricature of liberation theology, for example, in the monstrous Christian 'base camp' that was Canudos? Or how can one fail to read in the 'Counsellor's' confused proto-socialism a fundamentally reactionary cult of the personality? It is very unlikely that the, on some level admirable, fanaticism of the *jagunços* with its horrible consequences was not inspired very directly by Vargas Llosa's own reading of Peru's Maoist rebels, *Sendero Luminoso* ('Shining Path').

People who study the twentieth century confront a period unlike any other in traditional literary study. Many of the period's social characteristics are quantitative extensions of characteristics already present in the nineteenth and early twentieth centuries — including the 'massification' of the literary audience, the identity of writer and critic, the systematic commercial and governmental regulation of artistic products. However, others are entirely new, particularly the growth of the international electronic media.

To study the literatures of global dependency is to study traditional cultures, which are especially sensitive to the effects of these media. The late twentieth century is witnessing the universal reach of a culture of unimaginable immediacy — a culture of 'instant' heroes, 'instant' tragedy, 'instant' record-breaking, 'instant' classics. This is, first of all, a function of the technologies which allow for 'instant' communication. But there is more to it than that; as always, the socially specific causes lie behind a facade of impersonal technology. That is, 'immediacy' is also the expression of the changeable policies of the institutions which have increasingly established control over the dispersal of images. At no time more than the present has it been possible to see the triumph of elusive 'forms', and imaginative constructs of color, sound, and words on celluloid, plastic, and paper — a triumph over the concrete acts these 'forms' resemble but cannot replace.

So the study of contemporary fiction, above all in these neocolonial contexts, is always a comment on the responsible practice of interpreting the images of *today* — how to place them, how to give them perspective, how to discuss the way they reflect a submerged history while turning it into a contemporary, instantaneous shadow.

Notes

1 Quoted in Peter Worsley, *The Third World* (Chicago: University of Chicago Press, 1964), p. 5.
2 Raymond Williams, *The Year 2000* (New York: Pantheon, 1983).
3 Armand Mattelart, 'Introduction', in *Communications and Class Struggle*, vol. 2 (New York: International General, 1983), p. 57.
4 Paul Ricoeur, 'Civilization and national cultures', in *History and Truth* (Evanston, Ill.: Northwestern University Press, 1965), pp. 276—7.
5 Hugh Seton-Watson, *Nations and States: An Enquiry into the Origins of Nations and the Politics of Nationalism* (Boulder, Col.: Westview Press, 1977), p. 5.
6 See, for example, Fredric Jameson's 'Third-World literature in the era of multinational capital', *Social Text*, no. 15 (Fall 1986), pp. 65—88. This essay was written before Jameson's piece, which appeared following a conference on 'The Challenge of Third World Culture' at Duke University in September 1986 at which sections of the present essay were delivered. See also the response to his essay by Aijaz Ahmad, 'Jameson's Rhetoric of otherness and the "National Allegory"' in *Social Text*, no. 17 (Fall 1987), pp. 3—25.
7 See Benedict Anderson's *Imagined Communities*, (London: Verso and New Left Books, 1983); as well as introductory chapters of overviews of so-called 'Commonwealth' literature, Bruce King's *The New English Literatures* (London: Macmillan, 1980). For a work not restricted either to English or Third World contexts, see H. Ernest Lewald's anthology *The Cry of Home*, 1972.

8 Examples might include Edward Said, Ariel Dorfman, Hugh Ridley, Amiri Baraka, Homi Bhabha, Jean Franco, Abdul JanMohamed, Cornell West, and others.

9 Gordon Lewis, *Slavery, Imperialism, and Freedom: Studies in English Radical Thought* (New York and London: Monthly Review Press, 1978), p. 304. For the French tradition see Barbara Harlow's *Resistance Literature* (New York and London: Methuen, 1987), p. 27, with its discussion of France-based North African writers such as Mehdi Charef, Driss Chraibi, and Rachid Boudjedra.

10 Salman Rushdie, 'The Empire writes back with a vengeance', *The Times*, 3 July, 1982, p. 8.

11 Ariel Dorfman, *The Empire's Old Clothes* (New York: Pantheon, 1983), p. 8.

12 For the purposes of this study, by far the best works on the nation are Benedict Anderson, *Imagined Communities. Reflections on the Origin and Spread of Nationalism* (London: Verso and New Left Books, 1983); Horace Davis, *Towards a Marxist Theory of Nationalism* (New York and London: Monthly Review Press, 1978); Hans Kohn, *Nationalism: Its Meaning and History* (New York and Cincinnati: Van Nostrand Company, 1965); Tom Nairn, *The Break-up of Britain: Crisis and Neo-Nationalism* (London: New Left Books, 1977); Peter Worsley, *The Third World*; and, Seton-Watson, *Nations and States* — particularly, Anderson, Worsley and Nairn.

13 Anderson, op. cit., p. 12.

14 See Elie Kedourie, *Nationalism* (Essex: Anchor Press, 1960), p. 63: '"Only one language," says Schleiermacher, "is firmly implanted in an individual . . . . For every language is a particular mode of thought and what is cogitated in one language can never be repeated in the same way in another"'. This was the philosophical foundation in Germany for a much broader social movement described by Carlos José Mariátegui citing Francesco de Sanctis: 'In the history of the West, the flowering of national literatures coincided with the political affirmation of the nation. It formed part of the movement which, through the Reformation and the Renaissance, created the ideological and spiritual factors of the liberal revolution and the capitalist order': *Seven Interpretive Essays on Peruvian Reality* (Austin, Texas; University of Texas Press, 1971), p. 183.

15 The phrase is Anderson's. See also Anthony Barnett, 'Salman Rushdie: a review article', *Race and Class*, Winter 1985, p. 94: 'The novel as a literary form, like the newspaper, was one of the conductors of, and remains part of, the essential chorus for the rise of nations and nationalism.'

16 The phrase is Anderson's.

17 Mariátegui, pp. 187–8.

18 Ernest Gellner, quoted in Anderson, p. 15.

19 See Worsley, op. cit., p. 130: 'To what extent does this ideological emphasis upon the "unity" of the nation and the homogeneity of society reflect a real absence of social differentiation in the new societies, and to what extent is it merely another instance of the familiar rhetoric of all nationalists who, from Fichte onwards, have always appealed to an often spurious solidarity embracing all classes and conditions of the nation . . .?'.

20 Eric Hobsbawm, *The Invention of Tradition* (Cambridge: Cambridge University Press, 1983), p. 7.

21 Anderson, op. cit., p. 35.

22 Michael Holquist (with Katerina Clark), *Mikhail Bakhtin* (Cambridge, Mass.: Harvard University Press, 1984) has tried to divorce Bakhtin from the tradition of the Russian school of social critics (Dobrolyubov, Chernyshevsky) and

fix him within Russian formalism and a kind of mystical enthusiasm for the complexity and plenitude of the 'utterance', by which Holquist means the principles of 'psychological depth' and 'political pluralism'. To do so, he ignores not only Bakhtin's explicit attempts to revise Russian formalism (to 'socialize' it), but his deliberate and savage attacks on literary modernism and psychoanalysis. As a whole, Holquist has interpreted Bakhtin's assault on the orthodoxies of fixed language to be veiled attacks on Stalinism; but it is much more likely that they were attacks on the belletrism, scientism, and obscurantism of western cultural practice. Tzvetan Todorov (*Mikhail Bakhtin: The Dialogic Principle* (Minneapolis: University of Minnesota Press, 1984)) emphasizes 'heteroglossia', and interprets it (incorrectly) to be a kind of prototype of Julia Kristeva's impersonal 'intertextuality'.

23 Mikhail Bakhtin, 'Epic and novel', in Michael Holquist and Caryl Emerson (eds) *The Dialogic Imagination* (Austin, Texas: University of Texas Press, 1981), p. 12.
24 Bakhtin, op. cit., p. 13.
25 Hobsbawm, op. cit., p. 5.
26 Anderson, op. cit., p. 19.
27 Regis Debray, 'Marxism and the national question', *New Left Review*, no. 105, Sept.–Oct. 1977, p. 26.
28 Debray op. cit. p. 27 (his emphasis).
29 See 'Populism', in Worsley, op. cit., pp. 118–74.
30 Erich Auerbach, *Mimesis: The Representation of Reality in Western Literature* (Princeton: Princeton University Press, 1953), p. 491.
31 Bakhtin, op. cit., p. 38.
32 Bruce King, *The New English Literatures* (London: Macmillan, 1980), p. 42.
33 Bakhtin, op. cit., p. 30.
34 Tzvetan Todorov, *Mikhail Bakhtin: The Dialogic Principle* (Minneapolis: University of Minnesota Press, 1984), p. 58.
35 Walter Benjamin, 'The storyteller: reflections on the works of Nikolai Leskov', *Illuminations* (New York: Schocken, 1969), p. 87.
36 Benjamin, op. cit., p. 88.
37 ibid., p. 89.
38 ibid., p. 97.
39 Typical of the better accounts of nationalism is this restless paradox of Nairn's: '[There are not] two brands of nationalism, one healthy and one morbid. The point is that, as the most elementary comparative analysis will show, all nationalism is both healthy and morbid', op. cit., p. 347.
40 Kedourie, op. cit., p. 54.
41 Kohn, op. cit., p. 9.
42 Fascism haunts the studies of Kohn, Kedourie, and Hayes especially.
43 Herbert Schiller, *Communication and Cultural Domination* (White Plains, NY: International Arts and Sciences Press, 1976), p. 1.
44 According to Eric Hobsbawm, for example, 'The evidence is overwhelming that at this stage [in the nineteenth century] the crux of nationalist movements was not so much state independence as such, but rather the construction of "viable" states [with the intention of creating] the internal conditions (e.g. a "national-market") and the external conditions for the development of "national economy" through state organization and action': Eric Hobsbawm, 'Some reflections on "The break-up of Britain"', *New Left Review*, no. 105. Sept.–Oct. 1977. On the contrary, he continues, 'the characteristic nationalist movement *of our time* is separatist, aiming at the break-up of existing states'.

Hobsbawm might have added — not only states, but empires.
45 Anderson, section on 'Dynastic nationalism' in *Imagined Communities*.
46 Nairn, op. cit., p. 311.
47 Kohn, op. cit., p. 89.
48 ibid., p. 11.
49 ibid., p. 12.
50 *Many Voices, One World* (Macbride Commission Report) (New York: UNESCO, 1980).
51 Schiller, op. cit., p. 1.
52 Edward Said, 'The mind of winter, reflections on life in exile', *Harpers Magazine*, vol. 269, no. 161, Sept. 1984, p. 50.
53 Harlow, op. cit., p. 14.
54 Jeffrey Meyers, *Fiction and the Colonial Experience* (Ipswich: Boydell Press, 1974), p. vii.
55 Terry Eagleton, *Exiles and Emigrés* (London: Chatto & Windus, 1970), pp. 9—10.
56 Eagleton, op. cit., p. 18.
57 Frantz Fanon, op. cit., pp. 247—8.
58 Mario Vargas Llosa, *The War of the End of the World* (New York: Farar Straus Giroux, 1984), p. 248.

5

Irresistible romance:
the foundational fictions
of Latin America

Doris Sommer

An archeology of the 'Boom'

When Gabriel García Márquez, Mario Vargas Llosa and Julio Cortázar, among others, apparently burst onto the world literary scene of the 1960s and 1970s, they gave the impression that nothing really notable preceded them in Latin America. That impression was reinforced at home by a regional euphoria created, in part, by Castro's triumph in 1959. Revolution promised immediate liberation after the frustrations and disappointments with the gradual evolutionism of older liberal projects. Together with the mass consciousness industries that spread the celebratory mood, the new politics produced an inflated belief that Latin America had finally come of age. It had finally begun to overcome economic dependency by naming it, and to formulate a cultural independence by cannibalizing the range of European traditions, turning them into mere raw material in purposefully naive American hands.[1] Believing that the new literature, known as the Boom, had *invented* a truly proper language, it seemed that the Adamic dream had come true. Latin Americans could finally (re)name the world and, in doing so, name themselves. Caliban could at last possess his own kingdom.

While some critics doubt whether the Boom was a literary phenomenon at all, arguing instead that it was a promotional explosion, the novels themselves show a distinct family resemblance, enough in fact to produce a checklist of Boom characteristics. These include a demotion, or defusion, of authorial control and tireless formal experimentation, all, it seems, directed towards demolishing the straight line of traditional narrative. That line generally coincides with the 'positivist' mainstream of Latin American thought which combines a reverence for positive or 'scientific' data along with the assumption that the social sciences should take the physical sciences as their models. Learning about European positivism in Latin American was like learning that people spoke in prose. It was already a habit of thought by the mid-nineteenth century which had developed, as it did in Europe, from certain disappointments with revolutionary idealism. Herbert Spencer's organicism was especially popular, along with a Comptian schema of progressive stages in history.[2] Though eclectic, positivists tended to favor biology as the hegemonic discourse for predicting and directing social growth. They became the doctors who diagnosed social ills and prescribed remedies. With this authority, they wrote, or projected, what Foucault would call a totalizing 'macro-history'.[3] One result was that national history in Latin America often read as if it were the inevitable story of organic development.

By the 1960s novelists were scorning this habitual naturalization of history. The Boom tried to demolish or trivialize the 'mythic' subtext of national development, letting it peek through the discursive debris as risible simulacra. As they looked back at disappointments and misfired strategies, the new novelists wanted to deny any intellectual debts at home. Their version of literary history described a clean break with Latin American tradition.[4] José Donoso, for example, may be protesting too much in his charmingly self-indulgent *A Personal History of the Boom*, when he writes that the 'monumental omnipresence of the mighty [literary] grandfathers engendered . . . fathers weakened by their preoccupation with their brief tradition'. The next generation was 'fatherless, but, because of that missing link, without a tradition which might enslave us'.[5] If there is an unspeakable anxiety of influence here, the self-proclaimed orphans were more than willing to acknowledge adoptive parents (James Joyce, William Faulkner, and the authors of chivalric romance were favorites); these would vouch for the world (class) stature of the new writers who could not be accounted for in local or even continental terms.

If all this sounds like resistance, it was. Paradoxically, the more the Boom protested indifference to tradition, the more it would send me back to the persistent attractions that caused so much resistance. What was it, I would ask, about earlier Latin American novels that provoked so much resistance and denial? What burden of narrative habits or embedded assumptions could account for so round a repudiation? I wanted, in other words, to locate the Boom's claim of literary discontinuity in a genealogy of Latin American literature that would recognize how, in Foucault's terms, the story of ruptures crosses sides and recognizes the story of continuity.[6] One measure of that recognition, and of tradition's tenacity, is the fact that rectilinear 'historical' narrative can fairly be reconstructed from the efforts to get beyond it. We can deduce, for example, that 'positive' reality was traditionally opposed to magic; otherwise the proto-Boom style of magic realism would represent no new departure. But the novelty is evident from Alejo Carpentier's preface-manifesto to *The Kingdom of This World* (1949), where he complained that 'magic realism' was everywhere in Latin American history except in its literature.[7] And what would account for the tragicomedy of self-defeating repetition in *One Hundred Years of Solitude*, or for the frustration and shame in *The Death of Artemio Cruz*, if not the epic assumptions about Latin American history? History was supposed to be going forward. Social ills were allegedly being cured. In several countries national productivity had apparently been rising, from the middle of the nineteenth century to the populist period of import substitution industrialization during the Second World War. For a change, foreign powers were too busy to supply manufactured goods.

But after the war Latin American history no longer seemed to be a story of progress, no longer a positivist national biography of growth and maturation that was overcoming some childhood or chronic illnesses. When western Europe, but especially now the United States, was again free to meddle in Latin American internal affairs, and when the industrial centers could again step up the production and exportation of goods, populist optimism waned. In the 1960s a school of Latin American economists was consolidating some lessons of populism, without the lingering organicist developmentalism, and insisting that the problems of dependency could be solved only by clear breaks with the past, not by patience. At the same time narrators were breaking or bending the traditional straight line of history into vicious circles. Fuentes made this observation early on, referring to the older generation of novelists as populist[8] and too hastily celebrated their demise. Given the geopolitical deadlock of the United States, however, anti-imperialism and nation-building populism have a long afterlife in Latin America.

My readerly paradox, taking denial as a symptom of unresolved dependence, would not only send me back to the foundational fictions that the Boom was resisting, but also to an entire tradition of resistances in which to locate the Boom. The paradox borders on a typical irony of writing (in) America. Successive generations may deny literary resemblances to the point that denial itself constitutes a resemblance. In this case, the new novelists were, in fact, affirming their place in a Latin American tradition precisely because they protested their independence from it. If the Boom novelists imagined themselves suddenly born into full maturity, other American writers had imagined the same. Jorge Luis Borges jokes about the repetitive circularity and the impossible pride of starting anew in an essay called 'The wall and the books'.[9] He hints that when the emperor of China ordered the Great Wall to be built and all books before his reign to be burned, he already sensed that a future emperor would erase his epoch-founding work with another new beginning. Borges, the American writer, is evidently amused, but also fascinated by the paradox of a tradition built on disdain for the past.

To appreciate this counter-tradition of repeated denials it is important to know that for a long time the main current of Latin American literature took its engagement with politics for granted. The 'unacknowledged' ties between writing and legislating that Shelley wanted to reveal are no secret in Latin America. Arguments can and will be offered here for the coincidence between establishing modern nations and projecting their ideal histories through the novel. But perhaps the most stunning connection is the fact that authors of romance were also among the fathers of their countries, preparing national projects through prose fiction, and implementing foundational fictions through legislative or military campaigns. At the turn of the nineteenth century, there was already a page-long list of Hispano-American writers who were also presidents of their countries.[10] A comparable list for lesser offices might seem endless. And despite important parallels, North American writers who were establishing a national literature often assumed a political distance that allowed for an apparently unfettered critique of society. Latin Americans seemed more integrated into partisan struggles than given to transcendent criticism of social evils. Their extra-literary debates, like their novels, cast particular social interests into clearly identifiable actors.

By the end of the last century, however, economic prosperity coincided with positivist state policies that preferred to engage real social scientists over writers. A standard but none the less useful literary periodization distinguishes between a traditional, politically active intelligentsia and the newer classes of professional statesmen and artists. The intellectual division of labor had swung a literary pendulum away from the affairs of state towards a realm of 'pure' art, where writers tended to be relieved of, or exiled from, political responsibilities, and free to develop the preciousness of *modernismo*.[11] But by 1941, when Pedro Henríquez Ureña delivered his now classic Harvard lectures on 'Literary currents in Hispanic America', it was obvious that the pendulum had swung back to engagement for many of the continent's writers. The younger generation was split between the poetic vanguard of Borges and early Neruda who inherited the 'splendid isolation'[12] of the modernists, and an exalted or rebellious neo-Romanticism which gradually led back to the 'old habit of taking part in political affairs',[13] though most of these writers seemed no longer to hope for political leadership. Instead they often wrote from a 'nativist' or reformist opposition in order to sway opinion about, for example, race relations or economic policy. Many dedicated themselves to reform through education, as had Domingo F. Sarmiento and the many nation builders who followed. Nevertheless, to cite only two examples of the tradition's resilience after the Harvard lectures, by 1948 the novelist Rómulo Gallegos became Venezuela's first freely elected president, and in 1962 the novelist and story writer, Juan Bosch, won a landslide victory in Henríquez's native Dominican Republic. This periodization is, of course, very rough. But — like so much Henríquez Ureña wrote — its boldness and clarity are anchored in a wealth of detail. So I don't presume to improve on the scheme; I am simply bringing it up to date by briefly considering how the Boom tried to depart from historical novels and novelized history.

The Boom's fine ironies and playfulness can be read as a rejection of positivist assumptions and a capitulation to the apparent chaos of Latin American history. Or, it is a giddiness that comes from reaching a premature end of history and finding that the word end ceases to be synonymous with purpose, a looking back without being able to distinguish any process to the movement. Since Fuentes' essay we have been used to thinking of these revisions of history as describing circles in which original tragedies repeat themselves as farce. But the image I prefer is one that Mario Vargas Llosa builds up to in *Aunt Julia and the Scriptwriter*: an earthquake that levels the most baroque architectural and literary construction imaginable. The construction helplessly confuses

Vargas Llosa's autobiographical romance with the scriptwriter's stereotypic, ever-escalating and mutually invading soap operas until it is impossible to distinguish one story, character, or moral from the others, until the poor scriptwriter cracks under the once multiple but now cumulative and mangled project that falls on his, their, our, heads.

For those of us who survived the Boom, it evidently could not have been the end of history. Time passes and pendulums swing. Even some writers who had written circles around history in the 1960s and 1970s began to experiment with new versions of more traditional forms.[14] This is also true of film, as Fredric Jameson shows by measuring the 'enfeebled' postmodern history of glossy nostalgia films in America against the historically dense Latin American cinema he calls 'magic realist'.[15]

A burden of feeling

The return of a repressed historical tradition in Latin American narrative may make us wonder why we had largely accepted the Boom's playfully pessimistic terms as literarily mature, which is perhaps to say consistent with the First World's taste for the postmodern. The echoes of (self-) congratulation, the almost narcissistic pleasure of having our ideal notions of literature returned to us, should make us ask what eluded our symptomatic reading of the fictions that the Boom deliberately left behind. The question moreover, forces itself on us now that history is back in style. This post-Boom period of the 1980s may therefore make it easier to understand and to *feel* the passionately political quality of Latin America's earlier great novels.

Those novels, so central to the positivist project, turn out, rather curiously, to be historical romances in whose intimate language Latin American nations were nurtured. By romance I mean a cross between our contemporary use of the word as a love story and a nineteenth century use that distinguished romance as more boldly allegorical than the novel.[16] Latin American romances are inevitably stories of star-crossed lovers who represent particular regions, races, parties, or economic interests which should naturally come together. Their passion for conjugal and sexual union spills over to a sentimental readership in a move that apparently hopes to win partisan minds along with hearts. The undeniable burden for the new novelists, then, was formal, sentimental, and political at the same time. To show the inextricability of politics from fiction in the history of nation-building is, then, the first concern of this essay.

I will certainly not be the first to notice this connection. Leslie Fiedler, for example, uses it to launch his study of the ethical and allegorizing penchants in American novels.[17] And, more recently, Benedict Anderson has indicated the ties between nation-building and print communities formed around newspapers and novels. The novels, he says, helped to create 'imagined communities' through their 'empty, calendrical, time', that accommodates an entire citizenry.[18] These analyses are admirably astute and provocative, but I cannot manage to make them suggest why Latin America's traditional novel is so relentlessly attractive. The attraction is practically visceral. It owes much, I believe, to a feature that I hinted at above, though until now it has evidently gone unremarked. I am referring to the erotic and romantic rhetoric that organizes apparently historical novels. This language of love, specifically of productive sexuality in the domestic sphere, is remarkably coherent despite the programmatic differences among the nation-building novels.

My second concern, therefore, will be to locate an erotics of politics and to show how the variety of social ideals inscribed in the novels are all ostensibly grounded in the 'natural' romance that legitimates the nation-family through love. I suggest that this natural and familial grounding, along with its rhetoric of productive sexuality, provides a model for apparently non-violent national consolidation during periods of internecine conflict. To paraphrase another foundational text, after the creation of the new nations, the domestic romance is an exhortation to be fruitful and multiply. It will be evident that many of these romances strive toward socially convenient marriages and that, despite their variety, the ideal states they project are patriarchal or hierarchical. Nevertheless, the question of degree and even style will make all the difference in considering the mixed political and esthetic legacy of romance.

Supplement as history

For the nineteenth-century writer/statesman there could be no clear epistemological distinction between science and art, narrative and fact, and consequently between ideal history and real events. Whereas today's theorists of history in the industrial centers find themselves correcting the hubris of historians who imagine themselves to be scientists, the literary practice of Latin American historical discourse had long since taken advantage of what Lyotard would call the 'indefiniteness of science',[19] or, more to the point, what Paul Veyne calls the 'undecidability' of history.[20] To be more precise, the novelty or, as some would say, the immaturity of post-independence history would bring it close to Veyne's position. In the epistemological gaps that the non-science of history leaves open, narrators could project an ideal future. This is precisely what many narrators did, producing books that can be considered the classic novels of their respective countries: Argentina's *Amalia*, Cuba's *Sab*, Colombia's *María*, Chile's *Martín Rivas*, Brazil's *Iracema*, Peru's *Aves sin nido*, the Dominican Republic's *Enriquillo*, among others. The writers were encouraged both by the need to fill in a history that would increase the legitimacy of the emerging nation and by the opportunity to direct that history towards a future ideal.

Andrés Bello, Venezuela's famed legislator and poet, suggested the necessary connection between fiction and history in an essay written in Chile and originally called, 'Historical method'.[21] There he observed that it was foolish to insist on writing 'scientific' — as opposed to narrative — history in the Americas. Not that empirical and 'philosophical' study was invalid, but that it was inappropriate or premature on a continent where even the most basic historical data were lacking. Instead, Bello supported the narrative option. '[W]hen a country's history doesn't exist, except in incomplete, scattered documents, in vague traditions that must be compiled and judged, the narrative method [is] obligatory. Let anyone who denies it cite one general or particular history that did not start this way.' And Bello wonders out loud if the narrative supplement itself isn't history's 'truest' form; narrative's acknowledgement of its own supplementary nature gives it a freer hand to construct history, not despite, but thanks to the gaps and absences. 'Do you want to know, for example, what the discovery of America was like? Read Columbus' diary, Pedro de Valdivia's letters and those of Hernán Cortés. Bernal Díaz will tell you much more than Solís or Robertson.' It is easy to see that Bello's endorsement of the narrative method in history isn't purely defensive. The narrative supplement has its own charm and free-wielding power because it becomes an origin of independent and local expression. No doubt this is why Bello changed the title of this essay to 'Cultural Autonomy of America'.

Other Latin Americans went beyond Bello's endorsement of narrative in history; they went as far as considering narrative to *be* history, and made calls for a literary action that would fit into the general challenge of building nations. In 1847 the Argentine historian, future general, and president, Bartolomé Mitre, published a manifesto promoting the production of nation-building novels. The piece served as prologue to his own contribution, *Soledad*, a love story set in La Paz shortly after the wars of independence. In that prologue he deplores the fact that 'South America is the poorest region in the world when it comes to original novelists'. More than an esthetic deficiency, this signals social and political immaturity, because, he observes, good novels represent the highest achievement in any nation (*The Iliad* figures in his list of greats). It follows that Latin American life will improve substantially once a number of good novels are written. The novel 'wakens profound meditation and healthy criticisms';[22] it will teach people about their history, about their barely formulated customs, and about ideas and feelings that have been modified by still unsung political and social events. Modestly Mitre protests that his own humble story is meant merely to stimulate other youths to write.

José Martí was another notable propagandist for the nation-building novel. Though he appreciated the literary accomplishments of contemporary European fiction, he felt that its ironies and pessimism would do more harm than good at home.[23] America needed an edifying and practical literature. No wonder he wrote a rapturous letter to Manuel de Jesús Galván upon reading the Dominican's idealizing *Enriquillo* (1882): 'What a Christ-like Enriquillo! How perfect a bride is Mencía! ... This is not a historical legend [Galván's subtitle] but a brand-new and enchanting way of writing our American history.'[24]

Given this kind of enthusiasm, some have speculated about the late appearance of Latin American novels. The most obvious reason is probably the best one: Spain had proscribed the publication, and even the importation, of any fictional material in the Americas. Whether for its own Catholic utopian vision of the New World, or for reasons of security Spain tried to police the colonists' imagination. Novels started to appear along with, and as part of, the emancipation movement which was triggered in 1808 when Napoleon's army reached Madrid. There, he forced the abdication of King Charles and exiled the royal heir Ferdinand VII. This usurpation gave the Creoles an opportunity to break away from Spain by appealing to the venerable Spanish norm of popular sovereignty in the absence of a legitimate king. The Americans' freedom, even responsibility, to rule locally thus provided a traditional framework for incorporating French and English republican philosophy. The first novel published in the Spanish-speaking New World was a good example of the amalgam. *El perriquillo sarniento* (1816, completed 1830), by Mexico's José Joaquín Fernández de Lizardi, is picaresque in genre and enlightened in spirit, a book that seems to come at the end of a literary tradition that runs from *Lazarrillo* to Lesage rather than to initiate a new one. More modern novels, sometimes called romances, did not appear until the mid-century, after independence had been won and national consolidation was the challenge of the day. The coincidence of romance and consolidation, along with the rise of the bourgeois nuclear family, was, as we will see, not merely casual. As Leslie Fiedler has already said for North America, the country and the novel were born together, as long as we take consolidation rather than emancipation to be the real moment of birth. The same can be said of the south. Perhaps this allows us to offer another and equally good reason for the absence of novels before independence. They would have been politically premature until well into the nineteenth century.

All this assumes that literature has the capacity to intervene in history, to help construct it. Generations of Latin American writers and readers assumed as much; and they have produced and consumed foundational novels as part of the more general process of nation-building. But since the 1960s, since Latin America's post-Borgesian Boom in narrative and France's self-critical ebullience in philosophy and literary studies, we have tended to fix on the ways that literature undoes its own projects. This, of course, is a healthy antidote for our centuries-long habit of ignoring or dismissing the gaps and the absence that partly constitute literature. To notice this shift in emphasis, though, is also to acknowledge that earlier writings/readings managed the tensions differently. In the particular case of Latin America's nineteenth-century 'historical' novels, the nagging insecurities that writing produces only peek through the more patent and assertive inscriptions. The tensions exist, of course, and they provide much of the interest in reading what otherwise might be an oppressively standard canon. But what I am saying is that those very tensions are appreciated because the overwhelming energy of the romances is marshalled to deny them.

When the job of writing America seemed most urgent, the question of ultimate author-ity was bracketed in favor of the local authors. They didn't necessarily worry about writing being a supplement; that is, a consciously produced and necessarily violent filler for a world full of gaps. Empty spaces were part of America's demographic and discursive nature. She seemed to invite writing. The fact, in other words, that later she seemed indifferent is notable. It indicates a lack of confidence or optimism among many of the region's important writers in the kinds of projects that earlier generations were helping to write.

Beyond the differences

Read individually, the foundational fictions are very different indeed, not only in time and place but also in terms of their social ideals and concomitant strategies. It seems difficult, in fact, to talk of the books' commonality when the projects they advocate are so varied, ranging from racism to abolitionism, from nostalgia to modernization, from free trade to protectionism. The following series of examples should give an idea of the range.

In *Amalia* (1851), the Argentine José Mármol opposes 'civilization', associated with the free-trading and Europeanizing Unitarian Party based in Buenos Aires, to the 'barbarism' of gaucho-like Federalists who dominated the interior. At the same time he was opposing white to dark skin, a privileged intelligentsia to the untutored masses who supported the Federalist dictator Juan Manuel de Rosas. The elite lovers, whose passion binds this episodic book together, cross no racial or class lines; but they do represent and reconcile rival regions. And, significantly, the hero of the piece is a crossover artist. He is not Amalia's unyielding Unitarian boyfriend from Buenos Aires, but her cousin, Daniel Bello whose sympathies are Unitarian but whose family credentials make him a respectable Federalist. Bello is something of a double agent, a sheep in wolf's clothing, showing allegiance to the Federalist dictator while organizing the opposition. Despite his elitism, Mármol knew that conciliation, flexibility, compromise as far as was possible, were the necessary first steps towards peace and progress.

The racism in Jorge Isaacs' *María* (1867) is more subtle, taking the tragic form of impossible love and inevitable extermination for an African couple; but it is no less necessary for Isaacs' vision of Colombia than it was for Mármol's Argentina. Yet Isaacs dwells nostalgically on what seemed to be some promising amalgams. One would have joined the protagonist, Efraín, to the title heroine who is revealed to be a converted Jewess; another binds Efraín's privileged family to their modest neighbors and friends.

Chile's *Martín Rivas* (1862), by Alberto Blest Gana, attempts to mitigate oppositions by matchmaking across class and regional lines. Martín is a law student whose father had lost a fortune in the northern mining center of Copiapó, while his love is the daughter of the Santiago usurer who had once been Rivas' silent partner. But mitigation depends on more radical change in the tragic Cuban *Cecilia Valdés* (1839, 1882) by Cirilio Villaverde, and *Sab* (1841), by Gertrudis Gómez de

Avellaneda, which show that slavery and racism are the obstacles to civilization, not the handmaids. The generous, selfless quality of Sab's passion for his master's daughter is the measure of his superior humanity and, consequently, an argument for abolition.

To complicate matters more, Clorinda Matto de Turner's *Aves sin nido* (1889) will use the traditionally elitist opposition between civilization and barbarism to insist that Peru's only hope for future justice is to bring enlightenment to the provinces in order to liberate not to exterminate the Indians. But the Brazilian slaveowner, José de Alencar, may be writing about integrating with Indians in order to avoid writing about Blacks. In *O guaraní* (1857) he narrates Brazil's possible idyll once Indians and Europeans learn to love one another. His later *Iracema* (1865) is a more pessimistic Pocahantas-like story that promises political reconciliation through love but faces insuperable odds. And though the white adventurer leaves his Indian princess, like Aeneas left Dido, he takes along their *mestizo* son, a living conciliation of opposites. In a similar move to displace Blacks for Indians, Manuel de Jesús Galván's *Enriquillo* (1882) recreates Spain's first conquest in the New World. Along with *Aves sin nido* and Alencar's books, this has been called an indigenist novel, though Galván could not possibly have been concerned to protect already extinct Indians. But thanks to his myth of an originary *mestizaje* between noble Indians who submit themselves to noble Spaniards under the Emperor Charles V, the Dominican Black and Mulatto masses 'are' Indians. This distinguishes them from the 'Africans' of Haiti who had threatened ruling whites like Galván by invading the Dominican Republic in 1822, freeing the slaves, and fomenting racial/social rebellions for a long time.

Long after national consolidation in the Southern Cone, which produced novels such as *Amalia*, and after Antillean movements for economic and racial solidarity that *Enriquillo* joins, some Latin Americans found that they had to re-establish their independence, not from Spain this time, but from the neocolonial power to the north. From now on the obstacles to independence were local dictators supported by the United States. In *Doña Bárbara* (1929), the future Venezuelan president Rómulo Gallegos projects a double emancipation, from an internal tyrant and her external ally; that is, from the local boss, Bárbara, and her North American accomplice, Mr Danger. And while the hero succeeds in winning back his legitimate control of the land, he is conquered in turn by Bárbara's part-Indian daughter, Marisela. The novel marks the moment under Gómez's dictatorship when oil was discovered and reformers demanded control over national resources and revenues from the foreign extractors.

Are we to assume that the particular national contexts and the partisan programs of the various novels cancel any shared ground? In that case we should ask, for example, how Andrés Bello can write about Chile and sustain an argument about cultural autonomy in the Americas, and why Mitre sets his story in Bolivia though it is relevant for his native Argentina, or why Martí celebrates a Dominican novel as a model for American writers in general. In fact, the novels share far more than their nation-building goals. Read together, they reveal remarkable points of contact in both plot and language, producing a palimpsest that cannot derive from the historical or political differences that the novels address. The coherence comes, rather, from their common need to reconcile and amalgamate national constituencies, and from the strategy to cast the previously unreconciled parties, races, classes, or regions, as lovers who are 'naturally' attracted and right for one another.

This produces a surprisingly consistent narrative form that is apparently adequate to a range of political positions; it describes a fundamental coherence in the nineteenth-century canon of novels and in the political discourse it helped to organize. It was an ideally hegemonic[25] discourse of the most 'enlightened' sector in a given country, meaning the sector that promised to respond to the desires of a broad national constituency. After the long civil wars, progress and prosperity depended on national consolidation which needed reconciliation, not exclusion, of differences. The hegemonic project of the class that would be dominant had to win the support of other interests for a (usually) liberal national organization that would benefit them all, just as the hero of romance won the heroine and her family through love and practical concern for their well-being. A white elite, often in the large port cities, had to convince everyone, from landholders and miners to indigenous, black, and mulatto masses, that liberal leadership would bridge traditionally antagonistic races and regions in a new prosperity.

Therefore, the ideal national marriages were often projected in romances between whites and Indians (the Guaraní and Iracema), or mestizas inspired no doubt from Chateaubriand's *Atala* (Doña Mencía in *Enriquillo* and Marisela in *Doña Bárbara*). The originally Jewish heroine of Jorge Isaacs' *María* is a variation on the interracial romance. The ideal of *mestizaje*, so pejoratively translated as miscegenation, was based in the reality of mixed races to which the positivists ascribed different virtues and failings, and which had to amalgamate if anything like national unity was to be produced. Unity, in positivist rhetoric, was not so much a political or economic concept as it was biological. Since growth meant modernization and Europeanization, the most extreme idealogues (like Argentina's Domingo F. Sarmiento) advocated a combined policy of white immigration and Indian or Black removal, while others (including most of our novelists) settled for redeeming the 'primitive' races through miscegenation and ideological whitening. Vasconcelos gave probably the most famous and utopian formulation in *Raza cósmica* (1925), written after the Mexican Revolution, after the Indian masses had forced themselves into any consideration of nationalism and progress. But as early as Simón Bolívar's famous discourse at Angostura, Latin Americans have at least rhetorically assumed a racially mixed identity. 'It is impossible to correctly determine', said the liberator, 'to which human family we belong . . . . Born all of the same mother, our fathers of different origins and blood'.[26] This is not to say that racism and economic conflicts ceased to exist. One has only to observe that Indian and *mestiza* lovers appear in books like *O guaraní* and *Enriquillo* in order to redefine Brazilian and Dominican peoples as indigenous, not Black, to see prejudice at work. Hegemony, after all, is not an egalitarian project, but one that legitimates the leadership of one social sector by winning the consent of others. Romance had, therefore, to give a loving cast to national unity, not necessarily to equalize the lovers.

Whether the plots end happily or not, the romances are invariably about desire in young, chaste heroes for equally young and chaste heroines in order to establish conjugal and productive unions which represent national unification and which can be frustrated only by illegitimate social obstacles. Overcoming those obstacles produces the desired end (as in *Enriquillo*, *O guaraní*, *Martín Rivas*), while failure ends in tragedy (*Sab*, *María*, *Aves sin nido*). Before proceeding to consider the erotics embedded in these national romances, let us notice that the form itself is something of a reconciliation between two apparently estranged genres, one public and often male-identified, and the other private and feminized.

A marriage of gen(d)res

By labelling these novels romances I do not mean to understate their public function. In the United States, at least, this label has traditionally underscored the ethico-political character of our most celebrated narrative. And given the erotic coding for political factors in Latin American romance, there is no need here to distinguish between epic and romance, even in our contemporary meaning as love story, between nation-building and refined sensibility. In Spanish America the two are one, Walter Scott and Chateaubriand in the same pot-boilers, *pace* Georg Lukács.

In *The Historical Novel* (1937)[27], Lukács set Scott apart from Chateaubriand by an unbreachable esthetic and political distance. During the Popular Front Lukács was reducing his own 1915 distinction between epic and novel[28] in order to defend the novel's construction of social coherence as no less binding than the epic. Novels, he now maintained, could be just as objective and historical. And Scott came closest to the 'great historical objectivity of the true epic writer' (p. 34) who respects and even celebrates historical necessity (p. 58) as progress. Chateaubriand, by contrast, 'chopped and changed his material at will' (p. 290), 'tr[ying] hard to revise classical history in order to depreciate historically the old revolutionary ideal of the Jacobian and Napoleonic period' (p. 27). Like other sentimentalists, he was writing what we now call romance when, Lukács implies, he should have been writing novels. Scott looks ahead; Chateaubriand looks back; Scott's heroes are average participants in historical change; Chateaubriand's are uniquely sensitive victims of history. How could the two possibly be reconciled?

The possibility seems even more remote when we remember that Anglo-American criticism traditionally opposed novel to romance in terms that now appear to be inverted. Novel was the domestic genre of surface detail and intricate personal relationships, while romance was the

genre of boldly symbolic events. The tradition probably originated with
Dr Johnson's definition of romance as 'a military fable of the middle
ages; a tale of wild adventures in love and chivalry'. The novel, on the
other hand, was 'a smooth tale, generally of love'. But Walter Scott
adjusted Johnson's definitions in his own article on romance (1823) for
the *Encyclopaedia Britannica*, stressing the novel's 'ordinary train of human
events (in) the modern state of society'.[29] That is to say, or imply, that
it is a lesser genre, fit more for lady writers and readers than for robust
men. Scott claims, and is largely granted, significance as an historian
because he is a 'romancer', concerned not only with the 'marvellous and
uncommon', but also with the extra-personal and social dimensions of a
collective past.

In the United States writers like Hawthorne and his admirer Melville
picked up this distinction, and insisted they were writing romance as
opposed to novels because of their dedication to America's mission. In
his preface to *The House of Seven Gables* (1851), Hawthorne says that:
'When a writer calls his work a Romance, it need hardly be observed that
he wishes to claim a certain latitude, both as to its fashion and material,
which he would not have felt himself entitled to assume, had he
professed to be writing a Novel.'[30] Undoubtedly, Hawthorne was
hereby distinguishing his ambitious and broadly social projects from
those sentimental novels of the 'female scribblers'. And Perry Miller was
convinced in retrospect that American romances were precisely not
novels because they were not love stories. '[T]he true burden of Romance
in America . . . was not at all the love story. What all of them were
basically concerned with was the continent, the heritage of America, the
wildnerness.'[31] The distinction, though, misses one of the most salient
points of the allegory to which Miller refers; the wilderness was woman,
the object of man's desire and thus the source of his guilt as a conqueror.

Cooper, at least, suggested the connection between the public good
and private desire when he boasted that the distinguishing characteristic
of romance was that it aimed to deal poetic justice all around, and thus
achieve a higher truth than any available from chronicles where too many
heroes marry the wrong girls.[32] North American critics have also
noticed that the apparently male romance and female novels keep very
close company.[33] For Meyra Jehlin, in fact, any distinction would be
moot, since all US fiction of the nineteenth century was some variety of
romance.[34]

But even Lukács, who in the service of the Popular Front[35] theorized
the opposition between 'heroic' narratives of historical events and romantic tales of lachrymose longing, showed, despite himself, how the genres
can combine in practice. Lukács admitted that novels of 'underdeveloped'
European countries could portray neither Scott's middle-of-the-road
modernity nor his celebration of past events. These were possible for
Scott, of course, only because England had already achieved its
'progressive' bourgeois formation. And the happy outcome of her history
produced an entire class of heroes; that is to say, winners. But for countries such as Germany or Italy, where the unification of a modern

bourgeois state was frustrated, so too was the project of writing celebratory Scott-like novels. As in Latin America, European foundational fictions sought to overcome political and historical fragmentation through love. Lukács points to the strategy, but doesn't call attention to the recurring pattern or to its relevance even for Scott: 'Thus, while Manzoni's immediate story [in *The Betrothed*] is simply a concrete episode taken from Italian popular life — the love, separation and reunion of a young peasant boy and girl — his presentation transforms it into a general tragedy of the Italian people in a state of national degradation and fragmentation [into] *the* tragedy of the Italian people as a whole' (p. 70). Gogol, too, concentrates the downfall of the Cossacks in the romance of *Taras Bulba*. It is the tragedy of one of the principal hero's sons who, in love with a Polish aristocratic girl, becomes a traitor to his people (p. 74).

Latin American 'historical novelists' found themselves in a similarly pre-modern situation, although, to follow Benedict Anderson, we should add that they did so before many Europeans, and became models in prose as well as politics.[36] Therefore, Latin American histories during the foundational period tend to be more projective than retrospective, more erotic than data driven. Their genre is romance, which is itself a marriage of historical allegory and sentimentality. Viewed from the margins, then, Scott's 'middle-brow' exemplarity becomes questionable.[37] Still, Scott was a model of what a fully integrated national culture could be, just as the extra-ordinary heroes of Latin American romance were. But to work for his willing heirs in many cases Scott first had to wed Chateaubriand, or Rousseau, or Stendhal. It was their passionate (and especially in Chateaubriand's exoticizing case) sentimentalism that helped to *supplement* the histories which lacked usable, that is, constructive and flattering, data.

Romance, then, is not only the generic brand of nineteenth-century American fiction, as Jehlen points out. In Latin America, at least, it is also the supplement or the correction for a history of non-productive events. Otherwise, why would the familiar form seem adequate to the task of nation-building? Why else would Latin American political and military leaders cultivate and promote the romantic novel as perhaps the most significant discursive medium for national development? Evidently they assumed an analogy, commonplace in political philosophy, between the nation and the family and, by extension, between ideal history and (domestic) romance. To marry national destiny to personal sentimentalism was precisely what made these books peculiarly American. On the one hand, little seemed to determine the direction of historical discourse from the middle to the end of the nineteenth century since, as Andrés Bello seemed to complain, basic data were lacking. But on the other hand, and this is my point, not just any narrative filler would have done.

The glee I surmise in Bello's exhortation to supplement history surely owes to the opportunity he perceives for projecting an ideal history through that most basic and satisfying genre of romance. What better way to argue the polemic for civilization than to make desire the relentless motivation for a literary/political project? To read on, to suffer and tremble with the lovers' drive towards marriage, family, and prosperity, and then to be either devastated or transported in the end, is already to become a partisan.

The historical differences that we have seen affect how the stock characters of romance are cast and how they fare more than they affect the structural relationships among the lovers and the antagonist who threatens to usurp the maiden from her legitimate partner. She is the object of desire. Whether she becomes rhetorically synonymous with the land, as she often does, or with the 'naturally' submissive and loving races and classes that the hero will elevate through his affection, woman is that which he must possess in order to achieve harmony and legitimacy.

A family affair

Romance and nation-building come together in very fruitful ways in Latin America. In Europe, too, love and productivity were coming together in the bourgeois household where, for the first time in the history of the family, love and marriage were supposed to coincide.[38] It is as if America and the novel were destined to be born together. This was Europe's ideal, Imaginary[39] realm for the bourgeois project of co-ordinating feeling with reason, passion with productivity. And no one was more convinced of the possibilities than the transplanted, American Europeans. Theirs was the space to realize the dreams of a corrupt and cynical Old World, the space where domestic 'novels' and ethico-political 'romance' could marry. For all Sarmiento's respect and envy of European models, he knows that Argentina can surpass them.[40] And for all the admiration of French and English novelists, the Latin Americans dare to improve on, or to correct, the tragic, extramarital, and unproductive love affairs of the masters. One example is Mitre's *Soledad*, named after the young heroine who reads and identifies with Rousseau's *Julie* to avoid an aged unpleasant husband and to prepare for an affair with an unworthy young man. She is saved, though, when her cousin and childhood sweetheart comes home from the war of independence and stays to marry her, after the repentant old husband blesses the couple and conveniently dies. Julie's impossible and incestuous dream to combine propriety with passion[41] comes true for Soledad.

Martín Rivas is another example of setting the romance right. It rewrites Stendhal's *The Red and the Black* by having the provincial secretary, Martín, actually marry his boss's daughter, Leonor. We should note that, in the American version, love is sentimental and not romantic in the sense of unrequitable and non-mutual that describes European literary affairs of the same period. René Girard writes that 'Romantic passion is ... exactly the reverse of what it pretends to be. It is not abandonment to the Other but an implacable war waged by two rival vanities.'[42] When, for example, Stendhal's Mathilde de la Mole finally admits her passion for Julien, when she considers herself his slave, the struggle for recognition between them ends and his passion cools. Before this scene he had temporarily made her indifferent by revealing his love. This kind of erotic power play is decidedly un–American. Leonor's adorably foppish brother gets the moral of the corrected story right when he quips: 'The French ... say: l'amour fait rage et l'argent fait mariage; but here love makes both: rage et mariage.'[43]

The object is not to tease but to make babies. The fathers can't afford to eliminate the mothers, but they tend to subsume them and to face the sterile trap of narcissism. And although Girard notes that the only enduring love for the romantics is narcissistic,[44] American domestic and productive love tries to keep the lovers balanced. If the French authors and, for instance, the Richardson who wrote *Clarissa* showed the strains and finally the cracks in the bourgeois ideal of family, the Latin Americans tended to patch up those cracks with the euphoria of recent successes or with the sheer will to project ideal histories.

The successes should not be underestimated; and they sometimes have more than a metaphoric relationship to the project of co-ordinating love and marriage in the foundational novels. In fact the marriage metaphor slips almost uncannily into metonymy when we consider how marriages bridged regional, economic, and party differences during the years of national consolidation. I am referring to data specifically about Argentina and Chile which, nevertheless, suggests a pattern for other countries too.[45] If the love matches in *Amalia*, binding the rival cities of Tucumán and Buenos Aires, and in *Martín Rivas*, where northern mining interests marry commerce in the capital, are an indication of historical accuracy because they coincide with data on regional alliances, other novels may similarly help to explain not only the project but also the process of bourgeois consolidation through literal and figurative marriage. Now we may understand the concept love of country as a metonymy, and the goal of productivity as implying reproductivity. Part of the conjugal romance's national project, perhaps the main part, is to produce legitimate citizens, literally to engender civilization. Evidently, the most stable and legitimate couples could already call themselves family, as in the novels that married cousin to cousin (*María, Soledad, Enriquillo, Doña Bárbara*). But when the incest motif reached the extreme form of love between siblings, a union that would make (economic, regional) intimacy redundant, the lovers enact the tragic dead-end of an unproductive environment. (See *Cecilia Valdés, Sab, Aves sin nido*.)

Let us remember that the challenges of the second half of the nineteenth century were more often internal than external conquest. The uncompromising and heroic militarism that expelled Spain from most of America was now a threat to her development. What America needed now were civilizers, founding fathers, not fighters. Juan Bautista Alberdi, whose notes for a constitution in Argentina became a standard of political philosophy throughout Latin America, wrote that 'glory has ceded its place to utility and comfort, and military heroism is not the most competent medium for the *prosaic* needs of commerce and industry' (as if to say prose were necessarily replacing poetry).[46] He and Domingo F. Sarmiento agreed, at least, on the need to fill up the desert, to make it disappear. What sense was there in heroically reducing warm bodies to dead ones, when Alberdi pronounced that, in America, 'to govern is to populate'.[47] Few slogans have caught on and held so well as this one. Husband the land and father your countries, he was saying; they have already been conquered and now they must be loved and worked.

Alberdi didn't stop at exhortation. His book was a practical manual, and its concrete measure for increasing the population, in good bourgeois form, reconciles affairs of the heart to affairs of state. Alberdi's proposal went like this: he observed, with other 'pre-positivists', that as children of Spaniards Argentines are racially disabled for rational behavior, while Anglo-Saxons were naturally hard-working and efficient. So Argentina should attract as many Anglos as possible. The problem was that the state recognized no religion but Catholicism and, without the legal sanction of intermarriage, these Protestants would inevitably desire Argentine women and debase them, producing illegitimate children. Another problem was how Argentines could maintain political power while encouraging foreigners to make fortunes. Alberdi showed how the double jeopardy could neatly be contained, if only Argentina would grant religious freedom. Then, almost unbelievably, the political architect argues literally that *romance* would conquer prosaic challenges:

> We need to replace our citizens with others more able to profit from liberty. But we need to do this without giving up our racial character, or, much less, our political control . . . . Should we, perhaps, bring in more enlightened conquerors than the Spaniards? On the contrary; we will conquer instead of being conquered. South America has an *army* for this purpose, its *beautiful and amiable women* of Andalusian origin and improved under the splendid sky of the New World. Remove the immoral impediments that *sterilize the power of America's fair sex* and you will have effected the change in our race without losing our language or our racial character.[48]

During the twenty years that Alberdi was matchmaking through these political *Bases*, turning from sword-wielding Joshuas to plough-making Isiahs, we have seen that novelists were also turning one thing into another: sentimentalism into valor, romance into epic, husband into hero. This helped to solve the problem of establishing the white man's legitimacy in the New World, now that the illegitimate conquerors had been ousted. Without a proper genealogy to root them in the land, the creoles had at least to establish conjugal and then paternity rights, making a *generative* rather than a *genealogical* claim. They had to win America's heart and body so that the fathers could found her and reproduce themselves as cultivated men. To be legitimate, their love had to be mutual; even if the fathers set the tone, the mother had to reciprocate. Unproductive eroticism is not only immoral; it is unpatriotic and often related to the barbarous prehistory of the American mission and can be represented by 'unnatural' women for whom sensuality is power. Because their power competes with that of the fathers, the active Doñas Bárbara of foundational romances have to be subordinated, or eliminated along with the gauchos, the local caudillos, and other anachronisms, including the perennially immature wards who are sexual subjects only if they are perverse. The interdiction against exercising power, usually coded as pursuing sexual desire, goes for any mix of Old World habits and the new acquisitiveness, because they threaten reasonable, chaste love and may block the liberal project of commercial development. Natural women (María, Amalia, Mencía, Marisela, Leonor, although this last one is wonderfully willful) of course don't need any power once they land the right men. Instead, they are husbanded by the firm but generous patriarchs. By contrast, the adversaries in romance are greedy — for example, Loredano (*O guaraní*), Ricardo (*Francisco*), Mr Danger (*Doña Bárbara*), Valenzuela (*Enriquillo*). They are almost always the brutish bosses, macho rather than manly and lustful rather than loving.

If the difference between masculinity and machismo is somewhat vague, the vagueness should suggest at least one trap in romance. In its late, anti-imperialist, and 'populist' expressions romance valorizes virility as a uniquely male attribute by definition, while it tries to distinguish between good and bad men. Yet in earlier versions, when romance reconciled equally legitimate members of the nation-family, rather than defending that family from outside threats, the heroes are remarkably feminized. Their brand of productive heroism, in fact, depends on it. Death-dealing machismo became a thing of the past. Almost Werther-like in sensibility, though never losing reason to passion, the romantic protagonists distinguish themselves by looking and feeling enough like women to create an intimate bond with them. Daniel Bello, for example, has such lovely hands that 'any coquete would envy them';[49] and 'the almost *feminine* delicateness of his features',[50] helps to idealize Rafael San Luis of *Martín Rivas*. The title character himself, a model of rational behavior and restraint, is capable of crying like a baby.[51] At the same time, the women are admirably principled and resourceful. Leonor's brother complains, for example, that 'she got all the energy that should have been mine, as the male and the first born'.[52] And Amalia stands up to Rosas' terror by telling his police chief that 'only the men are afraid; but we women know how to defend their forgotten dignity'.[53]

Even in a populist and defensive romance such as *Doña Bárbara*, where any bleeding between male and female categories is felt like a hemorrhage, the apparently ideal man who controls barbarism has a paradoxical lesson to learn. Santos has to become passionate in order to maintain control. 'When one is not a simple soul, like Marisela, or too complicated, which Santos was not, one needs practical solutions.' This means falling in love and getting married. 'Otherwise, you can lose control of feelings and become the plaything of contradictory impulses. This is what happened to Santos.'[54] After he learns to love Marisela, and to love staying home with her,[55] Gallegos can leave the rest to nature. Any doubt regarding the quality or legitimacy of a hero's masculinity is cancelled by the domesticating act of marriage.

Marriage not only projected an ideal state, but also helped to realize the family alliances that supported national governments. If marriage is a 'cause' of national stability, it is also an 'effect' of the nation. Without the concept of nationhood the alliances and the stability they brought would be beside the point. Seen from either angle, the mutual dependence of family and state in Latin America ideally could and sometimes did mitigate the tension between private and public allegiances that has dogged western political philosophy. From Plato, whose solution in *The Republic* was to abolish the family along with its divisive gender roles, and Aristotle, for whom the public man/private woman distinction was useful so long as it was hierarchical, through, for example the English contract theorists and Rousseau's more radical but still incomplete dismissal of family as the natural model for society, political philosophy has had to consider what was 'natural' about the family. One result has been so much debate about Nature, that the concept is continually exposed as a social construction.

By extension, we can see how the variety of 'natural' families celebrated in national romances project specific and sometimes radically different social constructs. In other words, the observation that foundational fictions are national romances tells us only the general political parameters of each novel. *Amalia*, written after Argentine Unitarians and Federalists knew that neither party could dominate and live in peace, projects a marital partnership to replace Rosas, the supreme *pater familias*. *Enriquillo*, by contrast, doesn't banish the father; it distances him in the person of Charles V. This creates a benign and extended patriarchal family that confers more rights than obligations and helps to justify Galván's support for Spain's reannexation of the Dominican Republic. With *Doña Bárbara*, the authoritarian father makes a clear comeback. Venezuela under Gómez seemed neither ready for conciliation nor desperate enough to defer her sovereignty. Instead, Gallegos prescribed a bloodless takeover by the country's natural leadership that would set the national family in order. Despite the similarities of foundational fictions as family romances, the novels offer a variety of options in theorizing the family as a microcosm of the state. Therefore, in the spirit of our novelists, we may develop further options, or at least imagine satisfying public and private relationships.

We can, I think, take a lead from the very foundational romances that helped prepare the familial and often hierarchical rhetoric that recurs in Latin American politics, to steer between the impractical Scylla of discarding the pervasive culture and the unpromising Charybdis of venerating it. One lead could be the sentimental qualities of the romance's heroes. We may remember that juxtaposed to the brutish machismo associated with barbarism, the civilizing fathers were feminized and sentimental. Of course that juxtaposition responded to a period when military heroism seemed anachronistic whereas today it does not. Latin America needs all levels of heroism now that the civilizers to the north look more and more like barbarians. But if we reread the early fathers of Latin America and see them practice the alterity of woman in themselves, if we stop ignoring the feeling side of our Doñas Bárbara or the passions of our Marías, there is no reason why only women should be gentle or only men be heroic. This acknowledgement of alterity might provide a wedge into the polarized gender roles of the populist political imagination we have inherited. Then family would not necessarily assume patriarchy and marriage could mean a non-hierarchical partnership that would exceed the duality Mármol imagined between equally privileged lovers.[56]

Pretty lies

But no matter how attractive utopian readings may be, nor how necessary if we dare to hope for a better world, the perils of the project to rewrite romance are clear form the populist examples. When lovers face greater challenges than mutual reconciliation, when they are threatened by real enemies, the eros of politics may lose the flexibility that made partnerships possible. In *Doña Bárbara*, for example, the authoritarian father's comeback makes sharing power seem unpatriotic or economically irrational.

From the 1920s on, nativist or populist novels, like this one, would coincide with the popular fronts of newly founded communist parties. And, to some degree, the culture of populism is prepared in narratives that recast foundational romances to bring the soldier-citizen back into history. He had been the hero of the wars of independence, and even of the civil wars that followed. But in the following period of national consolidation, which featured programs to populate the empty and ungovernable spaces, we have seen that the fighter was called home to be a father. In the foundational romances of the period manly independence gave way to domesticity. The fathers could not stay home long, though, not after the shocking 1898 intervention of the United States in Cuba's war of independence. And the geopolitical reality of US domination makes a new homecoming seem remote. Spain had finally given up her fight in the Americas; but the US assumes that the Americas are home. Populism, therefore, has an important narrative career in Hispano America, and a long afterlife even when the political culture changes its name. A good example is a Cuban revival of *Doña Bárbara*; I translate it, *Good-bye to Women and Hello to War* (1971) by Manuel Cofiño López.[57] This is again a heroic program of bringing progress to a province sunk in superstition and personalism. And although the title seems to get beyond the romance that organizes other foundational narratives, the story doesn't. It swings back and forth from focusing on the revolutionary girl who is evidently destined for the hero to a woman so magically sexy as to be helpless against perverting herself and her lovers. What is different is the fact that this hero is so gender-pure that salvation through eros does not work, which may account for a certain lack of poignancy.

The populist or nativist period stands out in even greater relief today than it did for Henríquez Ureña in his 1941 Harvard lectures on 'Literary currents', if only because the following generation of writers associated with the Boom were so categorical about breaking with the populist and positivist tradition. We are now prepared to understand their iconoclasm as an attack on romanticized history. The great Boom novels rewrite, or unwrite, the foundational fiction to show that in Latin America there was no romance, no political erotics that could bind national fathers to mothers. And no novel does this more programatically than *The Death of Artemio Cruz* (1964) by Carlos Fuentes.

At the beginning of his career, Artemio Cruz seems like a classic father. I think this is so, less because he was an officer in Pancho Villa's army (Zapata was clearly too radical an option, just as he would have been for the liberal heroes of romance) than because he was a lover. Artemio loved Regina; he braved battles in order to be with her. And she reciprocated, getting ahead of the army to prepare a cozy spot and a warm meal for her man, like so many other *soldaderas* of the revolution. As they made love, they thought back on the idyll of their first meeting, sitting on a beach, watching each other's reflection in the water. But this was a

> pretty lie . . . she had conjured up that she might feel clean and inno-
> cent and sure of love . . . . It had no trace of truth. Neither did the
> truth: it was not true that he had gone into that Sinaloan pueblo just
> as he had gone into so many others, ready to grab the first woman
> who incautiously ventured outside. It was not true that a girl of eigh-
> teen had been thrown helplessly across his horse and carried back to
> the officers' dormitory to be violated in silence.[58]

Later, Artemio faces the fact of his cowardice under fire. But before there is time to invent another pleasing story, perhaps about the consuming love for Regina which prevented him from accepting death, she dies and Artemio turns deserter and opportunist.

Perhaps, though, the 'hero's' greater failure in this unraveled romance is his inability to make the next erotic conquest, the one that would have given him legitimacy. When the revolution ends, Artemio tries to win Catalina Bernal, whose rich landowner of a father is willing to bless the uneven match in order to keep abreast of the times, to insure his holdings by appearing to join forces with the revolutionary victors. Catalina, though, refuses or is unable to make up pretty lies that would legitimate the union through the pretext of mutual love and a renewed foundational romance. She suspects Artemios's treachery against her brother; she is hurt by her father's acquiescence when she herself is proud enough to resist. But mostly she is unsure how real interested love can be.

In *Doña Bárbara* we can read out a hint of guilt. But the self-implication is made relentlessly self-conscious in Fuentes. Here, the foundational love affairs of romance are revealed as rapes, or as power plays that need to traffic in women. On a rereading, we may ask why Doña Bárbara's evil is sometimes hard to distinguish from just revenge, and why Santos' enlightened goodness seems tarnished by a burden of guilt. It is to Gallegos' credit that his 'archetypes'[59] are less, or more, than ideal. Bárbara, the child of a submissive Indian mother and a white adventurer, suffers a gang rape as a teenager after her assailants kill the youth she is learning to love. What she conceives then is a hatred for men and a need to revenge herself on them. Is it possible that Gallegos is suggesting a historical rather than a geographical explanation for the barbarousness of the llanos, that a history of original and consecutive rapes and expropriations of an indigenous population is somehow responsible for the confusion between rights and revenge? The guilt may go as far back as the beginnings of Venezuelan history, when white men began to conquer or exterminate the Indians, just as the half-Indian Bárbara was being conquered and removed by Santos. My speculation gets some grounding in the happy resolution of the plot. It is the romance and projected marriage between Santos and the *mestiza* Marisela. The marriage plans show Gallegos trying to patch up the problem of establishing a legitimate, centralized nation on a history of usurpation and civil war. Marisela offers no resistance; she is more than happy to marry the man on the make and to legitimate his conquest by allowing him to consolidate the nation-building process in an interracial marriage.

If only Catalina would do the same for Artemio, we may sigh. The pair seems perfect: a beautiful aristocratic girl and a willful but rational boy from the provinces with heroic credentials. Fuentes arouses and makes us confront the habits of romantic longing we have learned from national romance. But if she had given in, would Artemio have become more honest or admirable in reconstructing Mexico on a popular base? Or would he merely have seemed more legitimate while reproducing the class structure that equally shameless exploiters bequeathed to Catalina's more elegant father? The reader, perhaps reluctant to give up the romance, probably has few illusions about Artemio's possible career in a country that 'institutionalized' the revolution as a strategy of containment.[60] It is possible that the pretty lies of national romance are similar strategies to contain the racial, regional, economic, and gender conflicts that threatened the development of new Latin American nations. After all, these romances were part of a general bourgeois project to hegemonize a culture in formation. It would ideally be a cozy, almost airless, culture that bridged public and private spheres in a way that made room for everyone, as long as everyone knew where they fitted.

Notes

1 Julio Cortázar, 'Approach to Lezama Lima', in *Vuelta al día en ochenta mundos* (Mexico: Siglo XXI, 1967), recently translated by Naomi Lindstrom in *The Review for Contemporary Literature*, Fall, 1983.
2 See Leopoldo Zea's classic work, *The Latin American Mind* (Norman: University of Oklahoma Press, 1963), and his prologue to the anthology he edited, *Pensamiento positivista latinoamericano* (Caracus: Biblioteca Ayacucho, 1979).
3 Michel Foucault, *The Archeology of Knowledge and the Discourse on Language*, trans. A. M. Sheridan Smith (New York: Pantheon, 1972), pp. 9–10.
4 Foucault, op. cit., p. 5: '*Recurrent redistributions* reveal several pasts, several forms of connexion, several hierarchies of importance, several networks of determination several teleologies, for one and the same science . . .; thus historical descriptions are necessarily ordered by the present state of knowledge.'

5 José Donoso, *The Boom in Spanish American Literature: A Personal History*, trans. Gregory Kolovakos (New York: Columbia University Press, 1977), p. 12.

6 See Foucault, op. cit., p. 6: '[W]e must not imagine that these two great forms of description [continuous and discontinuous] have crossed without recognizing one another.'

7 Alejo Carpentier, 'De lo real maravilloso americano', *Literatura y conciencia política en América Latina* (Madrid: 1969), pp. 116—17.

8 Carlos Fuentes, *La nueva novela latinoamericana* (Mexico: Joaquín Mortiz, 1969).

9 Jorge Luis Borges, '*The Wall and the books,*' *Labyrinths: selected stories and other writings*, ed. Donald A. Yates and James E. Irby (New York: New Directions, 1964), pp. 186—8.

10 Pedro Henríquez Ureña, *Literary Currents in Hispanic America*, 'The Charles Eliot Norton Lectures, 1940—1941' (Cambridge, Mass.: Harvard University Press, 1945), p. 243.

11 Mexico's regime under Porfirio Díaz (1876—1911), whose cabinet was made up of *científicos*, is exemplary of the new positivist regime, but it is not unique. The fact that Rubén Darío, the Hispanic world's leading *modernista*, encountered similar climates combining what he and other poets called crass materialism and freedom to pursue for art's sake throughout much of Latin American and Spain, indicates something of the general nature of this phenomenon. See Angel Rama, *Rubén Darío y el modernismo (circunstancia socioeconómica de un arte americano)* (Universidad Central de Venezuela, 1970), especially pp. 29—30. It is important, however, to remember the exceptions, especially so notable an example as José Martí. Though Martí is usually considered a *modernista*, the term is stretched to include him. His poetry strived for a popular and simple tone, as opposed to the delicate complexities of contemporaries; and his prose maintained a radically ethical and nationalist motivation. Part of the reason for this difference, no doubt, is that Martí's Cuba was still a Spanish colony while other countries had long since won independence; for all his literary innovation, Martí still belongs to a tradition of literary nation-builders.

12 Henríquez Ureña, op. cit., p. 185.

13 ibid., pp. 187—8.

14 In some cases, the masters of the Boom themselves moved away from the canon. Both Cortázar and Vargas Llosa, for example, abandoned the extravagant formal experimentation of *Rayuela* (Hopscotch) and *La casa verde* (*The Green House*) and drifted toward certain modes of 'realism': *El libro de Manuel* (*A Manual for Manuel*) and *La guerra del fin del mundo* (*War of the End of the World*). Even García Márquez left behind the radical 'marvellous realism' and self-referential écriture of *Cien años de soledad* (*One Hundred Years of Solitude*) and moved on to the overflowing orality of *El otoño del patriarca* (*Autumn of the Patriarch*). Furthermore, the 'dictator novels' which appeared in 1974—5, García Márquez's *El otoño del patriarca*, Carpentier's *El recurso del método* (*Reasons of State*), Roa Bastos' *Yo el supremo* (*I the Supreme*) — Donoso's *Casa de campo* is later but could be included — recuperate a representational topic which had a certain ascendancy much before the heyday of the Boom (e.g. Miguel Angel Asturias' *El Señor Presidente*, 1946) but only to deconstruct the centralizing power that underlies the concept of dictatorship. See George Yúdice and Doris Sommer, 'Latin American Literature from the "Boom" On' in *Post-Modern Literature*, ed. Larry McCaffery (forthcoming, Greenwood Press).

15 Fredric Jameson, 'On magic realism in film', *Critical Inquiry*, vol. 12, no. 2

(Chicago, Winter, 1986), pp. 301–25. The label 'magic realism' is evidently borrowed from an earlier period, which Jameson acknowledges by referring to Carpentier's definition (p. 311). That style spills over to García Márquez's prose in *One Hundred Years of Solitude* and also into the recent novel by his compatriot Gustavo Alvarez Gardeazábal, *Condores no entierran todos los días* (1984), the book on which Jameson's exemplary 'magic realist' film is based. And Jameson is right to distinguish it sharply from postmodern nostalgia films. But it is not the only cinematic style that could offer a contrast with the 'historically enfeebled' postmodernism of the industrial west. Another way of pointing out the difference is to say that the protagonist, or subject, is not obsolete in Latin American film and literature. If the Boom problematized the authority and knowledge, it did not kill the subject off. That might be too great a luxury, or merely redundant, for those already marginalized by history. Instead, Latin American narrative is busy constructing multiple selves from the margins of postmodern cynicism.

16 See Richard Chase, *The American Novel and its Tradition* (Baltimore, Md.: Johns Hopkins University Press, 1983, originally 1957, Anchor), p. 13. 'Character itself becomes, then, somewhat abstract and ideal, so much so in some romances that it seems to be merely a function of plot. The plot we may expect to be highly colored. Astonishing events may occur, and these are likely to have a symbolic or ideological rather than a realistic plausibility. Being less committed to the immediate rendition of reality than the novel, the romance will more freely veer toward mythic, allegorical, and symbolistic forms.'

17 This is a paraphrase of the first sentence in Leslie Fielder's *Love and Death in the American Novel* (New York: Stein & Day, revised edn 1966), p. 23.

18 Benedict Anderson, *Imagined Communities: Reflections on the Origin and Spread of Nationalism* (London: Verso, 1983), p. 30.

19 Jean-Francois Lyotard, *The Postmodern Condition: A Report on Knowledge*, trans. Geoff Bennington and Brian Massumi, foreword by Fredric Jameson (Minneapolis: University of Minnesota Press, 1984).

20 Paul Veyne, *Writing History*, trans. Mina Moore-Rinvolucri (Middletown: Wesleyan University Press, 1984). In one chapter called 'History does not exist', Veyne makes a point similar to Bello's, but makes it more generally: 'Science is *de jure* incomplete; history alone can be allowed *de facto* to have gaps — because it is not a fabric, it has no weave', p. 18.

21 Andrés Bello, 'Autonomía cultural de América' (1848), in *Consciencia intelectual de América*, ed. Carlos Ripoll (New York: Eliseo Torres, 1966), pp. 48–9.

22 Bartólomé Mitre, 'Prólogo' a *Soledad* (Buenos Aires: Editorial Tor, Lecturas Selectas), p. 9.

23 José Martí, *Obras completas* (Habana: Editorial Ciencias Sociales, 1975), vol. 23, p. 290.

24 Martí to Galván, 19 September, in *Enriquillo* (Mexico: Editorial Porrúa, 1976), p. 5. And extrapolating from what he considered to be the sorry state of Mexican literary dependence, Martí asked the following rhetorical questions: 'Can there be a national life without a national literature? Can there be life for local artists in a scene always taken up by weak or repugnant foreign creations? Why in this new American land should we live an old European life?' See *Obras Completas*, vol. 6, p. 277.

25 For a succinct definition of this Gramscian concept, see Chantal Mouffe (ed.), *Gramsci and Marxist Theory* (London: Routledge & Kegan Paul, 1979), p. 181. '[A] hegemonic class has been able to articulate the interests of other social

groups to its own by means of ideological struggle. This, according to Gramsci, is only possible if this class renounces a strictly corporatist conception ... also presupposes a certain equilibrium, that is to say that the hegemonic groups will make some sacrifices of a corporate nature.'

26 Simón Bolívar, in José Luis Romero (ed.), *Pensamiento Político de la Emancipación* (Caracas: Biblioteca Ayacucho, 1977), p. 114.

27 George Lukács, *The Historical Novel*, trans. Hannah and Stanley Mitchell (Boston: Beacon Press, 1963), p. 70 (Lukács' emphasis). Other page references will be made in the text.

28 Georg Lukács, *The Theory of the Novel*, trans. Anna Bostock (Cambridge, Mass.: MIT Press, 1971), p. 60. 'The epic gives form to a totality of life that is rounded from within; the novel seeks, by giving form, to uncover and construct the concealed totality of life .... (T)he search which is only a way of expressing the subject's recognition that neither objective life nor its relationship to the subject is spontaneously harmonious in itself, supplies an indication of the form-giving intention.'

29 Walter Scott, 'Essay on romance', *Essays on Chivalry Romance and the Drama* (London: Frederick Warne, 1887), pp. 65—108.

30 Chase, op. cit., p. 18. Chase uses this distinction to announce his own version of the generic differences, especially as they distinguish the English narrative tradition from the American. He cites, for example, F. R. Leavis' comment that Emily Brontë's *Wuthering Heights* is a sport, and adds that it would fit rather well in the bolder American tradition that purposefully neglects to offer coherent resolutions to contradictions (pp. 3—4). Chase illustrates through his choices that the great American romance of Cooper, Hawthorne, Melville, Simms constitute the center of our tradition, whereas Scott is the sole great representative of romance in England. One reason for romance in America is that it accommodates 'Manichaen quality of New England Protestantism' (pp. 10—11).

31 Perry Miller, *Nature's Nation* (Cambridge, Mass.: Belknap Press, 1958), p. 252.

32 ibid., p. 250. And Scott, in his late musings, seemed not to care about the gen(d)eric differences. In 1829 when he reissued the *Waverley* novels under his proper name, Scott made little if any distinction between romance and novel in his 'Advertisement', 'General Preface', or his 'Preface' to the third edition'. The terms seem interchangeable despite the fact that a distinction had been brewing in England for decades before Scott wrote. Perhaps that critical difference owes to Scott's strategic denial of a penchant for the newer, bourgeois, and sentimental novel. Certainly his stories qualify as love stories despite their historical detail. He, in fact, helped to domesticate romance, to bring the adventurous hero back to earth and back home. And home was Rowena, not Rebecca; it was the legitimate pre-scribed family.

33 Leslie Fiedler points out that only several years before he wrote his great romances, Cooper was training himself as a writer by imitating, not the manly historical romancer Walter Scott, but that English gentlewoman and mistress of the domestic psychological novel, Ms Jane Austen. Cooper's earliest novel, titled like one of hers, *Persuasion* (1820), was no parody, but a serious attempt to study the problem of marriage; and this 'first maker of America's myths' continued to impersonate a female with the pseudonym of Jane Morgan until 1823. See Leslie A. Fiedler, *Love and Death in the American Novel* (New York: Stein & Day, revised edn 1966), pp. 186, 190.

In general Fiedler shows how the genres bleed into one another even in their own nineteenth-century terms. The idealizing 'new-comic' plot of the historical romance (boy gets, loses, and regains girl) is evidently a love story; while the sentimental tales of seduction, repentance, and female triumph are in America quite as allegorical and morally ideal as the patriotic romances.

34 Meyra Jehlin argues that, in the terms of our contemporary criticism, the difference between romance and novel becomes even more blurred, because today's theories of the novel tend to distinguish it from nineteenth-century American works in general. If novels resist or self-consciously construct a narrative closure, neither the high-minded adventure stories nor the sentimental tales of this hemisphere qualify as examples. Their desire is ultimately contained in the lap of family life. The strict and absent moral code that organizes American 'romances', through often equally abstract characters, makes Billy Budd bless his executioner for defending social stability; it also makes Henry James typically bring his heroines to the point of recognizing their error and choosing to be good and to fit into an established bourgeois society, while Flaubert's Emma Bovary can only learn that she has no good choices; not that American heroes expect to win, but that their losing is a martyrdom to the unquestioned values of a *status quo*. For the novelist Flaubert, the rise of capital was a historical catastrophe; for the romancer James, capital was simply a fact of life, because America offered a way of transcending class and history. Jehlen will further suggest that the core of America's stable and transcendent ethics is the bourgeois family which has 'inspired the strident masculinity, even the celibacy of its heroes'. We can say, in other words, that the domestication, or 'bourgeoisification', of romance in the Americans either assumes that the hero is a lover turned husband, or it assumes that he should be. Whether we fix on a notion of romance as an erotic quest for stable love or on romance as the quest for freedom that apparently gives up stability, the North American examples finally bring their heroes home or watch them self-destruct. See Myra Jehlen, 'New World epics: the novel and the middle-class in America', *Salmagundi, a Quarterly of the Humanities and Social Sciences*, no. 36 (Winter, 1977), pp. 49–68.

35 Georgi Dimitroff, probably the main cultural theorist for the Third International of the Communist Party in 1935, defended a similar popular front position. He announced that it was a mistake for communists to abandon national heroes and traditions to the manipulations of fascists, it became legitimate and desirable to address the masses in a familiar rhetoric of soil and blood (nation and family) despite the political ambiguity in the party's desperate appeal for mass support. And long after the Second World War, the nationalist 'communist' culture persists, perhaps because that very culture makes alternatives so hard to formulate. See Georgi Dimitroff, *The United Front* (San Francisco: Proletarian Publishers, 1975), p. 78.

36 Anderson, op. cit., p. 49. About the American states he writes: 'For not only were they historically the first such states to emerge, and therefore inevitably provided the first real models of what such states should "look like" but their numbers and contemporary births offer fruitful ground for comparative enquiry.'

37 Richard Chase considers this difference in register to be fundamental in singling out English literature: American writers, he says, are either 'high-brow' or 'low-brow', as opposed to the 'middle-brow' quality of English literature, 'the only one, it may be, in history'. See Chase, op. cit., p. 10.

It seems that by considering Scott to be exemplary, Lukács himself has followed Marx's example in *Capital*, where a discursive slippage begins by claiming merely to describe the case of England and then moves on to using that description as a normative model for other countries.

38 Michael Mitterauer and Reinhard Sieder, *The European Family: Patriarchy to Partnership from the Middle Ages to the Present*, trans. Karla Oosterveen and Manfred Horzinger (Chicago: University of Chicago Press, 1983).

39 Jacques Lacan calls the ideal harmony between mother and child, self and ideal mirror image, the Imaginary realm; it is where love coincides with its object, before love becomes a desire that always falls short of satisfaction. Even readers unfamiliar with Lacan can guess that the father disrupts this harmony. He dominates the Symbolic order, otherwise known as the Law of Language, that sends the child out of Eden. The agent of displacement is more specifically the phallus, that signifier of signifiers and harbinger of the rest of the Symbolic system. As the object of the mother's desire, the phallus destabilizes the Imaginary realm and sends the child out into the world of unstable signifiers where it attempts to become the object of the mother's desire so that harmony can be restored. Another way of plotting the shift from the Imaginary into the Symbolic is to observe that once the child learns that the image in the mirror or the mother can be absent, it tries to compensate for the loss by language; that is, by the very intrusion that both corrupts the harmony and seems to promise a restitution. See his *Ecrits: A Selection*, trans. Alan Sheridan (New York: Norton, 1977).

40 Domingo Faustino Sarmiento, *Life in the Argentine Republic in the Days of the Tyrants; or Civilization and Barbarism*, trans. Mrs Horace Mann (New York: Hurd & Houghton, 1868), p. 13.

41 See Tony Tanner, *Adultery in the Novel: Contract and Transgression* (Baltimore: Johns Hopkins University Press, 1979), 'Rousseau's *La Nouvelle Héloïse*', pp. 113—78, especially the section called 'La maison paternelle'.

42 René Girard, *Deceit, Desire and the Novel*, trans. Yvonne Freccero (Baltimore: Johns Hopkins University Press, 1965), p. 108.

43 Alberto Blest Gana, *Martín Rivas (Novela de costumbres político-sociales)*, Prólogo, Notas y Cronología por Jaime Concha (Caracas: Biblioteca Ayacucho, 1977), p. 249.

44 Girard, op. cit., p. 108. 'The egotistical love of Tristan and Isolde, the first of the romantic heroes, heralds a future of discord ... a false reciprocity, which disguises a twin narcissism'.

45 Diana Balmori and Robert Oppenheimer, 'Family clusters: generational nucleation in nineteenth-century Argentina and Chile', *Society for Comparative Study of Society and History*, 1979, pp. 231—61.

46 Juan Bautista Alberdi, *Las Bases y Puntos de Partida para la Organización Política de la República Argentina* (1852), in Tulio Halperin Donghi, *Proyecto y construcción de una nación* (Argentina 1846—80), pp. 84—111, p. 92.

47 Alberdi, op. cit., pp. 107, 100. There was no purpose at all in 'reducing a mass of men to its eighth part in a matter of hours'.

48 Juan Bautista Alberdi, *Las 'Bases' de Alberdi*, ed. Jorge M. Mayer (Buenos Aires: Editorial Sudamericana, 1969), p. 406.

49 José Mármol, *Amalia* (Madrid: Espasa Calpe, 1978), p. 96.

50 Blest Gana, op. cit., p. 41.

51 ibid., p. 349.

52 ibid., p. 345.

53 Mármol, op. cit., p. 295.

54 Rómulo Gallegos, *Doña Bárbara* (Buenos Aires: Espasa Calpe, 1975), p. 164.

55 ibid., p. 163. 'Marisela will be an obstacle to doing what I want with my life. If I decide, for example, to return to Caracas or to go to Europe, as I wanted

to do earlier and still feel like doing sometimes, what do I do with Marisela?'
56 One serious effort in this direction has been the recent feminist developmental
psychology of shared parenting. Nancy Choderow and Dorothy Dinnerstein,
among others, assume what the tradition of political philosophy suggests,
namely that our hierarchical public behavior is in large measure determined
by our training in gender-coded relationships at home.

The ideal erotic relationships that Mármol describes are truly radical in the
context of romance. Amalia is certainly Belgrano's equal and Florencia is a
resourceful counterpart to Bello. And, in general, the unitarian women in the
novel come off better than the men who run greater risks when they display
courage. Mármol's ideal was evidently extra-literary as well, from the
evidence of letters. His biographer, Alberto Blasi Brambilla, writes that 'he
was alarmed by the patriarchal atmosphere [in Brazil], by women's
dependence on their husbands, . . . although that was the norm in those
times'. See *José Mármol y la Sombra de Rosas* (Buenos Aires: Editorial Pleamar,
1970), p. 53. But we should ask whether the perverse society under Rosas
could be the background for ideal relationships. In other words, we may
wonder if general equality would be the norm in a natural society.

In preparation for a natural order it may not be coincidental that the hero
comes from Buenos Aires while the heroine is from the province. She will
certainly be a partner, but perhaps a junior partner. This adjustment of states
is consistent with Aristotle's distinction between public and private realms
that may share responsibility as long as they are coordinated by a clear division of labor and hierarchy.

Even Rousseau's radicalism stops at total equality, fearing that without a
chain of command there could be no stability: see Jean Bethke Elshtain (ed.),
The Family in Political Thought (Amherst: UMass Press, 1982), p. 18. This, of
course, was a serious consideration for Latin Americans constantly threatened
by civil war and rebellion. To a great extent, the writing of romance was
supposed to promote harmony and order through a projection of a just and
natural hierarchy.
57 *La última mujer y el próximo combate.* Originally published in Cuba in 1971, this
novel has already gone through fourteen editions, winning acclaim in Latin
America and in the Soviet Union. Unlike romantic heroes, who know or
learn that woman is not the irreconcilable other, but a part of oneself,
Cofiño's hero finds no common ground with them, nor does he fear being
seduced by the local vamp. Instead he may resemble the more puritanical
heroes of Soviet socialist realism.
58 Carlos Fuentes, *The Death of Artemio Cruz.* trans. Sam Hileman (New York:
Farrar, Straus Giroux, 1985; originally 1964), p. 76.
59 Rómulo Gallegos, 'La pura mujer sobre la tierra', *Una posición en la vida*
(Mexico: Ediciones Humanismo, 1954), pp. 396–425.
60 The ruling party of Mexico since the end of the revolution is the Partido
Revolucionario Institucionalizado (PRI).

6
Denaturalizing cultural nationalisms: multicultural readings of 'Australia'

Sneja Gunew

Canon 1. A rule, law, or decree of the Church; especially a rule laid down by an ecclesiastical council . . . . A general rule, fundamental principle, aphorism, or axiom governing the systematic or scientific treatment of a subject; e.g. canons of descent or inheritance. (*Oxford English Dictionary*)

What is a national culture? Is it not the expression, in thought — form or art — form, of the Spirit of a Race and of a Place?[1]

Thus 'the English language' and 'the national literature', in dominant definitions, represent ratifications of a selective sense of culture and history, or comfortable affirmations of a certain structure and forms of cultural authority.[2]

Objectives of the Multicultural Program
. . . To improve the accessibility to the arts of ethnic communities.[3]

Multiculturalism . . . is a theory (albeit vague) about the *foundations* of a culture rather than a practice which subsumes cultural ideas.[4]

The narrative of 'Australia' as it pertains to cultural and literary history is dominated by a cluster of organic images comprising, inevitably, new branches springing lustily from old family trees, though the degree of their lateral, sinister, or even autonomous existence varies and depends on whether or not the writer is a universalist who believes in *Weltliteratur* or a republican promoting national uniqueness. A further rhetorical turn roots these growths in the land itself for what, after all, differentiates a post-colonial Anglophone national culture if not 'the' land, the uniqueness of the landscape. And here the colonized, the Australian Aborigines, play a crucial, if highly mediated, role. The land, as we shall see, 'speaks' most authentically through the oral literature of the indigenous nomads: in translation.

In his book *The Function of Criticism*, Terry Eagleton has argued for the necessary construction of a counter-public sphere in which the role of the critic is that of 're-connecting the symbolic to the political'.[5] Purists who are aware of Eagleton's debt to Habermas's concept of the public sphere, which is regulated by reason but which allows for a variety of contending positions, rightly object to the notion that a 'counter'-public sphere could exist at all.[6] For the purposes of this chapter it might be easier to see the public sphere as comprising a series of discursive formations of legitimizing and institutionally endorsed public statements whereas a counter-public sphere qualifies and interrogates these authorizations.

Eagleton goes on to posit (without developing) the existence of such a counter-public sphere in 'the' women's movement. Andrew Milner, drawing upon the work of both Perry and Ben Anderson, as well as Eagleton, suggests that within Australia one of the totalizing discourses of the public sphere has been located in history[7] rather than in Leavisite literary criticism (as Perry Anderson had argued).[8] This paper will contend that a combination of literary criticism and history, in so far as this nexus has manifested itself in some recent compilations of literary and cultural histories destined for English and American readers outside Australia (as much as for an Australian audience), provides a comparable totalizing discourse which helps construct a public sphere of what constitutes legitimate culture. My further suggestion will be that a counter-public sphere may be located in those writings which are currently excluded from these literary and cultural histories for, as Edward Said reminds us, 'culture is a system of discriminations and evaluations ... it also means that culture is a system of exclusions'.[9]

In order to provide a quick overview of the public debate, so that the reader may situate dissonant narratives, I have tried to construct both a familiar expository structure and juxtaposed it with another fragmented narrative, a brief anthology drawn from poetry and some prose which counterpoints some canonical Australian texts with other writings. These fragments do not function as exemplary illustrations supporting the arguments in the expository section, but suggest another kind of narrative of a national culture governed by that relatively new cohesive term 'multiculturalism'.

Culture too is property and must be governed by the customary laws of ownership and inheritance. Multiculturalism, the very term, suggests paternal confusion and maternal promiscuity. In England the term appears often to be used as a euphemism for black—white relations[10] whereas in Australia the inclusion, or not, of Aborigines under 'multiculturalism' is a vexed issue for various reasons which will be explained in the course of this chapter.

Whereas Aboriginal cultural productions are mentioned (one might say appropriated) in several of these compilations in very specific ways, what is not being considered at all is the increasing body of writings from Australians of non-Anglo-Celtic background who are often bi- or multilingual and who write either in English or, if not, are translated into English.[11] If one takes into account this 'dangerous supplement'[12] deriving from a third or half (the figure varies considerably according to the criteria used) of the population, this inevitably changes the genealogy or legitimating myth of origins on which all national cultures are based. It also transforms the 'foundations' and 'standards' (in the sense of the figurative economy) of these literary and cultural histories and, in consequence, changes the nature of the ideological closures suggested by terms such as 'excellence', 'works of international standards', and so forth which are invoked but never, of course, defined, at least explicitly.

But at the outset, since this is addressed to readers outside Australia, two kinds of literary history must be sketched in quickly and, needless to say, positioned (in conscious part at least) from a non Anglo-Celtic perspective.

One of the most famous essays in Australian literary criticism was produced in 1935 by P. R. Stephensen in answer to an English professor's contention that there was no Australian literature and never would be because Australia lacked ruins and 'past glories'.

Australia

A Nation of trees, drab green and desolate gray
In the field uniform of modern wars,
Darkens her hills, those endless, outstretched paws
Of Spinx demolished or stone lion worn away.

They call her a young country, but they lie:
She is the last of lands, the emptiest,
A woman beyond her change of life, a breast
Still tender but within the womb is dry.

Without songs, architecture, history:
The emotions and superstitions of younger lands,
her rivers of water down among inland sands,
The river of her immense stupidity.

Floods her monotonous tribes from Cairns to Perth,
In them at last the ultimate men arrive
Whose boast is not: 'we live' but 'we survive',
A type who will inhabit the dying earth.[13]

Stephensen's 'The foundations of culture in Australia' established a series of tropes which surface in Australian critical writing to this day and thus testify to the endurance of certain values, a textual unconsciousness, which these figures betray. Stephensen argued that although Australian culture may have begun in Britain, 'a gum tree is not a branch of an oak'. The subsequent welter of organic images constructs a logic which suggests that the land itself will spawn this new culture, that 'race and place' are the 'two permanent elements in a culture, and Place . . . is even more important than Race in giving that culture its direction'.[14]

And her five cities, like five teeming sores,
Each drains her: a vast parasite robber-state
Where second-hand Europeans pullulate
Timidly on the edge of alien shores.

Yet there are some like me turn gladly home
From the lush jungle of modern thought, to find
The Arabian desert of the human mind,
Hoping, if still from the deserts the prophets come,

Such savage and scarlet as no green hills dare
Springs in that waste, some spirit which escapes
The learned doubt, the chatter of cultured apes
Which is called civilization over there.[15]

Only those who are native-born can truly follow this cultural directing and, furthermore, nationality is perceived as being the permanent and most worthy extension of the ego. English culture is perceived as being at best a fertilizer which must be used sparingly.[16] It comes as no great surprise that Stephensen concludes that landscape painters rather than writers have best captured the spirit of place since, presumably, visual representation is somehow less mediated than its textual equivalent. Another clue may well lie in the aside that art depends on the patronage of 'men of taste' whereas literature thrives on 'mass-patronage'.[17]

The explicit appeal to a leisured and discriminatory elite is implicitly repeated some twenty years later in an essay produced by one of Australia's most distinguished academic poet-critics, A. D. Hope. In 'Standards in Australian literature' (1956), Hope argued that Australian literature was in danger, on the one hand, of a premature impulse to construct a pantheon and, on the other, of being too much influenced by the 'marked forces' of mass-produced literature. To rescue it, 'adequate organs of informed literary criticism'[18] were needed which would be capable of recognising 'the work of genius . . . that "surpasses the snow-line"'.[19]

Literary standards are established by two things: the existence of undoubted and enduring works of genius and the existence of a body of critical opinion which can only be vaguely defined as the 'judgement of the best minds' which in turn constitutes something equally hard to define, called the 'level of taste'.[20]

That pronouncement constitutes the measure of the public sphere with respect to literary culture. The later image used to describe the work of genius is concretely attached in his essay to a specific Victorian mountain (the land speaks, albeit metaphorically, in ways reminiscent of Stephensen's spirit of place). But not, and this is my central point, univocally.

Australia
You big ugly. You too empty. You desert with your nothing nothing nothing. You scorched suntanned. Old too quickly. Acres of suburbs watching the telly. You bore me. Freckle silly children. You nothing much. With your big sea. Beach beach beach. I've seen enough already. You dumb dirty city with bar stools. You're ugly. You silly shoppingtown. You copy. You too far everywhere . . .[21]

Cultural closures are located in natural features and read as paradigmatic classic realist texts. Behind this essay, apart from Stephensen's, lay another short but highly influential piece by A. A. Phillips. 'The cultural cringe' (1950) placed Phillips with the nationalists who were trying to slough off the 'colonial' label. Hope tended to see Australian literature as part of English and European 'masterpieces' whereas Phillips argued for the abandonment of what he termed the 'cultural cringe' which he saw as being embodied particularly in Australian intellectuals who, because their spiritual home was England, refused to participate in Australian culture beyond the extent of setting up invidious comparisons. The essay ends with the exhortation that 'the opposite of the cringe is not the strut, but a relaxed erectness of carriage'.[22]

To summarize the recurrent rhetorical preoccupations: 'the' land itself will speak through and in an authentic Australian literature; both writers and critics needed to break free of the colonial shadow, though some felt that this should result in joining an international pantheon; a canon of masterpieces needed to be established. These motifs recur in recent formulations of the cultural public sphere. It is to the outside that one must represent a unified and purposeful subjectivity or nationalism, defined by Ben Anderson as 'an imagined political community — and imagined as both inherently limited and sovereign'.[23]

Like other parts of the so-called New World, white Australia has always been riddled with anxious cultural debates concerning its national identity. Since white settlement initially took the form of penal colonies, it was difficult from the outset to sustain the myth (as in America) of a new Eden. Australia was resolutely postlapsarian. The 'culture' represented by the white intruders was thus consistently opposed to a 'nature' designated hostile (a nature which included the original Aboriginal inhabitants who were not so much colonized as systematically exterminated along with other obstacles in the path of white colonization).

Now, after recent bicentennial celebrations of white settlement (1988) questions of national identity are being posed with a renewed urgency which is informed by a desire to confirm a coming of age and to establish 'consensus' (the rallying cry of the current Labour government). Alongside *The Oxford History of Australian Literature* and various new anthologies of Australian literature there exists the discursive domain of 'multiculturalism'. Implemented under an earlier Labour regime (which came to grief via the unexpectedly reanimated spectre of the British crown) multiculturalism was designed to lay to rest both the iniquitous White Australia policy and the official immigration policy of 'assimilation'. Belatedly, it was felt, national identity might benefit from acknowledging the realities of cultural diversity - but only within strict limits.

Speaking figuratively, postwar migration also finally gave credence to a myth of a New Eden (particularly since the American Eden, increasingly, had rather less credibility). Those victims of the Second World

War inferno in the north had constructed Australia as the beckoning promised land so that, out of the ashes of the penal colony and the murder of a people, a new Australia was apparently rising. Multiculturalism represented a wholesome spectacle of nutritious ethnic bread and finger-snapping ethnic circuses. Within this frame Australia was colourfully reconstructed as a liberal and pluralist nation.

No matter that the same Anglo-Celtic group continue to man the institutions which orchestrate national affairs. For them multiculturalism is useful in a number of specific ways:

1 It incorporates notions of European cosmopolitanism which help break the cultural nexus between Britain and Australia whose paternalism has always irked Australian republicans. The current Labour government is at pains to foster versions of this anti-British republicanism.
2 At the same time the multicultural banner obscures the battle for land rights currently being waged by the Aborigines together with a campaign for rescuing what they can of their own cultural history.
3 In practice, multiculturalism celebrates post-Second World War migration (white, professional, European) and distinguishes this new Establishment from more recent (and less acceptable) Asian immigrants whose arrival has sparked off a new grass-roots version of the racist White Australia policy.

But these tensions and contradictions are not, for the most part, visible in the series of critical gestures signifying purpose, order, closure, which have recently been choreographed by those who speak in the name of 'Australia'. Four survey texts will be juxtaposed: *The Oxford History of Australian Literature* (1981); *Review of National Literature: Australia* (1982); *Australia: The Daedalus Symposium* (1985); *Writing in Multicultural Australia* (1985).

Though published in 1981, *The Oxford History of Australian Literature* situates itself ten years before the bicentennial celebrations. In the introduction, the editor, Leonie Kramer,[24]echoes 'Standards of Australian literature' when she emphasizes the need to be less protective of the 'delicate plant' of Australian literature. The compilation, divided into Fiction, Drama, and Poetry, omits an extensive discussion of non-fiction even though, somewhat paradoxically, the editor states that, 'in general the more talented recorders of early Australia were not first of all literary men but explorers, surveyors, scientists, visitors and administrators.'[25] The task of the earliest writers was to 'find forms which could contain their experience', forms which came initially, and more appropriately according to the editor, from the public modes of eighteenth-century neoclassicism but arose subsequently from the more introspective conventions of nineteenth-century Romanticism. Veering to more recent fiction, the editor deplores the excursions into social realism as 'the sacrifice of artistry to mundane detail' and prefers the poetry of that period because it 'shows ... the stamp of individual minds confronting experience'.[26] Preoccupation with the past and a tendency to create myth at the expense of reality are also not endorsed. It is also pointed out that there needs to be a distinction between 'political' and 'cultural' independence (implicitly a retort to descendants of A. A. Phillips and the nationalists) and, later, that questions of 'Australianness' are at best 'extra-literary considerations in criticism'.[27] In the midst of a recognizably familiar humanism there is the comment: 'The diversification of personal histories that one would expect to result from the influx of migrants from many countries of the world has to yet become a marked feature of Australian writing'.[28] Although this could function as a cue for considering non-Anglo-Celtic writings it is not in fact pursued.

In Adrian Mitchell's section on fiction, Judah Waten, for example, is discussed simply as a social realist although his most famous collection, *Alien Son*, deals with the experiences of Russian-Jewish immigrants. The very few non-Anglo-Celts who do appear are not widely discussed in terms of their cultural affiliations, presumably because to intrude such questions would qualify the absolutist standards of excellence which purportedly transcend history and politics and which comprise the critical assumptions operating in this collection. The introduction concludes with a plea for canon formation as the consequence of a discriminatory 'critical survey' instead of the prevailing protectionism which is seen as being negatively prescriptive in so far as it lays down 'conditions in which literary values are less important than social attitudes'.[29]

In 1982 the *Review of National Literatures* devoted an issue to Australia. Under the aegis of the Council of National Literatures (with its headquarters in New York) it describes itself as being 'a forum of scholars and critics concerned with literature as the expression of national character'. Each issue focuses on 'a representative theme, author, literary movement, critical tendency'. The writer chosen is Patrick White who is described as drawing the paradigmatic 'contours of the Australian psyche'.[30] The contributors are drawn from a mixture of Australian and American academics. Echoing *The Oxford History*, the introduction describes Australian literature as 'coming of age' and thus no longer needing to apply double standards. Implicitly, the peak above the snowline has been provided by Patrick White (though A. D. Hope has not always been a supporter of this writer).[31] An essay on A. D. Hope in relation to T. S. Eliot and William Carlos Williams draws upon a genealogical model when it considers English literature in relation to colonial literature in English and attributes to Hope the contention that the 'maturing literature' should reintegrate 'back into the parent tradition'. If one pursues the kinship metaphor this is rather mind-boggling.

europe

i'm europe deluxe nougat bar i'm better than most i'm really special rich and tasty black forest cake this picture makes me think of germany make me made me europe made me i keep my europe i europe this town is just like my polish town where born where is where am here is europe all the time for me in me i europe i keep it i got it i get it in me inside me is europe ....[32]

The concluding essay assesses the massive two-volume *History of*

Australian Literature by H. M. Green which asserts in its preface that it in fact consciously does follow a 'double standard' and that it is interested 'not in the few peaks, but in the long range'.[33] Green's work is described as more 'architectonic' than the New Critical limitations of *The Oxford History*, and Green himself is favourably compared to that melancholic, Robert Burton.[34] Indeed the portrait of Green sounds illustrative of the man of letters Eagleton describes as existing before criticism became academic and professionalized, 'establishing its professional legitimacy at the cost of renouncing any wider social relevance'.[35]

The contributions by the Australian critics begin with an essay by Manning Clark famed for producing histories which resemble classic realist narratives replete with characters, plots, and guiding myths. Titled 'The forerunners', it deals with the earliest writers whose initial 'cry of horror' was eventually transformed into more equable responses to the land.

> The problem was to put forward an ideology, or a vision of the world which would be both inelligible, and relevant to those who were seeing themselves more and more as Australians, and not as exiled Britons . . . . The problem was the literature of the British-Australians was coming to read more like the literature of a foreign country to each succeeding generation of Australians.[36]

Horseless Rider

Your season
this burn in the wind
that I feel on my lips
this light, so self contained
in an unbearable indifference.[37]

From the explorers' cry there developed the mythologizing of the bush as the 'cradle of male bonding (mateship)' which, in excluding women, became implicitly, in its reference to cradles, a myth about couvade. The problem of the silenced black women (and men), who besides 'the mates' presumably also inhabited the bush, is addressed in the next essay by the anthropologists Catherine and Ronald Berndt who state categorically that: 'For the majority of Australians, the most authentically Australian literature is virtually a closed book'.[38] Thus we have not only the authenticity of speech but that this phonocentrism 'closes the book', so to say, on Australian writing. It does not, of course, because it is recorded as part of this written overview, thus, in some ways, recuperating such putative authenticity (the land speaks) for this particular literary history. The Aborigines signify immediate contact with the land, though a contact which by definition requires translation, mediation, speech into writing.[39]

To Miroslav Holub

Flying foxes are about again
grinding rocks
to encircle the world
with grains of sand.

Shrouded in dust
trees fall into oblivion.

What was that magic chant
to keep our heads
above the desert?[40]

Harry Hesseltine's essay on the 'uncertain self' re-establishes the motif
of white colonizers trying to represent unprecedented experience: 'In one
series after another, our novelists have endeavoured to authenticate their
still uncertain selves by submission to some dominant theme of wide
extent — time, national history, socio-economic fact, cultural aspirations.'[41] Thus a somewhat heterogeneous list of institutional interpella-
tions, a hailing into being of literary subjectivities.[42]

Were All Women Sex-Mad?

— You know I've travelled all over the world don't you — any place you can
name. Well I'll tell you this — Australia's great for a holiday but I wouldn't
want to live there. It's unique I'll say that. Anyone can feel at home there
because it has a strange character or atmosphere which is like an absence of
character, a kind of neutrality. I think it's very tolerant or maybe just very
anonymous. No really, I do *like* Australia. When I lived there I liked it. But
I realize coming away again that there's some strange pressure there. It's
subliminal, very subtle. I don't think I could describe it exactly because it's an
abstract quality which pervades everything there, the work situation, the
politics, the social life. It's a place that gets you down. The amount of drinking
the people do is phenomenal. And it's as though everyone's bitten by the same
bug — some kind of desperation or hysteria which is never expressed. They're
stoics, the Aussies. The most cynical people in the world. Beyond morality —
like the English but more sophisticated because they never say *anything*. The
English talk and talk and talk, endlessly trying to reason things out, playing
with words really but they're expressing attitudes. The *real* Australian attitude
is never expressed.[43]

Chris Wallace-Crabbe's essay 'The legend of the legend of the nineties'
reveals the racism and misogyny contained in the influential journal *The
Bulletin* and shows these to be the flipside of its espousal of
nationalism.[44] Scarcely any women, or writers from non-Anglo-Celtic
backgrounds, figure in this construction of the cultural public sphere.

The Daedalus Symposium, under the patronage of the American Academy
of Arts and Sciences, contains only two literary critics, Leonie Kramer
(writing in this case on the media) and Nicholas Jose on 'cultural identity'. The volume begins with Geoffrey Blainey who, with Manning
Clark (writing in this volume on 'heroes') is one of Australia's leading
historians. Their prominence recalls Milner's point that historians, rather
than literary critics, participate centrally in the construction of the totalizing discourses of the public sphere. In the preface,[45] the American editor
Stephen Graubard remarks that Australia is a 'cozy' society in which
people are loathe to take serious public issue with each other. He also

draws attention to the fact that, unlike the US, Australia has always been able to control its immigration and that, furthermore, some Australians fear the establishment of ethnic enclaves. (Those fears do indeed surface often in the debate around multiculturalism and the suppressed term here is 'assimilation'.) The reference to controlled immigration is the silent other of the Blainey essay which is contextualized by a recent controversy around Asian immigration.[46] Blainey states here what he has reiterated in greater detail elsewhere, that Australia is too dry to sustain further large-scale settlement than the ribbon of settlers clinging for 200 years to its edges. Only the Aborigines managed to be nurtured by the whole land and even they may not have lived bounteously. The essay concludes on the anticipated note that Asian migration needs to be monitored more carefully while Australia makes 'decisions' about whether or not it wishes to 'continue to belong primarily to European civilization' and 'whether it should remain a relatively cohesive society or whether it should ... become a multicultural and multisocial society'.[47] To put those concerns into a future (or to locate them in a past) is a classic technique of displacing social 'problems'.

wogs

You can't miss them they're everywhere they shout they're noisy they're dirty they put vegetables in their front gardens they eat garlic they shouldn't have come here in the first place they're strangers i want to be with my own kind with my brothers with people like i am there's too many of them here already you don't know how to talk to them they're not clean they annoy me funny names luigi they got their own ways they don't do as you do they're aliens they look wrong they use us they take us they take us for what they can get from us then they go away they're greedy they take our space they not us not our kind they after what they can get they stick together i don't know what they say they don't fit in they dress wrong flashy they don't know our ways they breed and breed they take what little we got what is ours what belongs to us they take ours and ours they're not us ...[48]

The poet Judith Wright's adjacent essay catalogues the European's despoliation of the land and contrasts it with the careful conservation over millennia by the Aborigines. Since Aboriginal land claims are not being recognized via legal arguments, Wright is constructing the case on moral grounds. Donald Horne, currently president of the Australia Council (the statutory body which administers federal funding for the arts), reiterates the republican case which had already surfaced in the Stephensen essay. In the provocatively titled 'Who rules Australia?' he explores the use of 'the Crown' as a metonymic occlusion of a powerful colonial dependency which still controls Australia. The answer to his question is that male WASPs rule Australia and serve the interests of Australian capitalists who are in turn part of the British Empire 'in both their economic life and their strategic imagination'. The essay concludes in a rhetorical mode of revelation which none the less remains detached from any precise naming: 'There is no Australian ruling class. There are ruling interests that seem naturally to prevail at some time of conflict. But these prevailing interests are not in Australia.'[49]

First Day at School

... Thankfully, he passes
the inspection
without a mark
against his appearance —
all the hours of care
and attention
his mother put into pressing
his clothes
    Eventually
paying off.

At his name
the teacher pauses
commences to pronounce it
and stops,
    hesitates for a moment
and the sly flicker of a smile
passes across his eyes.
Tongue-tying himself
cleverly,
he mispronounces it.
Tries again and again.
Voices laugh. No one objects
Finally, he asks:
'Tell me, boy, how do you pronounce that?'[50]

Leonie Kramer's essay on the media echoes her introduction to *The Oxford History* in arguing for rigorous standards in the media as distinct from the protection of mediocrity now operating, partly due to pressures coming from the commercial networks. Nicholas Jose, who at the end of his essay praises *The Oxford History's* advocacy of *critical* discriminations, sets up a group of contemporary writers dedicated to exploring 'the nature of their marginality'. Again echoing *The Oxford History*, Jose takes issue with a tendency to mythologize which he discerns in many Australian writers. On the issue of multiculturalism he states:

The status of England as 'onlie begetter' has been challenged by Celtic and Gaelic claims, and the primacy of the British heritage itself has been placed in a different perspective by the influx of continental influences. Even Greece and Rome as the wellsprings of civilization are seen to be part of a larger, variegated, non-linear story. In consequence, the patterns to be adopted by future Australian societies become less predictable and more open to experiment. It is not a move towards cultural relativism, so much as a matter of making cultural values the result of wider discrimination and choice. From the side, marginal in numbers, the new arrivals embody a deep dimension of memory and wisdom.[51]

He then quotes the poet Les Murray (editor of the most recent Oxford collection of Australian verse and of Anglo–Celtic provenance) writing *on behalf of* non-Anglo Celtic immigrants.

So we return to the issue of multiculturalism, mostly absent from these compilations though there are, as I've indicated, gestures towards this absence. To begin with Donald Horne, ostensibly a supporter of multiculturalism:

> I would now say that in the sense that they should seek Australian, not British, definitions of Australia, all multiculturalists in Australia should be as it were 'anti-British'. Failing this, there is a danger that multiculturalism becomes a way of keeping 'the ethnics' quiet while the 'anglos' can go on running things, as destiny demanded they should. If the aim is to define Australia as a multicultural society and to set multiculturalism as a national goal, how, at the same time, can Australia be declaredly monocultural, as, not only symbolically, but constitutionally, it still is? . . . Multiculturalism will have real meaning in Australia when the English are seen only as one group of ethnics among others and when Queen Elizabeth will be welcomed as a representative of one of Australia's honoured ethnic communities. Just as whites can be seen as *the* black problem, or men as *the* women problem, so, in a multicultural sense, those Australians who still define Australia by its Britishness might be seen as *the* ethnic problem: they are, in effect, the principal enemies of policies of cultural diversity.[52]

One might wish to take issue with these over-simplified oppositions and one might well also ask questions about who is to administer these changes and then one discovers that Horne's own institution, the Australia Council, is still unquestionably and predominantly staffed by Anglo-Celtic Australians.

Oh Lucky Country
. . .Together with the migrant masses I am contributing to the process of your civilization, to widening your horizon which doesn't extend any further than the point of your great ugly nose. I tear the weeds out of your ears. I give you a certain style. I teach you to eat, to dress, to behave and above all not to belch in restaurants, trains, buses, cinemas, schools. You probably don't know, but I'll tell you in confidence, for you information, that your country, which is now mine too, is based on a gigantic belch. Its flag flutters in the wind created by the toxic gases produced by your stomachs which are choked up like sewers. The myth about being happy and lucky is based on your drunken bouts. Go on, then, drink. You offend us. You don't like wine? You prefer beer? Waiter, a huge bottle of beer for the lady.[53]

Multiculturalism circulates in Australia as a series of discursive formations serving a variety of institutional interests, as indicated earlier. As has been argued persuasively and at length by Foster and Stockley,[54] the emphasis on *cultural* pluralism has often functioned to obscure class differences and has pre-empted the possibilities for *structural* pluralism.

Government documents arguing for multiculturalism have been careful to address the fears of divisiveness and social fracturing by insisting that institutions will be held in common.[55] In other words, the emphasis appears to be on what Smolicz has termed 'residual multiculturalism' which may well turn out to be a 'thinly disguised euphemism for assimilation.'[56]

Inheritance
High ceiling rooms
with oak doors, dark parquetry
closed smells.
My sealed tomb
travels in my dreams.[57]

In part the ambiguities surrounding the use of the term 'multi-culturalism' centre around who is considered to be included. Usually (and this even seems the case in a recent policy document emanating from the Australia Council)[58] the term is restricted to those from non-English-speaking backgrounds so that Anglo–Celts are not included. Even those 'ethnics' who do write in English are in a handicapped situation. By the same token Aboriginal writers using English (instead of being represented in translation) are also considered 'ethnics'. Such writers are perceived as mediating the 'migrant experience', or, in the case of the Aboriginal writers in English, of communicating the outcast experience. Immigrant writing, particularly that which is written in the first person, is read as the rediscovery of the promised land and helps to rescue Australian writing from its murky topology in the penal colony and the fallen waste land. Let me unpack this claim further . . . .

By definition Australia existed as a refuge and a promise to those waves of European emigrants who were fleeing the known world during and after the Second World War. How different already, figuratively speaking, was this metonymy compared to those projected by self-styled legitimate residents to this country who located their national origins in institutions which are incarnations of legitimacy: namely the prison, the penal colony, the biblical fallen. For one group, then, the raising of barriers, the crossing of boundaries, for the other, the boundaries had always been there and in that period of migration, of inundation (the image recurs), had to be restated and reinscribed in different ways. The boundaries of the penal colony had been internalized by its inhabitants to constitute procedures of normalization. On the other hand, the *emigrants*, who at some mystic Neptune's line became *immigrants*, had to be made aware that they were crossing boundaries and that, indeed, they would never stop crossing boundaries all their lives. By definition, to be a *new* Australian was to be a boundary crosser, a transgressor, in the eyes of those who like to think that they had already been t/here.

In their very being those new Australians represented boundaries, or margins, those marginal voices which bordered the known country and were themselves hybrids comprising both the known and the unknown. In so far as they functioned as representatives of the postwar world, the world of the fallen, they could be used as the second half of a binary equation in which, by definition, Australia was now, finally after the inundation, unfallen. After the *Sündflut* of fire and brimstone and the human flood of immigrants, here were the survivors of a regenerated new world. The penal colony (textually speaking) was on its figurative journey towards redemption and reincarnation into the promised land, the lucky country.

Another element in this marginalization of migrant writing is that, together with other aspects of migrant cultures, it provides what could be dubbed a European charter myth of origins. Multiculturalism becomes too often an effective process of recuperation whereby diverse cultures are returned homogenized as folkloric spectacle. This recuperation serves to legitimate a European charter myth of origins which, in the name of civilization and progress, condones those 200 years of colonial rule which were *not* celebrated by the Aborigines in 1988. In this formation, multiculturalism functions to amalgamate and spuriously to unify nationalism and culture into a depoliticized multimedia event.

Those who write in languages other than English are generally regarded as a dying breed.

Feliks Skrzynecki
... Growing older, I
remember words he taught me,
remnants of a language
I inherited unknowingly —
the curse that damned
a crew-cut, grey-haired
Department clerk
who asked me in dancing-bear grunts:
  'Did your father ever attempt to learn English?'
  ...
At thirteen,
stumbling over tenses in Caesar's *Gallic War*,
I forgot my first Polish word.
He repeated it so I never forgot
After that, like a dumb prophet
watched me pegging my tents
further and further south of Hadrian's wall.[59]

Either they are perceived as speaking 'Latin', as Walter Adamson ruefully argues with respect to his own preservation of an anachronistic German,[60] or they try to keep alive a language and culture in exile.[61] Culture and nationalism are not necessarily based solely on language but, as Renée Balibar's work has shown,[62] language often has a sacred function and is certainly often a signifier for cultural authenticity.[63] If the ethnic group preserves a language and culture separately from the original country then multiculturalism is often reduced to a custodial operation or becomes, as George Michelakakis argues, a type of costume of folkloric exotica and nostalgia firmly oriented towards the past so that it cannot possibly be seen to have relevance in the present.[64] The logic here is that eventually these cultures will die out (as Stephensen argued *vis-à-vis* the Aborigines at the beginning of this essay).

Those who do write in English suffer from different kinds of discrimination. Even when born into the English language they are seen as being at a disadvantage: they write well for foreigners. In so far as the experiences of those from non Anglo–Celtic backgrounds have been represented within Australian writing they are perceived as being adequately covered by Anglo–Celtic writers.

Barbecue
At our back
the forbidden house
and beyond
the convent on the hill
massive red

The street deserted,
only we, in the bald yard
with the young gum tree,
fanning itself nervously,
eating raw meat laced
with black flies
drinking the parched wind
and making polite conversation
while the light poured on us
sizzling.[65]

Non–Anglo–Celtic writers are themselves loath to accept the title 'ethnic' or 'multicultural' because they have absorbed the fear of 'double standards' or 'protectionism' which might be seen to qualify the absolute standards of 'excellence'. As Barthes stated it: 'Literature remains the currency in use in a society apprised, by the very form of words, of the meaning of what it consumes'.[66]

It is not easy to gain acceptance for attaching notions of the literary to non–Anglo–Celtic writing. What then are the implications if non–Anglo–Celts wish to participate in selecting the words which, according to Barthes, consolidate social meaning? What kind of signification is non–Anglo–Celtic writing permitted within Australia? The swift answer is that such writing is invisible in literary and cultural histories and is usually received as sociology (the 'migrant problem' leading inevitably to the migrant *as* problem) or as oral history (authentic first-hand accounts from marginal groups). Moreover, in these contexts, we are not dealing with writing produced by immigrants so much as writing by others on behalf of immigrants. In any case, such writing is not usually received as literature which, for the moment, might be described as a textuality which is visibly more worked over than other forms of writing and whose implicit opposite is the apparent 'disorder' of speech.[67] If we accept the suggestion that immigrant writing and, by extension, non–Anglo–Celtic writing, signifies only within the formations of sociology and history, then, paradoxically its value lies here with speech rather than writing. In other words, the immigrant's speech (rather than writing) is solicited and the more disordered it is the more authentic it supposedly sounds. In those terms immigrant or non-Anglo-Celtic writing is valued precisely in so far as it is inscribed with the marks of linguistic naivety and (even) incompetence: broken language being symptomatic of subjects not yet assimilated (rendered the same) or 'naturalized'.

In the face of the little writing that does get limited exposure (autobiographical or autobiographically based) any obvious signs of language being crafted are none the less read as relatively unmediated confessions. Complexities, if acknowledged, are those provided by life, the complicated history of the non-Anglo-Celtic subject, rather than any consciously wrought textuality. Therefore, to consider immigrant poetry, for example, is, under those circumstances, perverse. Even poetry, the least transparently functional manifestation of linguistic self-consciousness, will be read for sociological or historical content. In Barthes' terms, classical poetry is 'a speech which is made more socially acceptable by virtue of the very conspicuousness of its conventions'.[68] To write poetry means that one is staking a claim to the literary and hence to public cultural participation. On what grounds can this be legitimated, more particularly when the language used is patently either not English, or, if English, then filtered through a previous and other culture or language? Those 'conspicuous conventions', alluded to by Barthes, are not simply acquired when setting foot on this continent, nor are they part of the naturalization certificate. Rather, they belong to that chimeric cultural superstructure which floats above the home territory signifying a mystery only gradually comprehended after many rites of passage. Poetry? From immigrants? Classic realist narratives perhaps, and reluctantly, but not poetry.

In the last few decades, and in spite of the compilations I have been analysing, there have been considerable efforts to mark the discursive formation of Australian literature, in gendered and cultural terms, as predominantly Anglo-Celtic and male. Thus there has been the work of those who consider the implications of Aboriginal writing (oral, colonized)[69] and women's writing (throwing new light, for example, on foundation myths of mateship and the bush).[70] What further complications result when one inserts non-Anglo-Celtic writing? At the very simplest level this means that no language can be considered transparent or referential in the fullest sense, that is, offering direct access to the phenomenal or somatic world. Those who are able to think from the beginning in more than one language find it impossible to consider language as a 'natural' and unproblematic expression of experience. Neither does this hold true for those who have experience of more than one culture (and we are probably dealing with a question of degree here) for here too it is difficult to accept culture as 'natural'.

Is it possible then to reclaim multiculturalism as a possible counter-public sphere? The potential is certainly signalled in *Writing in Multicultural Australia*. The Chinese–Portuguese Australian writer Brian

Castro referred to the need for literature to function as dissidence and in the face of the national histories of literature and culture which I have been analysing it certainly seems possible for non-Anglo-Celtic writings to operate as dissident and not simply to be recuperated.[71] The dangers of recuperation surfaced when various Anglo-Celtic speakers invoked the totalizing piety that 'we are all migrants' but this was picked up, for example, by Jacques Delaruelle who warned of the logic which ran: 'There was a problem, there is no more problem, there has never been any problem.'[72] It was also addressed constructively by Martin Harrison:

> To ask for instance — a tactless question —: from where exactly does the presumption come that a theory of social development (multiculturalism), which addresses material, educational and social needs, *has* a direct application to literature: Who subscribes to that view? Who benefits from it in the long run? In what other circumstances, one might well ponder, have writers colluded with such progressive social planning for writerly purposes? Indeed, it might be exactly by recognising the *limited* value of 'multiculturalism' as a literary term, that we most confirm the term's actual efficacy as a means of criticising institutions, both political and discursive ones. Only, that is, if it is seen as a cultural theory which operates between heritages, language communities *and* institutions, and if the issue of representation is not fudged into universal declarations of brotherhood (e.g. 'we are all migrants'). Then, the unrepresentativeness of major cultural institutions in Australia (the publishing companies, the media, the Australia Council, the theatres, the universities, etc. . . .) will be challenged.[73]

Multiculturalism will only function as a useful expression of difference when it is seen as including Anglo-Celts. In the past, dissidence within the public sphere was limited to the split between those terms Anglo and Celtic. On the one hand Australians of British, pro-monarchist, and Protestant descent and on the other the Irish (and sometimes Catholic and working-class) dissidents. Whether or not all the terms sit easily together, the oppositional model dictated that conflicts aligned themselves on one side or the other. In this form the debate was also represented within cultural and literary histories. The discontinuities and radicalism within Irish writing *vis-à-vis* England were linked with Australian dissidents who fed into the republican movement and who were seen as favouring a generalized anti-authoritarianism. To insert non-Anglo-Celtic traditions here would involve de-privileging this old opposition even when it surfaces in the guise of a debate between the nationalists and the putative internationalists. As David Carter has recently argued:

> The opposite of nationalism in Australia has seldom been inter-nationalism. Nationalism, in any of its numerous forms, has never been just parochial, despite the manner in which, for example, from the 1940s to the 1960s it provided a language of hostile responses to

'international' modernism .... The opposite of nationalism has been, instead, what we might call *universalism*: that argument about art, about individuals and society, about culture and tradition which seeks to resolve all issues of difference by translating them into the realm of universal values. Nationalists have aligned themselves with diverse contemporary movements, internationally; the universalists speak from within a single, dominant (English) tradition. From this point they assume the right to claim that there are no questions of feminist politics, only politics; no questions of black rights, only individual rights; and, ... no question of Australian art or migrant art, only good and bad art.[74]

To use multiculturalism effectively in the construction of a counter-public sphere in debates around culture or literature would mean deploying texts in such a way that they could not easily be recuperated in the name of nostalgia or absorbed into an Anglo-Celtic canon.[75] Instead it would mean that the whole tradition of Australian literature would need to be reread differently so that the positionality and history involved in all cultural productions be foregrounded.[76] Tracing the 200 years of non-Anglo-Celtic writing has already begun.[77] My own readings of these cultural and literary compilations have been determined by multicultural concerns. The texts I have inserted have not simply been examples quoted to illustrate certain arguments with supposed transparent meanings. Rather they offer counter-readings to an avowed public monoculturalism. Thus of reading here a reading which does not evoke Anglo-Celtic origins and which undoes the secular/sacred closures of cultural histories and canons, confounding those who believe that the land speaks ... literary nationalism.[78]

> Except for what memory recalls
> there is nothing to commemorate our arrival —
> no plaques, no names carved on trees,
> nothing officially recorded
> of parents and children that lived beside
> the dome-shaped, khaki-coloured hills
> and the red-dust road that ran between Parkes and Sydney.[79]
>
> ★ ★ ★
>
> Naturalized more
> than a decade ago
> we became citizens of the soil
> that was feeding us —
> inheritors of a key
> that'll open no house
> when this one is pulled down.[80]
>
> ★ ★ ★
>
> don yoo tel dem troowth
> dai dozn belif yoo.[81]

Notes

1 P. R. Stephensen, 'The foundations of culture in Australia', in J. Barnes (ed.), *The Writer in Australia* (Melbourne: Oxford University Press, 1969), p. 206.
2 B. Doyle, 'The hidden history of English studies', in P. Widdowson (ed.), *Re-reading English* (London: Methuen, 1982), p. 18.
3 A. Kefala (ed.), *Multiculturalism and the Arts* (Sydney: Australia Council, 1986), p. 7.
4 M. Harrison, 'On a poem of Gun Gencer's', in J. Delaruelle and A. Karakostas-Seda (eds), *Multicultural Australia* (Sydney: Australia Council for the Literature Board, 1985), p. 128. The volume comprises the proceedings of two conferences held in Melbourne and Sydney in 1984.
5 T. Eagleton, *The Function of Criticism* (London: Verso, 1984), p. 123.
6 I am indebted here to Dr I. Veit-Brause and Ron Gilbert for drawing these arguments to my attention.
7 A. Milner, 'The "English" ideology: literary criticism in England and Australia', *Thesis XI*, 12 (1985), pp. 110–29.
8 P. Anderson, 'Components of the national culture', *New Left Review*, 50 (1968), pp. 52–9.
9 E. Said, *The World, The Text, and the Critic* (London: Faber, 1984), p. 11.
10 J. Batsleer *et al.*, *Re-writing English* (London: Methuen, 1985), pp. 163–4.
11 Some are of course published in their original countries but not those political refugees whose original worlds exist no more.
12 The reference is of course to J. Derrida, *Of Grammatology* (Baltimore, Md.: Johns Hopkins University Press, 1980), pp. 141–64. The notion of the redefining supplement was used by me in an earlier critique on Australian cultural orthodoxies, S. Gunew, 'Migrant women writers', in C. Ferrier (ed.), *Gender, Politics and Fiction* (St Lucia: University of Queensland Press, 1985), pp. 163–78.
13 One of the most famous: so it is quoted in full, A. D. Hope, 'Australia' (1939, *The Penguin Book of Australian Verse*, ed. H. Heseltine (Sydney: Penguin (Australia), 1972), p. 190.
14 Stephensen, op. cit., pp. 205–6.
15 Hope, op. cit.
16 Stephensen, op. cit., p. 218.
17 ibid., p. 241. That Stephensen was later interned for 'allegedly profascist' activities is pointed out in Ian Reid's, 'From fertilisers to foundations', *The Age Monthly Review* (Dec./Jan. 1985), p. 16.
18 A. D. Hope, 'Standards in Australian literature', in G. Johnston (ed.), *Australian Literary Criticism* (Melbourne: Oxford University Press, 1962), p. 11.
19 ibid., p. 13.
20 ibid., p. 1.
21 A. Walwicz, 'Australia', in D. White and A. Couani (eds), *Island in the Sun 2* (Sydney: Sea Cruise Books, 1981), pp. 90–1.
22 A. A. Phillips, 'The cultural cringe', in C. B. Christensen (ed.), *On Native Grounds* (Sydney: Angus & Robertson, 1968), p. 451.
23 B. Anderson, *Imagined Communities: Reflections on the Origin and Spread of Nationalism* (London: Verso, 1983), p. 15.
24 Kramer is Professor of Australian Literature at the University of Sydney and was Chairman of the Australian Broadcasting Commission.
25 L. Kramer, 'Introduction', *The Oxford History of Australian Literature* (Melbourne: Oxford University Press, 1981), p. 8.
26 ibid., pp. 18–19.

27 ibid., p. 23.
28 ibid., p. 18.
29 ibid., p. 23. Note that the companion volume *The Oxford Anthology of Australian Literature*, ed. L. Kramer and A. Mitchell (Melbourne: Oxford University Press, 1985), contains about half a dozen non-Anglo-Celtic writers within its 600 or so pages. *The Oxford Companion to Australian Literature*, ed. W. H. Wilde, J. Hooton, B. Andrews (Melbourne: Oxford University Press, 1985), contains articles on feminism and the Aborigines but nothing on non-Anglo-Celtic writing or migrant writing.
30 A. Paolucci and L. Dobrez (eds), *Review of National Literatures: Australia*, vol. 11, (Council on National Literatures, 1982), p. 120.
31 See, for example, A. D. Hope, *Australian Literature 1950–1962* (Melbourne: Melbourne University Press, 1963), pp. 12–13.
32 A. Walwicz, 'Europe', in P. Skrzynecki (ed.), *Joseph's Coat: an Anthology of Multicultural Writing* (Sydney: Hale & Iremonger, 1985), p. 195.
33 H. M. Green, *A History of Australian Literature*, vol. 1, *1789–1923* (Sydney: Angus & Robertson, 1974), p. xix.
34 R. Clark and A. Paolucci, 'The achievement of H. M. Green', in Paolucci and Dobrez, op. cit., p. 247.
35 Eagleton, op. cit., p. 57.
36 M. Clarke, 'The forerunners', in Paolucci and Dobrez, op. cit., p. 29. Presumably the allusion in the title is to Vance Palmer's poem 'The forerunners', which is also about mountain peaks.
37 A. Kefala, 'Horseless rider', unpublished poem.
38 C. Berndt and R. Berndt, 'Aboriginal Australia: literature in an oral tradition', in Paolucci and Dobrez, op. cit., p. 39. It is useful here to recall J. Peacock, 'Writing and speech after Derrida: application and criticism', in F. Barker *et al.* (eds), *Europe and its Others*, vol. 2 (Colchester: University of Essex, 1985). Peacock discusses the exchange value of literacy in contexts where literate and non-literate cultures meet.
39 In the Paris exhibition at the Musée d'Art in 1983 the French 'discovered' Aboriginal Australia. See J. Montgomery, 'Australia — The French discovery of 1983', *Art and Text*, 12 and 13 (1984), pp. 3–15.
40 B. Wongar, 'To Miroslav Holub', *Bilma* (Columbus: Ohio State University Press, 1984). The author grew up in Yugoslavia but claims Aboriginal descent and has spent many years living a tribal existence.
41 H. Heseltine, 'The uncertain self: notes on the development of Australian literary form', in Paolucci and Dobrez, op. cit., p. 105.
42 The reference here is to Althusser's concept of interpellation. See L. Althusser, *Essays in Ideology*, London: Verso, 1984). I explore interpellation more fully with respect to non-Anglo-Celtic writing in 'Authenticity and the writing cure', in *Crafts*, ed. S. Sheridan (London: Verso, 1988), pp. 111–23.
43 A. Couani, *Were All Women Sex-Mad?* (Melbourne: Rigmarole Books, 1982), pp. 29–30. Couani is a third-generation Australian who writes from a self-consciously Greek–Polish cultural background.
44 That *The Bulletin* is continuing its tradition is illustrated by a recent issue containing an article by D. Barrett, 'How the bloated ethnic industry is dividing Australia', *The Bulletin*, 18 February 1986, pp. 58–62.
45 S. R. Graubard (ed.) *Australia: The Daedalus Symposium* (Sydney: Angus & Robertson, 1985), pp. v–xii.
46 The Blainey controversy has generated a great deal of print. See A. Markus and M. C. Ricklefs (eds), *Surrender Australia? Essays in the Study and Use of*

History: Geoffrey Blainey and Asian Immigration (Sydney: Allen & Unwin, 1985). See also S. Gunew, 'Australia 1984: a moment in the archaeology of multiculturalism' in Barker *et al.* op. cit., pp. 178—93.

47 G. Blainey, 'Australia: a bird's-eye view', in Graubard, op. cit., p. 26.

48 A. Walwicz, 'wogs', in S. Gunew (ed.), *Displacements 2: Multicultural Storytellers* (Victoria: Deakin University Press, 1987), p. 133.

49 D. Horne, 'Who rules Australia?', in Graubard, op. cit., pp. 194—5.

50 P. Skrzynecki, 'First day at school', *The Polish Immigrant* (Brisbane: Phoenix Books, 1982), p. 2.

51 N. Jose, 'Cultural Identity', in Graubard, op. cit., p. 335.

52 D. Horne, *The Perils of Multiculturalism as a National Ideal* (Melbourne: Australian Institute of Multicultural Affairs, 1983), pp. 3—4.

53 R. Cappiello, *Oh Lucky Country* (St Lucia: University of Queensland Press, 1984), pp. 192—3.

54 L. Foster and D. Stockley, *Multiculturalism: The Changing Australian Paradigm* (Avon: Multilingual Matters, 1984).

55 For all its good intentions this is clearly signalled in J. Zubrzycki, *Multiculturalism for All Australians* (Canberra: Australian Council on Population and Ethnic Affairs, 1982). Horne, op. cit., argues a similar line with the addition that Australian institutions should be seen as European in origins rather than as simply English.

56 J. J. Smolicz, *The Rhetoric of Multiculturalism*, Occasional papers, 7, (Ethnic Affairs Commission of NSW, 1985), p. 6.

57 A. Kefala, 'Inheritance', in M. Jurgensen (ed.), *Ethnic Australia* (Brisbane: Phoenix, 1981), p. 59.

58 See note 3.

59 P. Skrzynecki, 'Feliks Skrzynecki', op. cit., p. 18.

60 W. Adamson, 'Some problems of multicultural writing in Australia', in Delaruelle and Karakostas-Seda, op. cit., pp. 43—5.

61 This was shown by the speakers on Latvian, Estonian, Lithuanian literatures, ibid.

62 R. Balibar, 'National language, education, literature', in F. Barker *et al.* (eds), *The Politics of Theory* (Colchester: University of Essex, 1983), pp. 134—47.

63 Anderson, op. cit., discusses the importance of language disseminated in print. That 'purity of language' is a potent issue in Anglo-Celtic Australia is clearly shown in S. J. Barber, *The Australian Language* (Melbourne: Sun Books, 1966), particularly pp. 404—9, where he discusses the survival of 'the' Australian language even in the face of 'waves' of immigrants!

64 G. Michelakakis, 'Literature and the Greek migrants in Australia', in Delaruelle and Karakostas-Seda, op. cit., pp. 58—63. See also my chapter, 'Homeland: nostalgia in migrant and non-Anglo/Celtic writing', in P. Foss (ed.), *Island in the Stream* (Sydney: Pluto, 1988).

65 A. Kefala, 'Barbecue', in Jurgensen, op. cit., p. 58.

66 R. Barthes, *Writing Degree Zero* (London: Cape, 1967), p. 38.

67 ibid., p. 25.

68 ibid., p. 48.

69 See, for example, J. Davis and B. Hodge (eds), *Aboriginal Writing Today* (Canberra: Australian Institute of Aboriginal Studies, 1985), and K. Benterrak, S. Muecke, P. Roe, *et al.*, *Reading the Country* (Fremantle: Fremantle Arts Centre Press, 1984).

70 For example, D. Modjeska, *Exiles at Home* (London and Sydney: Sirius, 1981), and Ferrier, op. cit.

71 A move which may have been unconsciously signalled when the Chairman of the Literature Board, Tom Shapcott, reinvoked Stephensen's metaphor when he argued for a cross-fertilisation in order to produce 'hybrid vigour'. T. Shapcott, 'Multicultural literature and writing in Australia', in Delaruelle and Karakostas-Seda, op. cit., p. 7.

72 ibid., p. 52.

73 ibid., pp. 128–9.

74 D. Carter, 'The natives are getting restless: nationalism, multiculturalism and migrant writing', *Island*, 25/6 (1986), p. 3.

75 That this is a danger is argued by Michelakakis, op. cit. That it can happen is shown by the recent anthology *Australian Women Poets*, ed. S. Hampton and K. Llewellyn (Sydney: Penguin (Australia), 1986). For all its virtues in rectifying a gender imbalance in previous anthologies of poetry this compilation does tend to subsume non-Anglo-Celtic cultural differences under an Anglo dominance.

76 See Carter, op. cit., p. 8. See also my own contribution in Delaruelle and Karakostas-Seda, op. cit., pp. 15–23.

77 ibid., section dealing with 'Literature of particular language groups in Australia'.

78 My thanks to the Humanities Research Centre at the Australian National University for awarding me a fellowship which gave me time to write this paper.

79 P. Skrzynecki, 'Migrant centre site', *Joseph's Coat*, p. 151.

80 P. Skrzynecki, '10 Mary Street', *The Polish Immigrant*, p. 14. Also in S. Gunew (ed.), *Displacements: Migrant Storytellers* (Victoria: Deakin University Press, 1982).

81 Pi O, 'Untitled poem', in Gunew, op. cit., p. 135.

Acknowledgements

The author and publishers would like to thank the following copyright holders for permission to reproduce material in this chapter: Angus and Robertson Publishers/Collins for 'Australia' by A. D. Hope from his *Collected Poems 1930–1970*, © A. D. Hope, 1966, 69, 72. Ania Walwicz for 'Australia' and 'europe'. Ohio State University Press for 'To Miroslav Holub', reprinted by permission from B. Wongar, *Bilma*, copyright 1984 by the Ohio State University Press. Anne Couani for 'Were all Women Sex-Mad?' *Mattoid* for 'wogs' by Ania Walwicz. Phoenix Publications for 'First Day at School', 'Feliks Skrzynecki', and 'Naturalized more ...' by Peter Skrzynecki. Peter Skrzynecki for 'Except for what memory recalls ...' and 'don yoo tel dem troowth'.

7

Postal politics and the institution of the nation

Geoffrey Bennington

Approaches

It is tempting to try to approach the question of nation directly, by aiming for its centre or its origin. And there is almost immediate satisfaction to be had in so doing; for we undoubtedly find narration at the centre of nation: stories of national origins, myths of founding fathers, genealogies of heroes. At the origin of the nation, we find a story of the nation's origin.

Which should be enough to inspire suspicion; our own drive to find the centre and the origin has created its own myth of the origin — namely that at the origin is the myth.[1] In this story, narration comes too easy, too soon; investigating the nation is here complicit with the nation's own story. The problem is no doubt a result of the pretension to reach the centre directly, whereas such access is in general illusory: the approach to the nation implies borders, policing, suspicion, and crossing (or refusal of entry) — try to enter a country at the centre (by flying in, say), and the border is still there to be crossed, the frontier shifted from periphery to centre.

But the need to approach the nation via its edges immediately complicates the problem, in so far as it implies a difference, not merely between centre and circumference, but between inside and outside. The frontier does not merely close the nation in on itself, but also, immediately, opens it to an outside, to other nations. Frontiers are articulations, boundaries are, constitutively, crossed or transgressed. This formal point has been made clearly by Edgar Morin:

> The frontier is both an opening and a closing. It is at the frontier that there takes place the distinction from and liaison with the environment. All frontiers, including the membrane of living beings, including the frontier of nations, are, at the same time as they are barriers, places of communication and exchange. They are the place of dissociation and association, of separation and articulation.[2]

At the centre, the nation narrates itself as *the* nation: at the borders, it must recognize that there are other nations on which it cannot but depend. It follows that the 'origin' of the nation is never simple, but dependent on a differentiation of nations which has always already begun. The story of (the institution of) the nation will be irremediably complicated by this situation.

'Method'

This type of formulation of the problem, with its insistence on margins as against centres, on difference as a prior condition of identity, can quickly be labelled 'post-structuralist' in its inspiration. The label 'post-structuralist' (which is not itself a post-structuralist label) cannot, however, be simply applied from a methodological or theoretical 'outside' to designate a particular way of approaching a predefined question (in this case, that of 'nation and narration'): for the question of 'post-structuralism' *itself* immediately involves questions of nationality (French, American, English, German . . .), but also general questions of *institution* which cannot be separated from those involved in the problem of the nation. More especially, the name 'post-structuralism' immediately raises temporal or historical questions which will further complicate the spatial complications of frontiers sketched out above.

In more than one way, the name 'post-structuralism' is improper: it is an English name for an essentially (apparently, originally) French movement; it designates as 'literary theory' a complex set of work in philosophy, psychoanalysis, literary studies, and so forth; the thinkers grouped together under this name are in fact more or less violently opposed to each other. With the exception of Lyotard (and I shall return to this exception) none of these thinkers has, to my knowledge, laid claim to (or even used with reference to their own work) a name beginning with 'post-'. It is no doubt necessary to investigate the naiveties and misunderstandings induced by the use of the term 'post-structuralism', to write the history and sociology of this phantom movement or institution.[3] The institutionalization of 'post-structuralism' (which begins at least as early as the invention of the name) is a complex enough phenomenon to be worth this type of study: and as it seems that this English name for a French movement has itself been recently reimported into France,[4] then that complexity would immediately engage with the questions of nationality (notably via the question of translation) which are the concern of this volume.

However necessary and difficult such an analysis, and whatever refinement it showed, it would encounter, sooner or later, a necessary and troubling limit. Any socio-historico-institutional analysis of post-structuralism (or the postmodern) would rely on an understanding of the prefix 'post-' as designating 'what comes after', 'what supersedes', possibly even 'what sublates'. A first, parodically 'post-structuralist' observation would reply that, from the point of view of what is still, mistakenly, called 'the materiality of the signifier', the 'post-' is 'pre-': it is a prefix, and thus comes before and not after. The post is at the beginning, and precedes, in a certain linear order of the signifier, the name (structuralism, the modern) with respect to which it is thought to come after. This type of observation is not just a joke, however, and the (serious) claim that the post comes first, at the beginning, at 'the origin', does not imply that the truth is to be found in that so-called 'materiality of the signifier'. Take for example a slightly perplexing tension to be found between Lyotard's *The Postmodern Condition* proper, and the essay 'Answering the question: what is postmodernism?', printed as an appendix in the English translation of the book.[5] On the one hand, *The Postmodern Condition* tends to give the impression that the postmodern does indeed come after, in the order of history, and this conforms to the presuppositions of the type of analysis just mentioned. According to this obvious and apparently unproblematical schema, we enter the post-modern condition as we enter so-called postindustrial society, after a modern condition and an industrial society. This move from modern to postmodern seems to go along with a certain view of technical and technological 'progress', notably in the domain of computer technology. But on the other hand, if we are to take seriously the critique of 'grand narratives' which is the philosophical core of Lyotard's book, then it is difficult to accept this type of representation, which Lyotard has himself subsequently described as being itself 'modern'.[6] If the postmodern involves the decline or the loss of credibility of grand narratives, it is difficult to describe it in terms of a grand narrative of technology. And in the 'Answering the question . . .' essay, it becomes clear that the post-modern is no longer to be thought of in terms of such narratives, nor in terms of some break that would simply *separate* the modern and the postmodern. 'A work can become modern only if it is first postmodern. Postmodernism thus understood is not modernism at its end, but in the nascent state, and this state is constant' (p. 79). The post does indeed come first, then, and Lyotard goes on to elaborate this strange logic in terms of a temporal paradox of the future perfect.[7]

Can the same be said of post-structuralism? Apparently so, if we follow Robert Young's analysis,[8] which plays elegantly on the temporal sense of 'post' ('what comes after'), and its spatial sense ('what is placed behind'), and concludes that post-structuralism, coming after struc-turalism, none the less comes *behind* it, and therefore, in a bizarre sense, *before* it. Robert Young quite rightly invokes Freud's *Nachträglichkeit* to describe this situation.

History begins to lose its grip at this point: or rather history (which suffers from an inability to answer the question 'When?' asked of a text, or from an inevitable tendency to believe that there could be a *simple* answer to this question) only maintains its grip by a violent reduction of this scandalous instability of the prefix 'post-', which raises philosophical questions in excess of history. On the other hand, it cannot be denied that there are indeed historical and socio-institutional *effects* of post-structuralism, and these have to be addressed: this is a *political* question, and it is via the effects of the post- that it can best be approached. It is no accident that most of the adverse reactions to post-structuralism have been dictated by political concerns, and it may well be that the political question put to philosophy always demands simplicity, and that the philosophical answer to that question always insists on complexity. To the extent that the present essay is more on the side of the philosophical, then it too will stress complexity, in part by suggesting that the 'method' of the enquiry cannot here be separated from its 'object' (post-structuralism as an institutional phenomenon can itself only be understood in terms of postal politics). But in so far as this 'complexity' might only be another name for 'the political', then maybe a certain simplicity will emerge after all to satisfy current demands: and as such demands increasingly invoke certain values (clarity, communication, dialogue, rationality) which are those of the Enlightenment,[9] it is to authors of the Enlightenment that I shall turn for some help in elaborating the complex of spatial and temporal problems raised so far.

Postal politics

In order to approach these questions of politics, institutional effects, of nation and narration, I shall insist on another network, or translation, of 'post'. I have already suggested that the prefix 'post-' disturbs history, and even that in some sense it comes 'before' history. What now of the post as postal network? Eugène Vaillé's monumental *Histoire générale des postes françaises*[10] provides the following definition on page 1:

> [The post] can be defined as a regulated and usually governmental institution, which ensures, in conditions established in advance, both for the duration and price of transport and for its regularity, the transmission of the thought of the sender as he has transcribed it himself on a material support. (p. 1)

Just before this definition, Vaillé states that 'the post has the essential advantage of carrying out the transport of the very support which bears the thought of the sender as he has formulated it himself, which is a guarantee of absolute authenticity' (ibid.). This does not prevent him, two pages later, from 'making the transportation of thought a postal affair without waiting for the appearance of the material support which will receive the writing' (p. 3). This comes down to privileging the messenger or the postman, the transport over the support, and this 'extended' definition allows Vaillé to deduce the existence of the post at the dawn of civilization: 'As an institution indispensable to social life, the post, whose utility is manifest from the beginning of civilisation, must have appeared along with the constitution of that life' (p. 18). In his effort to locate and define his object, Vaillé all but makes communication *in general* a postal affair: and thereby postal affairs a precondition of history — it is perhaps significant that the first part of Vaillé's book is entitled 'The post before history'.[11]

What, then, of postal politics? A starting point can be found in a short text by Montesquieu, entitled *Of Politics*, which probably dates from 1725, and which is the only remaining fragment of a lost *Treatise on Duty*.[12] This text contains a strange and obscure statement, made all the more strange and obscure by being isolated in the text by blanks which cut it off from its immediate context. In its disturbing simplicity, this sentence reads simply: 'It is the invention of the post which has produced politics' (p. 174). We should immediately note the catastrophic reversal which this sentence operates on a reflection by Vaillé, for whom 'no doubt political necessities were behind the creation of the post'. For Vaillé, the post is *posterior* with respect to politics, its servant or follower; for Montesquieu it comes before, in an absolute anteriority which is our whole problem.

Montesquieu's statement is a little intimidating because of its aphoristic or gnomic aspect: this impression is not diminished by the discovery of two almost identical sentences in the collection entitled *Mes Pensées*,[13] and therefore in a more explicitly gnomic context (assuming that it is possible to speak so simply of 'context' for this type of sentence). These two sentences are to be found under the rubric 'Politics' (third sub-section in the eighth main section of the collection, 'Political education and political economy'). This sub-section contains other sentences which do not immediately appear very 'political', and one might wonder what brought Montesquieu's first editors to place them here, were it not for the fact that the text explicitly entitled *Of Politics* also contains such sentences, on chance, on the unforeseeable and overdetermined nature of effects — for example, in *Mes pensées*, 'There are few facts in the world which do not depend on so many circumstances that it would take the eternity of the world for them to happen a second time' (no. 1,763), and the following, in *Of Politics*: 'Most effects come about in such singular ways, or depend on causes so imperceptible and so distant, that one can scarcely foresee them' (p. 172). I cannot here attempt to establish the links, which I believe to be tight,[14] between this type of reflection and the sentence on the post, and its two displaced repetitions in *Mes pensées*: 'The invention of the post produced politics: we do not politick with the Mogol' (no. 1,760), and 'Politics, as it is today, comes from the invention of the post' (no. 1,761).

We do not politick with the Mogol, first because he does not belong to the same network as us, but also, perhaps, because he does not belong to any network, because he practises a politics which is other than postal, and thus other than 'politics as it is today', which is supposed to come from the invention of the post. These two sentences thus, unlike the version in *Of Politics*, give a glimpse of, on the one hand, the possibility of a Mogolian politics, and on the other of a politics anterior to that of today: in both cases, of a non-postal politics. Montesquieu does not say whether all non-postal politics would be necessarily Mogolian (and therefore despotic), although this is clearly enough the essential question: it would be no exaggeration to claim that this is the whole problem of the Enlightenment, and the whole problem of politics.[15]

The argument of this strange essay *Of Politics* is that politics, 'as it is today', suffers from being too complicated, too refined, too secretive, too full of detours, too postal. But Montesquieu's examples are far from being clear and univocal. I shall quote what is perhaps the simplest of them:

It is said that M. de Louvois, wanting to organise an expedition in
Flanders, sent a packet to the intendant, forbidding him to open it
before receiving orders to do so. It was a matter of organising the
march of troups dispersed on all sides, and the packet contained orders
for all the people subordinate to the intendant in the execution of this
project, so that the intendant would only have to sign, and so that the
messengers would not reveal the secret. This is pitiful. Did not this
packet, which remained for two weeks in foreign hands, expose its
secret? What purpose did it serve except that of exciting curiosity?
what is more, could the secretaries of the minister not be unfaithful as
much as those of the intendant? Was the two-hour period needed to
write these orders enough to reveal the secret of an expedition? It is
often more petty to show off useless precautions than not to take
enough. (p. 174)

We could say that in this description politics primarily involves secrecy.
But as the secret is that of an 'expedition' (the word has a strong postal
connotation in French), and as it must be sent, *expédié*, committed to the
postal network, there is the risk that the secret be lost or disseminated:
even though it remains sealed during its time in this network, the packet
or letter opens none the less, becoming an open letter or a postcard (as
Derrida would say),[16] while it waits for the signature or counter-
signature of the addressee, here the intendant. The letter, the aim of
which was to order or subordinate a dispersion, runs the risk of being
itself dispersed. This brings with it a proliferation of letters or *expéditions*
which all aim to avoid the dispersion of the first letter, to keep the secret
of that expedition: alongside the sealed packet, there must be an order
which states openly that the packet must not be opened (this order could
be written on the outside of the packet), and later there must be a second
order authorizing the opening of the packet which contains the real
orders . . . . Too many *expéditions*, too much politics, too much post, too
much secret: which, because of this very excess, opens and is lost.
Montesquieu thinks it better to do things more directly. As he says a
little earlier in this same essay: 'a simple and natural conduct can just as
easily lead to the aims of government as a more devious one' (p. 173).
   There follow two examples designed to illustrate the excesses of the
political behaviour of the Cardinal de Richelieu:

I have often heard praised the action of the Cardinal de Richelieu who,
wanting to pay over 2 millions in Germany, had a German come to
Paris, sent the 2 millions to one of his men, with an order to give
them, without a receipt, to a man with no name, of such-and-such
dress and appearance. How is it that people don't see in this a
ridiculous affectation? What was more simple than sending good *lettres
de change*, without loading onto this German such a large sum, which
could expose him infinitely; or, if he wanted to give the money in
Paris, why did he not give it himself?
   This minister, who used to buy comedies so as to pass as a good
poet, and who used to try to swindle all sorts of merit, was always

tormenting himself to find ways of getting new esteem.

Here is another show of bravado!

A man in whom he had confidence having remained in his office while he went out to accompany someone, the Cardinal remembered that he could have read some important papers that were on his table. He immediately wrote a letter which he gave him to take to the governor of the Bastille, which letter gave the governor orders to hold him for a month, at the end of which time the secret would expire: which was done, and, after a month, the prisoner was released with a large reward. Pure bluster, prepared and set up at leisure, and even without much judgement. Firstly, one does not receive several people in an office where there are papers of such importance. Prudent people write such letters in code. Finally, there were a thousand less showy ways of repairing this gross error. But he wanted to make a noise and be a great minister, at whatever price. (p. 174)

I cannot here comment on these examples as fully as they deserve: there would be much to say about the nameless and yet infinitely exposed German, and about what could be called the Bellerophon effect (or Hamlet effect) of the second example, from which it might be possible to deduce that the post always in some sense desires the death of the postman.[17] But if Montesquieu seems to be attacking a 'political' effect which depends on too much post, it is not clear that the remedy implies a simple quantitative reduction of postal complications. Writing *lettres de change*, and especially letters in code, surely complicates the network rather than simplifying it. What Montesquieu reproaches politics with is apparently not so much the post as such, as the fact of wanting to achieve, by postal means, effects on a secondary addressee, the public, by means of 'making a noise':[18] politics cannot want absolute secrecy, but the open, expiring secret constituted by a letter in the post. The secret is never absolutely secret, but announces itself as secret, and this can be the sign of the skill of a 'great minister'. (No doubt this schema remains valid for the analysis of a number of recent political events in Britain, around the Secret Services or so-called 'official secrets'. It will be remembered, for example, that one episode of the British 'Westland affair' of 1986 turned on the interpretation of the words 'secret and confidential' written on the outside of a letter, on whether these words referred to the *content* of the letter, or to its very *existence*. The fact that the ensuing 'noise' was taken to be the sign of an *incompetent* minister simply confirms Montesquieu's point.)

Montesquieu's analysis is not simple. On the one hand he appears to recommend a reduction of postal effects, a political simplicity which would have to do with a certain postal directness. But the remedies proposed appear to increase these same effects in the very effort made to avoid them. It is not hard to imagine that such a structure would produce paradoxes according to which an absolute reduction of postal politics would give rise to an absolute increase of postal political effects: 'In our own time we have seen another minister who never had a single paper on his desk and who never read any. If he had succeeded in his principal projects, he would have been looked upon as an intelligence who governed a state as would the spirits' (p. 174). And this paradox will allow us to read the final two sentences of Montesquieu's text: 'There is nothing so easy for a man in certain positions as to astonish people by a great project: there is something false in this. It is not the means which should be brilliant, but the ends. True politics consists in getting there by obscure routes' (p. 175).

True politics is not then simply the absence of the post, but a postal network which would itself be secret, distributing the mail in the dark, without exhibiting its expeditions and letters *en souffrance*, an underground network keeping the secret secret. The logic implied here also governs the *writing* of Montesquieu's text, which is thus also '(An example) of politics': at the outset, Montesquieu declares that 'it is useless to attack politics directly', and that 'it is better to take a circuitous route' (p. 172) — the structure of the argument thus repeats the structure of its object.[19]

Autonomy

The post wants the letter to arrive at its destination, at what Montesquieu calls its 'brilliant end': this end is the death of the postman and the end of the post. As postal network, all politics wants politics to end. The arrival of the letter should erase its delivery. The end of politics is the end of politics. All of this would have to be inscribed more generally in a notion of *nature* as a postal network, in which, as Montesquieu says in a near-contemporary text, 'toutes les créatures . . . s'entretiennent par une correspondance qu'on ne saurait assez admirer'.[20] For a whole Enlightenment, what is admirable in this natural correspondence is that it is ruled by inflexible and necessary laws: the end of politics would be to be absorbed into a *simulacrum* of this natural and necessary network. Through a slippage in the sense of the word 'law', positive laws are assimilated to the laws of nature, via the notion of 'natural law'. This type of schema rules, for example, the first book of Montesquieu's *De l'esprit des lois*, and also famous readings of Montesquieu by Auguste Comte and Louis Althusser. Kant too works within the same structure, which he complicates, certainly, but maintains.[21]

If such a simulacrum were to be achieved, then there would be no question of nation and narration, but only of nature and no narration. This can be shown by a brief consideration of Rousseau's political thought, which never, to my knowledge, makes the kind of direct appeal to the post made by Montesquieu, but which none the less presents a more rigorous and less anecdotal account of the same structure. Rousseau's aim, as formulated in *Emile*, is indeed to provide a model according to which the state would attain the necessary functioning of the Newtonian universe:

If the laws of nations could have, like those of nature, an inflexibility that no human force could ever overcome, then dependency on men would become again dependency on things, in the Republic all the advantages of the natural state would be linked with those of the civil state, to the liberty which maintains man exempt from vice would be joined the morality which raises him to virtue.[22]

In the *Social Contract*, the doctrine of the general will is designed to achieve this: in the light of the reading of Montesquieu, it seems possible to describe the general will as the sending of a letter (a circular letter) by the citizen as member of the sovereign to that 'same' citizen as subject. The citizen does not pre-exist the sending of this letter, but is created by it: 'sovereign' and 'subject' are Rousseau's names for the sender and addressee of the legislative letter, and 'citizen' the name which implies that the structure of the law allows the identity of sender and addressee to be asserted.[23] Given this postulated identity, Rousseau can claim that 'the Sovereign, by the simple fact that it *is*, is always what it *should be*', and that 'the general will is always right'.[24] The citizen sends himself the law, and in this sending names himself as citizen: this structure is that of autonomy in general, and implies a concomitant autonomination.

From the 'post-structuralist' perspective assumed earlier, we can see that this theory presupposes that letters arrive at their destination. If this were so, then the desire of politics to end the post would have been achieved, and there would be no need of politics at all — if the legislative letter always reached its destination (always in fact being returned to the sender), then there would be no need for it to be sent, for it would have always already arrived. The fact that this is not the case is sufficiently proved by the existence of Rousseau's theories, which presuppose that politics has come adrift from the natural network and can only attempt to reproduce it in the form of a radical fiction.[25] The immediate implication is that politics is a name for the necessary possibility of the failure of autonomy to close into the circuit which names the citizen as citizen, and that the designation 'citizen' is always inhabited by an element of impropriety. This impropriety is both the condition of possibility of politics and the reason why autonomy can never be achieved: this margin, which can be called 'freedom', is also the ground of differentiation which allows for the fact that 'citizens' are always in fact bearers of so-called 'proper names', and are not just isomorphic points. Rousseau also recognizes this in so far as he cannot let the law remain in its pure generality, but formulates the need for a government or executive power to allow its particular applications: the government being something like a central sorting office, 'an intermediary body established between the subjects and the Sovereign for their mutual correspondence'.[26] But more importantly for our concerns here, this necessary failure of autonomy also denies the absolute closure of the circuit of the general will in the form of the absolutely autonomous state. If the doctrine of the general will were not troubled by the necessary possibility of the letter's not arriving, then the state would be absolute and have no relation to any outside: it could not strictly speaking be a *nation*, and it would have no history, and thus no narration.[27] In order to have a name, a boundary and a history to be told at the centre, the state must be constitutively imperfect. The closure of the state becomes the frontier of the nation, and, as we have seen, the frontier implies that there is more than one nation.

We have to go further, and say that this complication is not an *accident* which befalls the state in its ideal purity, but that it is originary: just as, for Derrida, the possibility that the letter not arrive or that the performative misfire is not an empirical but a *necessary* possibility,[28] so national differentiation does not come along to trouble the state *after* its perfect constitution, but precedes the fiction of such a constitution as its condition of possibility. Rousseau also recognizes this, implicitly in the *Social Contract*, more clearly in, for example, the *Project for a Constitution for Corsica*. This text has, for us, the considerable advantage of recognizing national difference in its very title, while none the less maintaining a proximity to the theoretic rigour of the *Social Contract* itself. Corsica had in fact been named within the *Social Contract* as the only country in Europe still capable of legislation,[29] and the text of the *Project* duly lays down demands of autonomy and self-sufficiency:

> With whatever aim the Corsican nation wants to organise itself politically [*se policer*] the first thing it must do is to give itself all the consistency it can have. Whoever depends on another and does not have his resources within himself cannot be free. Alliances, treaties, the faith of men — all this can tie the weak to the strong and never ties the strong to the weak. So leave negotiations to the powers and count only on yourselves . . . .
>
> Here, then, are the principles which in my view should serve as a base for their legislation: make of their people and their country as much as is possible; cultivate and assemble their own forces, rely on them alone, and think of foreign powers as little as if none existed. (pp. 903—4)

The 'as if' in the final recommendation marks an awareness of fiction in the notion of autonomy: and, earlier, the text has in fact recognized that Corsica is practically at the mercy of foreign powers and would be the more so were it to prosper. There is here at work an insidious logic which De Man has analysed in a different fragment of Rousseau's political writing, and which can be found taken to an extreme in the Marquis de Sade: briefly, in Rousseau, autonomy is defined in part by independence from other nations — but this independence implies that the other nations in turn become dependent on, and jealous of, the 'autonomous' nation, whose autonomy is thus measured in terms of the other it is supposed to ignore. In Rousseau, this means, ideally, as in his recommendations to the Corsicans, that other nations in fact be forgotten in what we can now see to be a vain attempt to achieve the closure of autonomy and self-sufficiency: in Sade, the same logical process leads to the conclusion that the only consistent *internal* policy is one which encourages depravity, corruption and permanent insurrection.[30] These two conclusions are, clearly enough, dialectical opposites, and the possibility of such a dialectic depends on some recognition of a relation with an outside, repressed in Rousseau, invasive and pervasive in Sade.

Some progress beyond this dialectic can be made, typically, via Kant, who takes the crucial step of recognizing that these problems do not simply befall the autonomous state but constitute its possibility and its limit: implicitly in his *Perpetual Peace*,[31] where we find the following:

> Even if people were not compelled by internal dissent to submit to the coercion of public laws, war would produce the same effect from outside ... each people would find itself confronted by another neighbouring people pressing in upon it, thus forcing it to form itself internally into a *state* in order to encounter the other as an armed *power* (p. 112)

and explicitly in the seventh proposition of the *Idea for a Universal History with a Cosmopolitan Purpose*:

> The problem of establishing a perfect civil constitution is subordinate to the problem of a law-governed *external relationship* with other states, and cannot be solved unless the latter is also solved. What is the use of working for a law-governed civil constitution among individual men, i.e. of planning a *commonwealth*? The same unsociability which forced men to do so gives rise in turn to a situation whereby each commonwealth, in its external relations (i.e. as a state in relation to other states), is in a position of unrestricted freedom. Each must accordingly expect from any other precisely the same evils which formerly oppressed individual men and forced them into a law-governed civil state. (p. 47)

The state of nature is a state of war, or of the necessary risk of war,[32] and, again, this is constitutive and not accidental: and if it is difficult for us to accept the transcendental optimism of Kant's teleological view of nature progressing towards a perpetual peace, then that state of war is permanent, and susceptible only of degrees of more or less, never of final solution.

Nation is, then, always opened to its others: or rather, it is constituted only in that opening, which is, in principle, violent. The status of the individual nation and, within it, of the individual citizen, is derived from that primary 'global' violence by a process analogous to the 'morphogenesis' of catastrophe theory.[33] Faced with this situation, the nation resorts to narration of one sort or another, and proceeds by the sort of *Nachträglichkeit* constitutive of institutions in general, and which we saw above to be operative in the very name of post-structuralism. The social contract is one such narrative, projecting, aporetically, an impossible moment of foundation and legitimation: another narrative is that of the legislator, the giver of laws, the founder of the state. In Rousseau, the legislator comes from outside and leaves again:[34] in the time of his coming, it is impossible to decide as to his legitimacy — in view of quite traditional paradoxes of authority, the final establishment of that legitimacy can only be projected into an indefinite future.[35] The radically performative laying down of the law by the legislator must create the very context according to which that law could be judged to be just: the founding moment, the *pre-*, is always already inhabited by the *post-*. In the absence of final criteria for such a judgement, the nation narrates the founding moment and produces effects of legitimacy through repetition. These two narratives (that of the contract and that of the legislator) are not independent: the essential postal possibilities we have recognized in the mechanism of the general will open it to the coming of the legislator — and, more importantly, will prepare the state in question to extend its demand for autonomy by playing the legislator to all other nations. The doctrine of the social contract is essentially intolerant of national differences, and will attempt to absorb them in the creation of an autonomous 'humanity', for example. The American and French declarations duly formulate a confusion between the names of their respective nations and postulated universal 'rights of man', on the basis of which they have felt able to play the legislator the world over.[36]

The idea of the nation is inseparable from its narration: that narration attempts, interminably, to constitute identity against difference, inside against outside, and in the assumed superiority of inside over outside, prepares against invasion and for 'enlightened' colonialism. In this structure, the legislator is never far away. In Rousseau's doctrine, the legislator is always, undecidably, also a charlatan: and no doubt that insistence of the charlatan is becoming increasingly visible in international politics today. The arrival of the legislator is proof enough that the law to be laid down will never achieve its desired identity with the laws of nature, and that politics will never reach its goal (which is always that of wresting a realm of necessity from a realm of freedom), and to this extent is probably not simply to be deplored. But it should no doubt still be a source of amusement: legislators in general cannot fail to lay down the law and cannot fail to be laughable as they do so — this is no less true of the 'legislators' of institutions such as 'post-structuralism' than of any others, with the difference that the law they lay down allows some understanding of the necessary imperfection of legislation in general, and undercuts the faith in origins and ends which narration perpetuates. It also allows us to understand 'post-structuralism' more as a *movement* and less as an *institution*, while enabling an understanding of the effects of institution which necessarily ensue. And whether the law be formulated as *différence* or *différend*, it is also a law of the inter-nation (though not as international law), with which to negotiate a survival.[37]

March 1986

Notes

1 'We know the scene: there are men gathered round, and someone telling them a story .... They were not gathered before the story, it is the telling that gathers them .... It is the story of their origin .... We know this scene well. More than one story-teller has told it to us, having gathered us into learned fraternities, destined to find out what were our origins .... These stories have

been called *myths* .... We also know, henceforth, that this scene is itself mythical': Jean-Luc Nancy, *La Communauté désoeuvrée* (Paris: Galilée, 1986), pp. 109—13. See too Lyotard's analyses of the narratives of the Cashinahua Indians: *La Condition postmoderne: rapport sur le savoir* (Paris: Minuit, 1979), pp. 38—43 (tr. *The Postmodern Condition* (Manchester: Manchester University Press, 1984), pp. 18—23); *Au Juste* (Paris: Bourgois, 1979), pp. 63—6 (tr. *Just Gaming* (Manchester: Manchester University Press, 1986), pp. 32—3); *Le Différend* (Paris: Minuit, 1983), pp. 219—23; *Le Postmoderne expliqué aux enfants* (Paris: Galilée, 1986), pp. 56—9 and 73—5: and, for a brilliant analysis of Freud's version of the story, Mikkel Borch-Jakobsen, *Le Sujet freudien* (Paris: Aubier-Flammarion, 1982), especially pp. 159—292.

2 Edgar Morin, *La Méthode*, vol. 1, *La Nature de la nature* (Paris: Seuil, 1977; reprinted collection 'Points', 1981), pp. 203—4: the structure is also that of the 'hinge' (*la brisure*) described by Derrida in *De la grammatologie* (Paris: Minuit, 1967), pp. 96—108 (tr. *Of Grammatology* (Baltimore and London: Johns Hopkins University Press, 1976), pp. 65—73).

3 I am not aware off any serious attempt to do this: a precondition of such an attempt would be the recognition that it could not, by definition, constitute a critique (and *a fortiori* not a refutation) of the work labelled 'poststructuralist'. An earlier condensed version of the analysis of the 'post-' offered here appeared in French as 'Post', in D. Kelley and I. Llasera (eds), *Cross-references: Modern French Theory and the Practice of Criticism* (London: Society for French Studies, 1986), pp. 65—73.

4 Historically speaking, the word might have been used in French first: the earliest usage I am aware of in either language is in Jean-Joseph Goux's *Freud, Marx: Economie et symbolique* (Paris: Seuil, 1973), p. 47, where the word already appears in quotation marks. The Anglo-American use of the term seems to have become common after about 1979, and seems from its earliest uses to have commonly appeared in the form 'so-called poststructuralism'. This situation has been analysed by Robert Young in an unpublished paper called 'The improper name'. The reimportation into French seems to begin with Vincent Descombe's *Grammaire d'objets en tous genres* (Paris: Minuit, 1983) (tr. *Objects of All Sorts: A Philosophical Grammar* (Oxford: Blackwell, 1986)), is massively implicit in Jacques Bouveresse, *Rationalité et cynisme* (Paris: Minuit, 1985), and, under the name 'the thought of '68', in Luc Ferry and Alain Renaut, *La Pensée '68: Essai sur l'anti-humanisme contemporain* (Paris: Gallimard, 1985): the simplistic nature of this last book has been sufficiently demonstrated by Jean-Francois Lyotard and Jacob Rogozinski, 'La Police de la pensée, *L'Autre Journal*, 1 (1986), pp. 27—34.

5 Lyotard, *La Condition postmoderne*; 'Réponse à la question: Qu'est-ce le postmoderne?', *Critique*, 419 (1982), pp. 357—67 (reprinted in Lyotard, *Le Postmoderne expliqué*, pp. 13—34). The implicit reference of this title is of course to Kant's famous article of 1784, 'Beantwortung der Frage: Was ist Aufklärung?' (tr. 'An answer to the question: "What is Enlightenment?"', in *Kant's Political Writings*, ed. Hans Reiss (Cambridge: Cambridge University Press, 1970), pp. 54—60).

6 'Defining the postmodern', in *Postmodernism*, ICA Documents 4 and 5 (London: Institute of Contemporary Arts, 1986), p. 6. A slightly reworked version of these initially improvised remarks appears in French as 'Note sur les sens de "post-"' in Lyotard, *Le Postmoderne expliqué*, pp. 119—26 (pp. 120—1).

7 '*Postmodern* would have to be understood according to the paradox of the future (*post*) perfect (*modo*)', Lyotard, 'Réponse', p. 33 (*The Postmodern Condition*,

p. 81, tr. mod.). The various possible readings of the expression 'future perfect' are the object of work in progress.

8 Robert Young, 'Poststructuralism: the end of theory', *Oxford Literary Review*, vol. 5, nos 1—2 (1982), pp. 3—25, p. 4.

9 This (apparent?) shift from Marxist to Enlightenment demands seems to stem from Habermas's notorious Adorno prize speech of 1980: 'Modernity — an incomplete Project', in *The Anti-Aesthetic: Essays on Postmodern Culture*, ed. Hal Foster (Port Townsend, Washington: Bay Press, 1983) (reprinted as *Postmodern Culture* (London: Pluto Press, 1985)), pp. 3—15; *The Postmodern Condition* and the 'Answering the Question' essay are of course partially written against Habermas. The importance of what is at stake can be judged from the large amount of discussion this 'confrontation' has already received: see, most interestingly, Philippe Lacoue-Labarthe, 'Où en étions-nous?' in J. Derrida, V. Descombes *et al.*, *La Faculté de juger* (Paris: Minuit, 1985), pp. 165—193 (reprinted in Lacoue-Labarthe's *L'Imitation des modernes (Typographies II)* (Paris: Galilée, 1986), pp. 257—85) (tr. 'Talks', *Diacritics*, vol. 14, no. 3 (1984), 24—37); Richard Rorty, 'Habermas and Lyotard on postmodernity', *Praxis International*, vol. 4, no. 1 (1984), pp. 32—44 (and the subsequent discussion between Lyotard and Rorty at the 1984 Johns Hopkins 'Case of the Humanities' conference, printed in French in *Critique*, no. 456 (1985), pp. 559—84); Peter Dews, 'From poststructuralism to postmodernism', in *Postmodernism*, pp. 12—16; see, too, various articles in *New German Critique*, no. 33 (1984). In the ICA volume, Lyotard suggests, in response to Terry Eagleton, that 'We must recognize that Marxism is one of the versions of the Enlightenment' (p. 12): it would be interesting to test this statement against the eighteenth-century nostalgia of Eagleton's *The Function of Criticism* (London: Verso, 1984), itself of course heavily influenced by a particular account of Habermas — Eagleton's own discussion of the postmodern ('Capitalism, modernism and postmodernism', *New Left Review*, no. 152 (1985), pp. 60—73, reprinted in *Against the Grain* (London: Verso, 1986), pp. 131—47) does not address the question, though it is very critical of Lyotard.

10 Eugène Vaillé, *Histoire générale des postes françaises*, 6 vols (Paris: PUF, 1947—53).

11 The full title of this part of Vaillé's book is 'La poste avant l'histoire et la poste gallo-romaine': a less tendentious translation of the first part of this title would be, 'The post in prehistory', which would still make the point well enough. Given the inevitable regressions of Vaillé's attempts to define his object, it is clear that from our perspective his project is inconsistent — if the post precedes history, it cannot be an object of history.

12 Montesquieu, 'De la politique', in *Oeuvres complètes*, ed. Daniel Oster (Paris: Seuil, 1964), pp. 172—5. All references to Montesquieu will be to this edition and will be included in the text. All translations from Montesquieu are my own.

13 *Oeuvres complètes*, pp. 853—1082: the collection consists of 2,204 numbered fragments taken from Montesquieu's notebooks and organized into thematic groups by a late nineteenth-century editor.

14 The immediate reference in Montesquieu would be to the final two books of *De l'esprit des lois*, which contain a notoriously long historical discussion of feudal law and the birth of the French monarchy, the structural role of which in Montesquieu's work as a whole has baffled the commentators. The tension can be immediately pointed out and linked to the problem at hand, by placing the title of Book 30 ('*Theory* of Feudal Laws ...' (my emphasis)) against its

first sentence, which claims, against the generality promised by the word 'theory', that its object is 'un événement arrivé une fois dans le monde, et qui n'arrivera peut-être jamais' (literally, and mysteriously, 'an event happened once in the world and which will perhaps never happen') (p. 755): this 'event' is inseparable from the invasion of Gaul by the Franks, and engages Montesquieu in a polemic with Boulainvilliers and Dubos which is too complicated to summarize here, though it is precisely to do with telling a story which would ground the identity of the French nation. The problematic nature of the founding 'event' might be linked to Derrida's remarks on the 'singular event' of the institution of psychoanalysis (*La Carte postale de Socrate à Freud et au-delà* (Paris: Aubier-Flammarion, 1980), p. 7; see too p. 17 on 'une seule fois') — the present essay could be situated as an approach to the question of the event in recent French thought.

15 Montesquieu's *Lettres persanes* dramatizes this problem, but can do so only by having already drawn the figure of the Oriental 'despot', Usbek, into the postal network which gives the novel its existence, and simultaneously into the progress of 'enlightenment'. A despotic system of government is in principle, apparently non-postal: the despot's will has *immediate* force of law. But this concentration of all power in the despot is simultaneously, according to the *De l'esprit des lois*, the possibility of absolute delegation of that power: 'It is a result of the nature of despotic power that the single man who exercises it have it exercised similarly by a single man . . . . It is thus simpler that [the despot] abandon that power to a vizir who will, first of all, have the same power as he' (II, 5, p. 536); 'In the despotic government, power passes entirely into the hands of him to whom it is given. The vizir is the despot himself; and each individual officer is the vizir' (V, 16, p. 553). The despotic model is thus both absolutely postal and absolutely non-postal, and this is why it is the object of such fascination and loathing for Enlightenment thinkers. This structure also accounts for the inherent capacity of utopias to undergo catastrophic reversals into dystopias.

16 See *La Carte postale*, passim: the analysis offered here presupposes recognition of the force of Derrida's arguments against Lacan ('Le Facteur de la vérité', ibid., pp. 441—524 (partial tr. 'The purveyor of truth', *Yale French Studies*, no. 52 (1975), pp. 31—114).

17 On the story of Bellopheron, see Derrida's note in *De la grammatologie*, pp. 379—80 (tr. p. 349, n. 1), and especially the comment, 'In an endless chain of representations, desire carries death through the detour of writing' (tr. mod.): Bellopheron does not in fact die as a result of the message he carries, and his death is not reported in the *Iliad* at all. Hamlet does not die in this way either, though in his case the postal effect does work, on Rosencrantz and Guildenstern. Following the fate of the messenger would soon return us, beyond *Hamlet*, to *Oedipus Rex*; but also, via the Greek ἄγγελος (messenger) to a community of angels, which could again be shown, in the thought of both Rousseau and Kant, to be a purely postal polis returning to a pure absence of post.

18 'Noise' here can be understood in a quasi-cybernetic sense; what Montesquieu condemns in Richelieu's politics is its interference with the clarity of the message — at the second level (the public as meta-addressee) this 'noise' is converted into information, according to a logic laid out by Michel Serres in 'The origin of language', *Oxford Literary Review*, vol. 5, nos 1—2, pp. 113—24 (pp. 118—19).

19 In their opening text to the collective volume *Rejouer le politique* (Paris: Galilée,

1981), Lacoue-Labarthe and Nancy radicalize this 'uselessness' of attacking politics directly into an impossibility (p. 23): this guarantees, beyond any slogan, that writing on the political is itself necessarily political. Thomas Pynchon's *The Crying of Lot 49* might be read as an allegory of all the issues raised here.

20 'Essai touchant les lois naturelles et la distinction du juste et de l'injuste', *Oeuvres complètes*, pp. 175–81 (p. 175). Literally, 'All creatures support each other by a correspondence it is impossible to admire enough': but the French verb 's'entretenir' also has the sense of 'to have a conversation', 'to talk about'.

21 The complication in Kant stems from his explicit insistence on the originality of the ethical (and thereby political) with respect to the natural world as a mechanism: in the immediate context of the discussion here, see his *Perpetual Peace: a Philosophical Sketch* (1795–6), in *Kant's Political Writings*, pp. 93–130, and especially pp. 122–5, where the distinction between the 'political moralist' and the 'moral politician' depends on the fact that the former views questions of right in merely 'technical' or 'mechanical' terms, whereas the latter sees them as properly moral questions. More succinctly, the argument suggests that were the simulacrum of laws of nature to be achieved, there would be no freedom, and hence the concept of 'right' would be empty (ibid., p. 117). That this simulacrum would not be incompatible with despotism can be seen by grafting in another quotation from *De l'esprit des lois*: 'In despotic states the nature of government demands extreme obedience; and the will of the Prince, once known, must have its effect as infallibly as a ball thrown against another must have its effect' (III, 10, p. 539: Hume, billiard-balls, oughts and is's are not far away). But Kant none the less maintains the structure in all his moral philosophy, via the operator of *analogy*: one of the formulations of the categorical imperative demands that I act as if the maxim of my action were to be a 'universal law of nature'. The 'as if' in this formulation raises complicated questions of what Kant calls the 'type': see Lyotard, *Le Différend* (Paris: Minuit, 1984), pp. 181–3.

22 Jean-Jacques Rousseau, *Emile*, in *Oeuvres complètes*, ed. Bernard Gagnebin and Marcel Raymond, 4 vols appeared to date (Paris: Gallimard, 1959–), vol. 4, p. 311. All references to Rousseau are to this edition, and all translations are my own. What follows on the *Social Contract* is largely a summary of the more detailed argument presented in my *Sententiousness and the Novel: Laying Down the Law in Eighteenth-Century France* (Cambridge: Cambridge University Press, 1985), pp. 159–71.

23 'The words "subject" and "sovereign" are identical correlations brought together in the single word "citizen": *Oeuvres complètes*, vol. 3, p. 427.

24 *Oeuvres complètes*, vol. 3, pp. 363 and 373.

25 This fiction can be called 'radical' simply because it is at the root of the political: it thereby leads us back to the question of narration and myth from which we began.

26 *Oeuvres complètes*, vol. 3, p. 396.

27 The time of the sovereign is that of a succession of pure presents. The intermediary body of government attempts to deliver the post which would allow that time to exist, but in so doing takes time, breaks open the time of the sovereign, and gives rise to history and the possibility of the nation's narrating to itself what it should have been. For a useful derivation of the aporias of the idea of absolute autonomy or immanence, see Nancy, *La Communauté désoeuvrée*, pp. 16–19.

28 This much-misunderstood distinction is made most clearly by Derrida in

'Limited Inc.', *Glyph*, 2 (1977), pp. 162–254.

29 *Oeuvres complètes*, vol. 3, p. 391: 'There is still in Europe a country capable of legislation; the Island of Corsica. The valour and constancy with which this brave people managed to recover and defend its liberty would merit that some wise man teach them how to conserve it. I have some premonition that one day this little island will astonish Europe'.

30 For a fuller analysis of the structure in Rousseau, see Paul de Man, *Allegories of Reading: Figural Language in Rousseau, Nietzsche, Rilke, and Proust* (New Haven and London: Yale University Press, 1979), pp. 254–7: and for a summary of Sade's arguments, see *Sententiousness and the Novel*, pp. 198–9.

31 For a slightly different use of Kant's essay in a similar context, and an appeal to Rousseau's *Considérations sur le gouvernement de Pologne* rather than the text on Corsica, see Victor Goldschmidt, 'Individu et communauté chez Rousseau', in Bénichou, Cassirer *et al.*, *Pensée de Rousseau* (Paris: Seuil, 1984), pp. 147–61: it is worth pointing out that the volume in which Goldschmidt's text appears is presented (by Todorov) as in opposition to the whole 'post-structuralist' movement.

32 See Kant, *Perpetual Peace*, p. 98: 'Man (or an individual people) in a mere state of nature robs me of any ... security and injures me by virtue of this very state in which he coexists with me. He may not have injured me actively (*facto*), but he does injure me by the very lawlessness of his state (*statu iniusto*)', and §54 of the selections from the *Metaphysics of Morals* translated in the same volume (p. 165). Rousseau's insistence that the state of nature is *in fact* a state of peace would not trouble this argument at the level of right.

33 See Lyotard's presentation of this aspect of René Thom's thought, *La Condition postmoderne*, p. 96 (tr. p. 59). this 'analogy' must be treated with care, lest it return to us a new desired simulacrum based on a post-Newtonian account of 'nature': this problem haunts *The Postmodern Condition*'s appeal to 'postmodern science' as something of a model for a postmodern justice.

34 Rousseau tells some good stories about this essential feature of the legislator, and especially of Lycurgus, forced to resign all position of power, put up with hostility and eventually leave Sparta in order to enforce his legislation. Moses too is an object of admiration for Rousseau, essentially because of the durability of his legislation: it is not easy to see how the principles of Mosaic law could be reconciled with an ideal of autonomy, but a detour via Freud would rapidly confirm the importance of all the problems raised here. The incorporation of the essentially foreign legislator into the founding narration of an institution is pervasive, and returns, notably around the figure of Derrida, in accounts of post-structuralism: Frank Lentricchia's *After the New Criticism* (Chicago: University of Chicago Press, 1980) is a particularly blatant example.

35 For a succinct formulation of these paradoxes, see Lyotard, *Le Différend*, §203.

36 This tension is analysed by Lyotard with respect to the French declaration of 1789 in *Le Différend*, pp. 209–13, and, with a different emphasis on the question of the *signature* (which would be an important focus for any attempt to analyse the figure of the legislator), by Derrida in the first part of *Otobiographies: l'enseignement de Nietzsche et la politique du nom propre* (Paris: Galilée, 1984).

37 This survival is discussed by Nancy in *La Communauté désoeuvrée* around a notion of 'community' conceived of *against* or *beyond* the themes of autonomy and narration I have been concerned to question.

8
Literature – Nationalism's other? The case for revision

Simon During

Patriotism, in modern times, and in great states, is and must be the creature of reason and reflection, rather than the offspring of physical or local attachment. It was once said by an acute observer, and eloquent writer (Rousseau), that the love of mankind was nothing but the love of justice; the same might be said, with considerable truth, of the love of our country. It is little more than another name for the love of liberty, of independence, of peace, of social happiness.[1]

Some years ago Edward Said complained: 'if the body of objects we study – the corpus formed by works of literature – belongs to, gains coherence from, and in a sense emanates out of, the concepts of nation, nationality, and even of race, there is very little in contemporary critical discourse making these actualities possible as subjects of discussion'.[2] His remarks have born fruit, and discussion already shows signs of congealing into orthodoxy. It is becoming a commonplace that the institution of literature works to nationalist ends. This chapter works in the spirit of revision (in part – as we shall see – because it is written in Australia). I want to draw attention to the ways that, at least since the founding of the modern state, literature has operated in different social spaces than nationalism, employing different signifying practices. Furthermore I want to argue that literary criticism canonizes those texts which do not simply legitimate nationhood.

This is not to deny literature's ability to function as a signifier of national identity or heritage. One must also accept that in so far as the history of the West is a tale of exploitation of other societies, all European cultural practices are touched by imperialism. Yet nationalism is something other than imperialism writ as large as this. It is, quite specifically, the battery of discursive and representational practices which define, legitimate, or valorize a specific nation-state or individuals as members of a nation-state. Nationalism attaches to the modern state, revealing itself fully in subjects whose being is saturated by their nationality.

One can certainly be nationalist without being imperialist. Indeed, as the citation from Hazlitt indicates, nationalism has often seemed a mode of freedom. Its most powerful form — cultural nationalism — was in fact developed *against* imperialism. Herder, who invents the word 'nationalism' (in German), links a series of concepts — *Volk*, *Bildung*, lanaguage-as-consciousness-and-act, empathy, organic form, in an effort to connect with, and respect, what we must now call other cultures.[3] But this conceptual chain immediately penetrates imperialism — in a twist indicative of the way a single discourse may work to contradictory ends. For the notions 'culture' and 'nation' align, early-nineteenth-century Europe becoming a scene of individual cultures chasing after nationhood. Imperialist thought possesses itself of culturalism then, too, because cultures are even more worth fighting for than nations; hierarchies of cultures seeming to fix identities, whereas hierarchies of nations merely seeming to belong to history and politics. Under this dispensation an imperialist nation, competing with others, must regard itself as having a world-historical culture.

Despite the anti-imperialist intentions of culturalism at its founding moment, another dispensation — that of a nationalism *not* connected to culturalism — stands as this chapter's point of departure. I refuse the position, shared by most humanists, modernists, and Marxists, that nationalism is an essentially nasty ideological formation. It is important immediately to remember that nationalism has different effects and meanings in a peripheral nation than in a world power. Against the Hazlitt of my motto, nationalism is perhaps reason's creature least of all in 'great states'. And let us also remember that the nation-state is, for better or worse, the political institution which has most efficacy and legitimacy in the world as it is. Modernity reproduces itself in nation-states, there are few signs of it happening otherwise. To reject nationalism absolutely or to refuse to discriminate between nationalisms is to accede to a way of thought by which intellectuals — especially postcolonial intellectuals — cut themselves off from effective political action.

So I believe that today, in writing in a First World colony like Australia, one ought to be nationalistic. This is a position all the easier to take in Australia, because here, unlike many Third World countries, nationalism is not used *against* large minority racial/tribal groups. Here nationalism can retain a link with freedom in allowing us to resist cultural and economic imperialism, and to remain outside the technology of nuclear war which, with modern communication systems, largely defines internationalism today. It reminds us that we are *not* historically or politically, simply on the side of the major powers. These are important points which I simply state here — and they lead us at once to ask: what is one defending *against* the encroachments of cultural, economic, military imperialism if not a culture?

Less and more. One is defending a set of customs, memories, possibilities for controlling, developing, and redistributing one's own resources, some of which make up units in what becomes, for culturalism, a totalizing web, others of which do not. This means that nationalism may operate for a wide variety of different groups within the nation — though it need not imply 'multiculturalism', a concept which retains ties both to liberal pluralism *and* to culturalism.

One is also defending one's right to make particular and local appropriations of reason. We can take it for granted that reason today is neither a dream of order nor an instrument, as it was for the Enlightenment; still less the grounds of the real as it was for idealism. We can best characterize it as a self-reflective mode of reading what lies either present to hand or stored in the archive. Today reason is 'theory', and, in a familiar list, it undercuts claims to identity, belief in origins as defining essences and the view that language is a transparent tool for expression or communication. When one defends the local within given political institutions at the same time as one heeds reason as theory then it is unproductive simply to denounce, for example the literary canon as nationalistic. At the very least it becomes important to examine varieties of nationalism as well as the historical dislocations between literature and legitimations of nation.

These remarks, which indicate a point of departure, have been general and tendentious. I would like to develop them by offering an account of the relations between one form of literature and nationalism in the UK during the eighteenth and early nineteenth centuries. This period is crucial because it is then that both literature and nationalism take on modern forms. But given time limits, this account cannot help but be synoptic and abstract in turn. This is more than a self-serving apology. For the difficulty of the task is determined by the fact that when one no longer regards nationalism negatively, when one stresses politics against culture, and when, thus, one finds oneself unable to treat names such as 'literature', 'nationalism', and most of all, 'culture' itself as if they connect unproblematically to the production of discourse, then one is again in the situation that Said describes. The shorthand used by current thought seems no longer adequate.

Nationalism is often said to start in the period of the French Revolution.[4] This is too simple, for even if one grants that modern nationalism is a moment in the immense upheavals of that era, it retains ties with a history of legitimation of the nation-state which goes back at least into the Renaissance. For my purposes the best moment to interrupt this history is by considering the use of the word 'patriotism' in the early eighteenth century, as it is there that the home country, as a concept, enters into modern political debate, and thus into those aspects of nationalism which retain their vigour.

The word 'patriotism' first became current as part of the Tory resistance to Walpole headed by Bolingbroke, author of *The Idea of a Patriot King*. Here a patriot is a person defined in a classical sense by his love of country rather than personal ambition. For Bolingbroke, Walpole's Whigs forego the name 'patriot' in ruling through the new financial institutions — the Bank, the Stock Market, the Public Debt, and a Parliament semi-independent of the monarch; in short, by the post-1688 economic and political order. Thus patriotism is given value in an anti-statist, anti-economist (though not anti-mercantile), anti-urban discourse. A patriot is neither an 'enthusiast' concerned with his or her inner life and relation to God, nor an urbanite interested in money and civility. The patriot king (who, unlike the Hanoverians, should be a native) would communicate directly to the people, without mediation by the state or politicians, in unison with the aristocracy. His constituency is not of course the population at large but those who own land. Thus the word 'country' here tends to oscillate between naming the sum of estates in the realm and the object of sentiments self-consciously borrowed from Roman formulations of *patria*.

This does not, of course, make Bolingbroke's concept of patriotism coherent. For him the word is ultimately used in a game whose aim is political power. Thus, too, the slipperiness of his discourse:

> Patriotism has, in all Ages and Nations, been acknowledged a glorious virtue, and the more generous the Genius of a People is, the more Honor do they pay to those Fathers of Mankind, who, being actuated by the noble Principles of universal and unconfin'd Benevolence, have made the welfare of their Country, their great and only Care ....[5]

Here patriotism merges both toward a notion of a people's genius, which is not quite a national character, and toward 'universal and unconfin'd Benevolence'. How can such benevolence operate only for the welfare of one country? More than a ghost of an invisible hand is at work here as local benevolences produce universal order; there are particular and determining discursive absences. What is missing is the concept of a 'humanity' transcending mere nationality, and the concomitant concept of 'culture' as moulding specific peoples and individuals. These notions are connected: only when individuals and their practices are perceived to be wholly informed by cultures do abstract notions like humanity arise. Humanity is what belongs to peoples beyond culture. Also missing is 'liberty', the central attribute of humanity for Enlightenment thought. Benevolence is a private, oligarchic virtue, not a right as the Enlightenment conceived liberty to be.

So Bolingbroke's patriotism stands outside humanism, cultural nationalism, and enlightened rationality. It is itself a virtue *everywhere*, making a claim to universality even as it attaches to specific English legal and social institutions: to the constitution.[6] Bolingbroke appeals to the civic and legal rights of the 'freeborn Englishman': trial by jury, *habeas corpus*, the right to privacy, in a list which varies according to context. These rights, which predate the Norman yoke, shape English liberty. The 'constitution' stands for institutions which resist the state power being used by the Whigs to make room for the free play of the market.[7] But given its rhetorical force against the new order, the discourse which valorizes the constitution soon changes hands, coming to signify a wider liberty. As the century proceeds, it works as the official mark of enlightened opposition and by the 1780s dominates the discourse of English radicalism.[8] A constitutional patriot is no longer a Jacobite Tory but a reformer — even a revolutionary.

When one considers all this in the light of eighteenth-century literary writing familiar today, it is clear that these shifting notions of patriotism are lost to English departments. Canonized literature operates elsewhere, even in Tories like Fielding, Swift, and Pope. Take, for example, Pope's 'First Dialogue' in his *Epilogues to the Satires*, an important repository of early patriot wit though I suspect not much taught or remembered these days. It is on this unusual occasion of overt patriotism, that Pope includes his encomium for Ralph Allen, the private founder of the modern public postal system. As the explicit, if idealized, model for Allworthy in *Tom Jones*, Allen becomes the symbol for a kind of Englishness in another literary mode. This is not surprising: Allen's work is crucial in the development of modern communication systems, in the homogenizing of Britain. His work is the precondition not only of the epistolary novel, but of the radical corresponding societies later in the century. When Fielding and Pope make him a symbol of Tory patriotism they join the effort to manage the shift into modernity from the side of the old order.

What has happened to the discourse of patriotism itself? It is not just a part of the archive which remains uncanonized — in the poem itself Pope's patriot wit quickly shifts into a proto-nationalist symbolization. Allen's reputation is tuned to literary use, in an early instance of a different kind of signifying practice, one rare in canonized literature. An actual person becomes an icon of a particular kind of universal modernizing benevolence whose acceptability lies in its vague Englishness. But the shift from universal benevolence to Englishness *fully* occurs only later when, after the Napoleonic wars (Pope having acquired quite another kind of reputation),[9] Fielding's work enters the world of 'Merrie England'. 'Fielding's novels are in general ... thoroughly English' as Hazlitt will say.[10] Little here remains of radical patriotism.

At its centre, however, writing in eighteenth-century England is not dominated by polite letters nor by the production of 'Englishness'. It begins to form a new cultural space — which I shall call, not very satisfactorily, the civil Imaginary. This is a notion, though not a word, I take from recent work on the history of the novel inspired by Foucault.[11] The term names prose writings which provide representations of social existence from the beginning of the eighteenth century through the period of the classic realist and novel and beyond. At its beginnings the civil Imaginary does not cover just what we would today call fiction: Addison and Steele's journalism stand at its point of emergence. What these writings have in common with Defoe, Richardson, and Fielding's novels is the production of narratives, moral cruxes, a linguistic decorum, and character types which cover the social field of the post-1688 world.

The civil Imaginary is an attempt to order what Steele calls 'the uncontrollable jumble of Persons and Things' in that society.[12] Thus its purpose is in part ethical in the Foucauldian sense. It produces representations of manners, taste, behaviour, utterances for imitation by individual lives. Its sphere is secular — that is, not religiously enthusiastic. It is *not* political (it relies on what Habermas has called the modern split between politics and ethics),[13] it is not dominated by the old caste system, not determined by classical and Renaissance *virtu*. Its prime value is a sociability which cannot be expressed in terms of moral laws. It reproduces everyday life in the public domain, reducing the gap between the divine/moral order and actual behaviour, thereby replacing the old science of casuistry by the modern domination of the life-world by style and civility. One might say that the older aristocratic humanism becomes bourgeoisified in it; one might say that it is part of a process of the feminization of society; one might say that it replaces the law of the father, the absolutist order, with autonomous subjects regulated by internalized representations ... many such descriptions are available. More important to my purposes: writings carrying this system of ethics take the form of letters, memoirs, travellers' tales, club papers, histories. Their 'truth' or 'falsity' is secondary to the task of representation itself. And they remain in the formalist sense, 'motivated'. The narrator is explicitly socially located in the writing, the text's occasion being made apparent.

These remarks leave many gaps open. Let me attempt to fill one. Representations are produced from certain points of view. And it is clear that the civil Imaginary emerges in the writings of Whigs — Addison and Steele, Richardson. Their texts are a sympathetic attempt to circulate images of the forms of social existence available to the urban bourgeoisie of the time. They are Whigs both in their unpatriotic tolerance of the market — money and consumption; and their sense that the present and future belong to them. They reject the network of social obligations and duties which informed the official attitudes of the landed gentry. And publicly to circulate representations of the workings of the legal, medical, and military institutions (as even Fielding and Smollett do) is to provide grounds for certain reforms, that is, once again, for the transfer to modern power. Whiggish, too, is their susceptibility to the sheer glamour of the process of social representation, the drawing of the new into the recognizable, and their blindness as to the consequences of their exclusion of the 'vulgar'.

In an act of implicit resistance, Fielding and Smollett offer representations and narratives which both cover more diverse social range than their forbears and present images of more static social and individual drives. Fielding in particular can *narrativize* the civil Imaginary just because he wishes to insist that the limits of society and morality are also the limits of nature and tradition. The Fielding plot, so much stronger than that of his peers, enacts the closure of society-as-nature on society-as-manners each time the illegitimate or 'natural' son becomes a legitimate heir. (Of course, the narrative's energy derives from the fact that the hero has no father until the very end.) Yet such differences, and the political nuances behind them, become lost in the space of the Imaginary itself — as Sir Andrew Freeport, Roderick Random, Partridge, Lovelace, Moll, Parson Adams, and their stories, along with journalistic and novelistic descriptions of things, streets, houses, towns, and the presentation of tricky moral situations acquire their own effectiveness and being.

The power of representations to disencumber themselves of their politics does not merely testify to the gap between mimetic systems and intention. That power is also an effect of the linguistic vehicle which carries the civil Imaginary. It is adumbrated by Steele in his advice to letter writers: 'no rule in the world [is] to be made for writing letters, but that of being as near to what you speak face to face as you can'.[14] This immediacy, marked on the one side by an absence of traditional rhetorical topoi, and on the other by the represented presence of an observer, constitutes and links the novelty of the novel and journalism. (Its precondition is of course the technology of letters.) Unlike older forms — the comic, the tragic — the modern civil Imaginary consists of characters who do not have stories told of them again and again. Characters in novels live and die once — in *their* novel. Ethical representations are immediate to the degree that they trace themselves on the consciousness of an observer — either invisible and omniscient like Mr Spectator, or a historian like Fielding's narrative voice, or a character with a personality and a lingering debt to the old rogue tales like Moll. Their realism then is dependent on a certain subjectivity, even if it remains, when fullest, the subjectivity of instances of a type. As the civil Imaginary responds to social and political forces, this subjectivity will hollow itself more and more into the substance of the observed, as well as the observers, until it becomes the focus, and, more importantly, the legitimation of modern representation in its own right.

The civil Imaginary lives on. Poetry has gone through several revolutions since Pope, but fiction — though it has been transformed — occupies recognizably the same discursive space in Defoe and Richardson as in, say, Christina Stead and Pynchon. It is this continuity, this immense social effectiveness, that places the civil Imaginary at the very centre of the institution of modern literature. I hope it is already clear that its task has not been the task of nationalism. For it works *within* a society as part of the effort to know (and thus, in part and at several removes, to control) a particular social field. Being embedded within a society, it assumes and works on a set of social connections rather than promotes a national character. Comparisons of national types, dependent upon a cosmopolitan or a 'meta' point of view, are not essential to it.

We have arrived at the moment of the French Revolution. Now both English nationalism and the civil Imaginary (within its basic continuity) undergo profound shifts. Let us consider nationalism first. For revolutionary France, in the words of Abbé Sieyes, 'The nation is prior to everything. It is the source of everything. Its will is always legal . . . . Nations on earth must be conceived of as individuals outside the social bond, or, as is said, in the state of nature.'[15] Opposing classes become the nation whose own rights are natural rather than civic or legal. In France the replacement of the ancient concept 'people' by abstract rights granted to the nation is all the easier because there never was a constitutionally 'freeborn' Frenchman to stand alongside the 'freeborn Englishman'. There, following Rousseau, natural rights do not immediately replace civic and legal ones at the level of the individual.

The nation derives its legitimacy from nature and reason; each individual must act in terms of the general national will. It is English radicals like Paine who, drawing on Locke, appeal to the *individual*'s natural rights as the standard for, and roots of, civic ones.

The French legitimation of the nation has profound effects. In replacing custom by rights it denies history, as counter-revolutionary voices were quick to note. Politics becomes inadmissable as a way of negotiating social conflicts, for as members of one nation, all individuals have the same interest.[16] Civil society and the state merge into one realm of general will and rational freedom. Individuals as nationalized subjects become not a diverse and hierarchical mixture of different manners and customs, but transparent and equal to one another. And a whole range of symbolic practices enter the public sphere: the wearing of liberty caps, planting of liberty trees, images of the republic as Marianne, the tricolour, carnivals .... These are not the representations of the civil Imaginary, which are based on the circulation of mimetic images, on the dissemination and ranking of social differences, but non-mimetic emblems ('allegoric shapes' Wordsworth called them)[17] intended, as Abbé Grégoire put it, to penetrate the soul and mould the national character.[18]

With the birth of the new French nation, other European nationalisms shudder and change. Each state acquires a national identity which covers *all* its activities in imitation of, and differentiation from, the French contraction into national unity. It is now that each country has, for example, as Heine says parodically, not only 'its own cuisine and its own kind of woman' but that 'considered from the point of view of high idealism' women have 'a resemblance to their country's cooking'. He continues exuberantly, taking sexual and nationalist chauvinism to their very edges: 'Are not the British beauties as wholesome, nourishing, substantial and inartistic, yet as excellent as good Old England's simple, honest fare: roast beef, roast mutton, pudding in flaming brandy; vegetables boiled in water, with two kinds of sauces, one of which is melted butter?'[19] Analogies tie the field of national stereotypes together, to help form a culture.

At the same moment, nation and freedom become indivisible. Each nation lays claim to its unique brand of freedom. Passing over profound struggles in each country, we can say that France acquires liberty as national will; Germany — at least in Fichte — liberty as presuppositionless national self-determination. In England liberty exists in and as the historical heritage, which makes it, at once, a liberty which *determines* — with all the difficulties such a paradox implies. Certainly there the counter-revolution gears up its attack on the old discourse of patriotism as liberation. Hazlitt's fragment 'Patriotism' from which my motto comes is one of its last flickers. Indeed, as Linda Colley has argued, the British government resisted using even the new nationalist symbolic practices just because they might lead to revolution at home.[20] And in the burgeoning of the state apparatus to fight the wars, repress opposition, and spur on a rationalized market, common law is eroded, replaced through the 1820s by an extended legal code. The constitution, though appealed to still, becomes an increasingly abstract signifier for national liberation as radicals demand, more narrowly, representation in a parliament which 'represents the nation'.[21]

Burke sets the agenda for counter-revolution in England. He emphasizes preservation rather than reason. 'We do now wish to derive all we possess as an inheritance from our forefathers' he claims, and that implicit turn to family composes the very basis of his thought.[22] For him, civil society must be defended against the state, whose operation begins to require unpalatable notions of bureaucratic rationality. Such a defence is found in the hierarchical structure and filiative possibilities of the family. Because he believes the family to be both a natural and a social form, it provides the site at which nature and society meet. This enters more deeply into his thought than the effort to make of the 1689 Bill of Rights a binding contract. For it begins to solve the problem of authority which besets him. The instance just given indicates his quandary. Does the 1689 contract provide authority to defeat a rational, and totalizing, national will? Does nature? Tradition? The appeal to the family screens the conflicts between, and difficulties in, these alternatives, providing a substitute for theories of natural law.

Burke belongs to *political* nationalism in so far as he too accepts the nation as the legitimizing socio-political unit. 1688 is vitally important for him because then the *nation* agreed on a decentred political system. But, he figures the nation in institutions which resist the appeal of enlightened nationalism, turning to the family, the church, civil society, a hatred of theory rather than to common law, the state, freedom, language, reason. Indeed his discourse enacts this resistance. For he locates liberty not in thought, not in a national will, ultimately not even in tradition, but, almost unawares, in a personal freedom embedded in the act of writing. It goes without saying that to find liberty there is not to require socio-political change, it is barely to find liberty at all.

The *Reflections* take the form of a letter to a French acquaintance. In the middle of a diatribe against abstract liberty he writes: 'Indulging myself in the freedom of epistolary intercourse, I beg leave to throw out my thought, and express my feelings, just as they arise in my mind, with little attention to formal method'.[23] Almost invisibly, freedom moves from reason and politics to self and language — subjective and sociable, rather than rational or bookish, language. The style evoked a furor despite journalistic and novelistic precedents. In a personal letter his friend Francis scolded: 'Once for all, I wish you would let me teach you to write English ... why will you not allow Yourself, to be persuaded, that Polish is material to preservation?'[24] while, from the other side, the *radical* Hazlitt said of Burke's writing that 'it has the solidity, the sparkling effect of a Diamond; all other *fine writing* is like French paste or Bristol stones in comparison'.[25] Under the pressure of revolution, preservation requires solidity as subjective force, not polish; it depends on reproducing an effective prose — that of the civil Imaginary. Burke's is finally the authority of personal and paternal reasonableness, in a style equidistant from both theory and symbol.

Counter-revolution, then, brings with it a crisis of legitimation whose discursive solution is a subjective, wideranging tone; a foregrounding of personality in propositions which deny freedom and individualism. Its ultimate conceptual solution is an appeal to a familial filiation. These were strategies successful enough to help prevent both nationalism and reason gaining a grip on English high literary culture until our own time. (It is clear that recent British disdain of French poststructuralism has its roots in Burke's detestation of French 'men of theory'.) And Burke's intervention had an immense impact on the sphere of the civil Imaginary. This assertion I wish to develop in the rest of this chapter.

In 1812 Scott published *Waverley*. Like the revolution itself, contemporaries considered it to be without precedent. Goethe's remarks are typical: 'I discover in [Scott] a wholly new art, which has its own laws.'[26] What are these laws? A particular technical device stands as their precondition: Scott's texts are not motivated. Unlike *Tom Jones* to which it is much indebted, *Waverley* does not explain the occasion of its own writing.[27] The past world it describes is like, but adjacent to, archival history. Austen invents the unmotivated novel simultaneously — constructing present adjacent worlds with a realism Scott himself marvelled at. The purpose of these texts is not to construct ethical representations which directly address their readers, but a kind of mimesis for mimesis's sake. It is this autonomy, this retreat from ethics, which Henry James, who shares such values, indicates in his understated description of Scott as 'the first English prose story teller'.[28] With this lack of motivation comes a new principle of organization and delimitation — organic unity. This does not reproduce emerging state totality, nor is it, like Fielding's plot, a sign of the imposition of the natural on the social order. It operates as a formal requirement of autonomous texts intent on providing a scene adjacent to the nation-state. The text's unity is the unity of culture — a set of overlapping, unprogrammable connections and analogies within the strictly delimited frame of the work itself.

Scott and Austen's novels emerge from the civil Imaginary, on the back, as it were, of the Burkean style which now becomes — with its new authority — the 'narrative voice' or 'English prose'. They accept the counter-revolutionary burden of preservation with all its difficulties. As a consequence, they stage peculiarly modern forms of impotence: the inability to reconcile reasons of state and a private morality in Scott; community values and individual self-determination in Austen. In both, personal, presuppositionless acts of will have become impossible. Scott sees individuals as products of a social and cultural inheritance, thus, characters, viewed externally, become instances of large formations — moral, socio-economic, national. The 'international' theme unfolds. But even in Scott, whose characters often are national types, the text itself stands apart from nationalism. Its identity lies with the narrative voice which is, unlike the characters, and like Mr Spectator, everywhere and nowhere; and reproduces, in a new register, an earlier period in the civil Imaginary. The narrative voice becomes available to the abstract humanism which transcends nations and cultures. That ethical power which produced new images internal to a social framework is transformed into a renunciatory withdrawal into custom, culture, soul-making.

Of course these novels create hierarchies, that is at the very centre of their purpose. They are Burkean civil societies *in petto*. Here is Burke:

> Each contract of each particular state is but a clause in the great primaeval contract of eternal society, linking the lower with the higher natures, connecting the visible and invisible world according to a fixed compact sanctioned by the inviolable oath which holds all physical and all moral natures, each in their appointed place. This law is not subject to the will of those, who by an obligation above them and infinitely superior, are bound to submit their will to that law. (p. 195)

'Moral nature' here means in effect what is inherited by the individual — culture, dialect, class[29] — all of which are seen to be closed to choice and imitation. 'State' here means civil society, which these classic realist novels defend against the apparatus of the politicians and social managers in the name of submission.

Burke's immutable 'compact' is part of a defence of a cosmic *and* social 'establishment' which transcends reason and will. When he comes closest to defining this establishment's material being, however, the language of contract and law no longer suffices.

> Why should the expenditure of a great landed property, which is a dispersion of the surplus product of the soil, appear intolerable to you or to me, when it takes its course through the accumulation of vast libraries, which are the history of the force and weakness of the human mind; through great collections of antient records, medals, and coins, which attest and explain laws and customs; through paintings and statues, that, by imitating nature, seem to extend the limits of creation; through grand monuments of the dead, which continue the regards and connexions of life beyond the grave . . . (p. 272)

Here we have, in an economist trope, a 'surplus' which undermines its base. Note how paintings and statues *seem* 'to extend the limits of creation'; that 'seeming', however hesitant, undoing all the certainty of the 'primaeval contract' which, as the structure of creation, links both earth to heaven and individuals to society. The passage is extraordinary in its rhetorical effort to attach this valuable and unmanageable simulacrum to law and nature. Here again we see the pressures which demand that the Imaginary must work as an index of nature and a guarantee of filiation and reproduction rather than an ethical and *productive* force.

Scott and Austen, too, 'imitate nature' and thus 'extend creation', but, in Burke's spirit, they assuage the danger of the enterprise by forcing their extensions of reality back onto the real. However much their techniques and interests differ; for both, to be imaginative is also to be realistic. Their work allows for the possibility that the more adjacent, the less actual, the textual object; the closer, the more real. In connecting them, not now to Burke, but to proto-modernists such as Flaubert and James, this constitutes the continuity of classic realism over the nineteenth century. Indeed, later complaints against Scott's being just entertaining and the comparative neglect of Austen are part of a Victorian forgetting of the modernist, aesthetic impulse which surprisingly — given conventional accounts of these matters — is a byproduct of Burkean counter-revolution.

Novels which retreat from the ethical are actually uncommon. Leavis's seminal *The Great Tradition*, which comments on them, does not, I think, select a few works from a mass of others broadly similar. Leavis praises those rare texts which carry out precisely the long task of counter-revolution — though why he ignores *Waverley* remains a mystery to me. This is to imply that the values of Leavisism are, in the relevant aspects, those of classic realism. (Many nationalist novels were written between 1800 and 1920, but they are not in his canon.) But in fact the connections between high Leavisism and classic realism are mediated through a highly specialized and also, in our society, almost unsustainable discursive practice — literary criticism.

To state a complex matter simply: literary criticism is not literary history, not interpretation, not theory, not reviewing. Developed by Eliot and Richards, it is an Anglo-American phenomenon with roots in the German moment of Kant and Schiller. At its centre lies the thesis that literary texts cannot be translated simply into propositions or beliefs, and thus neither 'mean' anything, nor are interpretable. Form saturates content, writing is enactment, literature communicates to no specifiable audience but is what is communicated in its own locutions. Such notions connect most closely to poetry, and it is with poetry in sight rather than prose or the theatre that literary criticism develops. Only with Leavis does criticism broach the problems posed by the novel. In his work the retreat from ethics in the civil Imaginary connects with literary criticism's ranking of linguistic energy over signification. Here again, literature is the repository of culture, tradition, the life in language itself — an identity which can only be asserted by a rhetorical shuttling back and forth between literature as propositionless force and literature as bulwark against dissolution. Literary criticism enters the project of preservation which works for subjectivity but against both individualism and theory. As such it shares the non-nationalist politics which inform the objects of its approval, maintaining them in the canon.

My argument requires me to indicate one last thread in this story of the relations between certain literary and nationalist zones. Where does nationalism connect with literature *after* the decisive moment of the counter-revolution in England? As the political structure becomes genuinely more democratic, nationalism shifts into modern popular culture. There, using national symbols, the network of analogies, stereotypes, it becomes available for manipulation up until the time of our own patriot monarchs — Maggie, Bob and Ronnie. At the beginning of this redistribution, Hazlitt who was able to write his fragment on patriotism, also produces trite pieces on 'Merrie England' and 'John Bull' for the *New Monthly Magazine*. As England emerges as a world power, nationalism comes to be defined increasingly in terms of action, work, war, masculinity, bodies, and less in terms of peace and rights. (It returns, one might say, to Elizabethan and aggressive 'heart of oak' formulations of Englishness.) Perhaps Carlyle's *Past and Present* (1843), with its implicitly racist emphasis on England as a body of active men and its explicit repudiation of literature as national culture, is the most important text in this development. (He writes: 'The English are a dumb people. They can do great acts, but not describe them. Like the old Romans, and some few others, their Epic Poem is written on the Earth's surface: England her Mark!'[30]) Nationalism, isolated from the domain of the aesthetic civil Imaginary, becomes the property of an apparently depoliticized mass politics. At particular moments, especially between 1867 and 1914, it can re-enter the art novel — with Meredith for instance. But he is precisely not secure in the canon. On the other side, the older patriotic and revolutionary discourse can periodically re-emerge, not applied to Great Britain but to those peoples, whose great year was 1848, struggling for their own independent nationhood.

No text I know represents literature's encounter with nationalism, at the moment they take modern form, better than de Quincy's 1849 reminiscence of the Napoleonic era: *The English Mailcoach*. As the mild ambiguity of the title indicates, the mailcoach which carries news of the British victories signifies the nation. In the forefront of postal technology, the coach represents not civil society but the state, the 'conscious presence of a central intellect' as the text has it. Ralph Allen's spirit lives on. As it races through the country with unwonted discipline and precision, decked in the insignia of victory, it appeals to nationalized subjects. 'One heart, one pride, one glory connects every man by the transcendent bond of his national blood.' But de Quincy is not writing an ode in prose to the spirit of England. He describes an incident in which he fails to prevent the speeding coach from killing a girl. At the moment preceding impact, de Quincy, opiated, and the coachman, asleep, are unable to act. They fail to display exactly that male trait central to the formation of militarized nationalism. The fault is not quite theirs. The mailcoach's power and discipline place it beyond the control of individuals whom it smashes in its way. Action may be the quality of Englishmen, English bodies may beat with one heart, but discipline, inertia, and a tolerance for destruction are now required by the British state.

These comments have not reached the core of the text. For the invocation of the modern state, its use of symbols to turn individuals into nationals and de Quincy's own failure to act are followed by accounts of dreams, repeating and interpreting the accident. In the phantasmagoria of the dream-work, the coach becomes a crocodile, de Quincy and the dead girl travel into fantasy colonial islands, the road becomes a cathedral (or a railway station?) and so on. The dreams expose another uncontrollable site for his subjectivity:

The dreamer finds housed in himself, some separate chamber in his brain . . . some horrid, alien nature. What if it were his own nature repeated? How if the alien nature contradicts his own, fights with it, perplexes it and confounds it. How again, if not one alien member but two, three, four, within what he once thought the inviolable sanctity of himself?[31]

We see those interconnected entities: the warrior nation-state, disciplined bodies, nationalized subjects open out into what de Quincy calls 'anarchy' — a series of allegorizing tropes, associative jumps, subjective depths, oneiric rereadings of conscious gaps which neither can be domesticated by classic realism, nor easily appropriated by literary criticism. The essay enacts a series of clashes between various subjectivities each set into a particular socio-political institution, some of which can legitimate precisely *nothing*. It is as if the nationalized subject — de Quincy as an Englishman — shatters that unity of the self needed and granted by the civil Imaginary. A new passivity comes into being — one of whose favoured sites is the dream.

This begins to open up a new field for speculation and historical delving. Here nation and culture fall way from each other, to produce both a fractured psyche, the ground of no authority, and an inorganic text no longer quite at home in the civil Imaginary. This returns us to our point of departure. From the concealments of counter-revolution we have recovered a history of a nationalism which is antagonistic to oppression. Counter-revolution has worked for filiation, culture, and a subjectivity which is not an individualism, against theory as reason and the connection of nations to universals. It not only permits but encourages misrecognition of literature as a national heritage. In it, nationalism is reproduced in the mass public sphere by becoming a poetry which is not poetry, authorized by the state. De Quincy's texts reveals disconnections implicit in this scene. But one can also learn lessons closer to home here. One can learn the need to return to a confidence in the values of theory, to a political sense of history, to a resistance to the retreat of the ethical which occurred in the names of criticism, culture, and realism.

This essay began by declaring that nationalism in postcolonial nations has virtues that perhaps it lacks elsewhere. In the same way, the history of the novel which I have outlined in such broad strokes has particular point for us too — I write now as a citizen of a First World colony. For the postcolonial novel has a specific relation to classic realism. It has used that realism's folding of the Imaginary into the real, to work within a *global* Imaginary. Global, because the postcolonial writer searches for an audience; a good, which means a metropolitan, audience. In that search messages are sent from (perceived) peripheries to the centre.[32] They move across the globe; picturing their societies so as to connect them to the world. These are not messages sent by mail or mechanical reproduction (like documentaries for instance), they are sent within the punctured, already marginalized forms of representation available to the contemporary novel.

Postcolonial novelists do not have an organized subjectivity which instantiates a type and permits the tones and authority of the old narrative voice, anymore than do other writers after modernism. But for them, while the grounds of classic realism are lost, the project of imagining goes on. It remains important for them to *witness* their society, and their writings, which produces images, remain firmly placed in the imagination either of narcissistic egos or of magicians. The postcolonial narcissists — the later Patrick White, for instance — have a double focus: on the one hand they describe peripheral societies conceived of as being either extraordinarily empty or extraordinarily full and alive; and, on the other, they foreground themselves and their own life stories as vehicles for representation. Often they exist in their novels both as narrators and as characters — sometimes as a whole series of characters. (They also like to write autobiographies.) The magic realists — in a much stronger move — no longer ground their messages in the authority of their persons, though they continue to trade in experiences which bear traces of feeling and memory. They deliver themselves up to the force of their images: theirs are experiences preternaturally unmoored from subjectivity.

Critics have long since, and for very good reason, given up the task of telling writers how or what to write. Yet it does seem to me that to read the novel's history as developing within the frame of the civil Imaginary and counter-revolution is to come to terms with the postcolonial novel, in particular, in ways which might have practical implications. The genre's origins as other to, or resistance against, nationalism should now be seen as a *limit*. To say no more: the interplay between subjectivity and representation which dominates the postcolonial novel, seems to have less force and direction than its societies deserve.

Notes

The first version of this paper was written for, and presented, at the 1986 ASPACALS conference on 'National Cultures and Literature' at Deakin University. I would like to thank all those who participated in the discussion for helping focus these ideas. In particular, I would like to acknowledge the help and encouragement of Dr David Bennett.

1 *The Complete Works of William Hazlitt*, ed. P. P. Howe (London: Dent, 1930—4), vol. 4, pp. 67—8.

2 'Reflections on American "Left" literary criticism', in *The World, the Text, the Critic* (London: Faber, 1982), p. 169.

3 This is something of a commonplace in liberal accounts of Herder — see, for instance, F. M. Barnard, *Herder's Social and Political Thought: from Enlightenment to Nationalism* (Oxford: Oxford University Press, 1965).

4 Hugh Seton Watson, *Nations and States. An Enquiry into the Origins of Nations and the Politics of Nationalism* (Boulder, Col.: Westview, 1977), p. 6.

5 Lord Bolingbroke, *Contributions to Craftsmen*, ed. Simon Varey (Oxford: Clarendon, 1982), p. 18.

6 See Isaac Kramnick, *Bolingbroke and his Circle: the Politics of Nostalgia in the Age of Walpole* (Cambridge, Mass.: Harvard University Press, 1968), p. 27.

7 For the complex (but relevant) history of constitutionalism before this period,

see Quentin Skinner, *The Foundations of Modern Political Thought* (Cambridge: Cambridge University Press, 1978), vol. 2, pp. 113—78.

8 See E. P. Thompson, *The Making of the English Working Class* (Harmondsworth: Penguin, 1968), p. 86.

9 See James Chandler 'The Pope controversy: Romantic poetics and the English canon', *Critical Inquiry*, vol. 10, no. 3 (1984), pp. 481—510.

10 *Works*, vol. 6, p. 112.

11 See Lennard J. Davis, *Factual Fictions: The Origins of the English Novel* (New York: Colombia University Press, 1983). This notion is not a version of Castoriadis' much more fully worked out 'social Imaginary', though they share a resistance to being reduced to a simple social *function*. See his *L'institution imaginaire de la société* (Paris: Seuil, 1975), pp. 162—204.

12 *Selections from The Tatler and The Spectator* of Steele and Addison, ed. Angus Ross (Harmondsworth: Penguin, 1984), p. 87.

13 See J. Habermas, 'The classical doctrine of politics', in *Theory and Practice*, trans. John Viertal (London: Heinemann, 1973), pp. 41—82.

14 Addison and Steele, op. cit., p. 90.

15 Quoted in Anthony D. Smith, *Nationalism in the Twentieth Century* (Canberra: ANU Press, 1979), p. 48.

16 See Lynn Hunt, *Politics, Culture, and Class in the French Revolution* (Berkeley: University of California Press, 1984), pp. 7—21.

17 *The Prelude*, VII, p. 179. Wordsworth is actually writing about advertisements.

18 Hunt, op. cit., pp. 91—2.

19 *Aus den Memoiren des Herren von Schnabelwopski* in *Werke*, ed. Wolfgang Preisendanz (Frankfurt am Main: Insel, 1968), vol. 2, p. 536.

20 Unpublished paper 'Whose nation? Class and national consciousness in Britain 1750—1830'. I am indebted to Professor Marilyn Butler for drawing my attention to this important paper.

21 See the 1821 Yorkshire petition cited in Olivia Smith, *The Politics of Language 1791–1819* (Oxford: Clarendon, 1984), p. 32.

22 *Reflections on the Revolution in France and on the Proceedings in Certain Societies Relative to that Event*, ed. Conor Cruise O'Brien (Harmondsworth: Penguin, 1968), p. 117.

23 ibid., p. 92.

24 *The Correspondence of Edmund Burke, vol. 6*, ed. Alfred Cobban and Robert A. Smith (Cambridge: Cambridge University Press, 1967), pp. 85—7.

25 *Works*, XVII, p. 10.

26 Eckermann, *Conversations with Goethe*, trans. John Oxenford (San Francisco: North Point Press, 1984), p. 394.

27 It is worth noting that the later 'Tales of my landlord' sequence does contain some such motivation, though it has become supplementary.

28 *Literary Criticism: Essays on Literature, American Writers, English Writers* (New York: Library of America, 1984), p. 1201.

29 As Edward Thompson has noted, the 1790s is the decade in which the modern language of class is developed. See the first chapter of *The Making of the English Working Class*.

30 *Past and Present* (London: Dent, 1960), p. 151.

31 *Collected Writings*, ed. David Masson (London: A. & C. Black, 1897), vol. 12, p. 292. This passage was deleted by de Quincy after the text's first appearance.

32 This is much less true of Canadian than it is of Australian, New Zealand, or South American literature.

9
Sir Joshua Reynolds and the Englishness of English art

John Barrell

I

Whether there really is such a thing as the Englishness of English art is not an issue addressed in this chapter, which is concerned with the terms on which the claim that there is such a thing could be made. I treat the problem of discovering the characteristics of a national culture in a painting as a part of the process of describing its meaning — whether by recognizing a meaning as immanent within it, or by attributing meaning to it, is for the purposes of this chapter immaterial. And I take it as axiomatic that in order for us to describe the meaning of a picture, of the kind which relates different aspects of it into a statement about its significance, there has to be available a discourse in terms of which that meaning can be described. This essay asks when, and in terms of what discourse, it first became possible to suggest that English paintings might have distinctive qualities of their own, which might contribute to, rather than detract from, their value; and it considers why it came to seem important to make that suggestion. After some fairly lengthy preliminaries, it will get down to arguing that the suggestion was first made by Sir Joshua Reynolds, in writings which, however, and for reasons I will discuss, were remarkably unsuccessful in persuading other writers on painting.[1]

Let me say a little more about what I am not concerned with. For a start, I am not concerned with the kind of claim, which we begin to find made around 1700, that England had produced a school of painters worthy to be recognized as having made a significant contribution to European art, if that claim does not also imply that their contribution had been of distinctive value by virtue of its characteristic Englishness. One of the earliest 'essays towards an English school of painters' of which I am aware was written by Bainbridge Buckeridge, and may be found attached to the English translation of Roger de Piles's *Art of Painting, With the Lives and Characters of the Most Eminent Painters*. This essay is simply an alphabetical arrangement of brief biographies, of the kind written by Vasari or de Piles himself. It excludes living painters, although its author claims that to have included them would have 'enlarged and adorned our school so much, that neither the Roman nor the Venetian would have had cause to be ashamed of its company'. But in whatever sense the painters recorded by Buckeridge may compose an English school, it is not in the sense I am concerned with.

I can make the point most easily by turning, in his alphabetical arrangement, to the letter 'V', where we discover that the painters whose names begin with this letter, and who, as Buckeridge puts it, are 'ours' and 'belong' to us, are Henry Venderborcht, John Vander-heydon, Adrian Van-Diest, Sir Anthony Vandyck, William Vander-velde, Francis Vanzoon, Herman Varest, and F. de Vorsterman.[2] Now 'V' is of course a special case, but is not *so* special: of the 106 painters accorded individual biographies by Buckeridge, some 55 per cent were immigrants or occasional or one-shot visitors to England, and the percentage is very nearly as high for the more than 300 painters whose lives were sketched by Vertue and Walpole in their *Anecdotes of Painting in England*.[3] These statistics make it clear that Buckeridge's aim, and Vertue's and Walpole's, was not to define a distinctively English school of painting, but to assemble the most prestigious possible list of painters who practised, for a time at least, in England, and whose works may be of value as they transcend national difference, and thereby become comparable with those of painters on the continent of Europe, in terms of a universal, a transnational idea of excellence in painting.

Nor am I concerned with the more common argument that the English school has a distinctive value by virtue of its success in portraiture — a claim frequently made in the decades around 1700, for example by William Aglionby and Richard Steele,[4] and which turns out to amount to an admission that what is distinctive about English art — indeed, what is valuable about it — is a function of its failure to make any significant contribution to the highest genre of painting, history, by which the universal and transnational tradition of painting was believed (was *necessarily* believed, as we shall see) to be constituted. This argument can best be seen, perhaps, as one of a sequence of arguments by which the characteristic quality of English painting is defined by contrast with the qualities of painting in its ideal or highest form. Thus, when, a hundred years later, William Hazlitt was arguing that the greatest excellence of painting was to be looked for in the representation of individual character and characteristic expression, it emerged that English painting was therefore bound to be deficient, because the national character was too phlegmatic to allow the passions that freedom of expression which they exhibited in the mobile features of the excitable Italians. The English might not be deficient in depth of character, but were certainly so in the surface, the outward visible marks of character; and without available models of animated expression, the painting of character had nothing to exercise itself upon, nothing to represent.[5]

And when, a hundred years later again, Roger Fry was locating the excellence of painting in the qualities of the distinctively painterly vision — especially in the representation of plastic form and in the articulation of the spatial relations between forms — then English art was again revealed to be deficient, because of its characteristic propensity to favour moral narrative, painting as the illustration of the literary, which, it then went without saying, was the opposite of all that painting as painting should be.[6] The English national character was now defined by that very preoccupation with painting as narrative, as rhetorical, the lack of which had defined it 200 years before; but, as in each of the earlier cases I have considered, it was still defined as incapable of achieving those qualities that make painting great and style grand. The Englishness of English art was characterized — and I am concerned neither to endorse nor to question this characterization — as a quality distinctive only by its inadequacy.

I can conveniently introduce what I *am* going to talk about by suggesting that it was Nikolaus Pevsner who interrupted this sequence of arguments, in the book whose title I have borrowed for this essay.[7] The book proceeds by a series of concessions accompanied by a series of redefinitions of what it is that might constitute the excellence of art. Pevsner concedes all that Fry alleges about the characteristic unpainterliness of English painting, but then asserts that one form of excellence open to painting is, precisely, its ability to be used as a 'medium for preaching', and for storytelling. He concedes also Hazlitt's point, that the characteristic reticence of the English forbids them the free play of expression enjoyed by other European nations, but then suggests that it is precisely in the difficulty of representing faces in which the marks of character are nearly invisible that English artists excel.[8] And so on. The sequence is broken by offering a new account, not of national character, but of excellence in painting, which is now conceived of in terms of a plural aesthetic and a qualified cultural relativism, so that one measure of the quality of works of art is their success in articulating and expressing the national character as it is at one time or another.

Pevsner's arguments are of especial interest for my purposes where he sets out the terms on which national character can be assessed. The delicacy with which such an operation had to be conducted, by an immigrant from central Europe writing only ten years after 1945, can easily be imagined. One the one hand, he evidently wishes to pay a generous compliment to the character — tolerant, democratic, leisurely, conservative, given to queuing, fair-minded, distrustful of the 'sweeping statement' — of the people among whom he has made his home, and to claim membership among them. On the other, he has good reason to be even more anxious than most of his audience — the book began as a course of Reith Lectures for the BBC — to avoid 'everything ... that glorifies obsolete national divisions', and especially to avoid appearing to define national character in terms of a cultural purity which must be preserved by cultural isolationism.[9] An accommodation between these two aims is negotiated by various strategies. Pevsner claims, for example that he is particularly well-qualified to discuss his topic, by virtue of the blend of familiarity and detachment that is the result of being an immigrant of over twenty years' standing. He offers continual reminders of the contributions made by immigrants to the national culture of

England — the same kind of reminders as were then being used to persuade the English to accept large-scale black immigration.

In particular, Pevsner proposes a critical calculus designed to find value in works of art as they manage at once to instantiate the national character, and to ventilate that character by the international wind of historical change — what Pevsner calls the 'spirit of the age'.[10] This calculus works like the graph of a function whose axes represent the national character and the spirit of the age — or, by another version of Pevsner's consistently binary method — the 'geography', as he calls it, and the history of art. The most valuable works of art are those to be found grouped in the top-right-hand corner of the graph: those which are most 'geographical', most expressive of the concerns and values of the national culture that produced them; but which are also most 'historical', the most conscious of an internationalism which delivers national character form provincialism or insularity. The least valuable are to be found hugging one or another of the axes, for in these the spirit of the age and the national character do not, he says, 'act in accordance', but 'interfere with one another until one seems to black out the other completely'.[11]

How does Pevsner believe that national character is constituted? The main determinants turn out to be (as they usually do) not political and institutional, but linguistic and climatic. The character of the English, who pragmatically request a mutton chop when the more fanciful Italians sing for their supper — *una costoletta di montone, per favore* — has at once determined and been determined by the monosyllabic nature of their language, expressive, Pevsner believes, of 'understatement, the aversion against fuss, the distrust of rhetoric'. If monosyllables are a permanent feature of English, however, the characteristic syntactical organization of the language continually changes, as sentence structure becomes more or less complex at one period or another. Thus the changing characters of different nations may also be conceived in the form of a graph, of the kind — I don't know the technical name — by which the changing fortunes of different political parties are represented by columns which rise or fall with the passage of time. On the horizontal axis are arranged different national languages according to the fixed rhythms of their lexis. The changing rhythms of syntax, at one period of another, fluctuate along the vertical axis.[12] A similar graph defines the changing characters of nations in relation to their climate: the horizontal axis arranges countries according to mean annual temperature, rainfall, and so on; the vertical axis registers modifications in the experience each nation has of its natural climate, according to its social practices at one time or another. Thus, as far as England is concerned, what is fixed and natural is its moist climate, an important determinant of the character of English landscape painting and of English sympathy with Venice and with Venetian art. What changes is the English experience of this climate, as it fluctuates with the figures for the domestic consumption of coal, and changing preferences for well-ventilated or draughtproof rooms.[13]

It isn't my purpose to comment here on Pevsner's general account of

national character, or on his application of that account in his analysis of
English art. I am concerned, as I have said, with the invention of a notion
that was invented more than 150 years before Pevsner was writing, and
I have spoken about him at such length because he chose to base his
claim for the Englishness of English art on exactly two grounds — those
of language and climate — in terms of which the characteristic inability
of the English to produce works of higher art had been debated in the
eighteenth and early nineteenth centuries. The climatological argument
had been used by Du Bos, Montesquieu, and Winckelmann to suggest
that northern Europe was unlikely to produce great painters; and it was
resisted fiercely in England by James Barry, Prince Hoare, and John
Opie, among others, on the grounds that if the imagination in moist
climates becomes too waterlogged to function properly, England could
never have produced a Shakespeare or a Milton.[14] The issue of language
they regarded as entirely irrelevant. 'If', asks Pevsner, 'the rhythms of the
language differ' in one nation and another 'so much and so tellingly', is
there not every reason to assume that the same will occur in art?[15] The
question is a rhetorical one, but it can hardly have been an English
'distrust of rhetoric' that prevented Barry, an Irish Catholic, from reply-
ing 'of course'. For it was, to Barry and perhaps to everyone who
considered the issue in the late eighteenth and early nineteenth centuries,
a fact constitutive of the nature of painting that it used natural signs,
universally understood, and did not labour under the limitation imposed
on the arts of language by the arbitrary and local nature of the signs they
were obliged to employ.

This is John Brown writing in 1751 of the language of the scriptures;
he concedes all that Pevsner was to claim about the variations over time
in the sentence structures favoured by the writers in a national culture,
but effectively denies that this tells us anything about the visual arts:

> There is, in Philosophical strictness, but one *unvary'd Language* or *Style*
> in *Painting*; which is 'such a modification of *Light* or *Colours* as may
> imitate whatever Objects we find in Nature.' This consists not in the
> *Application* of *arbitrary Signs*; but hath it's Foundation in the *Senses* and
> *Reason* of Mankind; and is therefore *the same* in every Age and Nation.
> But in the literary *Style* or *Language*, the Matter is far otherwise. For
> language being the *voluntary* Application of *arbitrary* Signs, according to
> the Consent of different Men and Nations, there is no *single uniform*
> *Model of Nature* to be followed. Hence *Gracefulness* or *Strength* of Style,
> *Harmony* or *Softness*, *copious* Expression, *terse* brevity, or *contrasted*
> Periods, have by turns gained the approbation of particular Countries.
> Now all these *supposed* Beauties of Speech are *relative*, *local*, and
> *capricious*; and consequently unworthy the Imitation of a divine Artist;
> who, to fit the Speech he *ordains*, to the great Work of *universal Instruc-*
> *tion*, would, we may reasonably suppose, strip it of every *local*, *peculiar*,
> and *grotesque* Ornament; and convey it unaccompany'd by all, but the
> most *universal* Qualities common to every Tongue.[16]

Whether or not it is possible for writers who are not divinely inspired to strip their style of local and temporary ornaments is not made clear; but it is clear that, if it is *not* possible, then they cannot avoid, but painters can, a style which betrays their national origins.

Thus neither the argument from climate, nor that from language, is allowed by writers on painting in eighteenth-century Britain as a factor which promotes the creation of a characteristically national art, but each is used, on the contrary, to argue that there is no reason why English artists should be unable to produce works of higher art, or should be constrained to produce paintings which speak the idiom of their native country. And this riposte to Du Bos and others is not a simple nationalistic reflex. Du Bos's arguments for the determining influence of climate, in particular, place limitations not simply on the ability of English artists but on the universal value of higher art itself, which they must represent as the product of the accidental circumstances of life in Greece and Italy. What Barry and his followers are defending is thus not primarily the possibility of a national school of English art, but the civic ideal of art, one of whose principal enemies is what Reynolds called 'locality'.[17] Seen in a civic, a universal light, the appearance of the local colour of one or another national school in a work of painting is an indication of its failure to achieve the universality of great art, which must speak to a universal human nature from which all the accidental accretions of nationality have been scraped away.

This is not to deny the patriotic fervour of Barry, of Opie, of Hoare, or of the Reynolds of the period before 1776. But it is a patriotism which is, they believe, entirely the opposite of nationalism, of the insularity which would claim that any part of the value of English art was its Englishness. Their hope that higher art will be restored in Britain is to them a *properly* patriotic hope, because it is also a civic hope. By its success in the restoration of the dying art of history painting in the grand style, England would win a legitimate contest for distinction, and become an exemplar of civic culture by which all the nations of Europe will benefit. If higher art is restored elsewhere than in Britain, that also will be an occasion for rejoicing, hardly qualified by the regret that the palm was not won by the English school. For in competitions for civic excellence, when one nation wins, they all win.

The fact that, throughout the eighteenth century in Britain, the principal, almost the exclusive discourse on the visual arts was the discourse of civic humanism, did much to encourage the hope for the establishment of an English school. By the civic humanist theory of painting in its paradigmatic form, as enunciated most notably by Shaftesbury, the republic of the fine arts was understood to be structured as a political republic; the most dignified function to which painting could aspire was the promotion of the public virtues; and the genres of painting were ranked according to their tendency to promote them. As only the free-citizen members of the political republic could exhibit those virtues, the highest genre, history, was primarily addressed to them, and it addressed them rhetorically, as an orator addresses an audience of citizens who are his equals, and persuades them to act in the interests of the public. The higher arts could be produced only by and for free men, and England, as 'the nation of the free',[18] was thus of all the nations of Europe most likely to restore to painting the power and prestige it had enjoyed in the free republics of renaissance Italy.

But the citizen whom painting was required to address was at the same time a universal man, man in his ideal realization as a 'political animal', and his abilities and virtues were not imagined to be modified by, or to change their character according to, the specific national culture in which he happened to be situated. Thus the civic humanist theory of painting denied that there could be anything of value in the distinctively English character of an English school. The national character of England would appear in the productions of its artists only as a civic independence of spirit; and that would be manifested in works which announced that they were English only by announcing that they were addressed to men who were free citizens. And this brings me, finally, to the main argument of this essay, which is this. There developed, towards the end of the eighteenth century in Britain, and for reasons I shall consider, a desire to establish that there might indeed be such a thing as the Englishness of English art, a quality which would characterize, without diminishing the value of, the works of English artists. But as long as the criticism of art in England derived its terms of value from those of civic humanist ethics and political theory, that desire could not easily find expression. The problem was the same with regard to English attempts to characterize the Dutchness of Dutch art, the Venetianness of Venetian art, even the Romanness of Roman art: in so far as the local origins of a painting showed up, they could only show the painting up as, to that degree, a failure.

But if the problem applied to any national school of art whatsoever, there was a solution at hand which could be applied uniquely to Englishness and the English school. For alongside the discourse of civic humanism in Britain, there was another language of value, provided by the discourse of custom, of the customary: a discourse which — largely because of the nature of the English legal system, of common and customary, as opposed to civil law — was thought to have a peculiar authority in England, and to attribute a value to Englishness which it attributed to the character of no other nation. If a claim for the Englishness of English art could be made, it would have to be in the terms of this discourse; and the draft of such a claim was sketched out, I want now to argue, by Sir Joshua Reynolds, at a time when, for specific historical reasons, there was an urgent revival of interest — I use the word with all its implications of partiality — in the discourse of the customary.

II

Reynolds had first elaborated what I shall call a customary aesthetic in the essays he contributed to the *Idler* in 1759, in which he borrowed from Claude Buffier, as paraphrased by Adam Smith, an account of the standard of beauty as 'common', or 'middle' or 'central' form, the form that a species — men, or women, or swans, or doves — exhibits more often, not than deformity itself, for that is encountered far more often than beauty, but than any particular kind of deformity. Beauty is thus that form of a species that we are most used to seeing, and so it derives its authority, as a standard, from custom or habit.[19] But when Reynolds came to redefine the central form in his third address to the Royal Academy, delivered in 1770, he entirely abandoned the customary aesthetic. All objects in actual nature were now more or less deformed; and to arrive at the central form is now no longer a simple matter of having a range of experience sufficiently broad to enable us to register what is the most common form of a species. It is now necessary to 'contemplate', to 'compare' the forms of actual nature, and to arrive at a conception of ideal beauty by an empirical process of abstraction. Only the painter who, 'by a long habit of observing what any set of objects of the same species have in common, has acquired the power of discerning what each wants in particular', is now 'enabled to distinguish the accidental deficiencies, excrescences, and deformities of things, from their general figures', and so to make out 'an abstract idea of their forms more perfect than any one original'. In the most famous statement of principle in the third address, Reynolds explains that 'the whole grandeur and beauty of the art consists . . . in being able to get above all singular forms, local customs, particularities, and details of every kind'.[20]

The chief enemies of the central form are the temporary and the local. In the *Idler* it had been freely acknowledged that the standards of beauty in Ethiopia and in Europe would be different. But now the ideal is the abstract of every local form in the universe. The 'prejudices in favour of the fashions and customs that we have been used to' must be 'regulated' by the 'eternal variable idea of nature', and just as, according to Imlac in *Rasselas*, the poet 'must divest himself of the prejudices of his age and country', so the painter too 'must divest himself of all prejudices in favour of his age or country; he must disregard all local and temporary ornaments', for 'he addresses his works to the people of every country and every age'.[21]

By these arguments, the civic humanist theory of painting, by which the task of the art is to teach the principles of membership in a political republic, was redefined for a period and for an audience which attributed a less exclusive value than had writers earlier in the century to public virtue. It was, as we have seen, by teaching public virtues, according for example to Shaftesbury, that the art of painting had earlier fulfilled its public function.[22] Reynolds has little interest, however, in the earlier mode of civic humanist criticism by which that function was primarily performed by the fable of a painting, and by its rhetorical form of address. In the early *Discourses*, Reynolds offers what I shall call a philosophical rather than a rhetorical aesthetic: the public spirit that painting can teach is a form of knowledge before it is a form of action, and it is taught by central forms. When we recognize — as, if we are men of taste, we will recognize — the representation of the central form of man (the argument works only for men) we recognize the ground of likeness between ourselves and all mankind, the universal character of human nature, and the ground of social affiliation. The central form reinforces our attachment to the society in which we live, but to that society conceived of not in merely national terms, but as the type of civic society.

For that reason, and in spite of Reynolds's lack of interest in the moral lessons imparted by the fable of a picture, the highest genre of painting is still, as it had been for Shaftesbury, narrative history painting. This is so because the highest function of art can evidently be performed only by representations of the human figure; the central form of which is a metaphor for the body of the public, and figures forth what we have in common with each other. In portraiture, this form is compromised by the need to embody a likeness, and in comic or genre painting, by the desire to represent deformity. Only history painting allows the complete representation of the ideal, unembarrassed by, divested of, the accidents of nature, among which — for I want to keep the phrase in mind — are 'local customs'. History painting — and this too will turn out to be important in Reynolds's later revision of his opinions — has another advantage, in that the interest it asks us to take in the figures it depicts minimizes the degree of attention we are inclined to pay to their settings. 'Figures', writes Reynolds,

> must have a ground whereon to stand; they must be cloathed; there must be a back-ground; there must be light and shadow: but none of these things ought to appear to have taken up any part of the artist's attention. They should be so arranged as not even to catch that of the spectator.[23]

For the figures to embody the universal, transnational, civic ideal that I have described, they must be no one in order to be everyone; and they must be nowhere in order to be everywhere.

That later revision of opinion begins in the seventh address, delivered in December 1776, and it is marked by a renewed interest in what I have called the customary aesthetic which can be seen as part of a general revival of interest in the discourse of custom. If, in the field of law, the nature of the English constitution and legal system had never allowed this discourse to be lost sight of, it had been given a more visible importance by the thorough exposition of English common law that had been offered by Blackstone in the 1760s, and by his determined preference for customary over statute law.[24] The year 1776, however, had seen the publication of Bentham's attack on Blackstone, *A Fragment of Government*, and it was the year, also, of Tom Paine's *Common Sense*, and, more crucially, of the American Declaration of Independence. The discourse of custom, to which these three writings were all, in different ways, inimical, had also been employed by Samuel Johnson, Reynolds's intellectual mentor, as the basis of his account of the English language, of his attacks on the Middlesex electors, and, especially, on the rebellious American colonists. It is, I suggest, crucial to the re-emergence of the discourse in Reynolds's addresses to the Academy, that Johnson's pamphlets of the early 1770s are directed against the use, by the various opponents he attacks, of a version of the discourse of natural rights as it had been employed in Locke's *Second Treatise of Government*, which was to be the basis of the declaration of the fourth of July. Johnson employs the discourse of custom not against the political theory embodied in civic humanism, but against the notion that the government of a particular country could ever be tried by 'a regular theory',[25] whose principles include the claims that governments derive their legitimacy not from the independence of the governors, but from the consent of the governed; that the payment of taxes necessarily involves a right to enfranchisement; and that political theory is a science, the truth of whose conclusions do not depend on where — to which state or nation — they are applied.

To these notions, and in order to assert the principles on which the integrity of nation and empire are based, Johnson returns the same, invariable reply. It is a matter of fact that governments are established, not on regular plans, but by chance or accident. It is a matter of fact that from wherever, in a narrowly theoretical light, governments should derive their authority, they derive it in practice from the respect which, by habit or custom, we pay them. It is not from an analysis of the principles of natural right, or of human nature imagined as uncontaminated by accident and contingency, that attempts at political reform should start; but from an understanding of how custom, or 'second nature' as it was proverbially defined, has differently modified the first, or essential and universal human nature, in different countries. For national customs and customary institutions so shape the mind of a nation that it may be said that they constitute a people *as* a nation. The effects of political reform on second nature are extremely hard to calculate, so that to reform the institutions of a nation is always to put its stability at risk; and it goes without saying for Johnson — though he says it often enough — that political stability is the greatest good that a government can secure to a people. To calculate the effects of reform on first nature, as the discourse of natural rights offers to do, is apparently a good deal easier, of course, but serves no serious purpose; for it assumes the impossible, that we can decompound an essential and universal human nature from the reality we actually perceive, which is of different nations differently modified by their different habits, customs, and institutions. It follows, for Johnson, that 'for the law to be *known*, is of more importance than to be *right*', and that 'all change is of itself an evil, which ought not to be hazarded but for evident advantage'.[26]

The same arguments had been made by Robert Lowth, appropriately enough in a 30 January sermon to the House of Lords in 1767, on the text, 'My son, fear thou the Lord, and the king; and meddle not with them that are given to change'.[27] 'Reasonable amendment', Lowth appears to concede, 'is always desirable':

and some amendment, through change of times and circumstances, is often necessary. But as great reformations, though right in themselves, though moved by proper agents, and conducted by proper [i.e. constitutional] measures, are often attended with violent convulsions, hazarding the safety of the whole system, the utmost caution must be used, even when the occasion may seem the fairest, and the necessity most apparent.[28]

Serious reform is to be undertaken only when its beneficial outcome is certain — which, granted the uncertainty of all human affairs, will be rarely if ever the case. The basis of social affiliation is to be the established, the customary, the national: the way things are in Britain, and allegedly always have been, however things may be elsewhere, or however reason suggests that they should be.

Because, in the 1770s, the discourse of custom is directed primarily against the political theories produced by a democratic reading of Locke, Reynolds is able to employ the discourse in the belief that his defence of the customary is directed solely against a pedantically rationalist theory of painting, and not against the civic humanist theory of his earlier addresses, which indeed he seems to believe will be strengthened rather than challenged by his new concern for the customary. To ensure the compatibility of the customary and the civic discourse, all he needs to do, it seems, is to redefine the 'universal principles of human nature' so as to allow human nature to include whatever in second nature could be described as universal and invariable. Opinions and prejudices which have no basis in nature, but which command universal credit, are thus made part of an enlarged idea of human nature, which could still be regarded as uncontaminated by the merely local or temporary.

Reynolds borrows an example from Lord Kames to explain what he means. In all countries, he argues, the manner of showing respect to one's superiors is different — this is done in one country by bowing, in another by kneeling, in a third by prostration, in a fourth by removing the hat. But in all countries respect is shown by the attempt to make oneself *less* than the recipient of that respect.[29] The particular means by which respect is shown is an accident of place, a local custom, but the general principle is universal; and a painter who wishes, in conformity still with the civic humanist theory of painting, to represent an enlarged idea of universal human nature, may represent not merely the central forms of mankind, but also those manners and customs so universal as to be, always and everywhere, second nature. Painting may not represent *local* customs, but it should represent general customs; criticism may not base its principles on temporary or local prejudices, but it should include among its principles opinions and prejudices which, though not in conformity with the original frame of human nature, are always and everywhere the same.

The difficulty of applying this new position to painting would have been obvious to Bishop Berkeley: a painter cannot represent the abstract idea of showing respect, but only one or another of the local modes of doing so. Thus to admit custom into the realm of the paintable may be of necessity to admit local customs. Reynolds never acknowledges this difficulty explicitly, but that it was somehow present to him is suggested by the continuation of his argument in the seventh address — an address which, I had better say now, is immensely mobile and complex, and whose shifts and negotiations of position can properly be described only by a paragraph-by-paragraph analysis. Suffice it to say that it is not long before we find Reynolds arguing that *local* customs, too, may be admitted in painting, and he lays down the principle by which their admission is to be regulated which is not much more helpful than that by which universal customs were to be allowed. Local customs — Reynolds uses the phrase to include whatever cannot be regarded as constituents of the universal first and second natures of mankind — may be represented in a picture, so long as they do not conceal from us the universal nature which it is still, apparently, the primary task of the painter to depict.

Reynolds's argument is that 'in no case' ought the taste for the 'narrow' the 'local', and the 'transitory' to be 'wholly neglected', if 'it does not stand, as it *sometimes* does, in direct defiance of the most respectable opinions received amongst mankind' (my emphasis).[30] This taste can, he suggests, best be taken into account in the painting of 'ornaments' — a term which, for Reynolds, refers to all the parts of a picture which exist as adjuncts to the naked central form of the body — dress, background, and so on; all those parts which should be managed, he had argued in his third address, so as not to catch the spectators' attention. In that third address, such 'ornaments' were necessary to make a picture a credible representation of a real action, but were to be represented only because their absence would be so troubling as to unsettle our appreciation of central form. But so would an emphasis upon them: to give an undue attention and prominence to ornaments, to paint in the luxurious, Venetian, 'ornamental' style as opposed to the truly civic, 'grand' style, is to threaten to catholicize the art of painting; by analogy to clutter it as the churches of Italy had become cluttered with 'ornaments'.[31] It is also to feminize an art which is properly masculine, civic, stoic — among the many and complex meanings of 'ornament' when Reynolds was writing is one whereby the word refers pre-eminently to feminine or (in the case of men) 'effeminate' adornments, of dress, jewellery, coiffure. The desire to possess such ornaments is in turn a desire to constitute oneself as an object to be displayed and to be seen, to signify at the level of surface and not at the level of depth. Thus for a visual art to be 'ornamental' is for it to remain *merely* a visual art, incapable of the transparency which enables its meanings to be more than merely sensual and superficial. It is to conceal what is essential with what is merely continent. 'Local' and 'peculiar' ornament, we recall, is what according to Brown, a writer should ideally 'strip' from his speech, if he is to aspire to 'universal Qualities'.

Reynolds's position is now very different: first, because ornaments are now to be objects of attention in their own right, and secondly, because, as we shall see, they may constitute the main interest, the main source of value of an art whose main concern is now to teach us the grounds of our affiliation, not to a universal republic of taste, but to a national community of customary taste. For despite Reynolds's continued insistence that local ornaments may be represented only where they do not distract from the universal, he is soon to decide that this is what they do, and even what they *should* do.

The argument needed to be conducted with some delicacy, for it is here especially that the discourse of the customary might appear to contradict the discourse of civic humanism. To the civic humanist theory of painting, ornament — and, most especially, the realistic representation of costly fabrics, not generalized into 'drapery' — distracts the spectator from the universal principles of human nature exhibited in the central form of the human figure. In doing so, it offers him an opportunity to indulge in his own singularity, his caprice. The public function of painting is to make us aware of ourselves as *citizens*, by teaching us to subordinate our private interests to the interest of the public, or to grasp the identity of the two. A spectator who is permitted by a painting to indulge an interest in ornament, which is always conceived of as appealing to his sensuality rather than to his intellect, will therefore be an insufficiently civic spectator, for he will be allowing his attention to be diverted from the universal public interest towards his own appetitive, personal, and economic interests. He will be admiring those aspects of the painting which are concerned with the inanimate, and can be regarded as representing objects as capable of being acquired and consumed. Painting and the enjoyment of painting is thus conceived of by the discourse of civic humanism in terms of an opposition between the ideal, the universal, and the public, on the one hand, and, on the other, the material, the individual, and the private.

The discourse of custom, however, inserts a third term into this opposition, the *national*. An attention to ornament may still of course be evidence of a private acquisitive spirit. But if it is an attention shared by all the members of a national community as they inspect a work produced within their own culture; and if the ornaments in the work are properly dematerialized by being represented in terms of their 'general character' rather than of their particular, material nature; then what the spectators are attending to will no longer be the materiality of ornament, but its capacity to indicate the national character of the work, and so the spectators' membership in a national culture. As Reynolds's argument proceeds, his first concern is to establish that this new conception of ornament may be grafted on to his civic concern for the universal, by being allocated, as it were, to one stage in an ascending process of civic education. The national is what enables us to transcend the merely personal, and it may then itself be transcended in our progress towards the fully civic. Ornament can thus be 'public ornament' — I have borrowed the phrase from Burke, who uses it to describe the Church of England, in which the English come together 'in their corporate character to perform their *national* homage to the institutor, and author, and protector of *civil* society ... with modest splendour and unassuming state' (my emphasis).[32] Once this intermediate function of ornament has been established, however, it can be further suggested that it may be wise for the second transition, the transition from the national to the civil, to be deferred, perhaps indefinitely. It may be a more useful political function for painting, that it confirms our membership of a national community, and not of a civic republic, of taste.

III

Reynolds begins to work through these positions by arguing that the arts receive their 'peculiar character and complexion' from ornaments. We find in ornaments 'the characteristical mark of a national taste; as by throwing up a feather in the air, we know which way the wind blows, better than by a more heavy matter'.[33] There is nothing in the bare statement of this position which is new, and the comparison of ornament with a feather appears to represent it as a thing unworthy of any weighty attention. Nevertheless, Reynolds makes this remark in the course of arguing that, though ornaments should not be ranked with the 'positive and substantial beauties' of painting, the art would be imperfect without the kind of pleasures they offer. Before, the characteristic and peculiar mark of a taste merely national was exactly what a public, a civic artist in the grand style, should strive to efface. Indeed, for Reynolds even in this seventh address, one way of distinguishing general from local customs had been by the test that Addison had proposed for the distinction of true wit from false, that it should be *translateable*.[34] Now, less than a page later, he is offering as a defence of ornament, alike in painting, poetry, and oratory, the fact that it *displays* national characteristics and peculiarities, and that it may be encouraged in doing this, if the accidents of nationality do not conceal the substance of the universal — which, in his earlier addresses, they were bound to do.

It is important to understand at this point that Reynolds has been conducting his whole argument about custom in this address by reference to an analogy — which would have been perfectly visible to his audience — between the representation of, and the appeal to, custom in painting and criticism, and notions of English customary law. Thus the phrase 'local customs' would have been recognized as a legal phrase, used to apply to the particular legal customs of a locality within a national community, which should, according to Blackstone, be 'sacrificed' to the general customs of the nation, in the interest of arriving at 'one uniform and universal system of common law'.[35] The argument of the seventh address begins by representing general customs as supranational, and local customs as the peculiar practices of individual nations within the universal republic of taste, as if general customs were not national, but were entirely compatible, and even virtually identical, with the universal principles of human nature, or 'first nature', on which Reynolds had earlier founded that republic. To ensure that the analogy with law runs on all fours, he also begins by relating local customs to the municipal law of an individual realm, 'the law', according to Blackstone, 'by which particular communities, or nations are governed', which in England of course is primarily common (in the sense of customary) law.[36] This obliges Reynolds to insist — as he does insist, early in the seventh address — that, in painting, local customs should be 'sacrificed'; for, according to Blackstone again, such customs are practices 'in contradistinction' to those of 'the rest of the nation at large', and 'contrary to the law of the land'. If England is merely a province in a universal republic of taste, its peculiarities should not be displayed in its painting.[37]

But the analogy with law equally allowed Reynolds the opportunity of approving the representation of local customs in English painting, by analogy with the approval so commonly evinced in England of the customary law as contradistinguished from the legal systems of other European states. The customary law of England was widely regarded as something so 'connatural' with the genius of the English, so much an emanation of the English disposition to be free, that for Reynolds to refer to the local peculiarities of the nation as 'local customs', and then to demand that they be 'sacrificed' to a universal aesthetic, would not easily have been countenanced by many of his readers. To indulge a district within a nation, or a nation within a universal republic, 'with the privilege of abiding by their own customs',[38] is inevitably to allow them not to subscribe, in certain particulars to the universal law. But if that nation is England, the case is entirely altered, and the indulgence may be difficult to withhold, for it involves the very survival of English liberty.

Thus to permit an English painter, at least, to represent local, in the sense of national customs, is to grant him a properly English liberty, and to encourage him to promote, at least to some degree, a national community of taste, whose members he encourages to recognize the similarity of their tastes and practices by becoming aware of how they differ from those of other nations. And well before the end of the seventh address, the analogy with law, and the customary discourse in which it is conducted, turn out to have a momentum of their own, to lead the argument in directions they themselves define, and either to threaten Reynolds's belief in the compatibility of the customary and the civic discourse, or to allow him, hesitantly, and with no clear sign that he recognizes what is happening, to move beyond its orbit.

I do not want to make too much of this issue. The argument that we may derive a certain pleasure from works of art which display 'the characteristical mark of a national taste' is an argument insisted upon in Reynolds's later essay on Shakespeare, which I shall soon consider, but it is not explicitly advanced in any of the addresses but the seventh. But it is, in a sense, repeated on every occasion when, in the later addresses, Reynolds suggests that 'a complete, whole, and perfect taste' will include a taste for the ornamental, and will not necessarily demand the exclusion of 'local and temporary prejudices' if it can be argued that these 'have still their foundation, however slender, in the original fabrick of our minds'.[39] In the context of contemporary arguments being mounted in defence, for example, of the identifiably English character of Shakespeare, our 'national genius'; or of the idiosyncrasies of the English language, as reflecting the 'genius' of the people; or of the English law and

constitution as 'connatural' with that genius — any admission of ornament as a legitimate object of attention in painting, and on the grounds
that it is a representation of a 'national' taste, necessarily implies that it
is proper for a painter to represent to a nation its own characteristics, and
so to confirm his spectators in their sense of belonging, no longer just
to a civic republic of taste, but also, in due measure, to a national
community.

Towards the end of the seventh address, this implication is at once
reinforced, and justified as compatible with the civic discourse Reynolds
seems now almost to have abandoned, by an argument he offers in
favour of the notion that a painter should not entirely neglect the
ornamental, and thus should to some extent acknowledge the narrow,
local, and transitory prejudices of his public. This argument is a conventional one in the criticism of art, and is derived, indeed, from a conventional defence of the moral character of the arts as a whole, as compared
with the sterner character of moral philosophy. It is that ornament, and
colouring in particular — for 'ornamental' painters are almost invariably
regarded as colourists — 'procures lovers and admirers to the more
valuable excellencies of the art'. The language here is well calculated:
ornament takes on the character of a procurer or, more likely, a
procuress, because (the assumption is) it can most easily move its potential public by an appeal to their sensual rather than their rational
nature.[40] But the ends will justify the means, because our taste, when
fully developed, will transcend the sensuality which first attracted it. By
exploiting its sensual nature, painting can lead us to apprehend it as an
intellectual, a liberal art; ornament, which in the earlier addresses was the
very agent of corruption, is now a double agent, and its true but covert
operation is to attract us to the 'more valuable' — the more liberal —
'excellencies' of painting. And it will follow, also, that if we can be
attracted into the civic republic of taste by ornament, so we may also be
attracted into it by a prior attachment to the local, in the sense of the
national. Thus the compatibility of the customary and civic discourses
can be reaffirmed: the first makes us aware of ourselves as members of
a national community of taste, and that is a necessary first step to our
becoming citizens of the universal republic.

But it soon emerges that the main point of reassuring us of the
compatibility of the two discourses may have been to allow the definition
of a national community of taste to proceed more smoothly, under the
cover of an apparently civic aspiration. For the reassurance offers
Reynolds the opportunity to claim that the main danger to the establishment of a civic republic of taste is the attempt create it too soon, without
paying sufficient attention to the frailty of human nature, and its attachment to the local and the familiar:

> Whoever would reform a nation, supposing a bad taste to prevail in
> it, will not accomplish his purpose by going directly against the stream
> of their prejudices. Men's minds must be prepared to receive what is
> new to them. Reformation is the work of time. A national taste,

however wrong it may be, cannot be totally changed at once; we must yield a little to the prepossession which has taken hold on the mind, and we then may bring people to adopt what would offend them, if endeavoured to be introduced by violence.[41]

The similarity of this position with the arguments by which Burke would advocate the slow reformation of the constitution, as opposed to revolution, is obvious — I am thinking, for example, of Burke's advice that 'time is required to produce that union of minds which alone can produce all the good we aim at. Our patience will achieve more than our force'.[42] Indeed, although a national taste, in so far as it *is* national, must be presumed to be vitiated, so great are the dangers of attempting to reform it that it may be the part of wisdom to allow men to linger indefinitely with their unreformed (but at least stable and established) taste. For, Reynolds suggests, and again in a tone reminiscent of Lowth, Johnson, and Burke, 'ancient ornaments, having the right of possession, ought not to be removed, unless to make room for that which not only has higher pretensions, but such pretensions as will balance the evil and confusion which innovation always brings with it'.[43] While Reynolds waits, then, for the universal republic of taste to be established, he will not be unduly disturbed if painting manages to confirm at least a national community of taste, in which our identity as individuals may be subordinated, not to a civic identity, but to our identity as Englishmen.

IV

The discourse of custom, and the licence it now allows to the representation of the local, the national, as contributions to the value of a work of art, continues to make sporadic appearances in the later addresses to the Academy, but still with no sign that Reynolds believes them to be in any serious way incompatible with his civic humanism, or as having any other enemy than a narrow rationalism he associates with the discourse of national rights. By the time, however, that he came to write the two essays that remained unfinished and unpublished at his death, the political situation had changed considerably. Word had arrived from France that the members of the constituent assembly had not only embraced a Locke-like belief that kings could be cashiered, but had appropriated the civic discourse itself. If the republican rhetoric of civic humanism could be represented as compatible with a highly democratic version of the discourse of natural right, then it could no longer be presumed easily compatible with the mixed constitution and limited monarchy of Britain. A version of the civic discourse was discovered in the writings of the arch-fiend Rousseau; and finally the Jacobins were identified, by Coleridge among others, as civic humanists. 'When a nation is in safety', wrote Coleridge in 1800,

men think of their private interests; individual property becomes the predominating principle ... and all politics and theories inconsistent with property and individual interest give way, and sink into a decline

.... But is the nation in danger? Every man is called into play; every man feels his interest as a *Citizen* predominating over his individual interests; the high, and the low, and the middle classes become all alike Politicians; the majority carry the day; and Jacobinism is the natural consequence. Let us not be deceived by words. Every state, in which all the inhabitants without distinction of property are roused to the exertion of a public spirit, is for the time a Jacobin State.[44]

Coleridge has no objection to the language of citizenship, of public spirit, and of public interests predominating over private, as long as this is deployed by those whose property is sufficient to buy them the right to deploy it. But if it is to be spoken also by improper persons, who cannot afford to buy the privilege, or the rhetoric, of civic self-sacrifice, then it had better be abandoned, along with the language of natural rights, original compacts, and popular consent, which had also been misappropriated by the unpropertied.

As the discourse of civic humanism was seen, by the proponents of customary wisdom in taste and politics, to have become inseparably intertwined with the discourse of natural rights, the incompatibility of the civic and the customary became strikingly apparent, to Burke especially who, with the death of Johnson, had become Reynolds's new mentor. And thus Reynolds came to argue that criticism now needed 'a new code', for he now clearly recognized that it was no longer the primary nor even the final duty of art to create a universal republic of taste. Art should create, instead, a customary community of taste, to develop in a people a sense of its nationhood, of belonging to one nation rather than another, and to provide the justification of social and political privilege which the civic discourse could no longer be relied upon to supply.

The 'Ironic Discourse', and its more interesting preface, were written in 1791 as a response to Reynolds's reading of Burke's *Reflections on the Revolution in France*. In both the preface and the 'discourse' proper, Reynolds sets out to attack the notion that political and aesthetic issues could be determined by an appeal to popular opinion. Nothing, he insists, can be determined by a majority of the 'half-educated', who would presumably — for Reynolds explicitly points out the connection between his 'Ironic Discourse' and the *Reflections* — prescribe laws to the republic or community of taste with the same degree of insight as was possessed by the 'country clowns', or the 'taylors and carpenters', 'of which', according to Burke, 'the republic (of Paris, for instance)' was composed.[45] Like Burke, Reynolds attempts to safeguard the right of the 'few' rather than the 'many' to act as legislators, in art, as well as in politics, and he does so by redescribing — by comparison with the early addresses — the means by which the principles of both are to be discovered. To ground them on reason is to risk appearing to make them open to be determined by 'common sense adapted to the meanest capacity', or by anyone who claims to be a rational man simply by virtue of being literate.[46] The battle cry Reynolds attributes to half-educated men of reason is deliberately couched in the language of the discourse of natural rights: 'Let us pull the whole fabric down at once, root it up even to its foundation. Let us begin again upon this solid ground of nature and reason'. It is reminiscent both of Paine's exhortation, 'Lay then the axe to the root', and of Burke's attack on the notion that the principles of liberty can be 'settled upon any abstract rule', or that the science of constructing or reforming a commonwealth can 'be taught *a priori*'.[47]

The 'tree of knowledge', writes Reynolds, on which the advocates of rational reform

> pretend to say that mankind now have battened, does not grow upon a new made, slender soil, but is fastened by strong roots to ancient rocks, and is the slow growth of ages. There are but few of strength sufficient to climb the summit of this rock, from whence indeed they may look down to us and the clouds below.[48]

An understanding of principles in taste and politics alike is available only to the few 'whose view extends to the whole horizon', and not to the 'near-sighted', capable only of the management of their own affairs, their private interests. Those who are not capable of the 'labour and study' necessary to an understanding of the science of politics must therefore be excluded from political assemblies, and on the same grounds as the vulgar are to be excluded from the Academy exhibitions; for in both political and aesthetic matters, the vulgar will reduce standards to the lowest common denominator or mass appreciation, and 'the worst will appear the best, as being within their narrow comprehension'. Reynolds's denunciation of those who are determined to 'rescue the world from the worse than barbarous tyranny of prejudice, and restore the sovereignty of reason' is particularly evident as a departure from the position developed in his early addresses, in so far as the prejudice he seeks to defend is always, in late-eighteenth-century political theory, a prejudice in favour of the customary.[49]

The starting point of the unfinished essay on Shakespeare is a defence of Shakespeare's practice of mixing tragic and comic scenes and characters within the same work. Reynolds bases this defence on a challenge to the demand made by 'theoretical systems' of ethics and criticism, that 'a man ought totally to keep separate his intellectual from his sensual desires'. Against this, he argues that the mind is 'accustomed' by 'long habit' to doing two different things at once. Indeed, it 'always desires to double, to entertain two objects at a time'; and the mixed drama is more in accord with the customary, the 'second', irrational nature of man than is the single drama. For 'man is an inconsistent being, a professed lover of art and nature, of order, of regularity, and of variety'; he 'loves novelty', and 'therefore cannot long continue his attention without some recreation'. Thus critics who 'seem to consider man as too *uniformly* wise', have formed their rules

> for another race of beings than what man really is. They do not form their rules always from experience of what does please, but what in

their great wisdom they think ought to please — as if they should say man ought to like what is regular only, his passion for variety is vicious.

But Shakespeare, who wrote his dramas by observing the actual desires and passions of his audience, had a more comprehensive understanding of human nature, which he realized was a mixture of the intellectual and the sensual. He is 'superior for universality of powers' to the dramatists on whose practice the rules of drama have been based; and when 'a great genius has continued for ages to please, and to please by means contrary to the established art of pleasing, it is then high time to overhaul the rules of art, that they pass a new examination, that they be made more agreeable to the nature of man'.[50]

This demand for 'new rules of art' is apparently of such importance to Reynolds that the text of the essay, unrevised as it is, repeats it on no less than three occasions. 'It may be a question worthy the consideration of critics whether this civilized age does not demand a new code of laws' — 'from universal approbation is it not time to make a new code?' — 'it is time for a new code of laws, or at least for the old to be fairly and candidly revised'.[51] So often, and so urgently, is the demand made, that Reynolds can hardly have helped now noticing the similarities, both between the position of the critics he has been attacking, with their insistence on the uniformity of mind and art, and the civic theory he himself had advocated in the early addresses, and between the position represented by Shakespeare's practice and the 'new code' he had begun to propose in 1776. The nature of the new code is unambiguous. The greater universality of Shakespeare arises from the opinion — never before so directly expressed by Reynolds — that 'art in its most perfect state is when it possesses those accidents' (the very accidents which it had before been the duty of the artist to discard) 'which do not belong to the code of laws for that art'. It is quite evident, here, that the rationalism of the discourse of natural rights has become entirely inseparable in Reynolds's mind from the rationalism of the civic humanist tradition; for it was that tradition which had drawn up the legal code which failed to allow for perfection and for genius, and which Reynolds is now so anxious to reform.

It is even more evident that the 'accidents' that the 'most perfect art' is now to admit include local and national customs. Thus, a writer 'will run the risk of being even ungrammatical in order to preserve the idiom of the language' — he will offend, that is, against what was called 'universal grammar' in order to safeguard the 'genius' of the national language. More importantly, for our purposes, the 'effect' of a picture is now found to reside in 'the background' — in the 'place', the 'occasion', the local site of the fable, which earlier had been circumstances to which only a minimum of attention should be paid.[52] The new code will clearly be framed in order to create and confirm a national community, as something opposed to a civic republic of taste. Its task will be to establish the Englishness of English art as a constituent — the prime constituent — of its value, to confirm the nationhood of the English, and to represent that nationhood as something which can legitimately be described only in the conservative language of custom and justifiable prejudice.

Reynolds is the first critic of painting, I believe, to propose such a task, but he seems to have gone unheard. To some extent, this is the result of the fact that the essays in which the discourse of custom was most fully mobilized against the civic tradition remained in manuscript: they were excluded from the posthumous edition of Reynolds's works edited by Malone and published in 1797. But Malone's decision to omit them may itself be an indication of the continuing authority of the civic discourse in the criticism of painting, an authority it maintained in spite of mounting suspicion of its political tendency. For without an appeal to the values of civic humanism, it would have been extraordinarily difficult to argue for the supremacy of history among the genres of art. This, no doubt, is one reason why the value-language of civic humanism never entirely disappeared from Reynolds's *Discourses*, and why his new customary aesthetic could be developed most fully in an essay on dramatic literature, not on epic, or on epic painting. To some extent, too, the failure of the discourse of custom to establish itself in the Academy, at least, may have been a result of the fact that the most thoughtful and thorough lecturers there in the decade after Reynolds's death were Barry and Henry Fuseli, both of whom had begun to form their theories of the public function of painting during the period when the earlier addresses were being delivered. Blake, who left off annotating his edition of the *Discourses* after the eighth address, showed no signs of having registered the new emphasis on the customary contained in that and the previous address. But more to the point, all three of these writers were more sympathetic than Reynolds had been to the radical political movements which the discourse of custom had been revived to attack.

Outside the circles of the Academy, the most influential writer on painting in the decades after Reynolds's death was probably William Hazlitt, who, despite his commitment to a variety of middle-class political radicalism, was concerned to confine painting — unlike literature, or the theatre — to a private sphere of experience, uncontaminated by the notion that it might have a public *or* a national function.[53] And perhaps it was especially the privatization of painting, the increasingly widespread belief that its function was to offer private satisfactions to a private audience, together with the declining authority of the discourse of custom in the decade preceding the 1832 Reform Act, which resulted in the next attempt to define the Englishness of English art being based, by Ruskin, in arguments from climate rather than from law and language — in the characteristic moistness of the English climate.

(1986)

Notes

1 The second half of this essay is part adapted, part borrowed, from the later sections of the first chapter of my book, *The Political Theory of Painting from Reynolds to Hazlitt: 'The Body of the Public'* (London and New Haven, Conn.: Yale University Press, 1986). The more general assertions in this essay about eighteenth-century theories of painting may be found described and contextualized in that work, as may an account of the androcentric character of the theories of painting discussed in this essay, which explains my continual reference to the painter, the critic, the spectator, and 'man' in general, as 'he' (pp. 65–8).

2 Buckeridge's essay first appeared in 1706; I quote it from the version in the second English edition of Roger de Piles's *Art of Painting* (London, 1744), 'Dedication', unpaginated.

3 Horace Walpole, *Anecdotes of Painting in England, with Some Account of the Principal Artists*, 4 vols (Strawberry Hill, 1762–71).

4 William Aglionby, *Painting Illustrated in Three Diallogues* (London, 1685), 'Preface', unpaginated; *Spectator*, 6 December 1712.

5 See, for example, William Hazlitt, *Criticisms on Art: and Sketches of the Picture Galleries of England*, second edn (London, 1856), p. 217.

6 R. Fry, *Reflections on British Painting* (London, 1934), p. 42.

7 N. Pevsner, *The Englishness of English Art* (1956); all quotations are from the edition of 1964 (Harmondsworth: Penguin, 1964).

8 Pevsner, op. cit., pp. 35, 36, 79.

9 ibid., pp. 20, 15.

10 ibid., p. 21.

11 ibid.

12 ibid., pp. 16–17.

13 ibid., pp. 18–21.

14 For Barry's attack on the climatological theorists, see his *Inquiry into the Real and Imaginary Obstructions to the Acquisition of the Arts in England* (London, 1775); for endorsements of Barry's arguments, see Hoare, *An Enquiry into the Requisite Cultivation and Present State of the Arts of Design in England* (London, 1806), pp. 190–210, and Opie, *Lectures on Painting* (London, 1809), pp. 91–3.

15 Pevsner, op. cit., p. 15.

16 John Brown, *Essays on the Characteristics of the Earl of Shaftesbury* (1751), second edition (London, 1751), pp. 375–6.

17 *Sir Joshua Reynolds: Discourses on Art*, ed. R. R. Wark, 2nd edn (London and New Haven, Conn.: Yale University Press, 1975), p. 69 (hereafter '*Discourses*').

18 James Thomson, *Liberty*, pt 4 (London, 1736), line 775.

19 See Adam Smith, *The Theory of Moral Sentiments* [1759], ed. D. D. Raphael and A. L. MacFie (Oxford: Oxford University Press, 1976), pp. 198–9; *Idler*, 10 November 1759.

20 *Discourses*, p. 44.

21 S. Johnson, *The History of Rasselas Prince of Abyssinia* (London, 1759), ch. 10; *Discourses*, pp. 48–9.

22 See Barrell, op. cit., 'Introduction'.

23 *Discourses*, p. 59.

24 William Blackstone, *Commentaries on the Laws of England*, 4 vols (Oxford 1765–9).

25 'The false alarm', in *Samuel Johnson: Political Writings*, ed. Donald J. Greene, (New Haven, Conn., and London: Yale University Press, 1977), p. 328.

26 S. Johnson, *A Plan of a Dictionary of the English Language* (London, 1747), p. 10; *A Dictionary of the English Language* (London, 1755), 'Preface', unpaginated. For the congruity of these statements about language with Johnson's political views of the 1770s, see J. Barrell, *English Literature in History, 1730–1780: An Equal, Wide Survey* (London: Hutchinson, 1983), pp. 144–8.

27 Prov. 24: 21.

28 *Sermons, and Other Remains of Robert Lowth, D. D., some time Bishop of London* (London, 1834), p. 118. I am grateful to Dr Harriet Guest for drawing my attention to Lowth's political sermons.

29 *Discourses*, pp. 134–5, and see Kames, *Elements of Criticism* (1762), 11th edn (London, 1839), p. 187.

30 *Discourses*, p. 123.

31 In 1773, Reynolds had initiated the abortive scheme for 'ornamenting St Paul's cathedral': see James Northcote, *The Life of Sir Joshua Reynolds*, 2nd edn (London, 1819), vol. 1, pp. 307ff.

32 E. Burke, *The Works of the Right Honourable Edmund Burke*, vol. 5 (London, 1815), pp. 186–7.

33 *Discourses*, p. 135.

34 ibid., p. 134; *Spectator*, 10 May 1711.

35 Blackstone, op. cit., vol. 1, p. 74.

36 ibid., p. 44.

37 ibid., p. 74.

38 ibid.

39 *Discourses*, p. 141.

40 ibid., p. 136; for the source of Reynolds's notion of colour as a procur*ess*, see Charles Alphonse Du Fresnoy, *The Art of Painting, with Remarks and Observations*, trans. Dryden (London, 1769), lines 261–6, and p. 27: colour 'has been accused of procuring Lovers for her Sister (viz. drawing)'.

41 *Discourses*, p. 140–1.

42 Burke, op. cit., vol. 5, p. 305.

43 *Discourses*, p. 139.

44 Coleridge, 'On Peace. IV', *Morning Post*, 4 January 1800, reprinted in *Essays on His Times*, ed. David V. Erdman (Princeton, NJ: Princeton University Press), vol. 1, p. 75.

45 Burke, op. cit., vol. 5, pp. 95, 104.

46 *Portraits by Sir Joshua Reynolds*, ed. Frederick W. Hilles (London, 1952), p. 144.

47 Thomas Paine, *Rights of Man* [1791–2], ed. Henry Collins (Harmondsworth: Penguin, 1969), p. 80; and see Matt. 3: 10; Burke, op. cit., vol. 5, pp. 123, 124.

48 *Portraits*, p. 128.

49 *Portraits*, pp. 129, 130, 142, and (for exclusion from the Academy exhibition) see Barrell, *Political Theory*, p. 77.

50 *Portraits*, pp. 117–19, 112.

51 *Portraits*, pp. 112, 122.

52 *Portraits*, pp. 109, 113.

53 For a further account of the political theories of painting of Barry, Blake, Fuseli, and Hazlitt, see the separate chapters devoted to each of them in Barrell, *Political Theory*.

10
Destiny made manifest: the styles of Whitman's poetry

David Simpson

Despite Walt Whitman's reputation as a socialist hero in some parts of the world, there is in American literary criticism a significant tradition that queries the integrity and coherence of his egalitarian assertions. One of the poet's recent biographers, Justin Kaplan, has suggested that Horace Traubel was largely responsible for the myth of Whitman the socialist;[1] but even if we spare him this anachronism, Whitman is constantly proclaiming or 'promulging' himself as the great democrat, a claim that has occasioned a good deal of disaffected scrutiny of the political logic of his writings. D. H. Lawrence appreciated the originality and force of Whitman's determination to plant the soul in the body, thereby challenging a common dualism of Christian doctrine; but he also felt that the American poet's attitude to other people and other forms of life was at root unhealthy. It was not true 'sympathy' but rather an insistence upon being one with everything, a 'merging' and self-sacrifice.[2] For Lawrence, this compulsion negated or avoided the fruitful recognition of *difference*, of the otherness of others. Hence Whitman supplanted the love of woman (difference) by the comradely appreciation of men (sameness), and eventually subsumed the love of everything into an extended hymn to death, the true egalitarian. Whitman failed to realize that forms of life, whether human or animal, 'have the instinct of turning right away from *some* matter, and of blissfully ignoring the bulk of most matter, and of turning towards only some certain bits of specially selected matter'. (p. 172).

Lawrence does not pursue the political correlatives of this peculiar blindness of Whitman's; but it consists, if Lawrence is right, in a failure to recognize the empirical facts of ethnic, social, political, occupational, and sexual differences within the American society whose features he was celebrating. Instead of standing back and thinking about the terms of the slave's or the prostitute's difference, Whitman wants to share the slavery or the prostitution. The appetite for identity is so omnivorous that there is nothing it will not assimilate and hence explain or justify.

In 1955, Leadie M. Clark published a strongly negative account of Whitman, arguing that he 'lost sight of the reasons back of "manifest destiny" in his obvious joy in the mere physical expansion of the country', and declaring that 'for no major problem of his age can one go to Whitman for a proposed solution'.[3] Clark's Whitman is anti-Catholic, anti-Semitic, ambiguous in his attitude to slavery, silent on the key problems of Native American rights, and a free trader with no sense of the divisive results of an industrial economy. Less assertively but with similar priorities, Quentin Anderson later identified Whitman as making 'a big leap forward in our imaginative desocialization', and his poems as nostalgic mementoes of a time 'before the world became hopelessly plural'.[4]

Other examples of the dissenting view could (and will) be given. But there is a much stronger and more enduring acceptance of Whitman's claims to democratic credentials. Emerson, recommending him for a government post, announced his work to be 'more deeply American, democratic, & in the interest of political liberty' than that of any other poet (Kaplan, p. 274); and, despite some serious qualifications, F. O. Matthiessen's influential *American Renaissance* (1941) was founded upon the common devotion of Whitman and four other writers to 'the possibilities of democracy'.[5] In the classroom and in the popular consciousness, Whitman's status as the bard of democracy often remains unchallenged. He is of course always ready to declare himself as such, both in his poetry and in the anonymous eulogies that he published under the guise of review of *Leaves of Grass*. As well as the claim to total originality for his works — 'there exists no book or fragment of a book which can have given the hint to them' — he asserts their egalitarian inclusiveness:

> His scope of life is the amplest of any yet in philosophy. . . . He is the largest lover and sympathizer that has appeared in literature . . . [he comes] to unsettle what was settled, and to revolutionize in fact our modern civilization.[6]

It will then be clear that in any examination of the relation between formal expression and political content, between narrative and nationality, Whitman must be a central case. He declares himself as the first properly confident poet of America, and, with a frequency that seems inevitable in the light of his formal idiosyncrasies, discussions of his politics have indeed been carried on by way of discussions of his style.[7] The poet himself constantly claims an immediacy or objectivity for his words, as if in the moment of utterance (or writing) they *are* or could become the things they denote. As his own reviewer, Whitman describes his 'working the muscle of the male and the teeming fibre of the female throughout his writings, as wholesome realities' (*Critical Heritage*, p. 37). And, in a famous passage in the *American Primer*, he relates how:

> A perfect writer would make words sing, dance, kiss, do the male and female act, bear children, weep, bleed, rage, stab, steal, fire cannon, steer ships, sack cities, charge with cavalry or infantry, or do any thing, that a man or woman or the natural powers can do.[8]

To query these claims, we should not accuse him, as did the Boston *Christian Examiner* (1856), of some 'impertinence towards the English language' (*Critical Heritage*, p. 62). Such reliance upon fastidious notions of decorum merely legitimates Whitman, by negation, as a greatly authentic spirit, one of the roughs. Rather, we must try to read him on his own terms, testing out the claims against the performance. Where some readers have seen 'the ebb and flow and interplay of vital emotion', others, like Knut Hamsun, have sensed only 'a pretentious game with savage words' (*Critical Heritage*, pp. 284, 209). Beneath these apparently aesthetic judgements there are of course political assumptions and preferences; it is these that a careful account of Whitman's style must try to make clear.

The first (1855) edition of *Leaves of Grass* is introduced by the famous portrait of the casually dressed author-loafer, one hand on his hip and the other in his pocket, head cocked jauntily to one side. This is followed by the title and the place and date of publication. Except in the frequently unnoticed copyright clause, no name is given. There is a long and largely unpunctuated poetic-prose preface, and then, as the volume 'proper', a succession of lines set as poetry but undistinguished part from part by titles or attributions. After some 500 lines, a name appears: 'Walt Whitman, an American, one of the roughs, a cosmos'.[9] The author's name is buried unpretentiously in the stream of language, embodying the poet's claim to be speaking from within rather than from above his America. In the prose as in the poetry, Whitman's favourite mode of punctuation is the string of stops (. . . .), denoting a voice or sentence that can potentially go on forever, and a field of inclusion or agglomeration that is infinite. If we have an expectation of syntactic subordination, then it is continually refused by the practice of accumulation. The shock value of this format is clear and undoubted, and in this respect we might rank *Leaves of Grass* along with Blake's prophetic books and *Finnegans Wake* as radically subversive of the conventions of ordinary literary language. The replacement of the name (in the front matter) by a visual image makes a claim to immediacy and presence — a response to 'logocentrism', as we now say. This attempt to turn writing into speech, the absent into the present, is enhanced by the vocalic markers and incantatory rhythms of the text, which thus seeks constantly to express itself as voice. Various critics have noted that Whitman never refers to his poetry as writing, as a material, textual object; it is always a voice, a chant, a yawp, an incantation.[10] Everything possible is done to create — by means which always of course remain graphic — a sense of the incarnate presence of the poet's voice and body. Whitman has little sense of the ironies and paradoxes generated by this graphic assertion of voice (as Blake and Joyce do, for example). For him, the illusion is offered in complete good faith. The poetic self is 'the one chanting or talking' (*PW* p. 299), and the achievement of such talking is the bringing into being of things, whether it be the person of the poet (p. 311), or the 'natural life' of things (*1855*, p. 7). As single words embody particular items in this celebrative geography, so the poet in his style embodies their collective being: 'When the long Atlantic coast stretches longer and the Pacific coast stretches longer he easily stretches with them north or south' (*1855*, p. 7).

The accompanying gesture that allows Whitman to carry off what might otherwise come across as an aggressive posture toward his reader is the familiar Romantic invitation that the reader become one with the poet, or a poet unto himself. Thus 'a bard is to be commensurate with a people' (p. 6), rather than an authority over it. Reviewing his own work, Whitman declared that he was doing no more than putting his reader in the position of knowledge, from which he might freely choose his own direction. The poet:

> comes to no conclusion, and does not satisfy the reader. He certainly leaves him what the serpent left the woman and the man, the taste of the Paradisaic tree of the knowledge of good and evil, never to be erased again. (*Critical Heritage*, p. 46).

Later in his career, he declared again that the reader 'will always have his or her part to do, just as much as I have had mine' (*PW*, p. 307).

One cannot but respect Whitman here as surely one of the earliest of writers to inscribe the feminine pronoun as equal to the masculine in the definition of 'the reader'. But it is hard to confirm him within the Protestant, existential tradition — practised so rigorously by the likes of Blake and Kierkegaard — that seeks to isolate its reader in a thrilling but dangerous free space for the exercise of critical choice.[11] In the final analysis, Whitman does not seem either to demand this freedom of his reader, nor encourage him or her to it. No more does he publicize the ethical dangers of individuality, as the Wordsworthian subject so often does. Whitman's mode is much more assertive:

> And what I assume you shall assume,
> For every atom belonging to me as good belongs to you.
> (*1855*, p. 25)

This gesture can only be regarded as 'democratic' in the most etiolated or mythologized sense. We may accept it as a polemical desire — the world might be a better place if it were true. But as a representation of either the actual or prospective life of America in 1855 it is an obvious mystification. C. Carroll Hollis (1983, p. 70ff.) has aptly described Whitman's propensity for *shall* and *will* in terms of J. L. Austin's vocabulary of 'illocutionary forms' or 'performatives'. His writing is an ongoing demand that the reader admit the presence of what is written (not written 'about'), and the assertion of presence is used to insist that the reader remain alert and attentive. The famous 'catalogues', so dominant in the earlier poetry, are the best example of this — long lists of things, persons and places, laid forth in a syntactic parallelism that completely eschews the subordinating energies of complex clauses and qualifiers. The reader is put into the position of *seeing*, of surveying an infinite series of quiddities:

You shall no longer take things at second or third hand ....
  nor look through the eyes of the dead .... nor feed
  on the spectres in books,
You shall not look through my eyes either, nor take things
  from me,
You shall listen to all sides and filter them from yourself.

(1855, p. 26)

Whitman's mode is simultaneously prescriptive and descriptive. It *tells* us to filter from ourselves and for ourselves, but it *shows* us the results of the poet's own filterings. One cannot quarrel with being told to be independent; but this instruction often seems hard to live up to in the face of the stream of already filtered things that Whitman throws at us. We do not see everything, but one man's selection from the social and geographical whole. And the sheer bulk and energy of that selection rather exhausts us into acquiescence than encourages us to search for more.

The invitation to differ or qualify thus seems to be deployed to insinuate a posture of authority. Larzer Ziff has observed that Whitman's claim to be able to synthesize all extremes and contain all contraries 'extends only to his dominating use of sight. Once he hearkens to other senses — hearing and touch — his prophetic power becomes entangled in self-doubt' (*Literary Democracy*, p. 235).[12] As Wordsworth and other Romantics knew well, the eye is the most despotic of the senses; its activity presupposes a distance between the seer and the seen, and thus opens up a space for the potential inscription or assumption of a hierarchy, a posture of lordliness of the seer over the seen. As I have said, Whitman does what he can to image himself as speaking from within rather than from above or outside; but he does not exercise those senses of touch, smell, and hearing that are most active when one is in close contact with the crowd. Once again, practice and profession are in tension. Hearing and touching are, in their different ways, both more intimate and more insecure than seeing. Hearing depends upon some degree of selection of significant from background noise for sense to be made; touching reminds us of the fragility of flesh, and hence of our own flesh. Both senses are less efficient than sight as modes of access to a *whole* world. We touch and hear only a few things at a time; sight surveys a much larger range, one that can pretend to totality. Perhaps it is not accidental that those poems in which Whitman's posture of mastery seems most threatened (even when it is vindicated) are those in which he describes himself among the Civil War wounded, and doing a lot of touching. Here one senses both the passivity of those touched — they cannot pull away even if they want to — and the violent genesis of that passivity in the war itself.

The priority of the sense of sight in Whitman's writing is further appropriate in that it is *only* as perceiving, visualizing beings that we are equal. This very limited idea of equality is continually substituted into the poetry as a representation or protestation of political, social, and economic equality — in short, of a complete equality. That the sense of sight might enter into a complex and redetermining relation with other forms of being in the world — body with society, eye with ideology — is a possibility that the poems only ever move towards, without exploring. This potential is most apparent in the war poems, where the social-somatic horror that composes the terribleness of war is repeatedly faced, but then simplified out into a triumph of *social* spirit, and a psychic-erotic *bodily* response. Whitman's oneness with the wounded and the dying subverts the possibility of his ever facing up to the implications, both personal and social, of a divided body politic. As long as a person has two arms and two legs, Whitman believes that he or she is capable of all and anything. The sight of the wounded showed him persons without their full ration of limbs, but did not persuade him out of a consoling metaphysic of wholeness.

I shall return to the subject of the war poems, which are more subtle than I have so far suggested. For now, it is worth stressing again that the accumulative style, with its denial of grammatical subordination and hence of the political struggles and debates that such subordination would inevitably dramatize, is Whitman's image of an undivided society. He does not choose to face the possibility that all are not given the same opportunities to do all things, and are perhaps not even effectively 'free' to exercise such opportunities as they do have. Whitman's occupations — traders, mechanics, farmers, and so forth — never interact *with* each other or confront each other. The poetry presents them within a chain of successive signifiers, *next to* each other but never interfering or challenging each other. This is the syntax of a non-competitive society functioning without division of labour. Randall Jarrell has written eloquently of this world as one that

> streams over us joined only by *ands*, until we supply the subordinating conjunctions; and since as children we see the *ands* and not the *becauses*, this method helps to give to Whitman some of the freshness of childhood. How inexhaustibly *interesting* the world is in Whitman.[13]

One could extrapolate from Jarrell's remark some saving explanation of the historical inevitability of this freshness of vision, invoking the 'childhood of America' or some such condition of innocence. But one must then recollect that this mood of vitalistic celebration, so common among the writers of the 1840s and after, was not without its critics at the time. It was also, it must be stressed, a departure *from* rather than a continuation *of* the tradition of much previous American literature. The 'childhood' syndrome thus begins to look like a case of wilful infantilism, a false innocence. Whitman's ebullience is not to be found in the writings of Fenimore Cooper, or Brackenridge, or Bird, or Paulding, or Irving. In their different ways, these writers and others like them face up to and record the strident divisions of interest and opportunity that constituted their 'America'. Whether the message is a dark one as Cooper's often is, or a satirical one as Paulding's and Brackenridge's are, or one framed by a fairytale good humour (itself not unqualified) as in Irving, the earlier

writers are aware of the degree to which the national identity seems
likely to consist in an uneasy collection of factions, each competing with
the others for recognition and for basic rights.[14] The speed with which
the tragical or at least conflicting literature of the Jacksonian period was
replaced by the affirmative visions of twenty years later (there are of
course exceptions and qualifications) is one of the puzzles of nineteenth-
century American literary history: I cannot attempt to address this question here. Suffice it to say that earlier writers had tended to recognize the
existence of a divided society, whose tensions could only be resolved in
one of two ways: either by the naked assertion of the power of the
stronger, or by a contractual compromise generated out of a rational
admission of differences. The melancholia of so much literature of the
1830s comes from its sense of the unlikelihood of the second of these
possibilities. Far removed from the boisterous (though by no means
unanimous) optimism of 1776, and not yet reconciled to the ethical
righteousness of the westward expansion, many of these writers see the
world as the site of conflict and chaos.

Not so Whitman, who chose (or was historically impelled) otherwise.
For him, the contractual approach is irrelevant because there is no *essential*
conflict, no disagreement whose inner unanimity cannot be relied upon
and made clear. Similarly, no apparent gesture of power is really such,
since every atom of each belongs to all. In 1860 he queries his reader's
preoccupation with formalities as a way of resolving differences:

> (Were you looking to be held together by lawyers?
> Or by an agreement on a paper? or by arms?
> Nay, nor the world, nor any living thing, will so cohere.)
>
> > (*1891*, p. 316)

It was an odd year to be predicting that the Yankee and the inhabitant
of 'hot Carolina' would be coming together in a spirit of manly com-
radeship; even in 1860, Whitman is sufficiently infused with the vitalist
faith to be able to see underlying unity beneath the surface of division.
In the context of the national move westwards, Whitman seems to have
no complex doubts at all. He had, of course, the paradigm of Carlylean
anti-self-consciousness to look to, with its bland assumption about other
places as territories with no previous owners or independent cultures:

> Must the indomitable millions, full of old Saxon energy and fire, lie
> cooped-up in this Western Nook, choking one another, as in a
> Blackhole of Calcutta, while a whole fertile untenanted Earth, desolate
> for want of the ploughshare, cries: Come and till me, come and reap
> me?[15]

Carlyle's system relies upon leaders, self-evidently superior beings before
whom we will willingly prostrate ourselves in this passage outwards;
Whitman, the spokesman of an egalitarian culture, does away with the
leaders but preserves the spirit of a system whose logical dependence
upon *some* sort of hierarchy (for its political implementation) yet remains
clear. That place is now filled by 'myself', the cosmos, and anyone who

cares to or can join him. The ethical questions that might have been raised by such uninhibited self-projection on the part of a dominant culture or individual — and were raised by many of the writers of Jacksonian America and by the British Romantics before them — are completely passed over by Whitman. Different voices are lost in or drowned out by *the* voice, awkward plurality is subsumed into singleness.[16]

The ideological climate within which Whitman was thinking and writing did of course make such gestures both feasible and explicable. Apologists of the habits of mind that are roughly definable under the rubric of transcendentalism saw no primary separation of the self from the world. Here is Henry Goodwin, in 1849:

> The poet does not bring his thoughts and impose them upon nature, or merely link them to its forms; they are there already, as truly as what are called natural or organic laws. He simply finds them, apprehends them by the power of imagination.[17].

If there is an essential identity of self and other, then there can be no imposition — all forms of self-projection are sympathetic to and one with what is already there. Emerson, extraordinarily, carries this idea as far as to suggest that we cannot do harm to the world even if we try:

> There is a soul at the centre of nature and over the will of every man, so that none of us can wrong the universe. It has so infused its strong enchantment into nature that we prosper when we accept its advice, and when we struggle to wound its creatures our hands are glued to our sides, or we beat our own breasts.[18]

In retrospect, these legitimations of the white American male's philosophical right to assume that all other forms of life are versions of himself just waiting to be realized seem almost parodic. But they were not, any more than were Carlyle's hymns to the energies of empire. We can see that Whitman must have felt a good deal of solidarity with such sentiments as those expressed here by Goodwin and Emerson. But ideological determination cannot account for the total conformity of a poet's work. It can, after all, inspire objections and counter-voices, as it did (I would argue) in Melville. The clearer the articulation of the dominant ideology, the more possible it is for an opposition to articulate itself. What, if any, are the counter-voices in Whitman's writing?

There are, I think, very few. In fact, the enormity of what is excluded from Whitman's representation of an exemplary America is quite staggering. One could, and critics have, go about this question by undercutting the poet's claims to a stylistic originality. Lois Ware set out long ago to prove that Whitman was a very conventional writer, his characteristic style coming from his use of standard poetic techniques to excess in densely localized ways. Similarly, Rebecca Coy contested that Whitman never produced the language whose existence he theorized, 'not the great representative American speech of which he dreamed, but only a Whitmanesque dialect which will remain forever personal and inimitable'.[19]

There are colloquialisms, indeed, but few genuine Americanisms, and a great many pedantic and archaic words.

After reading Longfellow and Whittier, it seems to me that one would not want to deny Whitman a certain stylistic distinction! However, a close look at the elements of this style is important, and does offer some evidence of its 'political' fabric. Whitman wrote at a time when the settlement of the west was the major demographic phenomenon; we might then expect, from a self-declared man of the people, some literal recognition of the languages and identities of those ethnic groups with whom white America was coming into anxious contact: most obviously, Hispanics and Native Americans. Not so — or hardly so. So little presence do these cultures have in Whitman's mind *as* cultures that scarcely any elements of their vocabularies find their way into the poetry. Texas, California, and the South-West contained hundreds of thousands of Spanish-speaking people, with traditions going back over 200 years. But if Louise Pound is correct in her count, Whitman uses only *two* Spanish words in his poems: they are *Libertad* and *Americanos*! Even if she missed some, the total is less than impressive. The language that most frequently features in Whitman's work is in fact French — perhaps a legacy of his time in Louisiana, perhaps also a remnant of some lurking desire to assume social-educational distinction. Pound has elsewhere shown that many of Whitman's neologisms are adaptations from the French (although they do not outnumber his coinage of agent-nouns, ending in '-ist', '-ite', '-ee').[20] The French in Louisiana and in New England certainly were, as they still are, a significant ethnic minority within the borders of the United States. But it would be hard to claim that their status was as historically urgent as that of the Spanish speakers of the west. Moreover, there is not much evidence of a clear political purpose in Whitman's rendering of their language.

The same goes for his representation of Native Americans. To the best of my knowledge there has been no statistical study of the Native American elements (always, of course, in some state of transliteration) in the vocabulary of the poems. Whitman was a conscious celebrant of the poetic appeal of aboriginal names. In *An American Primer*, written around 1855 but not published until after the poet's death, he writes:

All aboriginal names sound good. I was asking for something savage and luxuriant, and behold here are the aboriginal names. I see how they are being preserved. They are honest words — they give the true length, breadth, depth. They all fit. Mississippi! — the word winds with chutes — it rolls a stream three thousand miles long. Ohio, Connecticut, Ottawa, Monongahela, all fit. (p. 18)

In the spirit of this onomastic luxury, Long Island can become Paumanok and New York Manahatta — 'a word, liquid, sane, unruly, musical, self-sufficient' (*1891*, p. 474). The rivers of the South similarly excite a joyous intonation of sonorous epiphets: 'Dear to me the Roanoke, the Savannah, the Altamahaw, the Pedee, the Tombigbee, the Santee, the Coosa and the Sabine' (*1891*, p. 473). But one looks in vain for any registration of the facts and consequences of the Indian removal policies that had been going on since the 1830s. Whitman's most detailed image of the relation between white and red races is the marriage of the trapper and the red girl (*1855*, p. 33). As an instance of the best that could and did happen, this is benign enough. But it is a long way from what we have to reconstruct as a typical situation. Once again, our judgement hangs upon whether we read *Leaves* as an account of the state of affairs, or as an ideal prognosis — the poet himself is hardly clear on this question. And the way in which elements of aboriginal vocabularies enter into the poetry is clearly coincident with the high romanticism of *commemoration*. The names are mementoes of races that have apparently disappeared, and all the more appealing in that they do not require any urgent confrontation with an alternative ethnic reality. Even as a form of romantic racism, moreover, Whitman's transcriptions are conventionally facile. He does not, for example, show any awareness of the awkwardness of the native words and their incompatibility with the sound values of the English language. Lewis and Clark, more scientifically minded, tried very hard to preserve the otherness of the languages they encountered, as did Fenimore Cooper in some of his novels.[21] In Whitman's poems, all is comfortably sonorous and acceptable; native languages are forms of poetical English, high points of assonance and onomatopoeia. Lawrence had some justification for his image of Whitman at the wheel of a vehicle going out of control:

> ALLNESS! shrieks Walt at a cross-road, going whizz over an unwary Red Indian.
> ONE IDENTITY! chants democratic En Masse, pelting behind in motor-cars, oblivious of the corpses under the wheels.
>
> (*Studies*, p. 176)

Even more ambiguous — and more obviously so for anyone residing as Whitman did in the east — is his literary formulation of the slavery debate. There is a famous passage in *Leaves* where the narrator recounts his hospitality toward a wounded runaway slave, whom he allows to rest and recuperate for a week (*1855*, p. 34). But in general the complex question of black—white relations in the decade or so before the Civil War is once again reduced to a celebrative parallelism in which all potential conflicts are subsumed:

> The groups of newly-come immigrants cover the wharf or levee,
> The woollypates hoe in the sugarfield, the overseer views
>   them from his saddle;
> The bugle calls in the ballroom, the gentlemen run for their
>   partners, the dancers bow to each other;
>
> (*1851*, p. 37)

This is indeed the style appropriate to Whitman's idea of democracy: 'that paradox, the eligibility of the free and fully developed individual with the paramount aggregate' (*PW*, p. 532). Once again, it fails to ponder the fact, and fact it was, that the aggregate did *not* allow for the freedom and individuality of all within it. After the war he looks forward to the triumvirate of freedom, law, and peace 'all issuing forth against the idea of caste', and this includes a new 'solidarity of races' (*1891*, p. 489). This is however very poorly worked out; once again, Whitman's spiritually unanimous sense of history is able to avoid seeing the problems of reconstruction in both north and south. Reading back to *The Eighteenth Presidency*, his contribution to the crisis of 1856, we can see a clear commitment to the northern cause, but the reasons for this are not simple. In arguing against slavery, Whitman does not draw upon the absolute, morally imperative arguments of the abolitionists, but speaks from a concern for the wellbeing of southern whites, 'that great strong stock of southerners that supplied the land in old times'.[22] Slavery is presented as an evil less in itself than for its effects on the poorer whites, since its political role excludes 'the true people, the millions of white citizens, mechanics, farmers, boatmen, manufacturers and the like . . . from politics and from office' (p. 24), and produces a class of great proprietors who have no more regard for 'free races of farmers and work-people than there is now in any European despotism or aristocracy' (p. 32). This was a popular argument at the time, and it does not by definition exclude holding abolitionist views on other grounds. But it remains the case that Whitman is conspicuously silent, here as elsewhere, about those other grounds. His primary concern seems to be for those southerners who came closest to his own preferred version of 'the people': the tradesmen, artisans, and labourers in whom the efficient energy of the mercantile-capitalist society most obviously resided. There is more than a dash of nativism, not to say Saxonism, in this emphasis of Whitman's. He was an emancipationist, if not an abolitionist; but he does not in his poetry work out or represent such discriminations in detailed terms. The difficult postwar question of the often-perceived threat of free labour to the interests of northern workers is not addressed directly; but it must be said that Whitman certainly does not endorse this threat either. He continues to write of a world in which everything should be in its place, without specifying exactly what that place should be.

As he disavows or 'sees beyond' that fact of interracial conflict, so Whitman also feels no need to register the tensions within white society that resulted from capitalization, industrialization, and the division of labour. As a newspaper editor Whitman knew plenty about streetfighting between rival political factions in New York, and about the turbulent career of Locofocism and its descendants. Faced with problems consequent upon industrialization, Whitman chooses to sing the virtues of commerce — essentially a nostalgic gesture. Many eighteenth-century thinkers, Adam Smith chief among them, had believed that bartering and exchanging were productive of sociability at the national and international level. Countering the adverse commentaries of those who feared the decline of civic virtue as a result of luxury (seen by some as an inevitable corollary of the commercial economy), the Smithians could voice a perspective here set forth by Joel Barlow:

That every distant land the wealth might share,
Exchange their fruits and fill their treasures there;
Their speech assimilate, their empires blend.
And mutual interest fix the mutual friend.[23]

If this was a plausible view in the early 1800s, it was much less so later in the century. For Adam Smith's case for the positive benefits of divided labour depended upon two conditions that had clearly not been met by the factory economy as it had developed: that there be no 'bosses', so that co-operation might remain the basis of the division; and that there be no monopolies, lest the free circulation of wealth be impeded. In general, the psychological model that *The Wealth of Nations* offers as the rationale for its system does not take much account of the human propensity for hoarding rather than exchanging. In a theoretical political economist writing before the factory system had developed very fully, such 'oversights' or alternative ideas about human nature are understandable enough — though there was in fact a well-articulated counter-voice even by 1776. Nor is Smith himself totally univocal on some of these questions. But for Whitman to reproduce the poetics of Smithian *laissez-faire* in 1855 and thereafter suggests either a condition of myopia or a total participation in the most extreme formulations of the liberal-capitalist ideology. He too writes of a world in which no participant interferes with or exploits another:

> The pavingman leans on his two-handed hammer — the reporter's lead
>   flies swiftly over the notebook — the signpainter is lettering with red
>   and gold,
> The canal-boy trots on the towpath — the bookkeeper counts at his
>   desk — the shoemaker waxes his thread,
>
> (*1855*, p. 38)

and so forth. To detail this world in which each is 'singing what belongs to him or her and to none else' (p. 13), Whitman noticeably selects occupations that can be presented as self-sufficient. He does not list those producing on the production line. And he implies, by the unsorted enumeration of tasks and occupations within both professional and labouring classes, that all are equal. In Whitman's copious syntax, the bookkeeper and the paving man are made one. Thus his world can persist within a political credo that stresses not adjustment or discipline but simply *letting happen*. William Leggett, who died in 1839 but who has been argued to have been a formative influence upon Whitman,[24] had consistently advocated a government of non-intervention, and had done so from the position of one defending the rights of the average man, the 'farming and mechanick interests' whom he, like Whitman, saw as the essence of 'the people'.[25] Leggett is more clearly anti-commercial than Whitman, and does differ from him on some doctrinal points, but his case against a 'superabundance of legislation' (p. 7) does underwrite the implicit emphasis of Whitman's poetry.

The American spirit is deployed by Whitman as an energy able to synthesize disparate entities into a singleness of will and purpose; the image and agent of this process of manifest destiny is the American language. In the realm of words also, he is able to contend that a covertly hegemonic posture is in fact one of openness and accommodation:

Great is the English speech .... What speech is so great as the English?
Great is the English brood .... What brood has so vast a destiny as the English?
It is the mother of the brood that must rule the earth with the new rule,
The new rule shall rule as the soul rules, and as the love and justice and equality that are in the soul rule.

(*1855*), p. 144)

The English is the mother of the American. Compared to his predecessors, Whitman spends hardly any time worrying over how much of the American speech will be latently British. He does not feel the linguistic legacies of the parent culture as oppressive, but rather as initiatives now at last to be fulfilled. It is the Americans who will be 'the most fluent and melodious-voiced people in the world — and the most perfect users of words' (*American Primer*, p. 2). America must and will have its own words when it needs them (p. 5), and this right to *expansion* is indeed for Whitman the essence of the Anglo-Saxon legacy, one that 'spurns law' and becomes the 'most capacious vital tongue of all', an 'enormous treasure-house' composed of elements from all over the world. The core of this language is its ability to absorb, but there is a clear hierarchy that organizes this process of inclusion: 'its own sturdy home-dated Angles-bred words have long been outnumbered by the foreigners whom they lead — which is all good enough, and indeed must be' (p. 30).

The foreigners are many, but it is the few, the Angles-bred words, that lead. In a later essay, Whitman will similarly describe the English language as 'a sort of universal absorber, combiner, and conqueror'.[26] He displaces the question of improper conquest by placing the essence of this language in 'the people', users of slang, which is the 'lawless germinal element' of language. But this is the rhetoric of populism rather than the logic of democracy. Slang is spoken by white tradesmen and mechanics, not by everyone. Walt is always one of the boys — Hollis has rightly commented that we cannot imagine a 'Billy Bryant' or a 'Hank Longfellow' (p. 62) — but he chooses his company none the less. Populist rhetoric, in fact, had become so obligatory for the politicians of all parties since the late 1830s that it cannot be used to confirm any exact political stance. Everyone claimed to speak for the people, as they still do. Then as now, this rhetoric subsists on the unanalysed assumption that there is such a thing as 'the people', one and indivisible.

The awareness of words as the tools of power is even clearer in another passage from the *Primer*:

Names are the turning point of who shall be master. — There is so much virtue in names that a nation which produces its own names, haughtily adheres to them, and subordinates others to them, leads all the rest of the nations of the earth. (p. 34)

In the same spirit, William Swinton's *Rambles Among Words* (1859), much of which is thought to have been written by Whitman, is eloquent about an American English that 'absorbs whatever is of use to it, absorbs and assimilates it to its own fluid and flexible substance' in a 'rich copious hospitable flow'.[27] And again, we wonder what happens to what is not 'of use', and how limited the hospitality might be. Swinton (and/or Whitman) goes on to argue that:

The immense diversity of race, temperament, character — the copious streams of humanity constantly flowing hither — must reappear in free, rich growths of speech. From no one ethnic source is America sprung: the electric reciprocations of many stocks conspired and conspire. This opulence of race-elements is in the theory of America. (p. 288)

I have suggested that Whitman's speech, at least, does not show much evidence of an opulence of race elements. Even if it gestures further in that direction than the language of other contemporary poets, it still falls short of its professions, both in the range of its vocabularies and in its grasp of the complexities of race and class relations. The reviewer for *The Critic* (1881) seems to capture exactly the essence of Whitman's inclusiveness:

He shows crudely the American way of incorporating into the language a handy or high-sounding word without elaborate examination of its original meaning, just as we absorb the different nationalities that crowd over from Europe. His thought and his mode of expression is immense, often flat, very often monotonous, like our great sprawling cities with their endless scattering of suburbs. (*Critical Heritage*, p. 185)

The incorporation, when it happens, is crude, without regard for original meanings, and presents its diverse elements as struggling for space within an infinitely expanding but basically uncoordinated 'suburb'. Whitman thus postulates, at the same time, both the power of language and its hospitable inclusiveness — a rhetorical tension that perfectly mirrors the hegemonic energy within the profession of democracy.

Returning once again to the local features of style, F. O. Matthiessen noted Whitman's habit of writing line after line of poetry without a main verb, as if he felt that 'his identification with the object made a verb unnecessary' (p. 571). If we think of the verb as that part of speech dramatizing agency, then it is also that which most clearly posits the separation of self from other. As such, it threatens to raise the question of responsibility. Its absence suggests a state of innocence, a world in which self and other are sympathetic, and in which behaviour has no critical consequences. Many nineteenth-century linguists enthused over the apparent absence of distinct verbal elements in the Amerindian languages, seeing these languages as expressive of paradisal integration, of a oneness with the world that their own culture had probably lost. Whitman's disinclination for main verbs may be interpreted in the same way: he seeks to minimize the importance of agency, while simultaneously asserting, as we have seen, the conquering powers of the American language. By declaring the conquest to be benevolent and synthesizing, he can maintain the identity of two positions that an inspection of the events of the nineteenth century must suggest as effectively very different.

Again, in noting Whitman's preference for metonymy over metaphor, Hollis (pp. 154—203) suggests a further way in which Whitman glosses over the questions that might be raised by an admission of the critical implications of agency. He argues that 'metonymy tends to remind us of what we already know; metaphor of what we do not know or had not thought of until that moment' (p. 203). Metonymy is thus less aggressive. It suits Whitman's democratic imperative, in that it is less prone than metaphor to surprise a reader into a posture of admiring subservience to a poet who might then seem to be something more than 'one of the roughs'. Not for nothing has criticism so often tended to measure the 'greatness' of a poet by the force and originality of his metaphors. On the other hand, the surprise element in metaphor can also invite a reader to ponder the act of comparing and relating two otherwise disparate things; and any close scrutiny of this process is likely to lead to judgements about the propriety of the comparison. Any literature or criticism that is at all anxious about the ethics of representation — what it means to think of a man as a wolf, for example — is going to pay special attention to metaphor as at once the most persuasive and assertive of all forms of comparison. Whitman's (relative) avoidance of metaphor is therefore also an avoidance of dealing with the problems of integration and difference of which it is the stylistic correlative and vehicle. Metonymy, or synecdoche, is the trope of self-sufficient independence: each person or thing is imaged by a part of attribute of himself. The worker is complemented by his tool or voice, not put into interactive tension with any other tool or voice. It is the poet's eye and mind that holds them together in a non-competitive series.

The principle of non-contradiction is carried over into the poet's imaging of himself. Just as there is no perceived need to judge between or discipline the different parts of the body politic, so the poet's own identity is allowed to remain multiform:

I know I am august,
I do not trouble my spirit to vindicate itself or be understood,
I see that the elementary laws never apologize,
I reckon I behave no prouder than the level I plant my house by after all.

(*1855*, p. 44)

Again:

Do I contradict myself?
Very well then .... I contradict myself;
I am large .... I contain multitudes.

(p. 85)[28]

Only when the 'other' is recognized as having different needs or interests
do we worry over the consequences of our actions or words; only when
it is admitted that there is a debate, and that our words might have a
persuasive effect within it, do we concern ourselves about not publishing
contradictions. Whitman's capacity to remain totally unaware of any
difference between self and other marks him out as the voice of manifest
destiny, and of the most confident period of nationalist enthusiasm.
Whitman's compliance with this ideological schema also makes him in
some sense its victim; for the acceptance of contradiction is also a covert
admission of the ineffectuality of the poet's language. It is hard not to
suspect that there is a level at which Whitman makes a virtue of
necessity.

Whitman is even less prone than most poets to search out philosophical
legitimations of his writings; and it is not surprising that, when he does
so, he turns to Hegel, who demonstrates how 'numberless apparent
failures and contradictions' are held together by 'a central and never-
broken unity' (PW, p. 608). But not for nothing have Lawrence and
others remarked that the true reconciler of contradictions can only be
death. The poet's 'vast similitude' (1891, p. 261) is occasionally explicit
about its ultimate locus beyond space and time; and it is not merely
impressionistic to suggest that the whole machinery of particularities that
Whitman puts forward in ostensible celebration of life is in fact most
coherent when regarded as premised upon death. The details of people
and things do not modify with time and place, in ways that might suggest
growth and development; instead, they go on being forever themselves,
each individual wedded to his attributes in a manner that is often
alliterative — the pedlar with his pack, the ploughman with his plough
(1855, p. 38—9) — and one suggesting not only the aptness but also the
inflexibility of the union of man and task. This is not the image of a
society constantly opening itself to new challenges and situations, so much
as one that reproduces its own pre-established forms on its members, and
on other minds and places. At the heart of Whitman's representation of
movement there is then a condition of near-reification. Those who are
themselves imprisoned within fixed occupational categories cannot be
expected to perceive the integrity of strange faces and other minds. Whitman can in this way be seen to celebrate a condition of alienation, and
to wish it upon others. Only the narrator, being nothing, can participate
polymorphously in everything. As Santayana noted, Whitman made 'the
initial and amorphous phase of society his ideal' in the face of the growing 'fixity of institutions' (Critical Heritage, p. 268). But the fixity
inevitably appears in the very features of the amorphous.

This leads us to a question that has preoccupied much of the critical
literature on Whitman: the apparent change of style in mid-career. In

1936, Rebecca Coy noticed that colloquialisms and Americanisms, as well as terms deriving from trade and manufacture, were less prominent in the poetry after 1865 than they had been before. Others have echoed this judgement, and most recently Hollis has investigated it quite thoroughly. He finds that the proportion of negatives is very high before 1860 and closer to the norm thereafter, a fact which he interprets as an abdication of the prophetic-aggressive stance (p. 127–8). After 1865, he finds that the incidence of finite verb elements approximately halves, while that of romance Latin words — traditionally the markers of 'polite' diction — approximately doubles (pp. 218–20). Dependence upon catalogues, upon metonymy, and upon the illocutionary mode also declines, and archaisms become more common.

Hollis does not claim scientific accuracy for his findings, but they are supportive of the insights of other scholars. How might we explain this change? The civil war must obviously figure largely in any hypothesis. It did not destroy Whitman's optimism, but it does seem to have led him to be more specific about what we might hope for, and how. He also came to admit the existence of divisions within an American society threatening by 1871 to remain 'materialistic and vulgar' (*PW*, p. 369), and certainly seeming to require that a choice be made about who is after all most representative and worthy of nurture — now the 'aggregate' of 'middling property owners' (p. 339). At the same time, even if *Specimen Days* (1882) seems to have the wisdom of too much hindsight, it does yet manage to assimilate the horror of the war into a vision of unanimity. Both the creation and the disbanding of the Union armies leave Whitman with a sense of 'the majesty and reality of the American people *en masse*' (*PW*, p. 442). One can imagine how the sight of thousands of men in the same uniform, all seeming to act as one within the rigid parameters of military discipline, might have appealed to him as an image of the unity of many in one; and once again, Whitman always presents the orderliness of the army as emanating from spontaneous morale rather than from discipline. No element of coercion is allowed to intrude; all results from the 'common consent' (*1891*, p. 281) of Manhattan's volunteers and others like them.

Drum Taps, the collection of poems that deals most explicitly with the war, is a complex volume. It is able to represent the tragedies of war without accommodating them to some positive vision, to give credit to the 'cold dirges of the baffled' that 'lull nobody' (*1891*, pp. 308, 323). In this respect, it is untypical of most of the rest of Whitman's poetry, though it too has its share of saving gestures.[29] But it does not herald the end of the poet's optimistic view of America's energies. 'Pioneers! O Pioneers!' (*1891*, p. 229) does not speak for a more complicated view of the westward migration than that articulated before the war, and Whitman continues to be enthusiastically swept up by the vehicular novelties of an age of rapid movement — trains, steamers, and so forth (*PW*, pp. 551 and 556, for example). His journey to the West shows him a landscape in which he sees the law of his own poems, an 'elemental abandon . . . entire absence of art, untrammel'd play of primitive Nature' (p. 565), a world that 'silently and broadly unfolded' for days on end (p. 575).

This recognition of the emptiness of the West as the law of his own poems is interesting. It is as if Whitman's epiphanies no longer come from the close rub and friction of other bodies in tight urban spaces but from the solitary contemplation (through a train window?) of an unpopulated sublime. One suspects here an admission of the emptiness that had perhaps always underpinned the poet's celebrations of human plenitude, and a recognition of the anatomy of alienation within his own 'social' personality. Certain later poems do confirm this. The opening of 'Prayer of Columbus' (1874), for example, reads more like Tennyson than the Whitman we have seen so far:

A batter'd, wreck'd old man,
Thrown on this savage shore, far, far from home,
Pent by the sea and dark rebellious brows, twelve dreary months,
Sore, stiff with many toils, sicken'd and nigh to death,
I take my way along the island's edge,
Venting a heavy heart.

(*1891*, p. 421)

The 'I' no longer leaps into a copulative posture, asserting its desire to be and become everything, but declares in appropriately involuted syntax its burdens of prior experience and self-consciousness. This is of course a dramatic monologue, but we must none the less sense the subversion of what the younger poet might have seen as the most joyous moment in history — the discovery of America. Often, in the later poems, Whitman's leaping lines are tamed into meditative cadences and soliloquies, his conclusions more and more focused on other-worldly moments. 'Passage to India' (1871) still celebrates the age of technology, and includes within it an extravagant hymn to the positive possibilities of trade and communication in bringing together all the nations of the earth. But the 'chanting' and 'caroling free' (*1891*, p. 418) that seems to present the poet at his old vocalizing best is somehow not the final voice of the poem. Fascinated by the way in which the journey westwards, into a 'future', must finally end in a return to the true and primal past, India, Whitman writes himself out of the centrifuge of earthly determinations, and into a realm 'where mariner has not yet dared to go' (p. 421). It is death that beckons, and beyond.

The rhetoric of this poem and others like it will probably remain more appealing, to those uncomfortable with the politics of expansive nationalism, than that of the earlier poetry. But the distinction is not by any means as complete as the apparent change in style might suggest. For what we have here is the other side of that same energy, now transformed into melancholia. The ethnocentrism is just as implacable as before, but quieter. India, for example, is nothing in itself. None of its own cultural complexities enter into the poem. It is an image, a symbol for a solitary reverie. There is one great common factor connecting the early poetry, with its endless lists of things, and those of the later poems (by no means all) that subsume all detail into a meditative continuum directed at a life beyond 'the rondure of the world at last accomplish'd' (p. 414): in neither case is there any admission of difference. In *Drum Taps*, and in some other poems where death and destruction are allowed to be simply what they are, we may trace the profile of a different voice. But it never emerged into majority. For the most part Whitman remains the poet of manifest destiny. If, as Swinton (and perhaps Whitman) wrote, the 'great tidal moments in a nation's life are repeated in great tidal moments in its language' (p. 11), then Whitman's language remains best suited for the songs of individual selves, each pretending to stand for others, whether actively or passively. Only the Civil War persuades it that it needs to register the clashing by night of different armies; and even then it does not linger long upon the disturbing implications. Whitman remains a powerful and a persuasive poet; all the more important, then, that we examine what it is that we are moved by, besides the sounds of the words he singing made.

(1986)

Notes

1 Justin Kaplan, *Walt Whitman: A Life* (New York: Simon & Schuster, 1980), p. 41.
2 D. H. Lawrence, *Studies in Classic American Literature* (1923; rpt New York and Harmondsworth: Penguin, 1977), pp. 182f.
3 Leadie M. Clark, *Walt Whitman's Concept of the American Common Man* (New York, 1955), pp. 20, 33.
4 Quentin Anderson, *The Imperial Self: An Essay in American Literary and Cultural History* (New York, 1971), pp. 92, 96.
5 F. O. Matthiessen, *American Renaissance: Art and Expression in the Age of Emerson and Whitman* (New York, London, Toronto: Oxford University Press, 1941), p. ix.
6 Milton Hindus (ed.), *Walt Whitman: The Critical Heritage* (London: Routledge & Kegan Paul, 1971), pp. 36, 39, 40.
7 See, for example, Matthiessen, op. cit.; Larzer Ziff, *Literary Democracy: The Declaration of Cultural Independence in America* (London and New York: Penguin, 1981), pp. 237, 251; and Allen Grossman, 'The poetics of union in Whitman and Lincoln: an inquiry toward the relationship of art and policy', in Walter Benn Michaels and Donald E. Pease (eds), *The American Renaissance Reconsidered. Selected Papers from the English Institute, 1982–83* (Baltimore and London: Johns Hopkins University Press, 1985), pp. 183–208.
8 *An American Primer. By Walt Whitman. With Facsimiles of the Original Manuscript*, ed. Horace Traubel (Boston: Small, Maynard & Co., 1904), p. 16.
9 *Walt Whitman's 'Leaves of Grass': The First (1855) Edition*, ed. Malcolm Cowley (1959; rpt London and New York: Penguin, 1981), p. 48. I shall be citing from this and two other editions of Whitman's writings: the 1891–2 edition, published as *Leaves of Grass*, ed. Sculley Bradley and Harold W. Blodgett (New York and London: Norton, 1973); and *The Portable Walt Whitman*, ed. Mark van Doren, rev. Malcolm Cowley (1974; rpt New York and London: Penguin, 1981). These three texts will be abbreviated, respectively, as *1855*, *1891*, and *PW*.
10 See, for example, Louise Pound, 'Walt Whitman and Italian music', *American Mercury*, no. 6 (September 1925), pp. 58–63; Matthiessen, op. cit., pp. 554–9;

and C. Carroll Hollis, *Language and Style in 'Leaves of Grass'* (Baton Rouge and London: Louisiana State University Press, 1983), pp. 1—27, for example. The illusion of voice in writing pretends to offer as sociable (conversation or address) what is in fact solitary (writing).

11 The poetics of this tradition is the subject of my *Irony and Authority in Romantic Poetry* (London: Macmillan, 1979).

12 Tony Tanner, *The Reign of Wonder: Naivety and Reality in American Literature* (1965; rpt Cambridge: Cambridge University Press, 1977), pp. 65—7, had previously discussed the importance of sight in Whitman's poetry.

13 Randall Jarrell, 'Walt Whitman: he had his nerve', *Kenyon Review*, 14 (1952). pp. 63—79, pp. 77—78.

14 For a fuller exploration of this topic, see my *The Politics of American English, 1776–1850* (New York and Oxford: Oxford University Press, 1986).

15 *The Works of Thomas Carlyle*, Centenary edn, 30 vols (London: Chapman & Hall, 1896—9), vol. 28, p. 39. Benjamin Lease, *Anglo-American Encounters: England and the Rise of American Literature* (Cambridge: Cambridge University Press, 1981), pp. 230—1, has argued for the formative influence of Carlyle upon Whitman.

16 On the conflation of the many and the one in Whitman's poetry, see Larzer Ziff, 'Whitman and the crowd', *Critical Inquiry*, 10 (1983—4), pp. 579—91.

17 Henry M. Goodwin, 'Thoughts, words and things', *Bibliotheca Sacra*, 6 (1849), p. 283.

18 *The Complete Works of Ralph Waldo Emerson*, Centenary edn, 12 vols (Boston and New York, 1903—4), vol. 2, p. 139.

19 Lois Ware, 'Poetic conventions in *Leaves of Grass*', *Studies in Philology*, 26 (1929), pp. 47—57; Rebecca Coy, 'A study of Whitman's diction', *University of Texas Studies in English*, 16 (1936), pp. 115—24, p. 124.

20 Louise Pound, 'Walt Whitman's neologisms', *American Mercury*, 4 (February 1925), pp. 199—200; 'Walt Whitman and the French language', *American Speech*, 1 (1925—6), pp. 421—30. Frank Murphy has however pointed out to me that many of the words Pound records as neologisms are to be found in Webster's 1828 dictionary, where they are specified as already in use.

21 See Simpson, op. cit., pp. 202—29.

22 Edward F. Grier (ed.), *The Eighteenth Presidency* (Lawrence, Kansas: University of Kansas Press, 1956), p. 27.

23 William K. Bottorff and Arthur L. Ford (eds), *The Works of Joel Barlow*, 2 vols (Gainesville, Fla: Scholars Facsimiles & Reprints, 1970), vol. 2, p. 344.

24 Joseph Jay Rubin, *The Historic Whitman* (University Park, Pa, and London, 1973), pp. 39—44.

25 Lawrence H. White (ed.), *Democratick Editorials: Essays in Jacksonian Political Economy by William Leggett* (Indianapolis: Liberty Press, 1984), p. 265.

26 'Slang in America', *North-American Review*, 141 (1885), pp. 431—5, p. 431.

27 William Swinton, *Rambles Among Words: Their Poetry, History and Wisdom* (New York: Scribners, 1859), p. 12. Anderson, op. cit., pp. 88—165, is astute on the subject of Whitman's preoccupation with metaphors of fluidity and emission.

28 Compare Emerson: 'With consistency a great soul has simply nothing to do. . . . To be great is to be misunderstood' (*Works*, vol. 2, pp. 57—8).

29 A fuller account than this might explore, for example, Whitman's reports of wounds and dismembered bodies in terms of the capacity of the synecdochic-metonymic mode for imaging the interchangeability of body parts: another rhetoric of potential identification.

11

Breakfast in America –
Uncle Tom's cultural histories

Rachel Bowlby

Quaker State I

Freedom ... American Style

IT'S the feeling you have when you get up in the morning and stand at an open window—the way you breathe in God's sunlight and fresh air. It's whistling before breakfast, disagreeing with the bank over your monthly statement, leaving a tip for the waitress if you feel like it.

It's working hard now with the idea of quitting someday. It's living where you like. It's looking forward with confidence —even while you willingly put up with gas rationing — to packing a lunch again and piling the family in the car for an outing.

It's keeping your car in condition against *that day.* It's realizing this is a nation on wheels that must be kept rolling—and that *your* wheels are part of all the wheels.

It's an oil company spending more money to make a better motor oil. It's giving that oil a brand name like Quaker State and being able to call it to your attention at a time like this, when your car needs extra care.

It's stating facts—that Quaker State is refined from Pennsylvania Grade Crude Oil; that it has won for itself, by its performance over the years, a reputation second to none in the field.

It's asking you to *try* Quaker State—in order to care for your car for your country in the best way possible. And, of course, it's your right to disregard this friendly advice if you feel so inclined. That's freedom— American style! Quaker State Oil Refining Corporation, Oil City, Pa.

OIL IS AMMUNITION—USE IT WISELY

© Quaker State Corporation 1944

This advertisement for motor oil as a symbol of the American way of life is one of the exhibits in Marshall McLuhan's 1951 study of American cultural myths, *The Mechanical Bride*.[1] The picture shows a pastoral idyll in the form of a country picnic whose everyday accessibility has been temporarily cut off by the demands of the wartime economy. It features that peculiarly twentieth-century peacetime institution: the two-parent, two-child, white 'nuclear family', possessed of at least one car and a pet, with their harmony troubled only, perhaps, by the presence of a flattened female golliwog in the foreground.[2] While Junior brings up the radio and the cat, the all-providing Mom holds up a plate of sandwiches for the genuflecting couple of pigtailed daughter and beaming Pop. It is he who figures in the text as doing what comes naturally, exercising the prerogatives of the vaunted 'Freedom . . . American Style': such rights — wittily analysed in McLuhan's commentary — as 'whistling before breakfast', or having a fight with the bank manager.

The ad does not specify whether any freedom is American; whether only American freedom is freedom; whether all Americans are free; whether freedom is manifested by any one or only the sum of the actions and feelings enumerated as its predicates ('It's . . . It's . . . It's . . .'). Halfway through, there is a shift from the address to 'you' as exerciser of American freedom to the personification of that freedom in the form of a particular type of oil company (one that spends for America, like a good consuming citizen). This move is made possible by the intermediate paragraph establishing identifications between the free individual, his motor, and the nation as a nation of (not on) wheels. Although the text ends up once more appealing to the individual and his 'right' to disregard its 'friendly advice', it has meantime deprived him of his supposed autonomy by transforming it into an automatic duty, making him just a cog in the national machine: 'Your wheels are part of all the wheels'. It becomes difficult to determine whether this motoring man 'of parts' is free to choose or bound to buy: in what sense he is 'subject' (master or slave) to the wheeler-dealer ethos of the nation.

Cultural histories of the United States have different stories to tell about twentieth-century 'Freedom . . . American Style', which is often linked to some notion of a consumer society: America as *the* consumer society; global consumerism as the Americanization of the world. This may be read as America's destiny, or its fatal flaw, or both. Either the consumer dream is the fulfillment, potential or actual, of the democratic and economic freedom advocated at the start of the American state and achieved through the extension of the good life to more and more participants; or the authentic dream of the pioneers has become a super-market, turning into a weakly degraded artifice and simulation of itself. Either it is the real thing, finally delivered, or it is a fake, in which case it is all the more insidious for looking like exactly that freedom of which it is in fact the opposite.

The American Topsy

Probably the most famous nineteenth-century advertisement for 'Freedom . . . American Style' also includes a representation of a 'Quaker State', to which we shall return. It also raises many of the issues about the terms of American freedom which are sketched out in the ad for motor oil, and all the more significantly for its enormous influence.

In 1863, not long before Abolition, Abraham Lincoln called Harriet Beecher Stowe 'the little woman who made this big war'.[3] Apart from its acknowledged effects in provoking anti-slavery sentiment, *Uncle Tom's Cabin* has a leading place in publishing history: it was the first novel anywhere in the world to sell a million, appearing (in 1852) at the start of a decade in which the proliferation of bestsellers written by women has entitled it to be dubbed — with an ambivalence that is not unrelated to readings of its political significance — 'the feminine fifties'.[4] Stowe herself claimed, in a period when authors were alive and well, that 'God wrote it'; be this as it may, the novel that bears her name has continued to hold a crucial place, or places, in American popular mythology. For all these reasons, *Uncle Tom* has continued to be the object of heated critical debates, concerning both its literary stature, and the terms in which that might be established, and the interpretation of its various theories of American freedom.

There is at least one point where the novel anticipates just such questions about the interpretation of the text of American history:

> Topsy, who had stood like a black statue during the discussion, with hands decently folded, now, at a sign from Miss Ophelia, went on:
> 'Our first parents, being left to the freedom of their own will, fell from the state wherein they were created.'
> Topsy's eyes twinkled, and she looked inquiringly.
> 'What is it, Topsy?' said Miss Ophelia.
> 'Please, Missis, was dat ar state Kintuck?'
> 'What state, Topsy?'
> 'Dat state dey fell out of. I used to hear Mas'r tell how we came down from Kintuck.'
> St Clare laughed.
> 'You'll have to give her a meaning, or she'll make one,' said he.
> 'There seems to be a theory of emigration suggested there.' (20, p. 368)

Topsy's 'theory of emigration' itself goes some way from Miss Ophelia's prescribed text, and the questions 'suggested' by it are problems about the definition of a 'state' — be it of nature, innocence, or grace, be it 'Kintuck' or the amalgamated USA. Whatever the state of soul or nation, and whoever may be identified by Topsy's (or St Clare's) 'we', coming 'down' suggests some kind of decline. Not a moral decline for Topsy, who merely repeats her master's words, without interpreting them. Topsy must be given a meaning; and it could be said that Stowe's novel is the attempt to provide it.

Topsy's innocent or knowing questions reflect the novel's ambivalence in supplying answers to questions about the present state of America: whether, like Topsy, it just 'grow'd' (20, p. 356); whether its development should be interpreted as the fall from a state of natural goodness to a state of evil and corruption; or from a state of freedom to a state of slavery; whether it should be read as many states like 'Kintuck', or as just one state, or as a combination of, and perhaps a conflict between, those that are free states and those that are slave states. The 'theory of emigration' might refer to a movement from a place of origin and purity to a place of division and alienation; or it might refer to a movement towards a 'promised land' of arrival, the recovery or discovery of a new state of harmony. These questions are at once theological, political, and personal: Stowe's theories about the progress or decline of America reveal parallel question about the progress and decline of persons. In struggling with issues of identity and development on all these levels, the novel finds itself embroiled in complications of regional, racial, and sexual differences and the question of whether they are natural — God-given — or variable.

This is nowhere clearer than in the case of Topsy herself. She is set up in contrast to St Clare's daughter Little Eva, whose tearjerker death scene is one of the most famous episodes of the book. This contrast is made initially in racial terms:

> There stood the two children representatives of the two extremes of society. The fair, high-bred child, with her golden head, her deep eyes, her spiritual, noble brow, and prince-like movements; and her black, keen, subtle, cringing, yet acute neighbor. They stood the representatives of their races. The Saxon, born of ages of cultivation, command, education, physical and moral eminence; the Afric, born of ages of submission, ignorance, toil and vice! (20, pp. 361—2)

In marking the racial difference as social ('representatives of the two extremes of society . . . representatives of their races'), this passage avoids ascribing to all the characteristics that follow the visual opposition of 'fair' and 'dark' any natural or necessary consequences. And this is the overt force of Stowe's anti-slavery argument: to disprove the distinctions made by whites on the ground of race in favour of an appeal to a common humanity rooted in the Christian heart.

On this basis, the developments of Topsy and Eva should follow a similar pattern if they are exposed to the same 'cultivation' and 'education'. But it turns out that the raw, or human material is not the same. Topsy is introduced as a present from St Clare, the easygoing New Orleans slaveholder, to his New England cousin, Miss Ophelia, who has already evinced her disapproval of southern ways: the child will be 'a fresh-caught specimen' (20, p. 353), 'For you to educate' (20, p. 352): 'You find virgin soil there, Cousin; put in your own ideas — you won't find many to pull up' (20, p. 357).

Topsy's 'ideas' are to be introduced from outside by the agency of Miss Ophelia; at the start, she is seen as an open field for civilized cultivation or colonization. But where Topsy is 'virgin soil', a neutral territory yet to be sown with humanizing plants, Eva is a fully formed moral being from the beginning: 'A child's thoughts are rather dim, undefined instincts; and in Eva's noble nature many such were yearning and working, for which she had no power of utterance' (20, p. 362). Where Topsy has no meaning to attach to her words ('You'll have to give her a meaning, or she'll make one'), Eva does not have the words to express a meaning already there. She is already a grown plant, with a natural affinity to the Bible: 'her own earnest nature threw out its tendrils, and wound itself around the majestic book' (22, p. 380). Eva is also inviolable, unlike virgin soil: 'Evil rolls off Eva's mind like dew off a cabbage-leaf, — not a drop sinks in' (20, p. 365). Her incorruptible integrity automatically gives her the means to make immediate moral distinctions: where 'evil' leaves her untouched, stories of unjust suffering are directly incorporated: 'These things sink into my heart' (29, pp. 326, 347).

Topsy neither has this receptive heart nor readily acquires it, in the view of her appointed instructor. What she does is to pose a challenge to what, in the case of Little Eva, is assumed to be the natural bond between the meaning and its expression, or between the 'instincts' and their potential 'utterance'. She is like 'a parrot' (20, p. 369), with a 'talent . . . for . . . mimicry' (20, p. 364), repeating what she has heard to the letter, as in her open-ended 'theory of emigration'. When called upon to admit to a forbidden deed, she obeys by admitting it irrespective of whether she did it ('Why, Missis said I must 'fess' (20, p. 361)), thus suggesting that it is the obligation to make a confession which produces the verbal expression of guilt and not the guilt itself which comes first and is then put into words.

The most famous examples of Topsy's disturbance of the yokings of theories to meanings for those around her occur when she fails to come up with the expected answers to questions about her origins. Asked the identity of her mother and her birthplace, she does not say she does not know them, but that she 'Never had none!' and 'Never was born!' (20, p. 355). Asked to say who made her, she replies: 'Nobody, as I knows on . . . I spect I grow'd' (20, p. 356). Topsy consistently refuses to supply answers of the type expected, taking the questions literally and thereby showing up the conventionality of the responses habitually attached to them: that children can vouch for having been 'born' to, and 'made' by, particular mothers and divinities.

In the differences between Topsy and Eva, *Uncle Tom's Cabin* shows two irreconcilable theories of what 'makes' a human being. The question comes down to whether the child is born (or 'grow'd') with a 'heart', with a Christian disposition already in place, or whether it is born as 'virgin soil', ready to take (or not take) the impression of whatever cultivation is subsequently planted in it. The novel deals with its dilemma by making Topsy eventually respond to the goodness of Eva, who declares her love for the other child and elicits from her the 'tears' which are always taken to signify the expression of genuine human feeling: 'Yes, in that moment, a ray of real belief, a ray of heavenly love, had penetrated the darkness of her heathen soul!' (25, p. 410). But this resolution only works by reaffirming the initial difference between the two. Topsy has to be 'penetrated' by the 'heavenly love' that comes from Eva's nature, and the 'ray' that lightens the 'darkness' makes natural the opposition of 'fair' and 'dark' which was earlier represented as an effect of differing cultural heritage.

The American mother

Topsy's questioning of the question about her mother points to one of the major categories through which the case against slavery is 'made' in the novel. *Uncle Tom's Cabin* is replete with mothers — mostly absent and always significant. Time and again, the reader is presented with a harrowing account of some unregenerate slavedealer or overseer, only to find out that far from being an outright villain he is somewhere troubled by the image of a saintly mother dissuading him from evil, immoral ways. The most striking example of this is the overseer Simon Legree who, unlike most of the other characters similarly afflicted, does not ever repent or change his ways; he is haunted, none the less, by the figure of feminine purity who — like Uncle Tom when he beats him — warns or reminds him of the Christian virtues he has repudiated. Mothers, nature, tears, and human sympathy are intimately associated, and the sight of the mother lets her goodness shine through: 'hers was just the face and form that made "mother" seem the most natural word in the world' (13, p. 216).

There is however one mother in the novel who is seriously disruptive to this overall picture. This is Marie St Clare, the mother of Little Eva. Far from being a figure of maternal virtue and benevolence, Marie is presented as the exact inversion of that image:

> Marie had never possessed much capability of affection or much sensibility, and the little that she had had been merged into a most intense and unconscious selfishness. . . . It is a great mistake to suppose that a woman with no heart will be an easy creditor in the exchange of affection. (15, p. 242)

From the outset, Marie's 'sick headaches' and other ailments are represented as necessarily illusory. She masquerades as the good mother she clearly is not. As 'a woman with no heart', Marie is by nature incapable of true maternal feelings. Her protestations of motherly love after her daughter's death, though verbally indistinguishable from the genuine article, are represented as manifestly deceitful covers for her basic lack. Instead of being read as evidence of true feelings, they are read as the simulation of that evidence.

Marie's falseness is also indicated through its difference from the true womanliness of Eva's 'Mammy', of Augustine's saintly mother ('*she* was *divine*!' (19, p. 333)), and of her husband's former fiancée, 'a high-minded and beautiful woman' (15, p. 240). She enters the scene expressly as compensation for the loss of this first love, and the non-attribution to her of womanly qualities is made in this light: 'Had his wife been a whole woman, she might yet have done something — as woman can — to mend the broken threads of life' (15, p. 241). The place of 'woman' is to mend the threads broken by the man's separation from another woman: the loss of the 'whole' in the form of a 'woman' already renders second-rate the repair work of even the true woman Marie is not.

Marie's unfeminine nature is also distinguished from that of St Clare himself. like Uncle Tom and like George Shelby who cries after Tom's death, Augustine represents the properly 'feminine' man:

> In childhood, he was remarkable for an extreme and marked sensitiveness of character, more akin to the softness of women than the ordinary hardness of his own sex. Time, however, overgrew this softness with the rough bark of manhood, and but few knew how living and fresh it still lay at the core. (15, p. 239)

Augustine has an original femininity overlaid by the contrasting qualities of a 'manhood' which supplants it on the surface. But 'at the core' he remains more 'akin' to a woman than his wife. In both cases, the external signs are to be given a meaning different to their conventional one. With Augustine, the outward manly attributes hide an inner 'sensitiveness'; in Marie, the signs of femininity mean there is none. Femaleness is not the criterion, then, of the manifestation of those traits of (good) femininity which are also shared by the best of men.

That the bad mother is not a one-off monstrosity or a corrupt version of a once pure nature is made clear by the sentence which both damns Marie as heartless and generalizes her as a type: 'It is a great mistake to suppose that a woman with no heart will be an easy creditor in the exchange of affection'. In *The Key to Uncle Tom's Cabin*, Stowe's own explanation of the novel, published in 1853 in the wake of the book's unprecedented sales and popularity, she describes Marie St Clare as 'the type of a class of women not peculiar to any latitude, nor any condition of society'.[5] Countering the predicted accusation that her portrait of Marie expresses the anti-southern prejudice of a Miss Ophelia, she declares: 'Human nature is no worse at the South than at the North, but law at the South distinctly provides for and protects the worst abuses to which that nature is liable.'[6]

This statement not only extends the case of Marie to 'human nature' in general, but also makes problematic the status of law and the possibility of separating its 'southern' fostering of 'abuses' from its 'northern' protection of 'freedom'. Undercutting the originary status of the good mother, Marie's nature is thus a natural abuse of nature.[7] Not only is it a matter of exact opposites, the good and bad woman both rooted in a given 'nature'; but the goodness commonly accepted as natural can itself come to be represented as only the surface appearance covering a femininity that is basically evil and violent. St Clare: 'Tell me of the lovely rule of woman! I never saw above a dozen women that wouldn't half kill a horse, or a servant, either, if they had their own way with them! — let alone a man' (25, p. 407).

The human commodity

The language of Marie St Clare's introduction in the narrative is also significant, specifying her as 'a fine figure, a pair of bright dark eyes, and a hundred dollars' (15, p. 240). This listing of separable attributes puts Marie in the same category as the lavish furnishings of the St Clare establishment of which the newly arrived Miss Ophelia takes a rapid mental 'inventory' (15, p. 258). It makes her, in other words, equivalent to a purchasable article and such a description reinforces the narrative insistence that she is not 'a whole woman' (15, p. 241) integrated by the possession of a heart.

In an earlier chapter, while Augustine St Clare is travelling south with his daughter and engaged in purchasing Uncle Tom, he considers the ethics of slavery by speculating with the dealer about his own marketability;

> I wonder, now, if I was divided up and inventoried . . . how much I might bring. Say so much for the shape of my head, so much for a high forehead, so much for arms, and hands, and legs, and then so much for education, learning, talent, honesty, religion! (14, p. 237)

Particularized, marketable qualities make, in the novel's terms, not a human being but a commodity, and it is on the rejection of just such labelling that the argument against slavery depends: 'They buy 'em and sell 'em and make trade of their heart's blood' (17, p. 291). In the case of Marie, though, the commodity description is taken to be adequate. The lack of a 'heart' is what makes her different from the good woman in relation to whom she represents only a debased substitute in the St Clare family. The hearts of George and Tom are converted to and misrepresented as the properties accessible to trade, but Marie has no such heart in the first place. At the same time, she stands condemned as not 'a whole woman': '"Hang the woman!" said St Clare, mentally' (15, p. 258).

The novel thus endorses as equally natural both good and bad femininity, and both the 'heart' and the 'commodity' views of humanity, while its claim for the insupportability of 'the peculiar institution' is grounded in the priority of the good Christian mother and the sympathetic human heart.[8] And indeed when it is stated that the heartless Marie should not be expected to 'be an easy creditor in the exchange of affection' (15, p. 242), the implication is that there is no pure love, outside the terms of buying and selling.

Feminization American style

The differences between good and bad, superficial and genuine femininity are seriously troubled in this structure which attributes naturalness to either side of the two polarities. It would seem that the novel, in making its argument in terms of both sides — by appealing to the 'good' Christian woman and to her false, but equally natural counterpart or inversion, both substantiates and undermines readings which take as their starting point either position.

Recently, critical debate has indeed turned towards a questioning of the status of 'femininity' in Stowe's text. Ann Douglas's *The Feminization of American Culture* (1976) takes *Uncle Tom's Cabin* as paradigmatic of what she identifies as a decline in the qualities of American culture and literature.[9] In religious terms, this is represented by a move away from a morally forceful Calvinism to the sloppiness of the humanistic cult of 'gentle Jesus'; in literary terms, it is the difference between the resisting strength of male writers like Melville, Hawthorne, and Poe, and the second-rate, stereotypical output of the sentimental female bestsellers. The 'feminization' of the mid-nineteenth century marks for Douglas the beginnings of the artificial, consumerist society of the modern period which spells the ruin of the authentic, critical creativity of earlier American culture. Such a descent from a state of genuine endeavour leads to the 'fakery' (p. 12) of the sentimental style — all tears and no substance, and all the more insidious for resembling outwardly the real thing of which it is only a debased imitation. Douglas thus traces a story of the corruption of a pure origin, gendered in the form of a sliding away from tough masculinity to its feminine trivialization: hers is a 'good origins, bad ends' tale of the fatal decline of critical American values under the impact of mass culture.

It is with this aspect of her argument that Jane Tompkins takes issue, in an article entitled 'Sentimental power: *Uncle Tom's Cabin* and the politics of literary history'.[10] For Tompkins, Douglas misrepresents the significance of all those characteristics of sentimental fiction which she dismisses as 'trash': the emotional power of tears, the ethic of self-sacrifice, the angelic mothers and innocent little girls — all of which are epitomized in *Uncle Tom* by the death of Little Eva. Reconstructing the ideological context into which Stowe's novel was inserted, Tompkins shows how it could come about that the novel meant so much to its readers, contributing to the outbreak of the civil war and eventually to the abolition of slavery. Tompkins is not interested in the worthlessness or otherwise of the consumer culture of which Douglas sees a harbinger in *Uncle Tom*. Her argument is that those textual values which Douglas regards as artificial and symptomatic of the loss of national 'toughness' (p. 18) are in fact to be valorized as offering radical and progressive criticisms and alternatives in relation to an unsatisfactory present society.

Tompkins adopts wholesale the identification of morality with a (good) femininity attributed by extension to all victims and honest reformers. She perceives authentic intimations of a matriarchal civilization which would be the good nature presently buried or violently repressed by the patriarchal institutions of which slavery is one of the foremost. It is on this basis that she is able to claim that the abolition of slavery was not the ultimate aim of *Uncle Tom*: 'The new matriarchy ... constitutes the most politically subversive dimension of Stowe's novel, more disruptive and far-reaching in its potential consequences than even the starting of war or the freeing of slaves' (p. 98). The nature of the good, virtuous mother is the starting point for the spread by 'influence' of the new society where 'moral suasion will take the place of force' (p. 97).

This recovery or uncovering of an inherent goodness rooted in femininity and specifically in maternity is absolutely different from Douglas's narrative of the descent of American culture into a state of passive femininity imposed from outside. Tompkins's reading follows the rationale of the novel's attempted valorization of feminine purity; Douglas, while acknowledging its 'masterful' qualities (p. 295), sees rather what makes it a forerunner of Stowe's subsequent novels of the fashionable life of feminine superficiality. Far from anticipating the matriarchal 'mission' that Tompkins finds adumbrated in the novel, it is to be read as foreshadowing the commercialized America of 'a perpetual Mothers' Day' (p. 5), a 'manufactured utopia' (p. 79). Douglas's own siting of the authenticity from which sentimental feminine culture represents a deviation or a false direction is variously suggested as Calvinist theology and sermonizing, or (in literary terms) as a Byronic romanticism whose critical thrust is precariously maintained by certain male contemporaries of the sentimentalists. Words like 'saccharine' (p. 3) and 'rancid' (pp. 307, 309) are sprinkled through the text to indicate the general unwholesomeness — both artificiality and disease — manifested by the 'sentimentalism' expressly distinguished from 'genuine sensibility' (p. 307). It is a poor, substitute food or dose which can do no good to its duped consumers. This is a nostalgic view founded on the assertion of 'what has been lost: theology, feminism, and romanticism' (p. 305), 'feminism' here representing the possibility of women's admission to the sturdy masculine culture from which an unnatural 'feminization' disqualifies them, as well as weakening the foundations of culture in general. Following the 'heart to commodity' logic whereby a pure substance is transformed into a false substitute which looks the same but is only a fake, and whereby humanity is travestied in the commodity, Douglas glosses what she identifies as this process of 'feminization' as 'the commercialization of the inner life' (p. 308).

Both Tompkins and Douglas maintain that literary quality is related to social criticism. Their disagreement is over the criteria according to which this should be established. Douglas holds to standards of critical independence, whereby literature would naturally be opposed to the norms of a culture of sentimental 'kitsch'. The 'romantic impulse . . . involves a genuinely political and historical sense' (p. 308); and the difference between romanticism and sentimentalism can be tested in a simple way by deciding whether, like rancid butter, the language has 'gone bad' (p. 308). Tompkins rates literature according to a power for radical political persuasion. Against the 'modernist literary aesthetic' (p. 84) she criticizes as ahistorical in Douglas's system of values, Tompkins argues for the historical relativity of textual conventions. But the opposition of the aesthetic and the political (as seen from Tompkins's side) or of the properly contestatory and the banal (as seen from Douglas's) is structured around a fundamental consensus as to the possibility and desirability of determining what is truly critical literature.

For Tompkins, false values are located not in sentimental categories but in those criteria she identifies as the norms of subsequent literary evaluation and universalization 'determining the currently sanctified American classics' (p. 84):

I will ask the reader to set aside some familiar categories for evaluating fiction — stylistic intricacy, psychological subtlety, epistemological complexity — and to see the sentimental novel, not as an artifice of eternity answerable to certain formal criteria and to certain philosophical and psychological concerns, but as a political enterprise halfway between sermon and social theory, that both codifies and attempts to mold the values of its time. (pp. 84—5)

This exhortation positions the contemporary reader as bound within the false religion of the 'sanctified' categories of 'the modernist literary aesthetic' (p. 84) and calls for a conversion to the different interpretative criteria which this aesthetic is said to exclude and preclude. Tompkins's appeal to her readers, claiming the historical relativity ('currently sanctified') of a contemporary received idea that does not do justice to questions thereby overlooked, is thus identical in form to what she analyses as Stowe's appeal to hers: 'Stories like the death of Little Eva . . . enact . . . a *theory* of power in which the ordinary or "commonsense" view of what is efficacious and what is not (a view to which most modern critics are committed) is simply reversed' (p. 85). In the same way that Douglas deplores the false rhetoric of sentimental fiction, and in the same way that *Uncle Tom's Cabin* decries the false biblical rhetoric of religious defences of slavery, Tompkins argues for the superiority of sentimental novels by criticizing the speciousness of the fake theology of the modernism to which the reader pays lip-service.

The structure of mutual dependence in the figure of good and bad femininity is thus repeated in the dispute between Douglas and Tompkins about what constitutes good and bad literature. Douglas advocates the genuine critical capacities of the Romantics who preceded and the contemporary writers who opposed sentimentalism, Tompkins the equally genuine critical capacities of sentimentalism itself. While agreeing that social criticism is the mark of great literature, the two positions are exact inversions of each other. Each sees as surface rhetoric what the other valorizes as genuine.

Quaker State II

Tompkins exhibits as the keystone of her argument the chapter called 'The Quaker Settlement', featuring the making of breakfast in an exemplary household based on Stowe's travels in Ohio.[11] She takes it to signify or anticipate a kind of world revolution from the kitchen out:

The novel's deepest political aspirations are expressed only secondarily in its devastating attack on the slave system. . . . Embedded in the world of *Uncle Tom's Cabin*, which is the fallen world of slavery, there appears an idyllic picture, both utopian and Arcadian, of the form human life would assume if Stowe's readers were to heed her moral lesson. The home is the center of all meaningful activity, women perform the most important tasks, work is carried on in a spirit of mutual cooperation, and the whole is guided by a Christian woman who, through the influence of her 'loving words,' 'gentle moralities,' and 'motherly loving kindness,' rules the world. (p. 97)

The epitome of such a radical transformation is provided by the marginal spectacle of Simeon Halliday shaving in front of a mirror while everyone else prepares breakfast. Stowe calls this 'the anti-patriarchal operation of shaving' (13, p. 223); Tompkins takes off on a flight of prophetic exegesis:

> With this detail, so innocently placed, Stowe reconceives the role of men in human history: while Negroes, children, mothers, and grandmothers do the world's primary work, men groom themselves contentedly in a corner. . . . The import, as critics have failed to notice, is world-shaking. (p. 100)

What critics have managed to notice in this scene has indeed been less than 'world-shaking'. E. Bruce Kirkham, for instance, sees its significance simply in terms of thematic alternation:

> The kindly Halliday family was easy to portray with its quaint speech, its men in . . . 'shirt-sleeves,' . . . and its big breakfasts. After Haley and slave sales and suicides, these pleasant, quiet Quakers were a welcome interlude for both reader and author.[12]

The pastoral episode is here an 'interlude', as in conventional epic structure: a retreat or return to an idealized world represented as a holiday with the Hallidays for the reader tortured by too much unrelenting exposure to the horrors of slavery. A different response to Tompkins's claims would ask further how a world whose 'primary work' was done by 'Negroes, children, mothers, and grandmothers' would represent an alternative to the *status quo*, other than in the form of its positive valorization. If this is the buried, earthshaking politics of *Uncle Tom's Cabin*, its disturbing effect lies less in its difference from than in its point-for-point correspondence to what it turns upside down.

Tompkins does not limit the case to Stowe's first and best-known novel. She goes on to write in equally laudatory language of the domestic manual subsequently published by Stowe and her sister Catherine Beecher under the title *The American Woman's Home* (1869). This is precisely the kind of proto-consumerist text criticized in Douglas's book; and Tompkins, responding to this, confidently protests:

> The imperialistic drive behind the encyclopaedism and determined practicality of this household manual flatly contradict the traditional derogation of the American cult of domesticity as a 'mirror-phenomenon,' 'self-immersed' and 'self-congratulatory.'
> *The American Woman's Home* is a blueprint for colonizing the world

in the name of the 'family state' under the leadership of Christian women. (p. 99)

Tompkins apparently subscribes, wholeheartedly, to the 'imperialistic drive' and colonization scheme as if they accorded fully with the positive implications of her earlier opposition between 'suasion' and 'force'. But it is not easy to see how the imperialism of the domesticating 'mission' is to be distinguished — other than by an arbitrary assertion that one is good and the other bad — from other nineteenth-century projects to colonize the world usually characterized as anything but anti-patriarchal. As with Marie St Clare and her motherly counterparts, it is a matter of a difference maintained only on the basis of the claim to an underlying goodness: matriarchal and patriarchal missions and emigrations will follow the same ambiguous paths.

In Douglas's sense, 'feminization' implies a decline of American culture. Where a passive, narcissistic consumer attitude is contrasted with the tough, pioneering outlook of the past, 'feminization' means making men into the 'women' that society has made women all along. But in Tompkins's affirmative narrative of cultural change, the nurturing, anti-bellicose qualities associated with maternal femininity become the measure of how far the good and genuine values have developed, how much progress has been achieved by motherly 'influence'.

The contrast can be made more forcibly — or more (per)suasively — by asking how Tompkins' Quaker State compares with the image of the advertisement for Quaker State motor oil. All good things flow from the mother in McLuhan's advertisement, and she is an object of veneration to those around her. This goodness can at the same time be seen as the high point of the artifice of an image selling not matriarchy but motor oil, and offered as a nostalgic substitute for the man at the wheel, or for a nation of wheels and at war which prefers to see itself back in the benign state of nature in which it imagines it was born.

The birth of a nation

Like literature, femininity is either fake or real, evil or good; feminization is either a descent from a pure origin or a progression towards a redemptive end. But it is impossible to make a decision between the two versions, both of which are constituted on the model of a possible good and healthy state, whether lost or yet to be found, and neither of which is univocally underwritten by the text. *Uncle Tom's Cabin* holds in regard to its narrative of American freedom the same ambivalence that comes to the fore in the contradictory status of feminine nature in the text. In a reversal of the customary nineteenth-century image of Africa as the 'dark continent', America itself becomes 'that dark land to which fugitives fear to return' (43, p. 606). The last chapters appear to acknowledge that America cannot accommodate all its sons, and that the 'heart' will fail to constitute a sufficient basis for freedom. The former slave George Harris, having made his individual 'declaration of independence' (17, p. 298), eventually makes plans to depart for the new African state of Liberia, 'having no wish to pass for an American or to identify myself with them' (43, p. 608). His own 'theory of emigration' leaves the existing state of America behind and takes to the new country something else: 'In these days, a nation is born in a day. A nation starts, now, with all the great problems of republican life and civilization wrought out to its hand; it has not to discover, but only to apply' (43, p. 603).

The novel attempts to resolve its conflicting representations of the natures of persons and peoples by making a clean break and starting over in a new place. But it has already thrown doubt upon the practicability of the model according to which precepts are thought to be simply applicable to an innocent nature, whether psychic or territorial. Etymologically, both 'nature' and 'nation' come from the past participle of the Latin verb *nasci*, 'to be born'. Here, the principles of the nation are to be transported and applied to supposedly virgin soil, just as Topsy was supposed to 'take' the cultivation implanted in her — but didn't. Topsy refused to accept that she was ever born, and *Uncle Tom's Cabin* leaves it uncertain whether a nation, any more than a child, might have had such a pure beginning, except as a retrospective construction: a nation can only imagine it *was* born.

It is as if Stowe ends by recognizing the impossibility of mending the broken threads and making America whole, or whole again, by the influence of maternal Christian love. Her 'Concluding Remarks' to the novel return to the problem of slavery at home and to those supposed to give birth its futures. She appeals to the sympathies of 'Mothers of America' (pp. 624—5), but this is almost immediately followed by an assertion turning this on its head: 'If the mothers of the free states had all felt as they should, in times past, the sons of the free states would not have been the holders, and, proverbially, the hardest masters of slaves' (p. 624). In holding the mothers responsible for the social injustices of 'times past', Stowe also invalidates the very premise on which the accusation is based. 'As they should' admits that they might not, and did not, and shifts the determinations of what they 'all felt', so that maternal behaviour is now the response to a social injunction rather than the spontaneous accompaniment to the bearing of sons. Maternal feelings and motherhood are thus separate issues, and their separateness immediately abolishes the natural basis of goodness. The call to 'Mothers of America' only repeats this contradiction, acknowledging that mothers may fail to deliver the goods by the very fact of demanding that they do. With femininity as with race, it is only with its sunny, or 'fair' side up that 'Freedom . . . American Style' can be enjoyed.

(1986)

Notes

1 Marshall McLuhan, *The Mechanical Bride: Folklore of Industrial Man* (1951; rpt Boston, Mass.: Beacon Press, 1967), p. 116.
2 Or perhaps by the curious footnote: 'Oil is Ammunition — Use it Wisely'. The phrase seems at first sight to fit in with a theory of the complicity between

the domestic idyll and international aggression; but it could also be read as a reminder of the possibility of using the personal supply of ammunition on targets closer to home, albeit 'wisely' selected.

3 Quoted, e.g., in Ann Douglas's introduction to the Penguin edition of the novel (Harmondsworth: Penguin, 1981), p. 19. Page references to *Uncle Tom's Cabin* appearing in the text will be from this edition, preceded by chapter numbers.

Philip Fisher has recently described *Uncle Tom* as 'perhaps the single most effective political work of art in the history of literature' (*Hard Facts: Setting and Form in the American Novel* (New York: Oxford University Press 1985), p. 182).

4 The phrase was coined by Fred Lewis Pattee in the title of his book, *The Feminine Fifties*. See further Nina Baym, *Woman's Fiction: A Guide to Novels by and about Women in America, 1820–1870* (Ithaca, NY: Cornell University Press, 1978).

5 Harriet Beecher Stowe, *The Key to Uncle Tom's Cabin* (London: Clarke, Beeton, 1853), p. 57.

6 ibid.

7 Far from finding this problematic, one recent critic feels moved to endorse its truth to life. In *'Uncle Tom's Cabin' and American Culture* (Dallas, Tex.: Southern Methodist University Press, 1985), Thomas F. Gossett states that the description of Marie is not 'slander' but drawn 'from human nature in general', and then announces with all the ingenuousness of one who has made a new discovery: 'The cult of the noble woman in nineteenth-century literature sometimes had a curious corollary. When a woman is bad, she is horrid' (p. 131).

8 A similar double bind, which might be summarized by the formula 'get yourself a heart but have it in the first place anyway', is to be found in another staple of American popular reading from the somewhat different field of self-help psychology. On p. 228 of what claims to be the 'first cheap edition' of Dale Carnegie's *How to Win Friends and Influence People* (Kingswood, Surrey: Cedar Books, 1953), appears the following:

> Another word of warning. I know from experience that some men . . . will try to use [this] psychology mechanically. They will try to boost the other man's ego, not through genuine, real appreciation, but through flattery and insincerity. And their technique won't work. . . . Let me repeat: the principles taught in this book will work only when they come from the heart.

It is the Topsy/Eva dilemma again: either you have the heart already (in which case no need for the principles), or you must be given the principles (but they will remain a mechanical, insincere technique).

9 Ann Douglas, *The Feminization of American Culture* (1977; rpt New York: Discus, 1978). Quotations included in the text are from this edition.

10 Jane P. Tompkins, 'Sentimental power: *Uncle Tom's Cabin* and the politics of literary history', in Elaine Showalter (ed.), *The New Feminist Criticism: Essays on Women, Literature and Theory* (London: Virago, 1986), pp. 81–104. Citations in the text will be taken from this edition; the article first appeared in *Glyph*, 8 (1981), pp. 79–102, and has also been reprinted in Jane Tompkins, *Sensational Designs: The Cultural Work of American Fiction 1790–1860* (New York: Oxford University Press, 1985), pp. 122–46.

11 Stowe seems to have been particularly interested in the possibilities of breakfast. In her *Sunny Memories of Foreign Lands* (London: Sampson Low, 1854), she reports on one of its English manifestations:

Looking around the table, and seeing how everybody seemed to be enjoy-ing themselves, I said to Macaulay [he of *The Lays of Ancient Rome*, etc.], that these breakfast parties were a novelty to me; that we never had them in America, but that I thought them the most delightful form of social life. (p. 240)

12 E. Bruce Kirkham, *The Building of Uncle Tom's Cabin* (Knowville: University of Tennessee Press, 1977), p. 117.

12
Telescopic philanthropy: *professionalism and responsibility in* Bleak House

Bruce Robbins

In the decade of the 1840s, 'there occurred a cataclysmic event, far more dramatic than anything that happened in England, a very short geographical distance away .... That was, of course, the famine in Ireland — a disaster without comparison in Europe. Yet if we consult the two maps of either the official ideology of the period or the recorded subjective experience of its novels, neither of them extended to include this catastrophe right on their doorstep, causally connected to socio-political processes in England.' According to the editors of *New Left Review*, who offer this statement for Raymond Williams' consideration in *Politics and Letters* (1979), English fiction of the nineteenth century and the English criticism concerned with it have both privileged 'national experience,' and thus have omitted what by many accounts would be the most significant aspects of the period. Because the French Revolution of 1848, for example, is 'not a national experience in the direct sense', neither it nor other 'foreign or overseas developments' can turn up in Williams' account of the English literature of the 1840s. For Williams' interlocutors, the conclusion extends to literary criticism as a whole: 'It is not possible to work back from texts to structures of feeling to experiences to social structures.' Since literary texts are tied to 'experience' and since 'experience' seems to neglect whatever is distant or international, the study of literature cannot be asked to furnish knowledge of 'the total historical process' or of how human beings might act in and upon 'an integrated world economy'.[1]

In response to this challenge, Williams offers the counter-example of Dickens. Dickens' novels, he says, attempt 'to find fictional forms for seeing what is not seeable' (p. 171). If it is generally true that the novel produces knowable communities only at the cost of blindness to international effects, determinants, and analogues, it is no less true that Dickens managed to represent a world 'increasingly dominated by processes that could only be grasped statistically or analytically — a community unknowable in terms of manifest experience' (p. 247). In effect, Williams suggests, Dickens has made experience out of what seemed beyond experience — and in so doing has proved the possibility of continuing to write novels adequate to 'an integrated world economy'.

Whether or not a political defense of literary study rests upon it, this argument seems a valuable one to interrogate further. The current dialogue between Marxist humanism and poststructuralism, like the dialogue between Williams and *New Left Review*, hangs precisely on rival views of the achievement Williams ascribes to Dickens: occupation of the politically dangerous territory outside humanist 'experience', involving both the risks of wandering away from ethical home truths and the potential advantages of learning to understand and act in a dispersed global system which now exceeds experiential categories. This essay will try to follow Williams' lead into this 'post-humanist' domain. Taking the example of professionalism — a hinge joining these risks and advantages, a context for Dickens' social analysis, a site of his personal ambivalence — it will examine the way Dickens' political position is both jeopardized and enlarged by his willingness to imagine professional 'dehumanization' as a new (international, post-humanist) condition of 'action at a distance'.

Williams himself writes that imperialism still seemed 'distant or marginal' to Dickens (p. 262). Nothing could be more distant than the allusion to Africa in *Bleak House*. The fourth chapter, entitled 'Telescopic philanthropy', introduces the heroine and the reader to Mrs Jellyby, who is described as 'a lady of very remarkable strength of character, who . . . is at present (until something else attracts her) devoted to the subject of Africa; with a view to the general cultivation of the coffee berry — *and* the natives — and the settlement, on the banks of the African rivers, of our superabundant home population'.[2] Mrs Jellyby is 'too much occupied with her African duties' to brush her hair or take care of her children; her eyes have 'a curious habit of seeming to look a long way off. As if . . . they could see nothing nearer than Africa!' The moral is quickly drawn, and it pushes Africa farther into the distance. Esther Summerson, who narrates the episode, expresses the opposite philosophy of social action. Rather than neglect the near in favor of the far, she concentrates her efforts on what is close at hand. 'I thought it best to be as useful as I could . . . to those immediately about me; and to try to let that circle of duty gradually and naturally expand itself' (ch. 8). The satire of Mrs Jellyby — 'just the style in which vulgar men used to ridicule "learned ladies" as neglecting their children and household', John Stuart Mill wrote to his wife[3] — makes Africa a distraction, an ineligible elsewhere. Instead of founding piano-leg factories on the left bank of the Niger, enlightened English women and men should see to it that their offspring don't fall down the stairs at home or go without their dinner. Jo, the slum-child of Tom-All-Alone's, is representative: 'he is not one of Mrs Jellyby's lambs, being wholly unconnected with Borrioboola-Gha; he is not softened by distance and unfamiliarity' (ch. 47). It is not Mrs Jellyby but Esther, fully present to those immediately around her and refusing to be distracted into anything but personal, face-to-face contact, who takes care of him.

However naive Esther has seemed to later readers, there is no doubt that Dickens endorsed her amateurish, slowly dilating 'circle of duty' as a paradigmatic alternative to Chancery's expansive 'circle of evil'. In his article on the Niger expedition — the original of Mrs Jellyby's project — in 1848, he had written:

> The stone that is dropped into the ocean of ignorance at Exeter Hall, must make its widening circles, one beyond another, until they reach the negro's country in their natural expansion. There is a broad, dark sea between the Strand in London, and the Niger, where those rings are not yet shining; and through all that space they must appear, before the last one breaks upon the shore of Africa. Gently and imperceptibly the widening circle of enlightenment must stretch and stretch, from man to man, from people on to people, until there is a girdle round the earth; but no convulsive effort, or far-off aim, can make the last great outer circle first, and then come home at leisure to trace out the inner one. Believe it, African Civilisation, Church of England Missionary, and all other Missionary Societies! The work at home must be completed thoroughly, or there is no hope abroad. To your tents, O Israel! but see they are your own tents![4]

These expanding circles are the perfect contrary of what we mean by the verb 'to telescope': a forcible, sometimes violent compression in which circles collapse into one another and the result is closure and perhaps loss. Yet Esther's concentric gradualism, 'responsible' in that all action remains continuous with and answerable to its originary center, sounds more troubling when transposed into international terms. Like his older contemporary Michael Faraday, Dickens here refuses the concept of 'action at a distance', or rather sees it as inherently destructive. Mrs Pardiggle's charity, 'overturning, as if by invisible agency, a little round table at a considerable distance' (ch. 8), is a figure of telescopic destruction. Dickens' circles on the water, like Faraday's ether or the 'webs' of George Eliot, presume a full, dense medium which impedes 'convulsive' action and judges 'far-off aims' by their first impact at home. Like *The Little Drummer Girl*, which respects the authentic commitment of 'natives', whether Palestinian or Israeli, while scorning the consciously chosen, 'telescopic' commitment of a non-native to a distant struggle, these passages articulate a politics of presence whose appeal must by the same token exclude or discourage a good many of the connections, national and international, which today compose political reality. And yet if, as Le Carré's novel suggests, we continue to respond to this privileging of proximity, we should not be surprised that it has continued to inform the most frequent ethical and political readings of *Bleak House*, which agree in setting local responsibility, as exemplified by Esther, against the novel's many versions of irresponsibly telescopic philanthropy, of which Chancery's is the most evident.

Critics have remarked that in *Bleak House* Dickens moves away from the individual villains of his earlier novels toward an understanding of social evil as, in Terry Eagleton's term, 'systemic'.[5] 'The Law is administered by people who are at best, like Conversation Kenge and Guppy, absurdly, at worst, like Tulkinghorn and Vholes, wickedly inhuman', Arnold Kettle writes.

Mr Tulkinghorn may not have a very coherent personal motive for his vendetta against Lady Dedlock, but the point is that he is the agent of an impersonal system more potent and more sinister than any expression of personal spite or hatred. . . . It is this very impersonality that makes Mr Tulkinghorn so formidable. It is not his personal wickedness that Lady Dedlock is up against any more than it is the personal kindliness of the Lord Chancellor that determines the workings of the Court of Chancery. The sense of the Law as a force in itself, an independent business, self-perpetuating within its own closed circles of privilege and procedure, is basic to the meaning of *Bleak House*.[6]

But if personal motive and character have indeed become irrelevant, if agency has become transpersonal — as Kettle recognizes, in an Althusserian moment, when he observes that this is a revolutionary novel without revolutionaries — and if we are thus dealing with a new 'impersonality', then the 'responsibility' reading and the comfortable conflation of the ethical with the political which supports it would seem to require some rethinking.

The point made in *Politics and Letters* holds here as well: to clutch the ethical and experiential, while letting go of the global and the systematic, is to give up on teaching people how they can act in, on, and against System. Critics have largely done just this, escaping the strain between the ethical level of 'responsibility' and the analytic level of 'system', between the impersonal institution and the accountable individual, by accusing that institutional category to which they themselves largely belong, namely the professions. For many critics, the professions are the true villains of *Bleak House*. In a representative opinion, Robert Alan Donovan writes:

> the lawyer cares nothing for justice; he cares only for the law. Of the justice, that is to say, of the social utility, of his professional activity he is presumably convinced antecedently to his engaging in it, but he goes about his business secure in the knowledge that justice will best be served by his shrewdness in outwitting his adversary . . . the evil they give rise to is not a consequence of their abusing their functions but of them performing them as well as they do.[7]

In addition to all the incidental professional satire, there is of course a substantial case against the professions, and especially against the legal profession. It is by means of their profession that the Chancery lawyers evade the responsibility for their actions, that they shoot their daily arrows in the air without being obliged to consider on whom the arrows are falling. The Court of Chancery that sits at the center of the London fog in the first chapter and is the central symbol of English society throughout the novel is the court that is supposed to take care of the helpless, the widows and orphans who make up a large percentage of this novel's cast of characters. But instead of taking care of them, it takes care of itself. Dickens shows lawyers and judges getting rich off the notorious cases that go on for years, caught up in legal red tape and gobbledy-gook that it is of course in their interest to maintain, while Chancery suitors go mad, commit suicide or murder, and live in run-down Chancery-held properties like the slum Tom-All-Alone's. The profession could be defined as a sort of organized, legitimated irresponsibility.

Yet in several ways this indictment is both inaccurate and inadequate. To begin with, it ignores Dickens' own ambivalence about the increasingly dominant mode of institutional impersonality. The contradictory feelings that he entertained with regard to professionalism make themselves apparent before *Bleak House* even begins. In the preface to the first edition, dated August 1853, Dickens responds to 'a Chancery Judge' who has informed him that the 'Court of Chancery, though the shining subject of much popular prejudice ... was almost immaculate'. Dickens writes:

> This seemed to me too profound a joke to be inserted in the body of this book, or I should have restored it to Conversation Kenge or to Mr Vholes, with one or other of whom I think it must have originated. In such mouths I might have coupled it with an apt quotation from one of Shakespeare's sonnets:

> My nature is subdued
> To what it works in, like a dyer's hand:
> Pity me, and wish I were renewed!

This is a familiar view: it is in the nature of work to subdue the worker to its habits, tendencies, and interests. Professions distort, and judges are as subject to this professional deformation as dyers. One sentence later, however, Dickens marshals evidence that 'everything set forth in these pages concerning the Court of Chancery is substantially true, and within the truth' by appealing to no other authority than professional disinterestedness: 'The case of Gridley is in no essential altered from one of actual occurrence, made public by a disinterested person who was professionally acquainted with the whole of the monstrous wrong from beginning to end.' Is professionalism a proof of self-interest and distortion, or on the contrary of disinterestedness and impersonal clarity?

Much the same ambivalence animates the novel's plot. Esther herself is a firm believer in professions, as we discover when she pushes Richard Carstone into one and then worries that he 'has not that positive interest in it which makes it his vocation'. Devoting oneself to a profession, Richard remarks, is 'like making a great disturbance about nothing particular' (ch. 17). But Esther shares Mrs Bayham Badger's opinion that to feel 'languid about the profession' is to disregard a moral imperative:

> 'It was a maxim of Captain Swosser's,' said Mrs Badger, 'speaking in his figurative naval manner, that when you make pitch hot, you cannot make it too hot; and that if you only have to swab a plank, you should swab it as if Davy Jones were after you. It appears to me that this maxim is applicable to the medical, as well as to the nautical profession.' 'To all professions,' observed Mr Badger. (ch. 17)

Reference has just been made to Captain Swosser's ship as 'the dear old Crippler'. And what immediately follows is an example of the professional deformation of Mrs Badger's second husband, the archaeologist Professor Dingo: 'The Professor made the same remark, Miss Summerson, in his last illness; when (his mind wandering) he insisted on keeping his little hammer under the pillow, and chipping at the countenances of the attendants. The ruling passion!' Within the comic mode, Dickens takes pains to associate professional passion with violent inhumanity. What is remarkable is not that Richard could feel 'languid' about such professionalism, but that Esther, hearing all this, continues to urge him on. And yet, despite all the comedy, Dickens puts the plot solidly behind her. If lawyers, ministers, and politicians are devastating England by faithfully pursuing their callings without asking larger questions about what they ultimately achieve or destroy, the plot also suggests that not having a calling is likely to be fatal, as it is for Richard, and precisely because the individual is then forced to confront the question of ultimate consequences. Richard Carstone's tragedy is that in hoping for justice — that is, the speedy termination of the Chancery suit — he cannot devote himself to a profession, which would suspend issues of justice. Could he have done so, the novel suggests, could he have chosen Allan Woodcourt's limited but systematic professional action instead of a heroic but foolhardy confrontation with Chancery, he could have done more good to others as well as saved his own life; as Esther in a sense saves hers by marrying Woodcourt, a character so thin that in effect she is not so much marrying a man as his work. Work is salvation, in *Bleak House*, not despite but because of its evasion of ultimate questions about the system.

The Victorian gospel of work flirted with nihilism: the fear that local professional activity, though possibly meaningless in itself, must be pursued as a blind therapy, since despair and self-destruction waited upon anyone who dared interrogate its distant meaning or end. To the extent that it resigns itself to this nihilism, *Bleak House* would seem to advocate not responsibility but irresponsibility. And in the context of the 1840s, there are other reasons why this should not surprise us. Among those reforms with which Dickens sympathized were several that loosened rather than tightened the legal rigor of responsibility. The most obvious is the end of imprisonment for debt, which he had of course suffered with his family as a child and which he attacks head-on in *The Pickwick Papers*. In the year when imprisonment for debts of less than £20 was abolished, 1844 (the year after the Borrioboolan expedition), the Companies Act was passed, taking the first step toward limited liability. The same concept of responsibility that incarcerated a body in exchange for a business debt also of course precluded the modern corporation. For 'it was still widely felt to be immoral for an ordinary commercial business to be carried on under conditions which might allow the "partners" to escape paying its debts'.[8] The whole point of joint stock companies, as N.N. Feltes writes, was to produce 'a new form of business association in which the members might not know each other personally, need not necessarily work together, and could not "be called upon to contribute to the debts and liabilities of the company"' beyond what they had invested in it.[9] With some indirection, the joint stock company takes us back to Africa. For it was only by means of limited liability, the outstanding modern form of economic irresponsibility, that what Eric Hobsbawm calls 'the emigration of capital' could take place:

> businessmen and promoters (contemporaries would have said 'unsound businessmen and shady promoters') were now better able to raise capital not only from potential partners or other informed investors, but from a mass of quite uninformed ones looking for a return on their capital anywhere in the golden world economy.[10]

To say this, however, is not simply to identify the overcoming of ethical responsibility with capitalism and imperialism. Today, when millions of lives depend on decisions about such distant, all-but-invisible matters as the Third World debt, one of the tasks of the global imagination is surely to teach us to see beyond the personal ethical simplicities of an earlier system (you pay back what you borrow) and to prepare the way for such 'unethical' options as repudiation or restructuring. Such shifts were already characteristic of Dickens' time. The word 'responsibility' itself was in fact undergoing a notable transformation. In the eighteenth century, to be 'responsible' was not to possess a trait of character but to occupy a position, within a system of social relations, where one could be made to answer for oneself. A servant, to take Edmund Burke's example, could not be made responsible. According to the *OED*, the first use of the word in the sense of 'morally accountable for one's actions', that is, as an inherent moral quality, comes as late as 1836. In short, it was in Dickens' lifetime (the *OED* in fact cites *Bleak House*) that the meaning of the word came to inhere not in relations of accountability but in the individual character. There was of course self-consciousness about this ethical shift in the nineteenth century; the rebellion against it is generally associated with Nietzsche, whose *Genealogy of Morals* tells 'the long story of the origin or genesis of responsibility'.[11] In our own time, this history has been filled in by Michel Foucault's revisionary reading of the institutions which produce the modern individual. The liberal recorders of the nineteenth century, Foucault writes in *Madness and Civilization*, 'substituted for the free terror of madness the stifling anguish of responsibility':

> the madman, as a madman, and in the interior of a disease of which he is no longer guilty, must feel morally responsible for everything within him that may disturb morality and society, and must hold no one but himself responsible for the punishment he receives.[12]

For Foucault, what is wrong with modern society is not, as criticism of *Bleak House* tends to assume, that it permits so much irresponsibility, but rather that it produces so much responsibility.

Dickens was of course one of these liberal reformers, cheering when imprisonment for debt was eliminated and sneering at those who resisted the extension of the state's social welfare efforts; fear of 'centralization', he wrote, was a mere mask for 'irresponsibility'.[13] In turning to Chancery after the prison as his central image of society, Dickens' career followed the path of enlightenment as Foucault has described it: people are released from behind bars only in order to submit to a new, less visible mode of power. This power permeates rather than encloses its objects; the state can now afford to reform its prisons, for people carry their walls and surveillance around inside them. They have become responsible. And yet Dickens' social vision is not simply reversed by Foucault. To an extraordinary extent, *Bleak House* anticipates Foucault's own complex and difficult position. Dickens' critique of institutional modernity, like Foucault's, is wary of such humanist values as responsibility, which it shows to be produced by the system. And Dickens, again like Foucault, courts paradox by looking for new sorts of resistance in post-humanist forms which the system has also generated.

We know that Dickens planned to call *Little Dorrit* 'Nobody's Fault'. Samuel Smiles later used the same figure: 'When typhus or cholera breaks out, they tell us that Nobody is to blame. That terrible Nobody! How much he has to answer for. More mischief is done by Nobody than by all the world besides. Nobody adulterates our food. Nobody poisons us with bad drink. . .'[14] Smiles was speaking in favor of self-help, whose other side is the need to pin responsibility to a definite individual target. But Dickens would seem to have access to a more nuanced attitude toward responsibility. Not only does he devote a great deal of attention to the psychological damage done by an *over-acute* sense of responsibility, as in Esther's case, but he also directs much of *Bleak House*'s humour precisely at the misattribution of responsibility to individuals for phenomena that are clearly collective. One instance among many is Boythorn reducing the system of public transport to a matter of individual character and thus proposing that late coachmen should be shot:

> It is the most flagrant example of an abominable public vehicle that ever encumbered the face of the earth. It is twenty-five minutes after its time, this afternoon. The coachman ought to be put to death! . . .With two ladies in the coach, this scoundrel has deliberately delayed his arrival six and twenty minutes. Deliberately! It is impossible that it can be accidental! (ch. 18).

In the same line, there is the principle of treating collectivities as if they were responsible individuals. One of the first examples is the rebellious outburst of Mrs Jellyby's daughter, Caddy, who serves as her reluctant amanuensis: 'I wish Africa was dead! . . . I hate it and detest it. It's a beast!' Alternatively, there is a series of jokes on the habit of attributing agency to processes, like spontaneous combustion, which *have* no agents. 'You don't suppose I would go spontaneously combusting any person, my dear?' Snagsby asks his wife. 'I can't say', returns Mrs Snagsby. (ch. 33). In associating the novel's revolutionary hopes with Krook's spontaneous combustion, Dickens, like Althusser, proposed a vision of history as a process without a subject.

Althusser's anti-humanism is a curiously valuable touchstone at other points as well. Dickens offers a textbook illustration of ideology as interpellation, for example, in describing Chadband's

> pulpit habit of fixing some member of his congregation with his eye, and fatly arguing his points with that particular person; who is understood to be expected to be moved to an occasional grunt, groan, gasp, or other audible expression of inward working; which expression of inward working, being echoed by some elderly lady in the next pew, and so communicated, like a game of forfeits, through a circle of the more fermentable sinners present, serves the purpose of parliamentary cheering. (ch. 25).

As the word 'circle' suggests, this resembles Esther's version of 'responsibility': the 'answering' by a particular individual of a general 'hailing'. The mistake and the joke lie in the incongruity between the utter arbitrariness of the particular 'subject' thus brought into existence and the discursive system which generates these effects. 'From mere force of habit, Mr Chadband in saying "My friends!" has rested his eye on Mr Snagsby; and proceeds to make that ill-starred stationer, already sufficiently confused, the immediate recipient of his discourse.' Chadband asks one of his usual rhetorical questions: why is Jo poor? Snagsby 'is tempted into modestly remarking, "I don't know, I'm sure, sir." On which interruption, Mrs Chadband glares, and Mrs Snagsby says, "For shame!"' In being 'lured on to his destruction', Snagsby parodies and, one might say, refutes Esther's personalized philosophy of responsible action: thinking that the call is truly for him, he offers a personal 'response' that is 'battered' and 'smashed' by a systematic 'Terewth'.

Scapegoating, the misguided ascription to available local objects of responsibility for circumstances that are systematic or otherwise ungraspable, is explained succinctly by a debilitated member of the Dedlock family: 'better hang wrong fler than no fler'. Responsibility must be attributed to *someone*, if only to relieve feelings that have no other outlet. It is this principle that underlies the extraordinary violence of everyday life in *Bleak House*. According to Nietzsche, violence is in fact the source of responsibility: it is violence from the outside, he explains, which creates the reflexive relation to oneself which is the foundation of moral consciousness, of the right to make promises, and hence the guarantee of future action. In *Bleak House*, too, responsibility results from Chancery's release of surplus violence into society, which cannot be directed at the System itself and must find particular, inappropriate targets, often oneself. After saying that she hates Africa, Caddy Jellyby says 'I wish I was dead! . . . I wish we were all dead' (ch. 4). When Guppy says 'How do you do, sir?' to Krook, the old man, 'aiming a purposeless blow at Guppy, or at nothing, feebly swings himself round' (ch. 20). Guppy, in the same chapter, is shown stabbing his desk with a knife: 'Not that he bears the desk any ill will, but he must do something.' Richard blames Jarndyce for Chancery, unemployed brickmakers beat their wives, and at Mr George's Shooting Gallery, where people come to displace Chancery-generated violence, Phil Squod 'makes a butt' at his master 'intended to express devotion to his service' (ch. 26). In the 'Telescopic philanthropy' chapter Esther and her friends come upon a child with his neck stuck between railings 'while a milkman and a beadle, with the kindest intentions possible, were endeavouring to drag him back by the legs, under a general impression that his skull was compressible by those means'. Released into Mr Guppy's arms, the child 'began to beat Mr Guppy with a hoopstick in quite a frantic manner'. It is another comic refutation of Esther's philosophy: in the impersonal system dominated by Chancery, 'the kindest intentions' may be received as and rewarded with violence.

Bleak House does however contain an alternative attitude toward violence and responsibility. Skimpole, who declares himself to be irresponsible, also refuses to find others responsible. Skimpole rewrites the scene of Oliver Twist asking for more, for example, by putting responsibility not on the individual criminal but on the social system:

> At our young friend's natural dinner hour, most likely about noon, our young friend says in effect to society, 'I am hungry; will you have the goodness to produce your spoon, and feed me?' Society, which has taken upon itself the general arrangement of the whole system of spoons, does *not* produce that spoon; and our young friend, therefore, says, 'You must really excuse me if I seize it'. (ch. 31).

If Esther represents Dickens at the level of ethics, it is surely Skimpole who represents him better at the level of analysis. And the contrast may not work entirely in Esther's favor. At some risk to herself, Esther takes the sick Jo into her house; fearful for himself, Skimpole accepts a bribe from Bucket and helps turn Jo out of the house. But Skimpole is in effect placing the burden on the public, where Dickens would agree it ultimately belongs; and Esther, taking the burden upon herself, falls ill, nearly dies, and is scarred for life.

Skimpole imagines Gridley, before his final entanglement in Chancery,

> wandering about in life for something to expend his superfluous combativeness upon . . . when the Court of Chancery came in his way, and accommodated him with the exact thing he wanted. There they were, matched, every afterwards! Otherwise he might have been a great general, blowing up all sorts of towns . . . but, as it was, he and the Court of Chancery had fallen upon each other in the pleasantest way, and nobody was much the worse. (ch. 15)

This fanciful computation of the social cost and benefit of an individual tragedy depends, of course, on a detached, impersonal point of view which subordinates individual feelings to the perspective of the system as a whole. But such impersonality seems to have become indispensable. Otherwise, Chancery is reduced to the Lord Chancellor, who is 'affable and polite', as Esther sees him. To Esther, the army, Richard's second choice of profession, is no worse than medicine, his first choice. To Skimpole, on the other hand, society would certainly be 'the worse' for another 'great general, blowing up all sorts of towns'. Which of them would be a better judge of 'the dear old Crippler'?

It is interesting that Bucket, attempting the neat trick of arresting the dying Gridley and cheering him up at the same time, presents Gridley's case to him in exactly Skimpole's terms: 'You want excitement, you know, to keep *you* up; that's what you want. . . . What do you say to coming along with me, upon this warrant, and having a good angry argument before the magistrates. It'll do you good' (ch. 24). And in the ending, Dickens' narrator will again apply Skimpole's view of violence, this time in Boythorn's quarrel with Sir Leicester: 'Mr Boythorn found himself under the necessity of committing a flagrant trespass to restore his neighbour to himself' (ch. 66). The same insensibility that makes Skimpole's theories funny also makes them capable of discovering supra-ethical coherence in English society: here, the poststructuralist insight that ordinary individuality is constituted by a displacement of violence from the system to more or less arbitrary individuals. In fact, his theories sound very much like the statements of early sociology, and the parallel is more than parodic. Through the intermediaries of Comte, Spencer, and Durkheim, a common attention to the disparity between the morality of individual actions and their eventual social value or function provides a historical link between Dickens and Foucault.

Since it is social facts that must be altered, the argument must keep to the level of social desirability, which is not congruent with the domestic virtues. In terms of those virtues, Vholes, for example, who supports three daughters and an aged father in the Vale of Taunton, is an eminently moral, professionally respectable barrier to reform.

> Take a few more steps in this direction, say they, and what is to become of Vholes' father? Is he to perish? And of Vholes' daughters? Are they to be shirt-makers, or governesses? As though, Mr Vholes and his relations being minor cannibal chiefs and it being proposed to abolish cannibalism, indignant champions were to put the case thus: Make man-eating unlawful, and you starve the Vholeses! (ch. 39).

Face to face with Mrs Jellyby, Esther was not interested in Africa, but in how Mrs Jellyby was treating her family. Here Africa in a sense regains its rights: it is not proximate ethics but distant politics, Dickens' narrator declares, that should be decisive. The social system can neither be comprehended nor acted upon as long as one consults the wellbeing of Mr Vholes' family. Without a humorous, apparently immoral detachment from such questions, one is left with a moral purity that paralyses all supra-individual change.

Dickens' own humanism was of course troubled by this paralysis. Trying to be ethically responsible to everyone, it could not easily accept, for example, retributive violence, as Gridley's crucial speech indicates:

> The system! I am told on all hands, it's the system! I mustn't look to individuals. It's the system. I mustn't go into the court and say, 'My Lord, I beg to know this from you — is this right or wrong? . . . *He*

is not responsible. It's the system. But, if I do no violence to any of them, here — I may! I don't know what may happen if I am carried beyond myself at last! — I will accuse the individual workers of that system against me, face to face, before the great eternal bar! (ch. 15).

Like Mr Bumble, Dickens wishes the eye of the law to be opened 'by experience'. But Dickens' politics is not exhausted by 'face-to-face' confrontation, whether in this world or the next. Gridley demands that the judges 'have the face' to answer him directly, but instead he is tracked down by the disguised Bucket, the faceless or two-faced professional. As he dies he too becomes faceless: there is 'no likeness in his colourless face' to its 'former combative look' (ch. 24). Esther performs an act of responsible, face-to-face philanthropy when she opens the door to social forces that not even Bleak House can hold by taking Jo into her home. The result is that she literally loses her face. Self-effacement, it would appear, is both the price of amateurism and the definition of a more efficient professionalism. Abdicating his responsibility as a moral agent, Skimpole speaks of himself 'as if he were not at all his own affair, as if Skimpole were a third person' (ch. 6). Through the usurer Smallweed and his imaginary 'friend in the city' this phenomenon is associated, significantly, with the general irresponsibility of finance capitalism. However, the same detachment characterizes the virtuous Jarndyce, who proposes marriage to Esther as passionlessly 'as if he were indeed my responsible guardian, impartially representing the proposal of a friend' (ch. 44). And George Rouncewell, who is told after his indictment for murder, 'you talk of yourself as if you were somebody else!' replies, 'I don't see how an innocent man is to make up his mind to this kind of thing without knocking his head against the walls, unless he takes it in that point of view' (ch. 52). Given a social system which distracts attention from its own irresponsibility by distributing false accusations of responsibility among the innocent, these characters find their only freedom of thought and action in adopting the impersonality of Skimpole, of the lawyers, of professionals.

If the mode of action proper to the world of finance capital is not Gridley's self-assertion but rather, in Esther's words, 'the art of adapting my mind to minds very differently situated, and addressing them from suitable points of view' (ch. 8), then Bucket, whose 'adaptability to all grades' (ch. 53) is the institutional version of Esther's selflessness, presents professionalism as a necessary component of a new, impersonal mode of action. Although the professions stand for an impersonality that may provoke the individual to be 'carried beyond' himself into violence, they also suggest, in the same impersonality, a means of being carried beyond the individual's rage, madness, and impotence. Paradoxically, Bucket's suppression of any private self — he is childless, and his 'occupations are irreconcilable with home enjoyment' (ch. 53) — gives him both a professional deformation and exceptional powers of spontaneous, charming, manipulative action, a combination expressed in the paradox of a repetitive comic tag based on the non-repetitive variety of *ad hominem* address, as well as the 'fat forefinger', his powerful substitute for a full face. If the abandonment of a private household for a wider field of action makes Mrs Jellyby a telescopic philanthropist, then Bucket is another one, and despite all his reservations about Bucket's character, Dickens has come almost full circle. Like the 'unmoved' policeman looking 'casually about for anything between a lost child and a murder', Bucket's professional callousness is both morally questionable and socially powerful. 'Angel and devil by turns, eh?' he replies to Hortense. 'But I am in my regular employment, you must consider' (ch. 54). For *Bleak House*, this alternation seems to define regular employment. Even in Woodcourt, whose attachment to the medical profession seems an unqualified ideal, Dickens hints at a certain inhumanity. Woodcourt is introduced to the reader, at the deathbed of the man who would have been his father–in–law, through his 'professional interest in death, noticeable as being quite apart from his remarks on the deceased as an individual', and speaks 'in his unmoved, professional way' (ch. 11). Yet only his medical professionalism seems to answer directly the 'class revenge as disease' figure. Outside Krook's door a policeman 'stands like a tower, only condescending to see the boys at the base occasionally; but whenever he does see them, they quail and fall back' (ch. 11). To be subsumed by one's function is to acquire at once the blindness of comedy and the potency of a telescopic regard.

To speak of Dickens as endorsing telescopic philanthropy would be an overstatement. Yet his complicity in the inhumanity he attacks has been widely attested, if in other than 'post-humanist' terms. '*Bleak House* itself has the same structure as the society it exposes', J. Hillis Miller wrote in 1971.[15] Terry Eagleton, Jonathan Arac, and David Miller have developed the theme, which has become a critical commonplace.[16] Esther's ethical myopia is of course brought to the reader's attention by the contrasting version of the second, impersonal narrator, who like the far sighted Mrs Jellyby sees telescopically. Robert Garis calls this narrator's style 'a tyranny over us which is at least as oppressive as the tyranny of Chancery', while Robert Kincaid finds in this narrative detachment 'the central sin of remaining untouched'.[17] Indeed, this narrator often sounds a good deal like the Reverend Chadband; he too makes use of tautologies and answers all his own questions. Like the Law, his self-enclosed and systematic rhetoric mimics the social system it comes out of. We are speaking of course of Dickens' humour — but wasn't humour precisely Dickens' own professional secret as an entertainer? And to the extent that comic villains like Chadband are always slipping out of Dickens' ethical and political control, as generations of readers have observed, isn't humour also the special repository of his own 'irresponsibility'? The principle is familiar: 'a child is destroyed, as in *Dombey and Son*, by the subjection of a human being to a social role', Raymond Williams notes, 'but then Toodles or Cuttle are similarly subjected, by their author, who defines their whole reality by the jargon of their job'.[18] This is narrative at a distance: the distance, the withdrawal of sympathy, by which the Victorians themselves defined the comic, by which Dickens defined 'telescopic philanthropy', and by which we continue to define professionalism. The Dickens we hear or imagine behind the narrator is very clearly, as Gabriel Pearson has argued, a professional.[19]

To see Dickens' complicity with the social structures he deplored, however, is no longer the point. These complicities are only interesting — that is, they only impinge upon that balance between past contextualization and present celebration that makes up our usual treatment of cultural monuments — if the standpoint from which we now observe them is also thrown into question. Indeed, not to throw it into question seems both politically incautious and intellectually timid. For there are few topics which so insistently demand reflexivity as the question, addressed to a political interpretation by a professional critic, of the politics of professionalism.

Recent criticism of Dickens has made little headway with such questions, largely it seems because it has been unwilling to acknowledge its own institutional basis. F. R. and Q. D. Leavis, who of course did a great deal to professionalize literary study, make a case for Dickens as an earnest professional, but in so doing plunge headlong into inconsistency. Dickens himself is praised, in the preface to *Dickens the Novelist*, for 'his high standard of conscientious professionalism', while Inspector Bucket is later accused of 'bloodhound professionalism'.[20] We are given no significant way of distinguishing 'bad' from 'good' professionalism, and the latter is extracted from *Bleak House* in pure form only at the cost of an astonishing neglect of the novel's humour. Indeed, Q. D. Leavis takes the exchange on professions with Mrs Bayham Badger with full seriousness:

> Mrs Badger notices Richard's lack of the sense of vocation for medicine because, as her husband points out, 'her mind has had the rare advantage of being formed by two such very distinguished public men as Captain Swosser and Professor Dingo', her two previous husbands. She is therefore able to point to the Captain's maxim, 'that if you have only to swab a plank, you should swab it as if Davy Jones were after you' (a maxim which, Mr Badger says, applies to all professions) and to Professor Dingo's reply when accused of disfiguring buildings with his geological hammer, 'that he knew of no building save the Temple of Science'. No doubt Dickens felt that literature as he himself practised it was like the navy, science and medicine in requiring to be pursued in the spirit of these maxims, which he undoubtedly personally endorsed. (p. 140)

Criticism which does not flee self-contradiction by omitting Dickens' humour has tended to do so by labeling it anarchistic. V. S. Pritchett: 'All bureaucracies are tyrannies of the individual. Dickens' ridicule is the soliloquist's protest against institutions.'[21] The trouble is not only that those who happily agree are themselves professional critics firmly established in institutions, but also that — as this comfortable consensus indicates — anti-institutional anarchism on this level is indistinguishable from liberalism, and of no more use in teaching us how to deal with the institutions we inhabit than the symmetrical mobilizing of Dickens' humour against any and all political engagement. 'If we strain at accepting Dickens as a thoroughgoing rebel or outcast', John Gross comments, 'it is, above all, on account of his humour'.[22] Setting Stuart Tave's *Amiable Humorist*, which traces the rise of democratically inclusive, sentimental humour through *Pickwick*, next to R. B. Martin's *The Triumph of Wit*, which shows how in the rest of the century sentimental humour is replaced by unsentimental wit, the effect is to trace, from Carlyle to Bergson, the blunting of comedy as a progressive political instrument. This same trajectory also results from Roger Henkle's *Comedy and Culture*, which takes Dickens as paradigmatic. 'The shift from a comedy that exposes the excesses . . . of the members of a society to one that relies largely on the exploration of paradoxes', Henkle writes, is 'perhaps the greatest change in English comedy in the 19th century'.[23] Substituting *aporia* for paradox, the same turn separates Hillis Miller's epoch-making account of Dickens in 1958, where professional automatism and repetition signal 'dehumanization', from his equally influential preface to the Penguin *Bleak House* in 1971, where it is no longer the professions which 'assimilate the particular into a system' but language, and where the theme of the novel thus becomes the impossibility of interpretation: that is *aporia*.[24]

The replacement of 'comedy as ridicule of the professions' by 'comedy as *aporia*' has less political impact than one might imagine. Both are critiques of all system as such, and are thus unable either to acknowledge that their own critiques emanate from institutions, or to distinguish (*within* the system) between the times and places when institutions must be attacked and the times and places when institutions may be defended. They cannot concede that professions, as in *Bleak House*, might belong both to the problem and to the solution. There is some comfort, finally, even in the commonplace that all the social injustices of *Bleak House* can be traced back to the single center of Chancery. As the antagonist becomes all-encompassing, it becomes more difficult to imagine overthrowing it. Foucault's critique of current definitions of power makes this point: to think of power as a totality is to think oneself into impotence and passivity. Even so brilliant a Foucaultian reading of *Bleak House* as David Miller's 'Discipline in different voices' succumbs — as does Foucault himself, according to some critics — to this totalizing trap. Against 'the feasible politics of reformism', Miller writes, 'the total social reticulation of Chancery finds its corresponding oppositional practice in the equally total social negation of anarchism'[25] — the urge to see the court go up in flames. Anarchism of a subtler sort underlies Miller's own moral:

> it could be argued that, despite or by means of its superficially hostile attitude toward bureaucracy, a novel like *Bleak House* is profoundly concerned to train us — as, at least since the eighteenth century, play usually trains us for work — in the sensibility for inhabiting the new bureaucratic, administrative structures. (p. 76)

The point is that Miller's essay, like my own, comes out of a bureaucratic, administrative structure. It is easy but disingenuous, therefore, to leave the reader to assume one's unexpressed and unlocated horror before such structures. In pointing out the novel's undecidability, which resembles and resists both the openness of Chancery and the closure of the police, Miller leaves undone the job of instructing those who, when analysis is finished, must decide to act from positions within the system. His analysis discourages action by providing no room for it. As a practice of interpretation that respects the text itself to the exclusion of imperatives to action which may lie outside it, the 'close reading' that discovers *aporia* leaves the reader before an *aporia* — a 'No Way Out' sign.

An argument that would return to ethical responsibilities, therefore, would have to say something on behalf of distance. Today, a responsible criticism cannot run from distant structures into the illusory consolations of presence, but must learn to extend its range, teaching the imagination to deal with the apparent inhumanity of our new distances. 'Many writers have not yet forgiven the English nineteenth century', Jonathan Arac writes, 'for giving us not a workers' revolution but instead the practical basis, both in government and industry, of modern management and bureaucracy.' Professional or telescopic overview, as Dickens fashioned it, 'may be understood as part of a coercive, manipulative stance to the world that coincides with many of the economic and social relations of the nineteenth century most productive of misery for that time and ours', such as the Panopticon and factory organization.

> To find the techniques of overview evil in themselves is a strong metaphysical temptation, and to condemn all bureaucracy, administration, organization is an anarchist temptation almost irresistible in our society for the spirit that would be free. The fundamental historical issue, however, remains who is surveying whom and for what purposes.[26]

Instead of confronting 'system' with *aporia*, we need to look farther afield. If we require, say, new links between local constituencies and international actions, then we need 'systems' of our own, and we need to know how such 'artificial' collectivities of postmodern anomie as the professions might yet be harnessed to other ends than at present.

Taking my materials from a considerable distance, I will end by suggesting an ancient 'way out' of *aporia*. As many footnotes have mentioned, *aporia* comes from the Greek *poros*, which means path, passage, or ford; *aporia* is in fact a near synonym of 'no way out', But *poros* also means — in the definition of Marcel Détienne and Jean-Pierre Vernant — 'a stratagem, the expedient which the cunning of an intelligent being can devise in order to escape from an *aporia*'.[27] As Détienne and Vernant point out, this cunning is strongly associated with the skill or craft of specialized workers. Through its involvement in *metis*, the subject of Détienne and Vernant's *Les Ruses de l'intelligence*, *poros* belongs to 'the entire collection of technical activities represented in the world of men by a wide range of know-how from metallurgy and pottery to weaving and carpentry and including the skills of the charioteer and the pilot' (p. 280).

As part of the pilot's craft, *poros* belongs, by one of our oldest metaphors, to the very essence of politics. Unlike contemplative philosophy — a later invention — it is a practical and professional know-how associated not with universals but with particular local situations of conflict, danger, and rapid change, like those of the navigator, the doctor, the athlete, the politician, and the sophist. If *aporia* continues to judge the professions against a universal standard, *poros* is the 'way out' — one translation of the term — which, by ditching universals, both retains rationality and maintains professional respect.

I don't want to suggest that this local, professional form of rationality solves the political problem of the professions. As in *Bleak House*, the ultimate ends and values beyond its instrumentality remain obscure. The limits of *poros* are indeed part of the term itself, which combines the antithetical meanings of 'indication' — how to do it — with 'bond' and 'limit'. But the suggestion that knowing how to involves knowing limits seems a very useful one for the revaluation of the rational sub-universality of professional work. And as a provisional alternative to *aporia*, *poros* certainly seems a good working choice.

Notes

1 Raymond Williams, *Politics and Letters: Interviews with New Left Review* (London: Verso, 1979), pp. 165—70.
2 Charles Dickens, *Bleak House*, ed. Norman Page with an introduction by J. Hillis Miller (Harmondsworth: Penguin, 1971), ch. 4. Further chapter references will be given in the text.
3 Quoted in Edgar Johnson, *Charles Dickens: His Tragedy and Triumph* (New York: Simon & Schuster, 1952), p. 761.
4 Quoted in Humphry House, *The Dickens World* (London: Oxford University Press, 1942),p. 89. It is worth noting that in at least one sense Dickens was wrong. One year after *Bleak House* was published, an expedition up the Niger was successfully accomplished without deaths from malaria, thanks to the use of quinine. There were of course other things to say about such expeditions, but Dickens did not say them. Critics of American intervention in Central America should learn that the 'impracticality' argument is not strong enough. See Howard J. Pedraza, *Borrioboola-Gha: The Story of Lokaja, The First British Settlement in Nigeria* (London and Ibadan: Oxford University Press, 1960). Dickens in fact supported the emigration scheme of Caroline Chisholm, on whom Mrs Jellyby is partly modeled. See 'A bundle of emigrants' letters', in Harry Stone (ed.), *Charles Dickens' Uncollected Writings from Household Words 1850-1859* (Bloomington: Indiana University Press, 1968), vol. 1, pp. 85—96.
5 Terry Eagleton, *Criticism and Ideology* (London: New Left Books, 1976), p. 130.
6 Arnold Kettle, 'Dickens and the popular tradition', in David Craig (ed.), *Marxists on Literature: An Anthology* (Harmondsworth: Penguin, 1975), pp. 231—2.
7 Robert Alan Donovan, 'Structure and idea in *Bleak House*', in Ian Watt (ed.), *The Victorian Novel: Modern Essays in Criticism* (New York: Oxford University Press, 1971), p. 87
8 G. D. H. Cole and Raymond Postgate, *The Common People 1746-1938* (London: Methuen, 1938), p. 288.
9 N. N. Feltes, 'Community and the limits of liability in two mid-Victorian

novels', *Victorian Studies* vol. 17, no. 4 (June 1974), p. 359.

10 E. J. Hobsbawm, *Industry and Empire* (Harmondsworth: Penguin, 1968), p. 118.

11 Friedrich Nietzsche, *The Birth of Tragedy and The Genealogy of Morals*, trans. Francis Golffing (New York: Doubleday, 1956), p. 190.

12 Michel Foucault, *Madness and Civilization: A History of Insanity in the Age of Reason*, trans. Richard Howard (New York: Random House, 1965), pp. 246–7. See also Peter Dews, 'Power and subjectivity in Foucault', *New Left Review*, no. 144 (March–April 1984), pp. 72–95.

13 Jonathan Arac, *Commissioned Spirits: The Shaping of Social Motion in Dickens, Carlyle, Melville, and Hawthorne* (New Brunswick: Rutgers University Press, 1979), p. 183.

14 Quoted in Asa Briggs, *Victorian People* (Harmondsworth: Penguin, 1965 [1954]), p. 134.

15 Miller, in Dickens, op. cit., p. 29

16 For example, Eagleton, op. cit.: 'Dickens is forced in his later fiction to use as aesthetically unifying images the very social institutions (the Chancery Court of *Bleak House*, the Circumlocution Office of *Little Dorrit*) which are the objects of his criticism', p. 129. For Arac and Miller see Notes 13 and 25.

17 Robert Garis, *The Dickens Theatre* (Oxford: Oxford University Press, 1965), p. 117; R. Kincaid, *Dickens and the Rhetoric of Laughter* (Oxford: Oxford University Press, 1971), p. 63. For Dickens on work, see also Alexander Welsh, *The City of Dickens* (Oxford: Clarendon, 1971), pp. 82–4.

18 Raymond Williams, *The English Novel from Dickens to Lawrence* (London: Chatto & Windus, 1971), p. 58.

19 Gabriel Pearson, 'Towards a reading of *Dombey and Son*', in Gabriel Josipovici (ed.), *The Modern English Novel* (London: Open Books, 1976), pp. 54–76.

20 F. R. and Q. D. Leavis, *Dickens the Novelist* (London: Chatto & Windus, 1973), p. xvi.

21 V. S. Pritchett, 'The comic world of Dickens' in Watt, op. cit., p. 38.

22 John Gross, 'Dickens: some recent approaches', in John Gross and Gabriel Pearson (eds), *Dickens and the Twentieth Century* (Toronto: University of Toronto Press, 1962), p. xii.

23 Roger Henkle, *Comedy and Culture* (Princeton, NJ: Princeton University Press, 1980), p. 183.

24 J. Hillis Miller, *Charles Dickens: The World of his Novels* (Bloomington: Indiana University Press, 1958), p. 207; Miller, in Dickens, op. cit.

25 D. A. Miller, 'Discipline in different voices: bureaucracy, police, family and *Bleak House*', *Representations* 1 (February 1983), p. 61. See also Dominick LaCapra's 'Ideology and critique in Dickens' *Bleak House*', and Miller's reply, 'Under Capricorn', both in *Representations* 6 (Spring 1984)

26 Arac, op. cit., pp. 189–90.

27 Marcel Détienne and Jean-Pierre Vernant, *Cunning Intelligence in Greek Culture and Society*, trans. Janet Lloyd (Sussex: Harvester, 1978), p. 150. Further page references are in the text.

13
European pedigrees/African contagions: nationality, narrative, and communality in Tutuola, Achebe, and Reed

James Snead

languages are the pedigree of nations. (Samuel Johnson)

A nation, says Bloom. A nation is the same people living in the same place. ... By God, then, says Ned, laughing, if that's so I'm a nation for I'm living in the same place for the past five years. (James Joyce, *Ulysses*)

Our true nationality is mankind. (H. G. Wells)

The unclarity about the real nature of 'African' or 'European' writing participates in a more general quandary over the indefatigable, yet ultimately indefinable word 'nation'. There is no consensus about what a nation is. Arising in the late eighteenth century, and particularly in the French Revolution, the political theory of 'nation', as developed by Diderot and Condorcet and recorded by Abbé Siéyès in 1789 ('a union of individuals governed by *one* law, and represented by the same lawgiving assembly') speaks of a collection of individuals united in supporting a perceived interest; the hierarchical or privileging connotations of 'realm', 'country', 'kingdom', 'territory', and 'race' are smelted into the usage 'nation'. Yet a purely political definition of 'nation' would seem inadequate to cover the territorial and constitutional fragilities of nineteenth- and twentieth-century history. Even adding other criteria, such as 'common heritage', leaves things all too vague.

Johnson's idea of language as a nation's 'pedigree' does not so much define 'nation' in the present as call upon the already existing aura of other concepts, such as 'history' and 'race', to produce the sense that there are now lost, but recoverable, distinctions between disparate races of people. The full quote comes from Johnson's 1773 journey to the Hebrides, and it reads: 'What can a nation that has not letters tell of its original? ... There is no tracing ancient nations but by language, and therefore I'm always sorry when language is lost, because languages are the pedigree of nations.'[1] Such a use of linguistic traits to recover a 'lost' national identity is contemporaneous with the enunciation of a German nationalist ideology by Herder and Novalis, which Fichte and Schleiermacher later heightened to a frankly metaphysical level: language and nation express aspects of Divine Truth. A 'nation' was an irreducible and original quality, an almost transcendent reality, which we could best grasp through 'mother tongue' and national literature. Schleiermacher, anticipating twentieth-century theorists such as Whorf, was among the first to suggest such a notion: 'what is cogitated in one language can never be repeated in the same way in another'.[2] In this way, whatever else a group of people had since become, its 'nationhood' could be identified backwards to its linguistic source, a relatively well-defined form of distinction.[3]

'Language' here must be taken not merely in philological and etymological terms, but also as an entire pool of resources at the disposal of narrators, from the raw materials (vocabulary and syntax, as well as the repertoire of myths, rituals, folklore), to the processing tools (formal and structural devices, such as repetition or withholding, types of address, tropes of arrangement), to considerations of narrative reception (audience composition and feedback, marketplace). At each of these stages, Johnson's 'language' can be, and often is, usurped by the prerogatives of 'nation', particularly by literary historians. It will be the aim of this article to show that, despite the intermittent adoption of black nationalist credos by some African and Afro-American writers, many African and Afro-American (and indeed, many western) narratives often aggressively out-scheme any attempt at narrow nationalistic definition. These African and Afro-American texts exhibit a different approach to what new criticism, speaking of western European literature, often has called 'universality'. Writers in the African tradition seem inclined to display a certain linguistic and cultural eclecticism or *miscegenation* — even as their critical apologists, finding in African writers a 'universal appeal', still seek to assert the radical difference of black thinking and black writing from the racially-based, pure pedigrees of western European tradition. I shall use as my chief examples some texts by the Nigerians Amos Tutuola and Chinua Achebe, and by the black American, Ishmael Reed.

The national and the universal

It is no accident that the epigraphs' three improvisations on the theme of 'nation', taken together, delineate the almost humorous instability of the concept. By taking 'nation' as a form of spatial coherence, one inadequately addresses the problem of defining 'people'. Leopold Bloom, displaced Jew, has good reason to define his 'Irishness' by place instead of race. Yet he quickly encounters an objection to his words 'same people'. For, as Joyce's Ned Lambert wittily shows, the term 'nation' itself embodies a paradox: a 'nation' is coherent, specific, and local; yet a person, the atomic essence of a nation ('I'm a nation'), does not constitute a *population*. Nations require plurality, yet plurality dilutes all strict standards of differentiation: 'Civilization is a re-agent, and eats away the old traits'.[4] There seems a principle of necessary dilution whereby the 'nation' must apply increasingly more general rubrics to its population, while at the same time continuing to include an ever widening spectrum of people.

Imperialism — the accumulation of diverse 'nations' under a single flag — may be seen as an almost semantic imperative; 'force' replaces 'nature' in forging alliances; selective assimilation, rather than aggressive exclusion, allows the national concept to survive, despite the relative distance between concept and reality. For instance, the more successful the British Empire became, the less it was racially and linguistically pure 'British'. Indeed, from almost any starting point, national definitions include more than they exclude, precisely because of the internal contradictions of the term 'nation' itself, which, as the H. G. Wells quote shows, can sustain an almost self-annulling level of generality (one's 'true nationality is mankind').

As a result, the concept of 'nation' finds its meaning on the broadest, rather than on the most detailed, levels, even as it pretends to furnish us with the most specific segregations. It might be predicted, then, that the study of national literatures would involve similar contradictions. The temptation to regard 'language' or 'literature' as the guarantor of a nation's 'pedigree' (remember that *natio* has in Latin an almost eugenic connotation) recalls the similar (and frequently more destructive) employment of the concept of 'color'. In both cases an apparently exclusionary process is meant somehow to isolate the pure 'pedigree' of a race, a language, or a literature, even as that process ends up in a compensating search for some emblem of universality.[5] Johnson's remark is perhaps more understandable against this background, though his linguistic definition of 'nation' raises as many problems as Leopold Bloom's topographical one.

We are familiar enough with the practice whereby literary history or literary canons stand in for a notion of national spirit or character, but a countervailing tendency also needs to be discussed, one already implicit in Wells' comment. This tendency would valorize particular national authors not just to the extent that they speak for themselves or for their 'race', but also to the extent that they speak for 'mankind'. Authors such as Homer, Dante, Rabelais, Cervantes, Shakespeare, and Goethe are often seen as 'consummate geniuses' of a given national spirit, or 'founding fathers' of their respective national literatures, yet ultimately attract even greater interest because they seem in some way to have embodied 'universal truths'. Nation and nationalism, then, begin to dissolve their hegemonies with the formation of this larger grouping, defined by 'genius'. The Romantic conception of 'universal genius' has not waned even in the present day — in all cases, the favored designees of 'universal genius' are drawn not from a particular country, nor even from a given colonial power, but in fact from the 'nation' of Europe itself; this conception serves to proclaim the superiority of white thinking, white writing, and white culture.

Despite the general use of these authorial 'founding fathers' to stand for a white European cultural ideal, the actual texts they have written seem radically *mixed*, even syncretistic. *The Odyssey*, *The Divine Comedy*, *Don Quixote*, *King Lear*, or *Faust* would seem the last possible proof-texts for any *separationist* or *exclusionary* brand of racial or cultural hubris. It might seem a paradox, but the language of such texts — that subsequent literary canons have taken as the quintessence of 'Greek', 'Italian', 'Spanish', 'English', 'German', or simply 'European' genius — is radically heterogeneous and eclectic. These texts are extraordinary, not by virtue of the skill and confidence with which they *exemplify* a particular style or vernacular, but by the way in which their language *mixes* a variety of styles and vernaculars; they are not so much *universal* as *hybrid*, unifying previously scattered or dispersed dialects, colloquialisms, and oral traditions. They reach beyond the standard set of materials proper to a local sense of group cohesion, and make assimilationist gestures which abruptly break the mold of national languages. By such a liberal inclusiveness — indeed, by their impurity — even the major texts of western European literature have been able to furnish general reference points to other cultures, creating rich semantic fields within the common places of what were once canonized as national and European classics.[6]

Yet neither the new critical quest for texts embodying 'universal truths' nor even the formalist (Propp) or structuralist (Lévi-Strauss and Greimas) project to find 'deep structures' or 'grammars' which would describe a transnational level of narration have eliminated literary chauvinism. Albeit Edward Said has seen signs recently that 'contemporary criticism ... has no faith in traditional continuities (nation, family, biography, period)' in most places literary studies still designate themselves by nationalistic terms, with even the least naive of critics believing, with varying degrees of irony, in the essence of a particular body of literary works produced by people speaking the same language.[7]

As distinguished a scholar as Erich Köhler can begin a recent article on French literature by saying: 'whoever wishes to clarify the nature of the "French spirit" need only, as a first step, interrogate French Literature.'[8] The tradition of literary territorialism finds tautological expression in the first paragraph of *The Concise Cambridge History of English Literature*: 'Though echoes from Celtic Britain must have lingered in men's minds, English literature begins, at least, by being English'.[9] The notion suggested here of an abrupt break or alteration leading to an original, founding moment — while indispensable to a certain sense of literary historical plotting — is neither logically nor philologically plausible. The beginning is and must be arbitrary — pedigrees, linguistic or otherwise, never find a first instance: it is precisely out of the *loss* of absolute beginnings that the *need* for arbitrary beginnings flows.[10]

Just as the modern comparative philologist posits only provisional forms, marking them with an asterisk to denote that the forms are hypothetical, so too do these provisional and ultimately unprovable beginnings serve a crucial rhetorical and definitional aim. The *Concise Cambridge History* admits that indeed 'we do not know where or what the beginning is ... the earliest forms of English literature, like the earliest forms of other national literatures, have perished'.[11] Yet this gap in the narrative of literary nationalism makes even more imperative the mandate to find, or manufacture, a moment at which particular national literatures seem to have become distinctive, if only to guarantee the coherence of a now dispersed center of identity. An earlier philologist, who was both a beneficiary and a victim of this kind of performative nationalism, well diagnosed the problem in 1886: 'What is called a "nation" in Europe today, and is really rather a *res facta* than a *res nata* (and occasionally can hardly be told from a *res ficta et picta*) is in any case something evolving, young, and easily changed, not yet a race'.[12]

European nationalism, particularly in the nineteenth century, seemed to depend increasingly for its definition upon *cultural* criteria. Dedication to the idea of culture provided a kind of generalized *coverage*, insuring a group's identity against external or internal threats of usurpation, assimilation, or denaturement. One could classify various national cultures both in terms of the tenacity with which the coverage was maintained and the extent to which one culture projected an image of radical *difference* — defined as 'national' and 'natural' *superiority* — from another culture. Freud suggests, with Nieztsche, that the entire idea of national differences, far from natural or original, gratifies more immediate desires:

> Closely related races keep one another at arm's length; the South German cannot endure the North German, the Englishman casts every kind of aspersion upon the Scot, the Spaniard despises the Portuguese. We are no longer astonished that greater differences should lead to an almost insuperable repugnance, such as the Gallic people feel for the German, the Aryan for the Semite, and the white races for the coloured. ... In the undisguised antipathies and aversions which people feel towards strangers with whom they have to do we may recognize the expression of self-love — of narcissism.[13]

When confronted with non-western cultures, European 'narcissism', at first a mere 'repugnance' towards other peoples, develops into a myth of the past whose now embarrassing aspects non-industrialized cultures may be seen to represent.

Particularly in the nineteenth century — precisely the point at which colonialism and imperialism were making their most brutal inroads into Third World cultures — aesthetic nationalism and progressivism were keen factors in the European's narcissistic self-presentation, both within Europe and in the rest of the world. The progressivist conception of European history, in its ecumenical appraisal of non-western cultures as potential and primitive versions of European society, achieved a vision of global cultural development that elevated and separated white Europeans from the 'backward' cultures that they devalued. Yet this notion also, by a peculiar kind of magnanimity, needed to include the primitive within its imperial hoard. For eventually, the presumably flattering model of linear improvement tends to undermine itself. European artists and scholars began to suggest that if the non-western aesthetic is a potential, or primitive, or aboriginal manifestation of that which western man has brought to maturity, then it follows that potency, primacy, and originality themselves represent radically regenerative attributes that the mature post-Enlightenment west has already lost. Linearity, then, might as easily imply decay as progress.

While Diderot's *Encyclopédie* made sense as a chronicle of Europe's mature achievements through the late eighteenth century, the very notions of 'maturity' and 'accumulation' upon which it concentrated must have reminded the observant reader of their concomitants in the organic metaphor, 'senescence' and 'obesity'. Almost from the beginning, both incipient and full-blown modernism expressed a wish to return to primal roots as well as a somewhat troubling awareness that this return was inconsistent with the claims to 'newness' and 'progress' and often 'national genius' that had for so long been made about the history of western cultures, independently and as a whole.

Jean-Paul Sartre expresses these anxieties best in his 1948 preface to Leopold Senghor's anthology of French West African poetry: 'It is almost impossible for our poets to realign themselves with popular tradition. Ten centuries of erudite poetry separate them from it. And, further, the folkloric inspiration is dried up; at most we could merely contrive a sterile facsimile.'[14] Given the assumption of linear continuity between origin and maturity in western culture, it came to be suspected in the late nineteenth century that primitive states might possess greater power and energy than sterile nations, or that, in other words, western material progress had amounted to spiritual and artistic decadence.[15]

Major European artists began to have doubts about the linear model for purely formal reasons, as well. Richard Wagner, Gustav Mahler, Igor Stravinsky, James Joyce, Henry James, Thomas Mann, and others, in testing the quantitative capacities of aesthetic forms, and indulging early modernism's predisposition towards encyclopedic art, were also indirectly challenging the European nationalisms and even imperialisms that had allowed for only token levels of hybridization. These and other artists found it necessary to undermine the entire notion of formal and material accumulation and *development* — crucial to western historical, as well as musical and fictional plots — in favor of significant cycles and structural *repetitions* in their scores and texts. So the paradox of cultural coverage became clear: the more retrospective, encyclopedic, weighty, mature — indeed, *western* — the work of art became, the more it had to incorporate elements of futurist, non-western, primitive, repetitive, and minimal structuration, if it were at all to remain comprehensible.

Despite attempts to apply evolutionary terminology to art forms, it became clear that there could be no approach to human sensations and response that had a progressivist nationalism as its basis. Long before Freud, it had been noted that if inclusion were the working principle for much modern art, then 'primitive' repetition rather than 'mature' development had to be a corollary structural feature. Even if an art form developed within a national culture as the outpouring of some necessary racial vigor, who could guarantee that such an art form would continue to appeal to that same 'race'? The more complex the art work, the more vexing the problem of comparative reception between cultures becomes. That is to say: even if the European and the African respond differently to Benin bronze or Bayeux Tapestry, can there be a question here either of nationalism or of progress?

Versions of universality: collections versus contagions

When African literature is in question, literary critics use terms such as 'national', 'progress', and 'tradition' quite differently than in their discussions of European texts. In the first place, there is a flattening of the entire concept of 'nation' — and for all the wrong reasons. Although African poets and politicians have been keen to borrow political and linguistic criteria from Europe's repertoire (as in the only partially successful concept *négritude*), European literary critics and historians for the most part have been reluctant to deal with Africa in all its dazzling racial, tribal, and regional multiplicity.

A standard German encyclopedia of world literature for example — one which includes articles on Flemish and Serbian literature, and dozens on European and Asian literature overall — compresses its comments about Africa into two articles: 'The traditional literature of black Africa', and 'Neo-African literature' (which includes Afro-American writers as well!). Extravagant generalizations about 'the African' follow. Although the distinction, based on writing, between 'traditional' (oral) and 'modern' (written) African literature is common, more recent overviews have broken the continent down into more specific though scarcely more enlightening divisions such as 'West' and 'East' African, 'Anglophone' and 'Francophone', or even national ('Nigerian') or tribal ('Ibo') units. The conclusion that 'today there are at least two distinctive prose styles in African literature in English, the Yoruba and the Ibo' is either reductive or imprecise, or both.[16]

Despite their hesitancy about coming to terms with the specificity of African literature, few western readers seem unwilling to talk about its 'universality'. The new critical valorization of 'universal appeal', which we have seen conflicts somewhat with the literary historian's insistence on strict national delineations, is frequently applied to African works — where the issue of 'nation' is even less clear than in Europe — even though the word 'universality' seems often merely to function as a codeword meaning 'comprehensibility for the European reader'. As 'one non-African reader' puts it, in trying to assert his qualifications for interpreting African literature:

> ... accomplished works of art communicate in such a universal human idiom that they are capable of transcending their particular time and place and speaking to all mankind. One does not have to be Greek to understand Homer, Hindu to appreciate Kalidasa, or Japanese to enjoy Chikamatsu. So why should a person have to be black to respond to James Baldwin, George Lamming or Amos Tutuola?[17]

In some instances, the search for the 'universal' in the 'African' takes extreme forms:

> Like any other artist, the Nigerian novelist must achieve universality through a sensitive interpretation of his own culture ...
>
> the African writer [must retain] that international standard of English

which is required if his work is to be other than merely local in its effects.

Using his African background, [Wole Soyinka] explores the human condition . . .

The Lion and the Jewel, as comedy, depends on seeing humans in terms of their universal motivations of pride, power and sex . . .

Soyinka's writing, although firmly set in Africa, is universal in its themes.

Amos Tutuola's *The Palm-Wine Drinkard* is [among the] marvellous works of the human imagination . . . the impact of much of what he writes is supracultural.[18]

Attributing 'universality' to African writers — or expecting to find it in them — can merely be a question of (as in the case of political imperialism) a given observer projecting onto a neutral space a wish for power. That power, in turn, may be defined as the power to comprehend and systematize within a European scheme a wide and often perplexing range of non-European cultures and writings.

In his article 'Neo-African literature', the well-known Africanologist Jahnheinz Jahn brings a flattened perspective to modern African literature, further compresses variety into identity. Jahn's over-reliance on concepts such as 'the African way of thinking' or 'the African conceptual world' leads him to ostensibly laudatory, but occasionally outrageous conclusions, such as 'In traditional Africa, everyone who speaks is a magician of words, a poet'. As one observer comments:

Critics of African literature tend to be either racists, nationalists or individualists. The racists devoutly believe *africanité* of African Literature and usually seek to demonstrate that black African writers think alike, feel alike, and therefore write alike. . .so long as he is black and African his writing is regarded as an expression of *négritude*, a verbal manifestation of the negro African soul. . . . Nationalist critics, on the other hand, are preoccupied with mapping the geography of African literature. . .a literature conveniently contained within the arbitrary territorial boundaries drawn by the former colonial powers.[19]

In describing the 'African's' spontaneous poetry, Jahn comments on what he sees as an unusual juxtaposition of images in an African poem — and in doing so exposes his own ethnocentrism: 'An image like "black innocence" is not an oxymoron for the neo-African poet, but an imperative image that creates a new reality'.[20] Jahn never even seems to question his own culture's assumption that 'black' and 'innocence' are oxymoronic opposites here, seeming to think that the belief is universally held, even by black African poets.

In much western writing about African literature, theorizing about 'progression' of narrative forms is replaced by discussion of 'derivation'.

The journey from 'traditional' to 'modern' African literature, for this mentality, was entirely due to contact with Arabic and European cultures, the adoption of writing systems, and, most significantly, the transcription of African languages to European writing conventions: 'All languages of this giant area are originally unwritten. The first known written form in black Africa was Arabic'. Traditional narration included songs, improvisations ('forgotten as soon as they arose'!), myths, epics and sagas, riddles, prayers, incantations, panegyrics, drama, and so on.[21] These are often dismissed as either irretrievable or unworthy of serious discussion, while the introduction of 'writing' and European language prototypes gives us a beginning, a 'pedigree', at the same time less remote and more familiar than would be possible for European language and literature. Note comments such as 'A standard orthography for the Yoruba language was established by the missionaries of the Church Missionary Society of London working in Yorubaland in the period 1842–82', or 'it was only at the start of the twentieth century that written Hausa literature came into being'.[22]

The European, whose intervention 'begins' African literature, once more finds himself flatteringly represented as the 'author of progress', and it is now possible to speak of first-and second-generation African writers, who are alternately beatified and villified, depending upon their closeness or remoteness to this primal, 'traditional', African source, or what one writer calls 'the African personality of this literature'.[23] The notion of 'progress', then, seems tied not to any internal logic, but to a sense of closeness or distance from European influence: 'There may be traditional Nigerian dramatic forms such as the masquerade or various ceremonies, but outside [read European!] infusion is obviously needed if local forms are to be developed and given artistic permanence'.[24] The assumption that the novel as we know it is a European form – coupled with the notion that for the most part, Europeans changed African oral traditions into written traditions – permits a new progressivist thesis tailored to 'African realities': 'The modern Nigerian novel ... follows the main historical development of the English novel'; 'Just as each European nation has its own literature so each nation in Africa can be expected to produce its own literary tradition.'[25]

The critical reception of Amos Tutuola, and particularly of his first novel, *The Palm-Wine Drinkard* (1952), furnishes us with an interesting example of these critical habits. Tutuola, a Yoruba writer born in 1920, has presented us in his first work with an extraordinary text, a memoir of a search through fantastic terrains to 'find out where my palm-wine tapster who had died was':

> When I saw that there was no palm-wine for me again, and nobody could tap it for me, then I thought within myself that old people were saying that the whole people who had died in this world, did not go to heaven directly, but they were living in one place somewhere in this world. ... One fine morning, I took all my native juju and also my father's juju with me and I left my father's hometown to find out whereabouts was my tapster who had died.[26]

Often dream-like, often a hugely successful meditation on the syntactical possibilities of the English language, *The Palm-Wine Drinkard* is the quest-narrative of a disembodied 'I', through both physical and cultural terrains. In his astute and humorous mixing of African and European reference points — such as linking 'juju' with that all too English cliché 'one fine morning' — Tutuola both plays with and against the expectations of African and European readers.

Critics have had difficulties with Tutuola's decidedly non-Aristotelian narrative structure, as well as with his idiosyncratic style — or, more precisely, they have been uncertain whether Tutuola's style was an individual creation or rather an expression of a 'West African' or 'Yoruba' 'spirit'. When Tutuola's style has been in question, the typical response has been, as in the discussion of 'modern African literature' generally, to search for European or African precursors, but rarely to give the artist credit for willed craftsmanship:[27]

> It is obvious that *The Palm-Wine Drinkard* . . . is reminiscent of other works in world literature . . . Bunyan and Dante . . . Orpheus. . . . The two works with which *The Palm-Wine Drinkard* has most in common . . . are the *Odyssey* and *The Canterbury Tales*. . . . The last chapter of *The Palm-Wine Drinkard* shows Tutuola using a final blend of African and European myth.

Tutuola, borrowing from European or African models, depending on the critic, is seen as closer to the 'source' of 'Yoruba' than such writers as Soyinka or Achebe, who have been 'spoiled' by Western influence:

> There can be no doubt that Amos Tutuola is closer to the traditional esthetic of the Yoruba . . . . One would expect therefore, upon further study, to perceive a continuum of 'Yorubaness,' extending from Tutuola at the deeply Yoruba end to Wole Soyinka at the more Euro-peanized, modernized end.[28]

Yet this praise quickly reveals itself as an oblique denigration. Some readers say that Tutuola's more 'deeply Yoruba' narrative is closer to the 'African genesis', 'like drumming', and better than the writing of the 'more Westernized African . . . [whose] writing is more in the nature of a gloss; in Tutuola, it is intrinsic'.[29] Other readers compare Tutuola unfavorably to Soyinka, and on the same grounds: '[Soyinka's] English is impeccable; one would search his works in vain for the unconscious West Africanisms and innocent barbarisms that crowd every page of Tutuola's writing'. It is not uncommon to read of Tutola's 'bad English. . . . No doubt Tutuola stumbled on his style accidentally at first by translating Yoruba expressions into English; but it has become a conscious technique in his later novels'.[30] 'Conscious' artistic technique (a sign of healthy, individualistic, artistic vigor) vies with the 'unconscious' influence of 'proletariat' diction (the same communal 'popular tradition' lauded by Sartre and now criticized as 'clumsy' and 'ungrammatical'). Once more we see the paradox whereby the evolutionary model, applied to writing, both reveres and demeans sources of literary originality, especially when they are writers and poets.

Like Tutuola, Chinua Achebe has suffered from the imposition of national and even tribal categories. His novels — in particular *Things Fall Apart* (1958), *No Longer at Ease* (1960), and *Arrow of God* (1964) — have Nigerian settings, and employ storytelling devices (myths, proverbs, songs) from the Ibo oral tradition. In depicting the first encounters between black African tribes and white European colonialists, they already stake out a supra-national territory. They have variously been praised and derided as 'sociological' or 'anthropological', but their most interesting aspect is the almost casual manner in which they present African norms to primarily non-African readers. As in the case of Tutuola's works, Achebe's novels provide an unexpectedly tricky reading experience for their western audience, using wily narrative stratagems to undermine national and racial illusions. One wonders whether either author was prepared for the interpretive confusions resulting from their unexpected disregard of literature's earlier segregations. For Achebe's novels do not merely insinuate the unaware reader into a foreign and putatively inferior consciousness; they suggest a natural and indeed actual place for African cultures alongside or even admixed with European ones. The presence of 'anthropological' detail in Achebe might represent verisimilitude for a reader fluent in Ibo customs, but for a European reader, it constitutes a veritable declaration of war on the practice of dividing cultures and fictions into strict national groupings.

For one thing, Achebe consistently leaves crucial Ibo words untranslated (some editions append a 'Glossary of Ibo words and phrases', which, in its terse inadequacy, reminds one of the parodistic 'Partial bibliography' at the end of Ishmael Reed's *Mumbo Jumbo*). Many words can only be deciphered from the context:

> He could hear in his mind's ear the blood-stirring and intricate rhythms of the *ekwe* and the *udu* and the *ogene*, and he could hear his own flute weaving in and out of them, decorating them with a colorful and plaintive tune.[31]

Moreover, similes are based on African, not European realities: 'Okonkwo's fame had grown like a bush-fire in the harmattan' (p. 7). What is being defined here is not so much 'tribal' or even a 'national' language or sensibility, but a black sense of cultural prerogative, the converse of the normal relations of power between Europe and Africa. The European reader, feeling at the outset at home in a literary form that Europe has developed, is made to assume, without warning, the vulnerable position of the African in a European culture which he or she is expected to understand and absorb. Whites, perhaps for the first time, see themselves as Africans see them: 'It is like the story of white men who, they say, are white like this piece of chalk,. . .And these white men, they say, have no toes' (p. 71). The words 'white body' are no longer synonymous with 'innocence' (as Jahn might suggest), but (in the Ibo conception reported in *Arrow of God*) with 'leprosy'.[32]

Perhaps most importantly, Achebe's ability to shift points of view and narrative centering between white and black characters (there is no longer any question of simply peering into the machinations of a putative 'African mind') increases the ironic distance from both perspectives, and intensifies Achebe's ongoing elegy to segregationist discourse and narrative. The ill-fated assumptions of superiority in both black and white realms are the problem: interpreting between whites and the leaders of Umuofia village in *Things Fall Apart*, Okeke says 'We say he is foolish because he does not know our ways, and perhaps he says we are foolish because we do not know his' (p. 175). The segregation of black and white viewpoints in the novel's early chapters simply replicates a wider cultural gap, one which leads to an outcome of which the reader is already all too aware. *Things Fall Apart* expropriates and pre-empts (albeit only in fiction) the written form in which the English language has assaulted an unwritten Ibo reality. The ironic ending, in which the district commissioner decides to capture the entire tale in 'the book which he planned to write', recapitulates the ongoing process of cultural interpretation and redefinition which typically worked to the detriment of blacks:

> The story of this man who had killed a messenger and hanged himself would make interesting reading. One could almost write a whole chapter on him. Perhaps not a whole chapter but a reasonable paragraph, at any rate . . . one must be firm in cutting out details. He had already chosen the title of the book, after much thought: *The Pacification of the Primitive Tribes of the Lower Niger*. (p. 191)

Yet it is Achebe who, through writing *Things Fall Apart*, pre-empts an attempted white usurpation of his story and his culture, trapping the 'official version' within a more sympathetic history.[33]

By borrowing his title from Yeats' pessimistically cyclical poem 'The Second Coming', Achebe similarly rewrites the text both of European historicism and of the cyclical view that was its hopeful antidote (the title of his second novel, *No Longer at Ease*, performs a similar operation on T. S. Eliot's 'The Journey of the Magi'). If, for Yeats (as for Spengler and other modernist philosophers of history), the transition from barbarism (or paganism) to the Christian era would be followed by an unknown, presumably negative cycle, in which 'things fall apart', Achebe reverses this view to highlight the negative impact that this hypothetically 'positive' Christian phase has already had upon the 'falling-apart' of African culture:

> in evoking Yeats's themes, Achebe implies that the sense of history and tradition, the burdens of cultural continuity, decay, rebirth, have all been the African's lot as well as the Westerner's . . . the novelist has exploited the European's cultural criteria . . . in order to reverse the white man's exclusivist definitions of history and culture.[34]

Even as the west is bemoaning the internal collapse of some of its structures, Achebe is showing the British subversion of Ibo customs (already endangered by their own decrepitude). Achebe hereby does more than merely 'exploit' the 'European's cultural criteria'. Far more than merely borrowing the notion of historical cycles from Yeats, he is in fact reclaiming an age-old non-western cyclical conception that European writers had only recently annexed.

In *Arrow of God*, the intersection of narrative form and literary revision is even clearer. In Achebe's third novel, as in *Things Fall Apart*, we see the collapse of a certain traditional Ibo culture under both internal and external assault. There is no glossary of Ibo words this time, and African proverbs (and even entire fables) interlace the narrative. The *New York Times* reviewer called it 'long on native customs and idiom, and short on narrative interest', and yet this appraisal is a sort of inverse testimony to the seriousness and subtlety of Achebe's narrative design.[35] For this novel (in a way that parallels Wole Soyinka's 1980 film *Blues for a Prodigal*) gives a deeper analysis of both the black and the white worlds than Achebe had ever attempted before. It alternates rapidly between events in chief priest Ezeulu's village and the machinations of the imperious white man, 'Wintabota' (Captain T. K. Winterbottom), culminating in their tragic collision.

Achebe's 'white' narrative often assumes a disarmingly familiar modernist shading. For this accommodation, Achebe has been much praised by certain critics, happy to find that Achebe's 'voice' seems as authentic in the white chapters as it does in Ezeulu's 'tribal' scenes. Jamesian passages ('The vehemence with which she said this seemed so much greater than the cause of her annoyance', p. 152) vie with passages of Woolfian streams of consciousness ('From this point Clarke speculated briefly on the nature of knowledge. Did knowledge of one's friends and colleagues impose a handicap on one? Perhaps it did,' p. 131), convincing us (if his titles already had not) that Achebe is fully aware of the modernist project, and fluent in its craft.

Yet perhaps the more important and typically unnoticed thing about this novel is not the to-and-fro between the mutually interpolating versions of African and English reality, interesting as it is. Far more striking is the increasing velocity with which the 'white' narrative constantly interrupts and undermines the 'African' one, in a way perhaps not unrelated to the historical effects of slavery and colonialism on African village life and culture. Political appropriation and co-optation as historical fact here are mirrored in the insistence of white discourse: the attempt of the 'white' narrative to usurp or 'universalize' the 'black' one, with all its quaint heritage of 'native customs and idiom'. At best, one has single chapters (as in 13) in which blacks and whites vie, as it were, for the control of their own history.

As we have seen, a similar struggle leads Achebe in *Things Fall Apart* to pre-empt a proposed white version of the plot (the district commissioner's report mentioned at the end — *The Pacification of the Primitive Tribes of the Lower Niger*) by ironically encircling it within his own, African narrative. In *Arrow of God*, we see Tony Clarke reading the same report (p. 39), so in a sense, Achebe's initial gambit has not worked. Achebe, again in the second novel, feels obliged to inscribe possibly biased white readings within an African narrative framework. The repetition of the attempt seems to indicate a suspicion of its ultimate futility. Indeed, as the novel progresses, the number of chapters written in 'white' discourse (as in chapters 3, 5, 10, 13, 14, and 15) increases. In only a few chapters (which have both black and white narrative) is chapter-based segregation broken down, yet the final victory of white discourse in a more global sense is already foretokened in the immediate material conditions of Achebe's literary products: written in English; published in England. Thus the fateful historical intervention of the European in Ibo society, and the effects on the Nigerian village life and culture of slavery and colonialism, here find a striking and unsettling narrational and institutional resonance.

Despite all the problems that western critics have had with Tutuola's and Achebe's texts, the term 'universal' has been applied to both. It should be clear by now, though, that we are dealing with two versions of the 'universal', best differentiated by a term used in Ishmael Reed's *Mumbo Jumbo* (1972). Here, the Afro-American writer Reed accurately dissects what could be called the 'white' and the 'black' approaches to universality and communality. *Mumbo Jumbo* traces an imaginary history of western and non-western culture, wherein non-historical and non-material (hence 'primitive') elements insist on disrupting western culture's appetite for closed and secure progression. These disruptions of closed systems — which Reed typifies as 'eruptions of Jes Grew' — in fact renew rather than ravage what might have become stagnant ('They are calling it a plague when in fact it is an anti-plague', p. 27). Established institutions consistently view them as threats, however.[36] Hence, in Reed's conception, western history becomes a series of failed and misguided attempts to ignore gaps in systems of national, cultural, or racial cohesion (what I have elsewhere called *cuts*) or to prevent them altogether: 'You must use something up-to-date to curb Jes Grew. To knock it dock it co-opt it swing it or bop it' (p. 73).[37]

The European notion of 'universality' often takes on, as we have seen, the aspect of *collection*: it seems a drive to accumulate as many texts, artifacts, nations, peoples as possible, all under one roof, one rubric, or one ruler. *Mumbo Jumbo* somewhat cheekily suggests that the European notion of 'universality' is a mammoth power play, 'universal being a word co-opted by the Catholic Church when the Atonists took over Rome, as a way of measuring every 1 by their ideals' (p. 153). The twin imperatives 'exclude and accumulate' seem fitting under a kind of Hegelian linearism that wants to incorporate within one Spirit or mind ever greater areas of knowledge and material. 'Realm' becomes 'nation' becomes 'empire' becomes 'western' or 'European' civilization, but stays *white*. Accumulation, then, is an almost metaphorical movement, whereby things of differing values are lumped together under a single image or signifier for purposes of potential exchange, marketability, or common defense. Efforts both literary and political to include non-whites in this scheme have centered around white perspectives and maintained the dominance of the white narrative and white nations (at least until very recently).

Reed's portrayal of western 'museums' as penal institutions, or 'Centers of Art Detention' for some of the Third World's most sacred artifacts engages the whole question of artistic 'universality' and the motivations behind it, as exemplified in the epithet that the largest European and American galleries (such as New York's Metropolitan Museum of Art) apply to themselves: *universal* museums'. These museums, *collections* in every sense, would seem to enforce a residual aesthetic progressivism and political imperialism that is not unrelated to universalizing tendencies in other realms of western culture.

Opposed to this critical stance of a 'universality' that encompasses — yet also confines and dominates — well-defined national distinctions, we have what might be called an African approach to universality: not *collection*, but a benevolent *contagion*, not of disease, but a shared awareness of shared energy. The transcendence of segregationist barriers that much African writing — and Reed's *Mumbo Jumbo* — exemplifies is exactly 'the indefinable quality that James Weldon Johnson called "Jes Grew" . . . "It belonged to nobody," Johnson said. "It's words were unprintable but its tune irresistible".' (p. 239) The dominant metaphor for 'Jes Grew' in Reed's text is 'contagion': all cultures, colors, and nationalities are subject to the ubiquity of its 'pandemic' (p. 27). 'Jes Grew' (in a sense, the main 'character' of *Mumbo Jumbo*) is the elusive force that certain repressive people (whom Reed names the 'Atonists') are trying to co-opt, confine, or destroy. But what might be the determinants of contagion? Perhaps the most important aspect of cultural contagion is that by the time one is aware of it, it has *already happened*. Contagion, being metonymic (*con + tangere* = 'touching together'), involves — most appropriately for an African tribal context — an actual process of contacts between people, rather than a quantitative setting of metaphorical value. If *collection* exists as a guarantor of *pro*spective value, then *contagion* is a *retro*spective attempt to assess a propinquity that seems to have always been present in latent form and has already erupted without cause or warning. Opposed to Dr Johnson's 'pedigree' that sought to discover lost, but recoverable *differences*, contagion represents the existence of recoverable *affinities* between disparate races of people. It is perhaps a tiny inkling of contagion that Achebe shows when we seen the presumably austere Winterbottom in *Arrow of God* 'mystifying other Europeans with words from the Ibo language which he claimed to speak fluently' (p. 184). His fate was not uncommon in the chronicle of imperialism: even as they tried to collect ever newer local cultures and races, dominant powers found themselves caught up in the contagion they tried to put down. The sequence of contagion, collection (or repression) and new contagion furnishes the basic rhythm of Reed's various plots. Even as collection domesticates and organizes barriers and distances, contagion seems to have already made obsolete the barriers to its own spread.

Reed's narrative — together with Tutuola's and Achebe's novels — provides a well-targeted analysis of cultural cohesion as Europe and America have practiced it throughout 'written history' against the 'unwritten' strains of blackness that repeatedly threaten to spread. *Mumbo*

Jumbo deals with the temptation of western culture to fasten a sense of superiority or national cohesion to particular texts, tropes, or routines. Inexplicably to the western mind, these texts, tropes, and routines soon (for the sake of convenience, let us say at around 1900) come to seem unstable, tainted, as if they have all along belonged not to the west, but to a distinct and mocking oppositional sensibility.

Reed's narrative must struggle, however, with a fascinating tension between its own diachronic account of history and its ultimately anti-progressive moral. Jes Grew 'is seeking its words. Its text. For what good is a liturgy without a text?' (p. 9) — yet it is also clear that finding a material base for Jes Grew (for contagion), beyond the people it infects, would threaten it with ossification and even destruction. One of the hopes of the Atonists is that 'by burning the Book they would sterilize the Jes Grew forever' (p. 217). In so far as the novel *Mumbo Jumbo* itself is the temporary repository for the energies of Jes Grew, it becomes narratologically unique and intriguing, yet difficult to finally fix.

It is exactly Jes Grew's ability to displace local allegiances that allows it to stand for contagion. Its best counterpart in western literature (alluded to in *Mumbo Jumbo's* rewriting of western history) is the cult of Dionysos in Euripides' *The Bacchae*. Dionysos' first inclination always was to migrate: to invade or 'infect' (in King Pentheus' words) diverse regions and lands, a process that Thomas Mann called *Ausweitung* ('spreading out'), borrowing from Erwin Rhode's description of Dionysiac rites in his *Psyche*. These rites, like Jes Grew's contagion, nullified national, sexual, and racial barriers — Jes Grew 'knows no class no race no consciousness. . . . It is self-propagating and you can never tell when it will hit' (p. 4). Reed's narrative swings from Harlem to Wall Street to Harlem to Yorktown to Croton-on-Hudson — finally, the entire globe is the field of Jes Grew's (and Reed's) historical play.

The eclecticism of Jes Grew even resonates in the title *Mumbo Jumbo*, which, according to the etymology that Reed prints in his preface, is a hybrid phrase, an amalgam of several Mandingo expressions, themselves incorrectly transcribed and employed by the English as a synonym for anything that sounds portentous, but is really meaningless. Yet even here, the phrase shows how collection submits to contagion. In attempting to 'collect' these two primitive words and make them 'mean' something foreign, the English colonialist becomes the victim of the word's own contagion: its original Mandingo roots are still in force, and alongside the dictionary definition of 'meaningless language', the word still insists on another meaning — 'African language that Europeans compulsively collect, but will never understand'.

The philosophical implications of hybridizing can escape an unwary reader, however. For example, Christopher Lehmann-Haupt, in his *New York Times* review, well describes but poorly understands Reed's tack:

> The only trouble with the Reed grand design is that in trying to resurrect the Neo-HooDooist black esthetic, it keeps having to expropriate the tools of Western culture — the printing press, the photograph, the

European narrative tradition, the English language, and other such diabolical instruments of the anti-Jes Grew conspiracy.[38]

Lehmann-Haupt's language of 'black esthetic', 'European narrative tradition', and 'English language' echoes with the dilemmas of national and racial exclusivity which the apparently universalizing effects of the *collection* had seemed to remedy, but now only perpetuate. It is not so much that Reed finds himself 'having to expropriate the tools of Western culture' as that he is revising a prior co-optation of black culture, using a narrative principle that will undermine the very assumptions that brought that prior appropriation about. Yet this principle works both ways, criticizing black nationalists (such as Reed's character Abdul) and Pan-Africanists ('the essential Pan-Africanism is artists relating across continents their craft, drumbeats from the aeons, sounds that are still with us': pp. 94—5) alike: 'pandemic', not 'Pan-African' is the operative word.

The writers and their works that I have discussed have presented us with an aesthetic that critiques the European, exclusivist connection of nationalism with language and literature. Such narratives are no longer comparable to any European humanistic or socio-political model. Far from progressive, it seems that Jes Grew 'has no end and no beginning. . . . We will miss it for a while but it will come back, and when it returns we will see that it never left' (p. 233). Jes Grew is seeking its text, but without a text, it retains the possibility of non-exclusive contagion.

Notes

1 James Boswell, *Boswell's Journal of A Tour to the Hebrides With Samuel Johnson, LL.D.,* ed. Frederick A. Pottle and Charles H. Bennett (New York: Viking, 1936), '18 September 1773', p. 186.
2 Quoted in Stanley I. Benn, 'Nationalism', *The Encyclopedia of Philosophy*, ed. Paul Edwards, vol. 5 (New York: Macmillan, 1967), p. 443.
3 A modern version of this notion may be found in contemporary debates over whether to establish an 'official language' for countries such as the United States, where a shared 'mother tongue' is less and less to be taken for granted.
4 Ralph Waldo Emerson, 'Race', in *The Portable Emerson*, ed. Carl Bode and Malcolm Cowley (New York: Penguin, 1981), p. 407.
5 Few authors have described the simultaneous and contradictory processes of racial inclusion and exclusion as well as William Faulkner, whose novels show the inevitable linguistic, sexual, and psychological mixtures consequent upon any systematic social rhetoric of division. See my *Figures of Division: William Faulkner's Major Novels* (New York: Methuen, 1986).
6 Vernacular translations of the Bible by Tyndall in the English tradition or by Luther in the German tradition (Nietzsche called Luther's Bible 'the best German book', compared to which 'almost everything else is mere "literature"') are perhaps the pre-eminent versions of using texts as commonplaces for group cohesion. Religious texts configure a narrative about the Divine — absolute universality — into an enduring set of words which by their peculiar magnetism can be subjected to the narrower claims of competing language

communities. The Koran provides an even more extreme example, being a religious text which interweaves religious belief, the historical standardization of Arabic writing systems, the primary inventory of tropes of literary expression, and a certain supra-national identification into a broad discursive fabric shared by all speakers and writers of Arabic. It is not uncommon, however, for an 'outsider' precisely to uncover the hybridizing possibilities of a text which had hitherto been used only to consolidate a particular nationalist prerogative. The case of Wole Soyinka's 1973 translation and production of Euripides' 'classic', *The Bacchae*, at London's Old Vic is exemplary here.

7 Edward Said, 'Roads taken and not taken', in *The World, The Text, and the Critic* (Cambridge, Mass.: Harvard University Press, 1983), p. 146.

8 'Wer sich berät das Wesen des "französischen Geistes" klarzuwerden sucht, braucht zunächst nur die französische Literatur zu befragen'. See *Kindlers Literatur Lexikon im dtv, Band 1, Essays* (Munich: Deutscher Taschenbuch Verlag, 1974), p. 153.

9 George Sampson, *The Concise Cambridge History of English Literature* (Cambridge: Cambridge University Press, 1959), p. 1.

10 Freud, in the 'wolf man' case, reconstructed a *primal scene*, triangulating backwards, as it were, to plot a hypothetical 'original' moment important for the understanding of later events, but one whose reality he was always careful to leave in question. He begins his proof by saying 'I will only ask [the reader] to join me in adopting a *provisional* belief in the reality of the scene', and by the end, he still has no 'proof' of that fateful original moment: 'I intend on this occasion to close the discussion of the reality of the primal scene with a *non liquet*'. He has construed, not found, the starting point for his later case 'history': Sigmund Freud, *Three Case Histories* (New York: Macmillan, 1963), 'From the history of an infantile neurosis' (1918), pp. 224, 248.

11 Sampson, op. cit., pp. xi, 1.

12 Friedrich Nietzsche, *Beyond Good and Evil*, trans. Walter Kaufmann (New York: Vintage, 1966), sec. 251, p. 188. German title: *Jenseits von Gut and Böse*.

13 Sigmund Freud, *Group Psychology and the Analysis of the Ego*, trans. James Strachey (New York: Norton, 1959), pp. 33–4. German title: *Massenpsychologie und Ich-Analyse* (1921).

14 Jean-Paul Sartre, Preface to *L'Anthologie de la Nouvelle Poésie Nègre et Malgache de Langue Francaise*, ed. Leopold Sedar Senghor (Paris: Presses Universitaires de France, 1948).

15 For more on the relationship between philosophical progressivism and some formal characteristics of modernist European art, as compared with black artistic forms, see my article, 'Repetition as a figure of black culture', in Henry L. Gates (ed.), *Black Literature and Literary Theory* (New York: Methuen, 1984).

16 Bernth Lindfors, *Folklore in Nigerian Literature* (New York: Africana, 1973), p. 173.

17 Lindfors, op. cit., p. 2.

18 See Douglas Killam, 'Cyprian Ekwensi', p. 78; John Povey, 'The novels of Chinua Achebe', p. 98; Eldred D. Jones, 'The essential Soyinka', p. 113; all in Bruce King (ed.), *Introduction to Nigerian Literature* (Ibadan: University of Lagos and Evans, 1971); J. Z. Kronenfeld, 'The "communalistic" African and the "individualistic" westerner: some comments on misleading generalizations in western criticism of Soyinka and Achebe', in Bernth Lindfors (ed.), *Critical Perspectives on Nigerian Literatues* (Washington, DC: Three Continents Press,

1976), pp. 252–3; Bruce King, op. cit., 'Introduction', p. 6, and Robert P. Armstrong, 'The narrative and intensive continuity: *The Palm-Wine Drinkard*', in Lindfors, op. cit., p. 110.

19 Jahnheinz Jahn, 'Die Neo-Afrikanische Literatur', in *Kindlers Literatur Lexicon*, p. 695, my translation. Also, Lindfors, *Folklore*, p. 153.

20 Jahn, op. cit., p. 695, my translation.

21 See Jürgen Zwernemann, 'Die Traditionelle Literatur des Schwarzen Afrika', in *Kindlers Literatur Lexikon*, pp. 684–5.

22 Adeboye Babalol, 'A survey of modern literature in the Yoruba, Efik and Hausa Languages', in King, op. cit., pp. 57, 50.

23 Lindfors, *Folklore*, p. 4.

24 King, op. cit., 'Introduction', p. 9.

25 Killam, op. cit., p. 77; King, op. cit., p. 11.

26 Amos Tutuola, *The Palm-Wine Drinkard* (New York: Grove, 1980), p. 9. All subsequent page references are from this text.

27 See Armstrong, op. cit., pp. 112–13, and Anne Tibble, *African/English Literature*, quoted in Lindfors, op. cit., p. 10.

28 Armstrong, op. cit., p. 128.

29 Armstorng, op. cit., p. 127; O. R. Dathorne, 'Amos Tutuola: the nightmare of the tribe', in King, op. cit., p. 66.

30 Lindfors, op. cit., 'Yoruba and Ibo prose styles', p. 161; King, op. cit., 'Introduction', p. 2.

31 Chinua Achebe, *Things Fall Apart* (New York: Fawcett Crest, 1984), p. 10. All subsequent references are from this text.

32 Chinua Achebe, *Arrow of God* (London: Heinemann, 1964), p. 177.

33 A similar literary reversal takes place in Ferdinand Oyono's *Un Vie de Boy* (1960), in which by gaining literacy from the French Camerounian missionaries, he both registers the acts of colonialist cruelty that he can now read from written diaries, and keeps a diary in his own dialect (Ewondo) that comments on the colonizers' ethnocentrism and ruthlessness. The literary device of the diary — borrowed from those who tried to oppress him by limiting his access to writing — becomes the text of the novel itself; writing, once the tool of oppression, has become a tool of liberation.

34 Lloyd W. Brown, 'Cultural norms and modes of perception in Achebe's fiction', in Lindfors, *Critical Perspectives*, p. 135.

35 Ronald Christ, *New York Times Book Review*, 17 December 1967, p. 22.

36 Ishmael Reed, *Mumbo Jumbo* (New York: Doubleday, 1972). All subsequent references are from this text.

37 See my article 'Repetition as a figure of black culture', p. 67.

38 Christopher Lehmann-Haupt, Review of *Mumbo Jumbo*, *New York Times*, 6 August 1972.

14
English reading

Francis Mulhern

My task which I am trying to achieve is, by the power of the written word to make you hear, to make you feel — it is, before all else, to make you *see*. That — and no more, and it is everything.

(Joseph Conrad)

English ought to be kept up.

(John Keats)

What should we read, *how* should we read it, and *why*? Such questions are staple elements of any politics of reading. But they remain less than critical if they are put without consciousness of the unavowed answer they already insinuate. Issues of selection, procedure, and purpose are often settled in advance by the meanings assigned to the collective pronoun. So there is a further question: *as whom, as what* do 'we' read? Asked or not, this question is always answered, and on this occasion it may be worthwhile to consider the 'answer' given in an especially forceful practice of reading: the English literary criticism chiefly represented by F. R. and Q. D. Leavis.

I

Pressed for a philosophical defence of his criticism, F. R. Leavis offered a narrative:

The cogency I hoped to achieve was to be for other readers of poetry — readers of poetry as such. I hoped, by putting in front of them, in a criticism that should keep as close to the concrete as possible, my own developed 'coherence of response', to get them to agree (with, no doubt, critical qualifications) that the map, the essential order, of English poetry seen as a whole did, when they interrogated their experience, look like that to them also. ... My whole effort was to work in terms of concrete judgements and particular analyses: 'This — doesn't it? — bears such a relation to that; this kind of thing — don't you find it so? — wears better than that', etc.[1]

In this way, Leavis sought to elude the very terms of René Wellek's demand. There would be no 'explicit' and 'systematic' account of principles, no 'abstract' evaluation of 'choices': only reading, and dialogue with other readers.

The upshot was paradoxical. Apparently unforthcoming, Leavis's counter-move was perhaps more revealing than a more compliant response would have been. The founding assumption of Leavisian criticism, it turned out, was a rigorous humanism: the experiential merging of critic and poem, and of both with the experience of 'other readers', was scarcely thinkable without the 'philosophical' guarantee of a human essence — something constant, universal, and, like the Arnoldian 'best self', potentially decisive.[2] However, there is a logical strain in the notion of an essence whose efficacy is contingent, and this is evident in Leavis's narrative of 'the common pursuit'. The imagined scene is ideal: critic and interlocutor in informal, even intimate exchange. But the very informality of the critic-narrator's questions betrays the imposture of openness: negatively phrased, they presume assent — or what is imagined at another moment as corroborative self-'interrogation'. The interlocutor, meanwhile, is silent; the expected 'critical qualifications', never uttered, remain parenthetical concessions in the discourse of the critic. Lacking this interlocutor, the situation and its justifying event are jeopardized, and Leavis seems almost resigned to the loss: 'I hoped . . . I hoped . . . my whole effort was . . .', he writes, as if telling a story of what might have been.

Leavis's half-realized character — present, presumably assenting, yet silent — embodies a compromise between two incommensurable entities: the ideal interlocutor whose active, confirming presence is the necessary ground of Leavisian criticism, and an actual, contingent readership that is neither present to the author nor predictable in the range and substance of its 'qualifications'. This, abstractly speaking, is a logical dilemma: Leavisian criticism is a long-drawn-out fallacy, endlessly bent on establishing what it already assumes to exist. But practically, it is a problem of suasion. 'My task', wrote Conrad, in a declaration uncannily close to Leavis's, 'is, before all else, to make you *see*. That — and no more, and it is everything'.[3] If so little is 'everything', it is because there is indeed something 'more'. The preferred reading of the passage is clearly signalled in its syntax and typography: the goal is shared vision. But these indications of emphasis are crossed by the counter-emphasis of repetition: the task is 'to make you . . . to make you . . . to make you . . .'. In a characteristic movement of disavowal, Conrad's words admit the moment of dictation in all writing. To represent the object is, measure for measure, to position the subject, the clarity of the one depending on the stability of the other. To 'make' is at once to compel and to compose: to compel the actual reader by composing an ideal one, to *pre-scribe* the subjective conditions of 'seeing'. No less than of Conrad's fiction, this is the rhetorical task of Leavisian criticism.

Leavis's task is to determine the object ('the map, the essential order') and, as a necessary part of this, to position the subject. His critical writing must work to reduce the discrepancy between its ideal interlocutor and real readers, to compose the *normal* subject of Leavisian reading-writing. In other words, the writing must complete the half-sketched second character in the exemplary narrative of criticism. And it really will be a 'character', not an ontological cypher. The sponsors of humanism are, dependably, rather more than generically 'human', and so equally are the normative images of their writing. As Perry Anderson observed nearly twenty years ago, the real solidarities of Leavisian humanism are quite specific in time and place.[4] The 'character' whose features emerge in Leavisian criticism is a fully historical being, and 'normal' in every way.

II

This normalizing drive is sometimes declared, as on those occasions when critical attention turns from the literary object to the ('qualifying'?) reader: 'Here a few illustrations [from *The Prelude*] must suffice, as indeed, to point the attention effectively, they should: that once done, the demonstration is the reading, as anyone who cares to open his Wordsworth may see; the facts, to the adverted eye, are obvious'.[5]

But conspicuous interventions of this kind are only the periodic excesses of an activity whose signs are everywhere in the ordinary workings of Leavisian 'analysis and judgement'. For in this cultural zone nearly all seasons are bad ones. The imagined time of Leavisian criticism ('I hoped . . . I hoped . . . my whole effort was . . .') is that of impending loss. The ideal interlocutor is chronically prone to distraction by the spectacle of historical change. The meaning of modern history, for Leavis, was the dissolution of 'community'. Emerging in the period of the English Revolution and gathering strength in the succeeding century, a whole array of social forces had worked to undermine a traditional, integrated way of life, and then unleashed the industrializing dynamic that shook it apart. Where once there had been an 'organic' community, there were now two mutually opposed and unequal realities: 'civilization', the world of means and quantities, which drove forward according to the autonomous logic of industrial production, and 'culture', the world of qualities and ends, the memory of a 'human norm' that could never again find general social acceptance, and the only resource of those who fought to avert a final breach in 'continuity'. By the early twentieth century, the lot of 'culture' had so worsened that language, in its most demanding literary usage, was now the only element of continuity. Out of that history and that vital 'human' need came the cultural warrant of literary judgement and the objective responsibility borne by any who thought to exercise it.

Such representations of the past are not truly historical in mode. Processes of change are described and interpreted, but only as the corrosive, demoralizing environment of something that is held to be essentially changeless, and whose value is the decisive theme of the retrospect. This is the past not as history but as 'tradition'. Its characteristic mode is, so to say, *transjunctive*, its valued moments 'joined across' the objective order of what has been in the service of what now exists. Tradition, as Leavis himself noted, is akin to memory. And, as he did not add, their procedures and functions are the same. Tradition, usually said to be received, is in reality made, in an unceasing activity of selection, revision, and outright invention, whose function is to defend identity against the threat of heterogeneity, discontinuity and contradiction. Its purpose is to *bind* (and necessarily, therefore, to *exclude*). Tradition is prone to represent itself as custom, as the settled fact of continuity, but its real process is shot through with anxiety, as the history of Leavis's journal itself attests. *Scrutiny*'s watchword, as it tested the claims of writing in its own day, was 'for continuity' (the title of Leavis's first collection of essays). But its retrospects were no less wary, and the last years of the journal witnessed a restless probing of the 'organic community' itself, in its putative seventeenth-century setting. The essential strengths of that period were found to be residues of pre-Reformation culture, which in its turn was discovered to run back into a pre-Christian past. And so the deepest continuities of English literature seemed to be with a society and a culture that were not in any reasonable sense 'English'.

The poignancy of this conclusion deserves emphasis, for the sovereign *topos* of Leavisian discourse was precisely the continuity of Englishness. The basic categories of *Scrutiny*'s historiography were implicitly universal in application; as is manifest in the kindred sociological line descending from Tönnies's *Gemeinschaft und Gesellschaft*, they frame a certain interpretation of the transition to capitalism as such. But in Leavis' writing, their privileged reference is to England and the doom of English culture, and his key values are not so much 'culture' or 'literature' as a language and a people.

Shakespeare, Leavis affirms, is 'the pre-eminently (in his relation to the language) English poet',[6] and the decisive nuance of the adverbial is fixed in this tribute to Donne: 'This is the Shakespearian use of English: one might say that it is the English use — the use, in the essential spirit of the language, of its characteristic resources'.[7]

The attributes of this 'essential spirit' are celebrated again and again. Donne's poetry exhibits 'the sinew and living nerve', the 'strength of spoken English'.[8] Jonson evinces a 'native robustness', a 'rooted and racy Englishness'; his 'toughness is lively and English', going with his 'native good sense'.[9] In Jonson, these qualities are such as to subdue the external, 'classicizing' language of the Renaissance, his 'racy personal tone' turning 'erudition into native sinew'. Where classicism prevails, as in Milton, the outcome is 'rejection of English idiom', for which the critical penalty is exile.[10] The integrity that animates this English idiom has more than one specification. Leavis largely agrees with Gerard Manley Hopkins that Dryden's 'native English strength' is 'masculine' in its stress on 'the naked thew and sinew of the language', and compliments Crabbe on his 'generous masculine strength'.[11] The lapse from this idiom is a token of moral deficiency, as the case of Shelley shows. But Keats bears witness to the possibility of regeneration, finding at last 'a strength — a native English strength — lying beyond the scope of the poet who aimed to make English as like Italian as possible [and a] vigour such as is alien to the Tennysonian habit, and such as a Tennysonian handling of the medium cannot breed'.[12]

The steady connotative pressure of Leavis's idiom is quite remarkable. The literal emphasis on the specificities of the English language is developed, across an unvarying range of metaphor, association and (scarcely intended) pun, into a positive characterization of 'Englishness'. By the later stages of *Revaluation* an elaborate order of solidarity and antagonism has been enforced: the native, racy, vigorous, strong, masculine, and against these the classicizing, Italianate, alien, corrupt, voluptuous, effeminate, impotent. In vouching for Wordsworth as 'normally and robustly human', Leavis summarizes a whole anthropology of virtue.[13] 'The facts, to the adverted eye, are obvious'.

The Great Tradition was to do for the English novel what *Revaluation* had done for English poetry. Like the earlier work, it is concerned not to construct a history (it is expressly pitched against 'the literary histories') but to ascertain the 'tradition', the 'line' of the English novel as it comes down through the heterogeneous mass of narrative fiction in prose. The nature of the operation approaches self-consciousness in this sentence from the opening pages of the work: 'One of the supreme debts one great writer can owe another is the realization of unlikeness (there is, of course, no significant unlikeness without the common concern — and the common seriousness of concern — with essential human issues)'.[14]

The movement of this passage epitomizes the activity of binding and exclusion in which Leavisian criticism is involved. Heterogeneity is at first acknowledged, but is then reduced to 'significant' unlikeness, which turns out to be the deceptive sign of an inner consonance whose bearing (cognitive and ethical) is the essentially human — in short, the self-identical. And the medium of the essentially human, it turns out, is English. The nativism of *Revaluation* is equally, if less euphorically, evident in *The Great Tradition*.

Of Leavis's three chosen novelists, only one (George Eliot) was English. James was Anglophone but American; the language of Conrad's novels was his third; and both learned significantly from other literatures. A key purpose of *The Great Tradition* was to reduce these complexities of formation to biographical accident and to 'naturalize' James and Conrad as exponents of a transcendent language that must be understood as adequate, and finally as necessary, to the novelistic exploration of 'essential human values'. The story of the book is the victory of an English tradition over the circumstances of origin and, crucially, over the latterday Renaissance, French realism. Thus, James may be located in 'a distinctively American' line, but this is as it were a ruse of tradition: Hawthorne emancipated James from the influence of Thackeray and from Flaubert, making possible an authentic, enabling connection with Eliot.[15] Conrad did indeed learn from 'the French masters': the stylism and exoticism of his weaker writing is derived from Chateaubriand, and

Nostromo recalls Flaubert.[16] Yet Conrad's work, with its 'robust vigour of melodrama', is also 'Dickensian', 'Elizabethan' even.[17] And if he evinces that 'racy strength' it is because, his origins notwithstanding, his 'themes and interests' actually called for the English language rather than any other. He is 'unquestionably a constitutive part of the tradition, belonging in the full sense'.[18]

A second major theme of *The Great Tradition* is the novel as such. It was in the course of writing this book that Leavis substantiated his conception of the novel as linguistic art. 'The differences between a lyric, a Shakespeare play, and a novel, for some purposes essential, are not in danger of being forgotten; what needs insisting on is the community', he wrote in the early 1930s, and the criticism that ensued was to be interested not in 'character' and 'incident' but in the 'pattern of moral significances' that novelistic art might yield, in 'the novel as dramatic poem'.[19] Much of the meaning of this conception, and the polemical force with which Leavis promoted it, must be sought in the history of academic and lay literary criticism. Leavis, like others around him, was determined to redeem the novel from its common status as a cultivated (or narcotic) diversion and to establish its parity with the canonical arts of language. But his manner of doing so bears an interesting relation to his critical practice generally. His terminology disrupts the received classification of verbal art and redefines the novel (epic) as a combination of the two types from which it was classically distinguished, the lyric and the dramatic. The effect of this development — which reinforced an already well-established emphasis on the 'poetic' essence of verse drama — was to reorder the field of critical perception at the expense of *narrative*. All wider differences set aside, it can still be said that the greatest weakness of Leavisian criticism lay just here; and part of the sense of that weakness may be glimpsed in Leavis' reading of *Typhoon*.

The 'elemental frenzy' (Leavis's phrase) that occupies most of Conrad's story is a literal event: a British merchant ship is exposed to a devastating tropical storm and only narrowly escapes destruction. But from the outset it is metaphorized as a psychic and political ordeal. The ship's captain, MacWhirr, is an obsessional. Locks and charts are the emblems of his life; his letters to his wife are phatic observances, without value as registrations of feeling or incident; his speech, which he enforces as a shipboard norm, is laconic, literal, and untouched by the smallest acquaintance with pidgin. However, the circumstances of this voyage are not wholly routine. The ship has been transferred from the British to the Siamese flag; and the 'cargo' on this occasion is human — 200 Chinese coolies returning from periods of labour in various colonies. Sailing under 'queer' colours, its crew outnumbered by their freight of alien bodies, the *Nan-Shan* heads into 'dirty' weather. The storm attacks every established social relationship of the vessel. Masculinity is abandoned for hysteria; linguistic order fails, as speech turns figural or obscene, is blocked by superstition or swept away by the gale. MacWhirr and his first mate, Jukes, reach for each other in encounters that mingle duty and desire, resolution and bewilderment; while in the hold the Chinese have apparently gone berserk. The lowering of the British ensign brings on a storm that unfixes identity ('He started shouting aimlessly to the man he could feel near him in that fiendish blackness, "Is it you, sir? Is it you, sir?" till his temples seemed ready to burst. And he heard in answer a voice, as if crying far away, as if screaming to him fretfully from a very great distance, the one word "Yes!".'), and *Homo Britannicus* is abandoned to a chaos of effeminacy, homoeroticism, and gibberish — the terrifying counter-order of the Chinese labourers below. The ship survives. But the restoration of order is understood as a furtive improvisation, the hurried winding-up of an incident better forgotten. It is related not by the main narrator but in a chattily complacent letter from Jukes, who, in his uncertain sexual orientation (his regular correspondent is male) and openness to linguistic transgression (metaphor, pidgin), is socially perverse. Worse, the protagonist himself is fatally ambiguous: MacWhirr, as we have learned from an early narrative recollection, is not British but Irish. The chief officers of the *Nan-Shan*, ultimate guarantors of imperial order, bear the typhoon within themselves.

Leavis's account discloses virtually nothing of this. Where he quotes passages whose manifest sense discourages any other reading, he confines himself to dubious technical observations on 'a novelist's art', and his wider commentary on *Typhoon* strikes a directly contrary emphasis. It is the 'ordinariness' and 'matter-of-factness' of the ship's captain and crew that hold his attention, 'the qualities which, in a triumph of discipline — a triumph of the spirit — have enabled a handful of ordinary men to impose sanity on a frantic mob'.[20] Leavis's language reveals his ideological relationship to *Typhoon* and, at the same time, the strategy of his reading. Identifying himself with the norms of the text, he sets out to rewrite its ending and to *unwrite* the greater part of the narrative. *Typhoon* works through a fearsome 'return of the repressed'; Leavis's reading functions to assist repression, indeed to perfect it, simply silencing the anxieties that generated the story in the first instance.

Leavis's encounter with *Typhoon* may serve as a hyperbolic illustration of his critical relationship with narrative generally. Narratives vary, it need hardly be said; but the work of narrativity is always an opening and closing, a loosening and rebinding of sense. All but the most sedate or the most forensic narratives are in some degree unsettling — and *Typhonn* is neither. It may be ventured, then, that a criticism bent on affirming an essential human identity will be inhibited in the face of narrative, and will 'revise' its object-texts (as the ego is said to revise dreams and memories) in that interest. And it is apt that Leavis, confronted with a fictional dispersal of that identity, in a text of his own choosing by one of his canonical authors, should read with an averted eye.

III

The 'human' is a closely specified term in Leavisian discourse, as, in turn, is 'English': *Revaluation* makes this plain. They are normalizing terms that arrogate the common names of a species, a language and an ethnic formation as the honorific titles of particular social commitments and agencies. They are, in the necessary strict meaning of a slackened concept, ideological. The nature of these commitments and agencies is manifest in the social history of Leavis and his collaborators, and equally in their critical writing. The normal subject of Leavisian discourse is specified not only by nationality but also by class, gender, and sexual orientation.

The *Scrutiny* 'connection', as Leavis sometimes called it, was petty-bourgeois. Its leading members were generally such by provenance, as were its contributors and regular readers — teachers in the main — by occupation. The politics of the 'connection' were likewise suspended over the main national and international conflicts of the time. The anti-industrialism of the journal was inevitably shaded with anti-capitalism, sometimes markedly. But *Scrutiny*'s stand against Marxism is a legend; and notwithstanding social compassion and episodic political sympathy, Leavis and his collaborators rebuffed any suggestion that the industrial working class had the capacity to sustain or develop 'humane culture'. The class disposition of the journal was plainest in its constant attacks on the leisured academic rearguard of Oxford and Cambridge, and the part-*rentier*, part-commercial intelligentsia of the capital. One among many needling allusions to the former can be discerned in Leavis's repeated reference, in *Revaluation*, to 'the mob of gentlemen' who versified at the court of Charles I; and a more striking index of this academic class antagonism is the diction of Leavisian criticism, which quite character-istically qualifies the received idiom of cultivated leisure ('taste', 'sensibility', 'fineness') with a new and challenging idiom of effort ('strenuous', 'labour', 'collaboration' 'enactment'). The strategic prize in *Scrutiny*'s contention with the metropolitan elites was the status of 'centrality', which Leavis and his collaborators sought to invest with a strictly cultural, rather than 'social', meaning. Here too the polemical idiom was telling: in a metaphorical economy of intellectual life, the 'inflated currencies' of the capital were to be regulated by authentic 'stan-dards' and 'values', real measures of work and self-improvement.

Much of Q. D. Leavis's assault on Virgina Woolf can be read in this light. The latter's *Three Guineas*, she charged, exemplified the conceptions of a class-blinded 'social parasite'; Woolf's feminist critique of educa-tional provision was 'a sort of chatty restatement of the rights and wrongs' of propertied women intellectuals like herself, designed to 'penalize specialists' in the interests of amateur 'boudoir scholarship'. But there was more than righteous class hostility in a passage like this, which duly places Leavis's occasional concessions to feminism:

> 'Daughters of educated men have always done their thinking from hand to mouth . . . [Woolf had written]. They have thought while they stirred the pot, while they rocked the cradle'. I agree with someone who complained that to judge from the acquaintance with the realities of life displayed in this book there is no reason to suppose Mrs Woolf would know which end of the cradle to stir. . . . I feel bound to

disagree with Mrs Woolf's assumption that running a household and a family unaided necessarily hinders or weakens thinking. One's own kitchen and nursery, and not the drawing-room and dinner-table where tired professional men relax among the ladies (thus Mrs Woolf), is the realm where living takes place, and I see no profit in letting our servants live for us. The activities Mrs Woolf wishes to free educated women from as wasteful not only provide a valuable discipline, they serve as a sieve for determining which values are important and genuine and which are conventional and contemptible. It is this order of experience that often makes the conversation of an uncultivated charmless woman who has merely worked hard and reared a family interesting and stimulating, while its absence renders a hypertrophied conversation piece like *Three Guineas* tiresome and worthless.[21]

That Virginia Woolf was prone to *rentier* myopia is undeniable, and Q. D. Leavis's attack would be sympathetic were not its terms and tone those of a far more myopic, truculently conformist femininity. Not merely a self-pampering 'victim' of class privilege, the suggestion went, Woolf was deficient as a woman. In such judgements the Leavises stood side by side. Corresponding assumptions animate the language of *Revaluation*, with its ready gendering of poetic idiom and associated imagery of virility and procreation (or their vicious substitutes). Woolf did not lack male company either: F. R. Leavis's summarizing review of E. M. Forster, in one way a moving tribute, hesitated several times before the novelist's 'spinsterish' prose; and the most-lamented poetic wastrel of the 1930s, W. H. Auden, was cast out in an article deploring his 'inverted' development.[22] There were so many tests of what was 'normally and robustly human'.

The evidence of these canonical works — the critical books and essays — is supported by that of the apocrypha: the joint autobiography that occupied the Leavises (and those around them) all their lives. This 'work' was never written, in the ordinary sense, but as Raymond Williams has observed, it might as well have been: 'Most of those who have heard [the story] will know how compellingly it was told. It was a sustained structure of feeling through the only apparently random episodes. It was essentially composed, in a literary sense.'[23] Williams is referring to the institutional history of Cambridge, *Scrutiny*, the London 'literary racket', and so on. But the volume of memoirs from which his words come extends their sense to the sphere of the domestic and personal. What emerges from Denys Thompson's gathering of 'recollections and impressions' is how strongly, how theatrically, the Leavises emphasized the proprieties of gender and family, and with what impact on those who were close to them. Frank was vain to the point of boasting about his athletic prowess, as was Queenie about her domestic skills; his running and her scones are staple topics of their memoirists. Their famous intellectual 'collaboration' was subject to strict gender regulation and a corresponding division of domestic labour. This was not a trouble-free formula: Queenie, proudly a working woman intellectual but just as proudly the wife and mother who never broke a cup, suffered conflicts of identity and interest from which her husband was largely exempt, and she knew it. But, in all, it seems that the drama of Leavisian criticism was encoded also as a determined and conservative politics of 'mature', 'normal' gender and sexuality, whose ideal scene was the family. It is not merely that the Leavises lived in a certain way — that is of purely biographical interest. What is important is that they actively represented their life together as a further specification of the 'human norm'.

The style of life, thus organized and projected, joined the critical style in a discourse of formidable appeal, as grateful pupils soon began to testify. 'Sanity and vigour and masculinity and Britishness' were the qualities that compelled one early tribute — Martin Green's. F. R. Leavis seemed

> intensely and integrally British. Not Europeanized, not of the intelligentsia, not of the upper classes, not of Bloomsbury, not of any group or set. . . . [He] comes to us from generations of decency and conscience and reasonableness and separateness, of private houses hidden behind hedges, along the road from Matthew Arnold and John Stuart Mill. . . . Alone in all Cambridge his voice has echoes of the best things in my parents' England, makes connections between all the parts of my experience.[24]

These are ingenuous words, but they are apt. Their 'structure of feeling' is manifestly Leavisian. In such terms, the ideal interlocutor finds a social identity and begins to speak.

IV

The governing values of Leavisian discourse are class-restrictive, (hetero)sexist and ethnocentric. The 'human' image is caught in a sepia print of family life in lower-middle-class England. In this composition of values, the fixing element, the guarantee of integrity, was the notion of an abiding, self-evident Englishness. Ethnocentrism did much to frame the perspective of *Scrutiny*'s literary criticism — which in turn cannot fully be understood apart from its conditions of formation in mid-century England.

'Ethnocentric' need not mean stay-at-home. If *Scrutiny* was less cosmopolitan than some other literary journals of its time, it was not insular. The literature of England was always its major concern, but that was hardly an unreasonable option. French, German, and US literature were extensively discussed, and other national literatures were surveyed or sampled. Neither was the journal in any ordinary sense patriotic: on the contrary, opposition to British chauvinism was a point of honour during the Second World War. The traces of *Scrutiny*'s ethnocentrism are to be found not in the range of its international coverage, which by the standards of the day was merely unremarkable, but in its characteristic manner. Scrutiny was most confident when dealing with *native* literatures: those emerging from the home ground of their respective languages —

English, French, German, Italian. Inhibition and resistance became evident in the face of 'rootless' diversity. 'More and more does human life depart from the natural rhythms', Leavis wrote, in an early, qualified reference to Spengler; 'the cultures have mingled, and the forms have dissolved into chaos'.[25] Scrutiny's criticism — and more pointedly his own — attempted to restore integrity and order. Thus, the Renaissance was legitimate on its own territory, but not when it threatened to 'classicize' English poetic idiom; and whatever might be said for the French novel as a moment in the cultural history of France, it could not be granted a formative role in the novelistic tradition of England.

Within Anglophone culture itself there were special problems, for imperialism had made the metropolitan tongue a lingua franca whose users were, in majority, not ethnically English. The language had won its international eminence at the cost of its native integrity. The most salient foreign literary vernaculars in English at this date were those of the United States and Ireland. America was always important, and in many ways attractive, to Scrutiny. But attempts to characterize its literature were unresolved. The journal's most sustained effort to describe a distinctive American literary tradition — the work of an American contributor, Marius Bewley — ran a paradoxical course. Bewley's purpose, openly opposed to Leavis's, was to establish the 'essential Americanism' of Henry James. But this critical difference was not all its principals took it to be, for Bewley's thesis ended in bathos: setting out from the example of Jane Austen and returning to England in the person of James, the American 'line' turned out to be a loop circuit of 'the great tradition'.[26] Scrutiny's coverage of Irish writing, in contrast, was sparse and fragmentary. But its greatest interwar representative, James Joyce, was rejected early and decisively, and in telling terms. Joyce, for Leavis, was the anti-Shakespeare, his work the destructive antithesis of an authentic, 'rooted' idiom.[27] The charge was appropriate in a way, but the historical impetus of Joyce's work was not one that Leavis, in his own pregnant word, could easily 'recognize'. What is lost in Joyce is indeed any sense of the English language as second nature. Unlike James and Conrad, as The Great Tradition portrays them, Joyce was not relieved of his circumstantial beginnings by the language of Shakespeare. He was a product of colonial Ireland and wrote out of that formation. His writing is, in this respect, a dramatization of the 'native' as alien, the 'mother' language as another language. (Stephen, of the Dean of Studies: 'The language in which we are speaking is his before it is mine. How different are the words home, Christ, ale, master, on his lips and on mine! I cannot speak or write these words without unrest of spirit. His language, so familiar and so foreign, will always be for me an acquired speech. I have not made or accepted its words. My voice holds them at bay. My soul frets in the shadow of his language.') It is the writing of one for whom 'English' could not be self-identical, a literary practice whose 'roots' lay in the history of colonialism.

That history sank just as deeply into the metropolitan culture, sparing none, not even the 'disinterested' humanists of Scrutiny. All writing proposes a subjective 'place' of reading, but dictation is beyond its power. Many things may be written and read, but rather few are internalized, reiterated, elaborated, and applied. The ideal match of inscribed addressee and contingent reader cannot happen in the absence of favouring extra-textual conditions — whose shapes are, therefore, ultimately decisive for cultural history. The historical conditions of Leavisian discourse are those of Britain in the fifty-odd years between the Armistice and 'the end of empire'.

Scrutiny and its active audience emerged as part of a long re-formation of the dominant culture — its practices, orientation, and social equilibrium. One of the main constituent processes in this complex change was a recomposition of the intelligentsia. In the thirty years after the First World War, an established intellectual bloc was obliged to adapt or yield to an emergent formation of a quite distinct character. The old bloc was essentially Victorian. Lodged in the old universities and in the cultural centres of the capital, it cultivated a wide variety of interest without prejudice to its fundamental social unity. Even its most radical personalities tended to speak as if by right of inheritance, secure in the presumptions and licences of the class to which they directly or vicariously belonged. The postwar levies, in contrast, were not cohesive in much except their objective difference from this culture; both generational experience and typical class background estranged them. Drawn largely from the petty bourgeoisie, coming up through grammar rather than public schools and — more and more likely — the 'civic' universities rather than Oxford and Cambridge, they were perforce 'professionals', making livings and careers in a world still held by the mystique of effortless distinction. The forms and outcomes of this historical encounter were naturally various. There were stylistic accommodations on both sides, and mere generational turnover, reinforced by continuing educational reform, ensured the ultimate practical advantage of the new formation. But there were also passages of open conflict, of which the most acrimonious was the long 'affair' of Leavis and *Scrutiny*. The new 'provincialism' of British intellectual life was widely observed, and celebrated or deplored, in the 1950s. Martin Green's sentiments are a vivid expression of it, and an index of the critical role of Leavis in its emergence.

'Provincial', as used then by both the exponents and the misfits of the new ethos, was the summary term for a whole social complex: tributary terms like 'ordinary', 'serious', and 'decent' (or 'lower-middle-class', 'earnest', and 'puritan') were seldom far away. However, Green's catalogue of virtue is a reminder of another sense of the term, and of the fact that these internal shifts in British culture occurred in the context of a fundamental alteration in its global position. Another difference between the old and the new intellectual dispensations is that they matured respectively before and after Britain's withdrawal from India. The old intellectual bloc was part of an *imperial* elite: its collective imagination, patrician and cosmopolitan in tone, was nourished by the international eminence of the British state. The successor formation came of age in a palpably shrinking country, in the years of imperial retreat and the rise of a new, American hegemony. 'Britain' and 'England', in Green's vocabulary, are exclusive terms: summarizing 'all the parts' of his experience yet surrounded by emphatic negatives, they are in effect diminutives.

In this sense Green was already 'post-Leavisian' — or, for it comes to the same thing, Leavis was not, as Green was, subjectively 'post-imperial'. For there is nothing diminutive about the functioning of such terms in *Revaluation* or *The Great Tradition*. 'English', in these works, is both exclusive, socially and morally, and *universalizing*, systematically offered as the instance of a 'human norm'. It was not a given: the most rigorous discriminations were necessary. But these were for the sake of its unquestioned claim to moral sovereignty. Here, as in much else, Leavis was critically disaffected from a world to which, however, he could imagine no alternative. He had inherited the humanism of 'the intellectual aristocracy' but not its patrician ease; he asserted a specific and normative Englishness but was still too much a 'cosmopolitan' to settle for the gnawing, cheated chauvinism of Little England. Leavisian discourse in its high period — the *Scrutiny* years — cannot be assimilated either to the old, imperial literary culture or to its 'provincial' successor: its distinctive shape was that of the transition between them.

But transitions prolonged beyond their time are liable to decay. F. R. Leavis's 1967 Clark Lectures read in places like a desperate last struggle against silence. Rejecting all 'chauvinism' or 'patriotic nationalism', and any suggestion of a 'compensatory nostalgia for lost imperial greatness', he persisted in his appeal to a reality that could and should be valued as England's 'national greatness'.[28] His affirmation was almost literally hollow: so many disavowals englobing an inexpressible faith. His partner's late conclusions, on the other hand, were typically forthright. In 1980, Q. D. Leavis gave her last public lecture. Her theme, appropriately synoptic, was 'the Englishness of the English novel'; the venue was Cheltenham. As she neared the end of her presentation, she turned to reflect on the plight of 'our run-down Britain', and the deep harmonies of the occasion became audible:

> The England that bore the classical English novel has gone forever, and we can't expect a country of high-rise flat-dwellers, office workers and factory robots and unassimilated multi-racial minorities, with a suburbanized countryside, factory farming, sexual emancipation without responsibility, rising crime and violence, and the Trade Union mentality, to give rise to a literature comparable with its novel tradition of a so different past.[29]

Decadence, whose decadence? The 'humanism' that found words for that noxious elegy had decayed into simple misanthropy.

But Q. D. Leavis was right in this at least: the cultural bases of Leavisian discourse have weakened greatly in the thirty years since *Scrutiny*'s closure. This is so above all in schools, whose young population — most of them children of the working-class and of settled minorities from the ex-colonial world — cannot often be made to adjust their intuitions to the normalizing imperative of her kind of 'Englishness'. Most English teachers have long been aware of this, and many positively assert it as a premiss of their work. In the higher, exclusive reaches of the education system, however, old traditions are more durable. About 'the Leavisites' themselves, there is little to say: they abide. But too much radical theoretical and historical work still finds its terminus within the boundaries of 'English' and 'literary criticism', as if mistaking institutional confinement for intellectual fatality. The deepest assumptions of Leavisian (and kindred) criticism will tend to persist unless new objects and priorities of analysis are asserted against them. One of the most radical works of 'literary criticism' produced in England in recent decades is Raymond Williams's *The Country and the City*, and one of its most radical elements is precisely its refusal of that familiar condensation of a nationality, a state and a language in the spellbinding notion of 'English'.[30] It was by refusing it that Williams could begin to reread 'English literature' in its real formative conditions, and to read the words of the classes and populations, at home and on other continents, that it marginalized or silenced. Initiatives of this kind are indispensable for those of us who really believe that our common humanity is less a heritage than a goal, and that it will be defined, in its 'essential diversity', by all or by none.

Notes

1 'Literary criticism and philosophy', a reply to René Wellek's communication of the same title, *Scrutiny*, vol. 5, no. 4 (March 1936), repr. in *The Common Pursuit* (Harmondsworth: Penguin, 1972), pp. 214, 215.

2 My critical use of the term 'humanist' bears only on this kind of essentialism. As a Marxist, I believe simple 'anti-humanism' to be theoretically shallow and morally evasive. Here and elsewhere I have summarized material from my *The Moment of 'Scrutiny'* (London: NLB, 1979) — to which this essay is in some other respects a corrective. I am grateful to Michèle Barrett, Clara Connolly, and especially Homi Bhabha, for their encouragement and critical advice.

3 Preface, *The Nigger of the 'Narcissus', Typhoon, Falk and Other Stories* (London 1950), p. x.

4 'Components of the national culture', in Robin Blackburn and Alexander Cockburn (eds), *Student Power* (Harmondsworth: Penguin, 1969), p. 271.

5 *Revaluation* (Harmondsworth: Penguin, 1972), p. 146.

6 ibid., p. 12.

7 ibid., p. 58.

8 ibid., pp. 19, 21.

9 ibid., pp. 26, 29.

10 ibid., p. 55.

11 ibid., pp. 35, 118.

12 ibid., p. 245.

13 ibid., p. 160.

14 *The Great Tradition* (Harmondsworth: Penguin, 1972), p 19.

15 ibid., pp. 148, 151.

16 ibid., pp. 217, 218, 219.

17 ibid., pp. 241, 225, 227.
18 ibid., pp. 27, 29.
19 *Towards Standards of Criticism* (1933) (London: Lawrence & Wishart, 1976), pp. 19—20.
20 *The Great Tradition*, p. 214.
21 'Caterpillars of the Commonwealth unite!', *Scrutiny*, vol. 7, no. 2 (September 1938), pp. 210—11.
22 *Scrutiny*, vol. 7, no. 2 (September 1938), and vol. 13, no. 2 (September 1945) respectively.
23 Denys Thompson (ed.), *The Leavises: Recollections and Impressions* (Cambridge: Cambridge University Press, 1984), pp. 119—20.
24 'British decency', *Kenyon Review*, vol. 21, no. 4 (Autumn 1959), pp. 505—32.
25 *For Continuity* (Cambridge: Cambridge University Press, 1933), p. 139.
26 Marius Bewley, *The Complex Fate* (London: Chatto & Windus, 1952).
27 'Joyce and "the revolution of the word"', *Scrutiny*, vol. 2, no. 2 (September 1933), pp. 193—201.
28 *English Literature in Our Time and the University* (London: Chatto & Windus, 1969), pp. 33—5; and cf. Leavis, *Nor Shall My Sword* (London 1972), pp. 223—7.
29 G. Singh (ed.), *Collected Essays*, Vol. 1: *The Englishness of the English Novel* (Cambridge: Cambridge University Press, 1983), p. 325.
30 Raymond Williams, *The Country and the City* (London: Chatto & Windus, 1973).

15

The island and the aeroplane: the case of Virginia Woolf

Gillian Beer

England's is, so writers over the centuries have assured us, an island story. What happened to that story with the coming of the aeroplane? That larger question is central to my essay but my chosen example is a particular one: the writing of Virginia Woolf.

The advent of the aeroplane had profound political and economic consequences;[1] the object itself rapidly entered the repertoire of dream symbols, with their capacity for expressing erotic politics and desires. In the period between 1900 and 1916 Freud came to recognize the extent to which 'balloons, flying-machines and most recently Zeppelin airships' had been incorporated into two kinds of dream symbol: those which are 'constructed by an individual out of his own ideational material' and those 'whose relation to sexual ideas appear to reach back into the very earliest ages and to the most obscure depths of our conceptual functioning'.[2] His analysis of flying dreams is phallocentric (women can have them as the 'fulfilment of the wish to be a man', a wish which can be realized by means of the clitoris which provides 'the same sensations as men'). He identifies 'the remarkable characteristic of the male organ which enables it to rise up in defiance of the laws of gravity' as the reason for its symbolic representation as a flying-machine. If we pursue that line of argument what are we to make of Virginia Woolf's striking interest in her *Diary* in air crashes? Or of her description of the Zeppelin with an umbilical 'string of light hanging from its navel'?[3] Suffice it for the moment to say that the aeroplane in Woolf's novels is given a crucial presence in four of her works, *Mrs Dalloway*, *Orlando*, *The Years* and *Between the Acts*, all of which are concerned with the representation of England and with difficult moments of historical national change.

The destructiveness and the new beauty generated by the possibilities of flight are realized by Gertrude Stein in her book, *Picasso* (1938), in which she comments on the formal reordering of the earth when seen from the aeroplane — a reordering which does away with centrality and very largely with borders. It is an ordering at the opposite extreme from that of the island, in which centrality is emphasized and the enclosure of land within surrounding shores is the controlling meaning. Stein writes of the First World War thus:

Really the composition of this war, 1914—18, was not the composition of all previous wars, the composition was not a composition in which there was one man in the center surrounded by a lot of other men but a composition that had neither a beginning nor an end, a composition of which one corner was as important as another corner, in fact the composition of cubism.

Flying over America she thinks: 'the twentieth century is a century which sees the earth as no one has ever seen it, the earth has a splendor that it never has had, and as everything destroys itself in the twentieth century and nothing continues, so then the twentieth century has a splendor which is its own'.[4] The patchwork continuity of an earth seen in this style undermines the concept of nationhood which relies upon the cultural idea of the island — and undermines, too, the notion of the book as an island. Narrative is no longer held within the determining contours of land-space. Woolf's first novel is *The Voyage Out*, which opens with the ship leaving England — a journey from which its heroine never returns. *Between the Acts*, her last novel, takes up the multiple signification of the island, including that of the literary canon, and places them under the scrutiny of aeroplanes at the beginning and end of the work.

Woolf's quarrel with patriarchy and imperialism gave a particular complexity to her appropriations of the island story. At the same time her symbolizing imagination played upon its multiple significations — land and water margins, home, body, individualism, literary canon — and set them in shifting relations to air and aeroplane.

'If one spirit animates the whole, what about the aeroplanes?' queries a character in Woolf's last novel, *Between the Acts*, which is set on a day in mid-June 1939 and was written with the Battle of Britain going on overhead.[5] In the midst of its composition a last version of the island story as safe fortress was played out: an 'armada' (telling word) of little boats set out from England to rescue from the beaches of Dunkirk the British soldiers being strafed by German bombers. Woolf writes of the events with great intensity in her diary, as we shall see. In the public mythologization of that episode it has never been quite clear whether the topic is triumph or defeat.

Much earlier in the century H. G. Wells concluded his novel of coming events, *The War in the Air*, with Bert Smallways thinking that 'the little island in the silver sea was at the end of its immunity'.[6] Yet the myth of the fortress-island was sustained past the beginning of the Second World War, so that the sculptor and refugee Naum Gabo could note in his Diary in 1941:

The sea lies stark naked between my windows and the horizon. . . . The heart suffers looking at it and the contrast with what is happening in the world . . . how many more weeks will this peace last on this little plot of land? . . . Our life on this island, in this last fortress of the old Europe, gradually enters . . . into a state of siege.[7]

In *British Aviation: The Ominous Skies 1935–39* Harald Penrose reports a journalist as writing at the beginning of August 1939, a month before the outbreak of the Second World War: 'The dangers of air attack have been much magnified. This country is protected by stretches of sea too wide for the enemy to have an effective escort of fighters'.[8]

The advent of the aeroplane was by no means only a military phenomenon, of course. H. G. Wells was not far out when in the 1890s he wrote a forward fantasy, 'Filmer', in which the hero's mastery of the art of flying 'pressed the button that has changed peace and warfare and well nigh every condition of human life and happiness'.[9] In 'The argonauts of the air' he grimly foresaw the future of the flying machine: 'In lives and in treasure the cost of the conquest of the empire of the air may even exceed all that has been spent in man's great conquest of the sea.'[10] Later in his life, when he had experienced the pleasures of flying for himself, and when the diversity of uses for the aeroplane had become actual, Wells argues against the individualism of light aircraft and for large passenger airships in order that the freedoms and pleasures of flight should be opened to many. In 'The present uselessness and danger of aeroplanes. A problem in organization', in *The Way the World is Going* (1928), he writes:

> I know the happiness and wonder of flying, and I know that its present rarity, danger, and unattractiveness are not due to any defects in the aeroplane or airship itself — physical science and mechanical invention have failed at no point in the matter — but mainly, almost entirely, to the financial, administrative, and political difficulties of aviation.[11]

Unlike H. G. Wells and Gertrude Stein, Virginia Woolf never flew, though she fantasized the experience vividly in her late essay 'Flying over London'.[12] But the aeroplane is powerfully placed in her novels. It typifies the present day, and beyond that it is a bearer and breaker of signification, puffing dissolving words into the air in *Mrs Dalloway* to be diversely construed by all the casual watchers of its commercial task. In *Between the Acts* its presence is more menacing, breaking apart the synthesizing words of the rector at the end of the village pageant, rumbling overhead towards the imminent war. *The Years* represents the whole period of the First World War by the 1917 air raid. ('The first mass aeroplane raid took place on London on June 13, 1917', Gibbs-Smith informs us.)[13] *Orlando* ends with the sea-captain-husband transformed into an aeronaut, 'hovering' over Orlando's head. Menace, community, eroticism, warfare, and idle beauty: the aeroplane moves freely across all these zones in her writing. The pilot's eye offers a new position for narrative distance which resolves (as at the opening of *The Years*) the scanned plurality of the community below into patterns and repeats. Woolf was not alone in her invocation of the aeroplane, of course: we think across immediately to Yeats and Auden. But she was, I think, particularly acute in her understanding of it in relation to the cultural form of the island, and extraordinarily economical in her appraisal.

The story of Daedelus and Icarus — the craftsman father who made the flying machine and the flying son whose wings loosened disastrously when he flew too near the sun, which melted the wax that attached them

— revives in twentieth-century literature, very possibly accompanying the coming of aeroplanes. In the last pages of *Portrait of the Artist*, written in 1914, such imagery seems still entirely mythological and is related to ships sailing rather than aircraft flying.

> *April 16*. Away! Away!
>
> The spell of arms and voices: the white arms of roads, their promise of close embraces and the black arms of tall ships that stand against the moon, their tale of distant nations. They are held out to say: We are alone — come. And the voices say with them: We are your kinsmen. And the air is thick with their company as they call to me, their kinsman, making ready to go, shaking the wings of their exultant and terrible youth.[14]

In 'Musée des Beaux Arts' (1938) Auden makes of Breughel's *Icarus* an image of the insouciance with which suffering is surrounded, 'its human position'.

> In Breughel's *Icarus*, for instance; how everything turns away
> Quite leisurely from the disaster; the ploughman may
> Have heard the splash, the forsaken cry,
> But for him it was not an important failure; the sun shone
> As it had to on the white legs disappearing into the green
> Water; and the expensive delicate ship that must have seen
> Something amazing, a boy falling out of the sky,
> Had somewhere to get to and sailed calmly on.
>
> *December 1938*[15]

The discreet clarity of description here distances the disaster and mutes its specific reference to Europe at the time of its inscribed date 'December 1938', keeping the discrepancy between acute suffering and humdrum life permanently disturbing. In another poem written in the same year (which Auden did not retain in 'Sonnets from China' but which appears in the original sequence, *In Time of War*, as sonnet 15) Auden concentrates on the pilots 'remote like savants' who are preoccupied only with skill as they approach the city. (Fuller reads this poem as being about politicians, surely mistakenly.)

> Engines bear them through the sky: they're free
> And isolated like the very rich;
> Remote like savants, they can only see
> The breathing city as a target which
>
> Requires their skill; will never see how flying
> Is the creation of ideas they hate,
> Nor how their own machines are always trying
> To push through into life. They chose a fate
>
> The islands where they live did not compel.[16]

Auden and Yeats dwell on the human pilots of such planes: the isolation and aggression of such a position is inimical to Woolf, for it is dangerously caught in to the militarism it castigates. But she, like them, does explore the paradoxes in flight:

how their own machines are always trying
To push through into life (as Auden writes.)

The glamour that pervades 'An Irish Airman Foresees his Death' in *The Wild Swans at Coole* (1919) is riposted even within Yeats' own work in a poem called 'Reprisals', not printed in the definitive edition and first published after the Second World War, in 1948. It opens:

Some nineteen German planes, they say,
You had brought down before you died.
We called it a good death. Today
Can ghost or man be satisfied?[17]

One of Woolf's last essays, written as she was finishing *Between the Acts*, was 'Thoughts on peace in an air raid', prepared for an American symposium 'on current matters concerning women'.[18]

Woolf's opposition to patriarchy and imperialism, her determined assertion that she was 'no patriot', her emphasis on women's 'difference of view', all have their bearing on her figuring of the aeroplane and of flight in her writing. The diaries and the essays, as well as the novels, allow us, through her, to understand some of the ways in which the advent of the aeroplane reordered the axes of experience.

The island

The identification of England with the island is already, and from the start, a fiction. It is a fiction, but an unwavering one among English writers and other English people, that England occupies the land up to the margins of every shore. The island has seemed the perfect form in English cultural imagining, as the city was to the Greeks. Defensive, secure, compacted, even paradisal — a safe place; a safe place too from which to set out on predations and from which to launch the building of an empire. Even now, remote islands — the Falkland Islands or Fiji — are claimed as peculiarly part of empire history.

The island is equated with England in the discourse of assertion, though England by no means occupies the whole extent of the geographical island; Scotland and Wales are suppressed in this description and Ireland is corralled within that very different group, 'the British Isles'. In this century, of course, the disjuncture has become more extreme, with the division between Ulster and Eire, one assertively within 'the United Kingdom', the other an independent state. But Ireland has for far longer been the necessary other in the English description of England, 'John Bull's other island' which is determinedly *not* John Bull's.

Shakespeare's *Richard II* provided the initiating communal self-description, alluringly emblematic and topographical at once. Gaunt calls England:

This royall Throne of Kings, this sceptred Isle.
This earth of Majesty, this seate of Mars,
This other Eden, demy paradise,
This Fortresse built by Nature for her selfe,
Against infection, and the hand of warre:
This happy breed of men, this little world,
This precious stone, set in the silver sea,
Which serves it in the office of a wall,
Or as a Moate defensive to a house,
Against the envy of lesse happier Lands,
This blessed plot, this earth, this Realme, this England. (II. i. 42—52)

England is seen as supremely and reflexively *natural*: 'This Fortresse *built by nature for her selfe*'. The 'insularity' of the island is emphasized in this part of the speech: it is a 'little world', a moated country house as well as a fortress. It is both a miniature cultivated place, 'this blessed plot', and an extensive 'Realme'. It is 'this England' (as the *New Statesman* fondly titles its collection of symptomatic newscuttings each week). The less-quoted second part of Gaunt's speech turns into an accusation against the present state of this favoured island. First, he represents the noble fecundity of the land, 'this teeming wombe of Royall Kings', who are renowned for their deeds:

This Land of such deere soules, this deere-deere Land,
Deere for her reputation through the world,
Is now Leas'd out (I dye pronouncing it)
Like to a Tenement or pelting Farme.
England bound in with the triumphant sea,
Whose rocky shore beates backe the envious siedge
Of watery Neptune, is now bound in with shame

The country house or fortress is become 'a Tenement or pelting Farme'. The binding in of the land by the sea — a natural battle of repulsion and attraction in which 'triumphant' curiously attaches both to land and sea and suggests a sustained and wholesome matching — is instead constrictingly 'bound in with shame'. It is easy to see why the latter part of this speech is less often ritually recalled than the first. Value ('this deere-deere Land') and price ('Leas'd out') are here set disquietingly close. Shame — the shame of bad government — mars the perfect order of the island.

The imagery which Shakespeare employs is defensive, not expansionist, though there is a suggestion of the depradations of the crusaders at the centre of the speech which speaks of the 'Royall Kings':

Fear'd by their breed, and famous for their birth,
Renowned for their deeds, as farre from home,
For Christian service, and true Chivalrie,
As is the sepulcher in stubborne Jury
Of the Worlds ransome blessed Maries Sonne.

The punctuation in the first folio affirms that they are *renowned* 'far from home' rather than that their deeds took place far from home: but the ear receives both meanings. The passage has certainly been put to expansionist uses, though its insistence in context is on correcting the bad governance of the island so that its society may fulfil its demi-paradisal geography. In its later extracting from the play the passage has been repeatedly employed for self-congratulation rather than self-correction.

But the Shakespeare passage draws attention also to a fundamental tension in the idea of the island, one which has been to some extent concealed by the later phases of its etymology. The concept 'island' implies a particular and intense relationship of land and water. The *Oxford English Dictionary* makes it clear that the word itself includes the two elements: 'island' is a kind of pun. 'Isle' in its earliest forms derived from a word for water and meant, 'watery' or 'watered'. In Old English 'land' was added to it to make a compound: 'is-land': water-surrounded land. The idea of water is thus intrinsic to the word, as essential as that of earth. The two elements, earth and water, are set in play. An intimate, tactile, and complete relationship is implied between them in this ordering of forces. The land is surrounded by water; the water fills the shores. The island, to be fruitful, can never be intact. It is traceried by water, overflown by birds carrying seeds.[19]

The equal foregrounding of land and sea is crucial not only in understanding the uses of the concept in imperialism, but in the more hidden identification between island and body, island and individual. The tight fit of island to individual to island permits a gratification which may well rely not only on cultural but on pre-cultural sources. The unborn child first experiences itself as surrounded by wetness, held close within the womb. It is not an island in the strict sense since it is attached to a lifeline, an umbilical cord. It becomes an island, an isolation, in the severance of birth. Such conceptual power-sources are available for our speculation, even though they may not be directly represented. When Donne, in one of the most famous sentences in English, asserts that 'No man is an island' the words take their charge from their quality of paradox. They presuppose that the individual *is* ordinarily understood to be like an island.

In *The Tempest* Caliban's claim to the island condenses oedipal and land-descent discourses: '*by* Sycorax my mother'. The island is his progeny and his inheritance. It is also himself:

> This Island's mine by Sycorax my mother,
> Which thou taks't from me.   (I.ii.391)

His claim to possession is matrilineal. He is ab-original.[20]

The island has features of the female body; the map of the British Isles has sometimes been represented as taking the form of an old crone. But England is only intermittently a woman in the symbolic discourse of the nation. Britannia is a considerable displacement of the island idea, though she carries Poseidon's trident for pronging the fish and the foe. The sea, which encircles the land, can also bring enemies to its shores and occasionally, as when the Dutch sailed up the Thames in 1667, the island has been humiliated by foreign penetration. At such times the sexual imagery of invasion makes England for a while the 'mother-land' in the language of politics.

H. G. Wells astutely commented in 1927 on the contrast between the steamship and the aeroplane era: 'the steam-ship-created British Empire ... is, aerially speaking, decapitated. You cannot fly from the British Isles to the vast dominions round and about the Indian Ocean without infringing foreign territory' (*The Way the World is Going*, p. 131). In the Victorian period, he suggested, the sea-tracks of the long-distance steam-ships could foster the illusion that the British Empire dominated the entire world, because it was possible to set out from the central island and stay always within either British or international waters. This is an ingenious rationalization of the expansionist phase of the island story. Since the sea is as important as the land for the island concept, the sea offers a vast extension of the island, allowing the psychic size of the body politic to expand, without bumping into others' territory. The aeroplane, on the other hand, though offering access to almost limitless space, must overfly the territories of other nations. It cannot imitate the extension of the island, magically represented by the silver pathways in the wake of ships, threads linking imperial England to its possessions overseas.

To the Lighthouse is Woolf's island story. The family group and the house are themselves contracted intensifications of the island concept: and, in a further intensification, the final separation of the individual each from each is figured in the work: 'We perish each alone', Mr Ramsay obsessionally recalls. The island is displaced, a Hebridean place oddly like St Ives in Cornwall where Virginia Stephen spent her childhood summers and where the harbour island was much painted by the St Ives group at about the same time that Woolf was writing her novel. Throughout the book, sometimes louder, sometimes muted, the sound of the waves is referred to. The sea is as much the island as is the land. The fisherman's wife, in the story Mrs Ramsay reads to James, longs for possession and for dominance, for control: that last wish is shared with Mrs Ramsay, and perhaps the other wishes too. 'That loneliness which was ... the truth about things' permeates the book (p. 186).[21] The lighthouse itself is the final island, the last signifying object, amidst the timeless breaking of the sea: 'it was a stark tower on a bare rock', thinks James as they finally come close to the lighthouse in the last pages of the book. At the end of the book the First World War is over; the family is fragmented: the mother is dead, a son, a daughter; the fishes in the bottom of the boat are dead. Cam and James, looking at their ageing father reading, renew their silent vow to 'fight tyranny to the death'. But Cam's musing continues:

> It was thus that he escaped, she thought. Yes, with his great forehead and his great nose, holding his little mottled book firmly in front of him, he escaped. You might try to lay hands on him, but then like a bird, he spread his wings, he floated off to settle out of your reach

somewhere far away on some desolate stump. She gazed at the immense expanse of the sea. The island had grown so small that it scarcely looked like a leaf any longer. It looked like the top of a rock which some big wave would cover. Yet in its frailty were all those paths, those terraces, those bedrooms — all those innumerable things.

Distance and retrospect is achieved at the end of To the Lighthouse: 'It was like that then, the island, thought Cam, once more drawing her fingers through the waves. She had never seen it from out at sea before' (p. 174). The long backward survey to the politics of Edwardian family life, to England before the First World War, which began to unravel through the image of the abandoned house in 'Time passes' here reaches conclusion: 'It is finished' — Lily's words — and those of the Cross — mean also what they say. Things have come to an end. The period of empire is drawing to its close. The book ends; the picture is done; the parents' England is gone. In laying the ghosts of her parents Woolf clustered them within an island, a solitary island which no one leaves at the end of the book save to accomplish the short, plain journey to that final signifier, the lighthouse, whose significations she refused to analyse. The island is here the place of intense life and the conclusion of that form of life, both private and the image of a community from whose values she was increasingly disengaged.

To the Lighthouse is an elegy for a kind of life no longer to be retrieved — and no longer wanted back. In To the Lighthouse Woolf frets away the notion of stability in the island concept. The everyday does not last forever. The island is waves as well as earth: everything is in flux, land as much as sea, individual as well as whole culture. The last book of To the Lighthouse looks back at the conditions of before 1914. Implicit is the understanding that this will be the last such revisiting for the personages within the book.

The aeroplane

The absolute answering of land and sea to each other, which contributed ideas of aptness and sufficiency to the Victorians' understanding of 'England', will soon be disturbed by a change of axes: under water, in the air. Woolf is writing into the period at which the island could be seen anew, scanned from above. Her later writing shares the new awareness of island-dwellers that their safe fortress is violable. They look up, instead of out to sea, for enemies. Stephen Kern argues of the aeroplane:

> Its cultural impact was ultimately defined by deeply rooted values associated with the up-down axis. Low suggests immorality, vulgarity, poverty, and deceit. High is the direction of growth and hope, the source of light, the heavenly abode of angels and gods. From Ovid to Shelley the soaring bird was a symbol of freedom. People were divided in their response to flying; some hailed it as another great technological liberation and some foresaw its destructive potential.[22]

All felt its symbolic and its political power.

The old woman singing beside Regent's Park in *Mrs Dalloway* mouths a primal series of syllables which have persisted from the prehistoric realm, a sound composed out of 'the passing generations . . . vanished, like leaves, to be trodden under, to be soaked and steeped and made mould of by that eternal spring —

ee um fah um so
foo swee too eem oo.[23] (p. 90)

The aeroplane in the same novel, writing its message in the air, seems at first equally unreferential. Earth and air, sound and sight, resist signification though not interpretation. The people of the book set to, reading their messages into the community and into private need. The aeroplane is sybaritic, novel, and commercial. Its intended message is nugatory: an advertisement for Kreemo toffee, but it rouses in the watchers, many of whom do not appear elsewhere in the novel, thoughts, pleasures, and anxieties both glancing and profound.

In *Mrs Dalloway* the aeroplane is set alongside, and against, the car. (Both are observed by most of the book's named and unnamed characters.) The closed car suggests the private passage of royalty, and becomes the specular centre for the comedy of social class: the 'well-dressed men with their tail-coats and their white slips and their hair raked back' who stand even straighter as the car passes; 'shawled Moll Pratt with her flowers on the pavement'; Sarah Bletchley 'tipping her foot up and down as though she were by her own fender in Pimlico'; Emily Coates thinking of housemaids, and 'little Mr Bowley, who had rooms in the Albany and was sealed with wax over the deeper sources of life' (p. 23). All these briefly named characters respond to 'some flag flying in the British breast' and gaze devotedly on the inscrutable vehicle whose occupant is never revealed. The sharp description, as so often in Woolf's representations of the English classes and their rituals, inches its way towards hyperbole. At White's:

> The white busts and the little tables in the background covered with copies of the *Tatler* and bottles of soda water seemed to approve; seemed to indicate the flowing corn and the manor houses of England; and to return the frail hum of the motor wheels as the walls of a whispering gallery return a single voice expanded and made sonorous by the might of a whole cathedral. (p. 22)

The continuity of club and cathedral, of London institutions (White's and St Paul's), and of London typecast characters, mocks the self-esteem which expands from individual to nation, and which clusters upon an invisible and yet over-signifying personage inside the car.

In the next paragraph Emily Coates looks up at the sky. Instead of the muffled superplus of attributed meaning represented by the car, the aeroplane is playful, open, though first received as ominous. Its 'letters in the sky' curl and twist, offer discrete clues to a riddle whose meaning will prove trivial — and the writing teases the reader with the ciphering of 'K.E.Y.':

Every one looked up.

Dropping dead down, the aeroplane soared straight up, curved in a loop, raced, sank, rose, and whatever it did, wherever it went, out flut- tered behind it a thick ruffled bar of white smoke which curled and wreathed upon the sky in letters. But what letters? A C was it? an E, then an L? Only for a moment did they lie still; then they moved and melted and were rubbed out up in the sky, and the aeroplane shot further away and again, in a fresh space of sky, began writing a K, and E, a Y perhaps?

'Blaxo,' said Mrs Coates in a strained, awe-stricken voice, gazing straight up, and her baby, lying stiff and white in her arms, gazed straight up.

'Kreemo', murmured Mrs Bletchley, like a sleep-walker. With his hat held out perfectly still in his hand, Mr Bowley gazed straight up. All down the Mall people were standing and looking up into the sky. (pp. 23–4).

Everyone's attention is distracted from the car which '(went in at the gates and nobody looked at it)'. The repeated word 'up' disengages the people from society. In their gazing the whole world becomes 'perfectly silent, and a flight of gulls crossed the sky ... and in this extraordinary silence and peace; bells struck eleven times, the sound fading up there among the gulls'. The contemplative erasure of meaning accompanies the wait for meaning. Instead of the expansion of the car's hum to cathedral size, the plane produces a modest insufficiency of meaning, and amalgamates with sky and gulls, its sound fading instead of resonating. It becomes an image of equalizing as opposed to hierarchy, of freedom and play, racing and swooping 'swiftly, freely, like a skater'. It includes death, 'dropping dead down', the baby 'lying stiff and white in her arms', but it does not impose it. Then, as in *Orlando*, 'the aeroplane rushed out of the clouds again'. Each person reads the plane's message differently. To Septimus 'the smoke words' offer 'inexhaustible charity and laughing goodness'. The communality is not in single meaning but in the free access to meaning. The ecstatic joke is about insufficiency of import: 'they were advertising toffee, a nurse-maid told Rezia'. The message does not matter; the communal act of sky-gazing does. For each person, their unacted part becomes alerted: Mrs Dempster 'always longed to see foreign parts' but goes on the sea at Margate, 'not out o' sight of land!'. The plane swoops and falls; Mrs Dempster pulls on the thought of 'the fine young feller aboard of it'. The eye of the writer now expands the aeroplane's height *over the little island of grey churches*, St Paul's and the rest' until, with an easy and macabre shift of perspective, the plane reaches the 'fields spread out and dark brown wood.' (we are still soaring visually), then the eye of the writing homes downwards in magnification to 'where adventurous thrushes, hopping boldly, glancing quickly, snat- ched the snail and tapped him on a stone, once, twice, thrice'. The aggression of the aeroplane is displaced on to the bird.

The liberated, egalitarian extreme of the aeroplane's height, and the distanced eye of the writing, dissolves bonds and flattens hierarchies. The passing plane raises half-fulfilled musings in the thoughts of another momentary figure:

> Mr Bentley, vigorously rolling his strip of turf at Greenwich thinks of its as 'a concentration; a symbol' ... of man's soul; of his determination, thought Mr Bentley, sweeping round the cedar tree, to get outside his body, beyond his house, by means of thought, Einstein, speculation, mathematics, the Mendelian theory — away the aeroplane shot. (p. 32)

The comic and disturbing discrepancies now are between the tight 'strip of turf' swept in Greenwich and the yearning towards the newly insubstantial 'real world' of post-Einsteinian theory. So the aeroplane becomes an image of 'free will' and ecstasy, silent, erotic, and absurd. It is last seen 'curving up and up, straight up, like something mounting in ecstasy, in pure delight, out from behind poured white smoke looping, writing a T, and O, and F' (p. 33). Toffs and toffee are lexically indistinguishable, farts in the wake of lark, of sexual rapture. Virginia Woolf's disaffection from the heavily bonded forms of English society often expresses itself paradoxically thus as affection and play — and in this novel, as in Orlando, the aeroplane figures as the free spirit of the modern age returning the eye to the purity of a sky which has 'escaped registration'.[24]

The aeroplane in Mrs Dalloway is no war-machine. Its frivolity is part of postwar relief. It poignantly does not threaten those below. It is a light aircraft, perhaps a Moth. The D.H. Moth first flew in 1925 and, as Gibbs-Smith puts it, 'heralds the popularity of the light aeroplane movement'. At this period the aeroplane could serve as an image of extreme individualism and of heroism, as well as of internationalism. The hooded pilot becomes, in the 1930s, a trope in the work of W. H. Auden and it may be that Woolf's response to the work of Auden and his associates, sketched in 'The leaning tower', is more intense than has yet been charted. Certainly, the question of the individual artist's responsibility to produce revolutionary change in society becomes the matter of an impassioned argument between Woolf and Benedict Nicolson towards the end of her life. The argument is conducted in letters written with the drone of enemy aircraft overhead and in the period leading up to the evacuation of British troops from Dunkirk: that evacuation is a last island story, in which the little boats sailed by fishermen and amateurs from England impose a forlorn mythic victory upon a ghastly defeat. In the late 1920s and early 1930s, however, the aeroplane suggests escape and aspiration in her work.

Women were among the pioneers of early air travel and exploration. In the early 1930s came two individual exploits which drew immense acclaim: Amy Johnson flew solo from England to Australia in a Moth (May 4th–5th 1930), and in 1932 came the first solo Atlantic crossing by a woman (Earhart in a Vega).[25] The first woman to become a qualified pilot had been Baroness de Laroche as long ago as 1909. The figure of

the aristocratic woman escaping ordinary confines is powerful symbolic-
ally for Woolf at the end of the 1920s, fuelled by her love affair with
Vita Sackville-West, and permitting, as in dreams, an identification which
brings impossible freedoms within the range of the everyday.

Woolf was fascinated, too, in a mood between the sardonic and the
obsessional, with the failed dreams of escape, the Daedelean claims of
women: we see it, at this period, in her story of Shakespeare's sister in
A Room of One's Own. We see it also in the macabre comedy of her
description of 'the flying princess', crossdressed in purple leather
breeches, whose petrol gave out on a transatlantic flight in 1927 and who
drowned with her companions:

> The Flying Princess, I forget her name, has been drowned in her
> purple leather breeches. I suppose so at least. Their petrol gave out
> about midnight on Thursday, when the aeroplane must have come
> gently down upon the long slow Atlantic waves. I suppose they burnt
> a light which showed streaky on the water for a time. There they
> rested a moment or two. The pilots, I think, looked back at the broad
> cheeked desperate eyed vulgar princess in her purple breeches & I
> suppose made some desperate dry statement — how the game was up:
> sorry; fortune against them; & she just glared; and then a wave broke
> over the wing; & the machine tipped. And she said something
> theatrical I daresay; nobody was sincere; all acted a part; nobody
> shrieked; Luck against us — something of that kind, they said, and then
> So long, and first one man was washed off & went under, & then a
> great wave came & the Princess threw up her arms & went down; &
> the third man sat saved for a second looking at the rolling waves, so
> patient, so implacable & the moon gravely regarding; & then with a
> dry snorting sound he too was tumbled off & rolled over, & the
> aeroplant rocked & rolled — miles from anywhere, off Newfoundland,
> while I slept at Rodmell, & Leonard was dining with the Craniums in
> London.[26]

Woolf creates the incongruities of disaster: the clipped inhibited speeches
'nobody shrieked; Luck against us — something of that kind, they said,
and then So long'; 'the rolling waves, so patient, so implacable & the
moon gravely regarding'. The pernickety vengefulness of this description
and the glamour of the seascape make of flight a foiled escape, equally
from England and from the sea of death. Air and water alike place small
social life out of its element. The flying princess seems like a haunting
other imagination for her own fears of flying too high, as well as being
a savage pastiche of aristocratic claims to dominance.

Even Woolf's initial working title for *The Waves*, 'The moths', may
have had an additional resonance lost to our ears. Clearly it refers
predominantly to those flying creatures, so like butterflies to amateur
eyes, but so particularly phototropic that at night they cluster helplessly
towards any light source, even if it burns them to death; but in 1925 the
Moth aeroplane first flew. *Orlando*, published in 1928, recognizes the
aeroplane as an emblem of modern life, along with the telephone and

radio, the lifts. Going up in the lift in Marshall & Snelgrove, Orlando muses: 'In the eighteenth century we knew how everything was done; but here I rise through the air; I listen to voices in America; I see men flying — but how it's done, I can't even begin to wonder. So my belief in magic returns' (p. 270).

Accepting technology into everyday life renews the magical; explanation becomes unstable and unsought. On the book's last page Orlando's husband, Shelmardine, returns from his rash voyage 'round Cape Horn in the teeth of a gale'. In an invocation of ecstasy which is both euphoric and comic the moment of midnight approaches:

> As she spoke, the first stroke of midnight sounded. The cold breeze of the present brushed her face with its little breath of fear. She looked anxiously into the sky. It was dark with clouds now. The wind roared in her ears. But in the roar of the wind she heard the roar of an aeroplane coming nearer and nearer. 'Here! Shel, here!' she cried, baring her breast to the moon (which now showed bright) so that her pearls glowed like the eggs of some vast moon-spider. The aeroplane rushed out of the clouds and stood over her head. It hovered above her. Her pearls burnt like a phosphorescent flare in the darkness. (p. 295)

The plane 'hovers' like a bird, mingling erotic and hunting imagery: 'it stood over her head'. It hovers also like the spirit brooding creatively. Pearls and landing lights are here confused: 'Her pearls burnt like a phosphorescent flare' and there is no gap between sea and air, pilot and captain, bird and plane and man: 'It is the goose!' Orlando cried. 'The wild goose'. Time coalesces: the time of the fiction and the time of the hand concluding the writing of the fiction coincide: The book ends: 'And the twelfth stroke of midnight sounded; the twelfth stroke of midnight, Thursday, the eleventh of October, Nineteen Hundred and Twenty Eight' (p. 295).

In this confluence the aeroplane is the central image, here conceived as individualistic, erotic, and heroic. 'Ecstasy' is enacted as a brilliant ricochet of ancient and immediate symbol, which lightly draws on pentecostal signs; 'in the roar of the wind she heard the roar of an aeroplane'. Sounds become tactile: 'breeze, brushed, breath'. The labials and fricatives, 'br' repeated, lightly mimic the rumble of the approaching plane. The first stroke of midnight 'brushed' her face. 'The aeroplane *rushed* out of the clouds'. The man descends through the clouds at the conclusion here, but then, Shelmardine is 'really a woman' and Orlando 'a man', in their initial recognition of each other.[27]

The heady pleasures of air travel probably remained the more intense in Woolf's imagination just because she never flew. In her late essay she describes flying over London with a convincing ease and élan which mischievously resolves itself into fantasy at the end of the piece. She had been in London under bombardment; she had looked up anxiously after Vanessa vanishing by light plane to Switzerland. The aeroplane gave a new intensity to the upward gaze and the downward thump. Woolf saw the plane always from the point of view of the island dweller, aware of the intimate abrasion of land and sea, that intimacy now disturbed by the new pastoral of the aeroplane — pastoral because so strongly interm-ingled with breezes and country sights, lying so innocently 'among trees and cows', but sinister, too, ab-rupting the familiar lie of the land, the ordinary clustering of objects:

Monday 26 January
    Heaven be praised, I can truthfully say on this first day of being 49 that I have shaken off the obsession of Opening the Door, & have returned to Waves: & have this instant seen the entire book whole, & how I can finish it — say in under 3 weeks. That takes me to Feb. 16th; then I propose, after doing Gosse, or an article perhaps, to dash off the rough sketch of Open Door, to be finished by April 1st (Easter [Friday] is April 3rd). We shall then, I hope, have an Italian journey; return say May 1st & finish Waves, so that the MS can go to be printed in June, & appear in September. These are possible dates anyhow.
    Yesterday at Rodmell we saw a magpie & heard the first spring birds: sharp egotistical, like [illegible]. A hot sun; walked over Caburn; home by Horley & saw 3 men dash from a blue car & race, without hats across a field. We saw a silver & blue aeroplane in the middle of a field, apparently unhurt, among trees & cows. This morning the paper says three men were killed — the aeroplane dashing to the earth: But we went on, reminding me of that epitaph in the Greek anthology: when I sank, the other ships sailed on.[28]

Woolf uses 'dash' three times in this diary entry. She will 'dash off the rough sketch of the Open Door'; she saw 'three men dash from a blue car' and, last, 'the aeroplane dashing to the earth'. Lateral, vertical, horizontal: all these are figured by the one word. The hand writes; the men run; the plane falls. Speed unites them — a speed allayed by the last allusion to the sea. Imaginatively sky and sea are akin; and pilots are still *aeronauts*: sky–sailors. Anne Olivier Bell's note reads:

    Mount Caburn is the bare down dominating the Ouse Valley on the far side of the river from Rodmell. The crashed aircraft was an Avro 40K from Gatwick aerodrome, where the three dead men were employed. 'I am the tomb of a shipwrecked man; but set sail, stranger: for when we were lost, the other ships voyaged on.' Theodoridas, no. 282 in book VII of *The Greek Anthology*, Loeb edition.

Woolf experiences a totalizing of experience: air, sea, land, death, and life. Suddenly she sees 'the entire book whole', not an island, yet a totality.
    The island's identity depends on water. It is the sea which defines the land. Wave theory disturbed the land—sea antinomies: instead, over and under, inner and outer, stasis and flux, became generalized as motion. Thresholds and boundaries lose definition. Something of this can be read in *The Waves*, a book whose rhythmic life is the reader's only means of

pursuit. Instead of the 'man clinging to a bare rock', which was Virginia Woolf's image for herself as writer in the summer she began to write it, this book engages with an imaginative scientific world in which substance is unreal, motion universal.

This does not render *The Waves* an apolitical novel, but its politics are in its refusal of the imposing categories of past narrative and past society, its dislimning of the boundaries of the self, the nation, the narrative. In *The Waves* Woolf pushes on to the periphery all that is habitually central to fiction: private love relationships, the business of government, family life, city finances, the empire. Each of these topics is, however, marked into the narrative so that we also *observe* how slight a regard she here has for them. Instead she concentrates, as she foresaw women writers must do, on 'the wider questions . . . of our destiny and the meaning of life', instead of on the personal and the political. She does this by reappraising the world in the light of wave theory and the popular physics of Eddington and Jeans. Eddington writes in 1927: 'In the scientific world the concept of substance is wholly lacking. . . . For this reason the scientific world often shocks us by its appearance of unreality'. He opens his argument by asserting that 'the most arresting change is not the re-arrangement of space and time by Einstein but the dissolution of all that we regard as most solid into tiny specks floating in a void'.[29] Waves in motion are all the universe consists in: sound waves, sea waves, air waves — but as Jeans also observes in *The Mysterious Universe*: 'the ethers and their undulations, the waves which form the universe, are in all probability fictitious . . . they exist in our minds'. Jeans is thereby led to privilege fiction or equalize it with the outer world: 'The motion of electrons and atoms does not resemble those of the parts of a locomotive so much as those of the dancers in a cotillion. And if the 'true essence of substances' is for ever unknowable, it does not matter whether the cotillion is danced at a ball in real life, or on a cinematograph screen, or in a story of Boccaccio'. He concludes that 'the universe is best pictured . . . as consisting of pure thought'.[30]

Yet people drown and planes crash. The silver and blue aeroplane sits in a field intact, dead men invisibly inside it. The aircrash is a new form of death, and *thanatos* had great allure for Woolf. Septimus Smith and Percival both die falling from a height. However, 'when I sank the other ships sailed on'.

Motion is eternal, but the new forms of experience brought by flight also sharply focus social and national change. If, at one extreme, there is no island, only waves, at the other extreme the geographical ideal of England becomes more poignant in the Europe of the 1930s. Daedelus and Icarus — artificer, aeronaut, and unwilling sky-diver — were perhaps, I have suggested, imaginatively provoked into the writing of Joyce and Auden by the coming of the aeroplane. The conclusion of *Portrait of the Artist* foresees no aircrash. But Auden's poem, 'The Old Masters', combines the Bruegel image of Icarus falling through the air with attention to the unnoticeable disaster and its concurrence with the everyday. It is a poem which evades the allegorical and refuses to mark more than suffering and oblivion. Woolf's description of the crashed airmen in the field has the same blithe calm.

The island and the aeroplane

Woolf considered herself no patriot. On 29 August 1939 she wrote: 'Of course, I'm not in the least patriotic'. In January 1941, while she was revising *Between the Acts* she wrote in a letter to Ethel Smyth:

> How odd it is being a countrywoman after all these years of being a Cockney! . . . You never shared my passion for that great city. Yet it's what, in some odd corner of my dreaming mind, represents Chaucer, Shakespeare and Dickens. It's my only patriotism: save once in Warwickshire one Spring [May 1934] when we were driving back from Ireland, I saw a stallion being led, under the may and the beeches, along a grass ride; and I thought that is England.[31]

This passage occurs in a letter concerned with the repression of sexuality. We can gauge some of the counter-forces in Woolf's relations to the idea of England in the condensing of disparate elements within the remembered image: the invocation of Ireland as the necessary other island, the emphasis on maleness — the stallion — in the idea of England, and the sense of herself as exile. Only in London can she feel herself in kinship with the most 'English' writers, representing the phases of the literary canon (Chaucer, Shakespeare, Dickens).

The euphoric image of the aeroplane and the keen pleasure in its menace, which we have seen in her earlier responses, are set in a more difficult series of relations with the idea of island history in her novels of the later 1930s, *The Years* and *Between the Acts*. Virginia Woolf's insistence on her own 'unpatriotic' relation with England is nearly always formulated in relation to a concession. She resisted and deeply disliked the show of public mourning for the 'heroes' of the R101, lost in 1930 on an experimental flight from England to India — an attempt bound into imperialism and the wish to annex, beyond Wells's 'steamship empire'.[32] She disliked 'the heap of a ceremony on one's little coal of feeling': 'why should every one wear black dresses'. The sameness demanded by tight social forms always irritated her and roused her scepticism. Her use of plurals is a recurrent means of teasing island pomposity but it sometimes succumbs to a related social condescension: the opening of *The Years* employs the privilege of the narrative over-eye looking down on thousands of similar events. We begin with the sky: 'But in April such weather was to be expected. Thousands of shop assistants made that remark' . . . 'Interminable processions of shoppers . . . paraded the pavements' . . .

> In the basements of the long avenues of the residential quarters servant girls in cap and apron prepared tea. Deviously ascending from the basement the silver teapot was placed on the table, and virgins and spinsters with hands that had staunched the sores of Bermondsey and

Hoxton carefully measured out one, two, three, four spoonfuls of tea.[33]

Something odd and uneasy occurs in this writing with its mixture of Dickensian super-eye and the autocracy of the air, gazing *de haut en bas*. The aerial view affords a dangerous narrative position, too liberating to the writer and demeaning to those observed here. The levity of this socially bantering view of London is corrected in the 1917 episode with the brief account of an air-raid, unseen from the cellar where the characters finish their dinner and wait for a bomb to fall. It does not fall on them; the silence, the 'greenish-grey stone', the oscillating spider's web are all seized into the writing with intense reserve (pp. 313—4). The remembered episode re-emerges in the 'Present day' section when Eleanor looks up to where she saw her first aeroplane and muses on the degree of change it has brought, thinking how it first seemed a black spot, then a bird. Next she recollects the 1917 raid, and then her eye falls on 'the usual evening paper's blurred picture of a fat man gesticulating'. Eleanor rips the paper violently, shocking her sceptical niece who has been feeling superior. 'You see', Eleanor interrupted, 'it means the end of everything we cared for',

'Freedom?' said Peggy perfunctorily. 'Yes,' said Eleanor. 'Freedom and justice'. (p. 357)

Within the scan of two pages of memory the aeroplane has changed from bird to collusive war instrument, part of the oppression operated by dictators.

The writerly pleasure in the plane's fantastic powers, so prominent in *Mrs Dalloway* and *Orlando*, is now sardonically viewed. In *Between the Acts*, and in the diaries and letters which accompany its composition, Woolf works urgently on the problem of the artist's presence in society and in England's history. Outside the book she is in passionate controversy with her nephew on the artist's responsibility to bring about revolutionary change in society. In a caustic letter of 13 August 1940 she defends Roger Fry against Nicolson's charge of inaction.[34] As she writes *Between the Acts*, from May to August 1940, some of the worst of the war is going on directly over her head. On 9 June she writes: 'The searchlights are very lovely over the marsh, and the aeroplanes go over — one, a German, was shot over Caburn, and my windows rattled when they dropped bombs at Forest Row. But it's like a Shakespeare song today — so merry, innocent and very English.[35]

English literature and English weather form much of the material of *Between the Acts*. Despite her disclaimers and her sense of being the townie incomer, Woolf was clearly engaged and puzzled by English life in a quite new way at the beginning of the war. The Women's Institute asked her to produce a play for them; instead what she did was to write Miss La Trobe and *Between the Acts*.[36]

It proved harder to let go of the island story once it was under threat from invasion, and once it seemed that she and her friends might, through inertia, have contributed to its obliteration. In the excellent work that has been accomplished on the connections between *Three Guineas* and *Between the Acts*, critics such as Roger Poole and Sallie Sears have drawn attention to the connection Woolf makes between militarism bred in men through their education and the coming of the Second World War.[37] The novel itself offers a comedic threnody for an England which may be about to witness invasion, the final loss of 'freedom and justice', and the obliteration of its history. This sounds a solemn task, but that is not Woolf's way of either celebrating or disturbing. Within the work she alludes to and fragments the canon of English literature; she records a tight and antique village community in whose neighbourhood has recently been built 'a car factory and an aerodrome'; she places at the centre an ancient house, Pointz Hall; and she mimics the self-congratulatory forms of village pageants, then so often held on Empire Day:

'The Nineteenth Century'. Colonel Mayhew did not dispute the producer's right to skip two hundred years in less than fifteen minutes. But the choice of scenes baffled him. 'Why leave out the British Army? What's history without the army, eh?' he mused. Inclining her head, Mrs Mayhew protested after all one mustn't ask too much. Besides, very likely there would be a Grand Ensemble, round the Union Jack, to end with. Meanwhile, there was the view. They looked at the view. (p. 184)

Woolf surrounds the people of the book with the contours of historical landscapes no longer perceptible to the naked eye. On the second page we move from the conversation about the village cesspool to the new forms of aerial observation. The bird, singing, dreaming of the 'succulence of the day, over worms, snails, grit' is, as in *Mrs Dalloway*, linked in sequence with the aeroplane. Mr Oliver 'said that the site they had chosen for the cesspool was, if he had heard aright, on the Roman road. From an aeroplane, he said, you could still see, plainly marked, the scars made by the Britons; by the Romans; by the Elizabethan manor house; and by the plough, when they ploughed the hill to grow wheat in the Napoleonic wars' (p. 8).

The aeroplane, in this opening of the book, allows history to surface in the landscape and be seen anew. The acceptance of change, new use, and continuity, of village inconvenience and incomings, allows the inconsequent of middle-class life a homely poetry which is as close as Woolf comes to affection. In this work the 'future is disturbing our present (p. 100) Giles, returned from London, rages at the 'old fogies who sat and looked at views' when the whole of Europe was 'bristling with guns, poised with planes. At any moment guns would rake that land into furrows; planes splinter Bolney Minster into smithereens and blast the Folly. He, too, loved the view' (pp. 66–7). The swallows swoop as they have done since the world was a swamp, are caught into language as 'the temple-haunting martins' (instead of 'martlets' in the half-stirred allusion to *Macbeth* in the last serene evening before violence, just as this is the moment before war.) Their recurrence seems to offer assurance of continuity, perhaps as factitious in its way (there may soon *be* no temples) as *The Times* leader of yesterday:

> The swallows — or martins were they? — The temple-haunting martins who come, have always come. . . . Yes, perched on the wall, they seemed to foretell what after all the *Times* was saying yesterday. Homes will be built. Each flat with its refrigerator, in the crannied wall. Each of us a free man; plates washed by machinery; not an aeroplane to vex us; all liberated; made whole. . . . (p. 213)

But it is old Mrs Swithin who carries in her mind an awareness of the prehistory of England, of a voluptuous primal world even before England was an island; 'Once there was no sea', said Mrs Swithin. 'No sea at all between us and the continent' (p. 38). Now Giles reads in the morning paper of men shot and imprisoned 'just over there, across the gulf, in the flat land which divided them from the continent' (p. 58). So the lackadaisical conversations about how far it is to the sea from Pointz Hall also become part of a general dislimning of securities.

The land shifts, the sea dries up, the impermeable island is a temporary form within the view of geological time. English life and language, on its shorter scale, is similarly impermanent, and here Woolf uses the parody sequences of the pageant to point the shifting markers of the island literary canon. Isa musing on the library 'ran her eyes along the books. "The mirror of the soul" books were, *The Faerie Queene* and Kinglake's *Crimea*; Keats and the *Kreutzer Sonata*. There they were, reflecting. What? What remedy was there for her at her age — the age of the century, thirty-nine — in books?' (p. 26). The pageant opens with a small girl who pipes:

> *This is a pageant, all may see*
> *Drawn from our island history.*
> *England am I* (p. 94)

The child sticks there, having forgotten her lines. The pageant scenes that follow include traditional elements (Queen Elizabeth played by the local shopkeeper) but these images are ruffled and undermined, sometimes by chance events — the wind, the cows lowing — sometimes by the plethora of language. Beneath this spume lie inalienable emotions: Love. Hate. To them, Isa, in this book, adds, Peace.

In *Mrs Dalloway* the dallying light aircraft represented the reassuring triviality of peace after the war, which is still melting and freezing the consciousness of Septimus Smith. Here the aircraft, still mingled in imagery with natural forms and with happiness, also presage the future: a future that may not exist.

Nothing holds its full form for long: that is one reason why rhyme, which fleetingly hitches unlike together, is so prevalent in the language of the book. Isa, dreaming of her tenuous secret love, looks out of her bedroom window at her little boy George with the two nursemaids in the garden.

The drone of the trees was in their ears; the chirp of birds; other incidents of garden life, inaudible, invisible to her in the bedroom, absorbed them. Isolated on a green island, hedged about with snowdrops, laid with a counterpane of puckered silk, the innocent island floated under her window. (p. 20)

The fragile imagined island of security is succeeded by the image of arousal, here figured as aeroplane:

the words he said, handing her a teacup, handing her a tennis racquet, could so attach themselves to a certain spot in her; and thus lie between them like a wire, tingling, tangling, vibrating — she groped, in the depths of the looking-glass, for a word to fit the infinitely quick vibrations of the aeroplane propeller that she had seen once at dawn at Croydon. Faster, faster, faster, it whizzed, whirred, buzzed, till all the flails became one flail and up soared the plane away and away....

'Where we know not, where we go not, neither know nor care', she hummed. 'Flying, rushing through the ambient, incandescent, summer silent....'

The rhyme was 'air'. She put down her brush. She took up the telephone.

'Three, four, eight, Pyecombe', she said.

'Mrs Oliver speaking. ... What fish have you this morning? Cod? Halibut? Sole? Plaice?'

'There to lose what binds us here', she murmured. 'Soles. Filleted. In time for lunch please', she said aloud. (pp. 20–1)

Isa's habit of rhyming is skeined through the work without any satirical commentary and at times the same habit moves out into the communality of gossiping voices.

So abrupt. And corrupt. Such an outrage; such an insult; And not plain. Very up to date, all the same. What is her game? To disrupt? Jog and trot? Jerk and smirk? Put the finger to the nose? Squint and pry? Peak and spy? (p. 213)

The semantic cacophony of rhyme (auditory likeness without referential reason) suggests the reckless antiquity of the community. The forms of likeness are embedded in the sounds of the language, not in any reasoned relationships. The slippage between words and senses, and between separate units of speech, is constantly displayed in this work, where words collapse, reverse, become units of lexical play without sustained boundaries. In this passage, for example, the fish 'sole', effortlessly reverses in her next line of poetry into 'lose': '"There to lose what binds us here", she murmured. "Soles. Filleted"'. 'Filleted' takes up the sense of *binds* (a fillet is a ribbon which binds the hair); that sense flies loose, so to speak, beside the utilitarian boneless 'filleted' fish. The sole/soul fugue is elaborated a few pages later. The fugitive lightness of this linguistic play risks being lost in any act of analysis such as that I have just offered. But such inversions and smudging of semantic bounds are essential to the work's sense of smothered crisis. It has in itself contradictory functions: it signals collapse and fragmentation. Yet it also celebrates the insouciant resilience of the English language and of literary history: Woolf's one form of patriotism.

Poems do not survive intact in memory but single lines are absorbed and adapted. Past literature permeates the work, but as 'orts, scraps, fragments'. The canon of English literature is no tight island but a series of dispersed traces constantly rewritten in need, so that, for example, William Dodge misremembers Keats's 'Ode on a Nightingale' and is not corrected. Instead of the expected 'Grand Ensemble: Army; Navy; Union Jack; and behind them perhaps . . . the church' (p. 209) the audience at the end of Miss La Trobe's pageant is offered mirrors and the present moment. That moment fills with rain — nature takes its part — but is followed by interrupting aeroplanes. Nothing remains intact, and, within the gossip another idea emerges: 'The very latest notion, so I'm told is, nothing's solid' (p. 232).

At the end of the pageant, composed as it also is of 'scraps, orts, and fragments' of past writing, Miss La Trobe holds the mirrors up to the audience 'reflecting. What?'. 'Book-shy and gun-shy', all that is left to them is landscape and world gossip. Recurrence knits the island past together: the swallows fly in to the barn each year from Africa. 'As they had done, she supposed, when the Barn was a swamp' (p. 123). 'Before there was a channel . . . they had come' (p. 130). The skeined-out inter-connections of the work (Giles's youth in Africa, the flight of the swallows, '"Swallow, my sister, o sister swallow"', he muttered, feeling for his cigar case', the scene of the reported rape even) call to mind *The Waste Land*, though the mood is closer to *Four Quartets*: 'History is now, and England'. In this work, however, 'the doom of sudden death' oppresses all the characters, because it threatens the whole history of England. No longer is the island a sufficient geometry, a sustaining autonomy. 'The future shadowed their present, like the sun coming through the many-veined transparent vine leaf; a criss-cross of lines making no pattern' (p. 136).

In the intervals of the pageant the talk is of coming war, and of old roses, of refugees, and the falling franc, of the royal family and Queen Mary's secret meetings with the Duke of Windsor, and of 'the Jews, people like ourselves, beginning life again' (p. 143). Mr Streatfield, the clergyman, tries to draw the pageant together into coherent message: we act different parts but are the same, a spirit pervades beyond our own lives, 'Surely, we unite?' These hopeful utterances lead to his announce-ment of the collection for 'the illumination of our dear old church'. Woolf's first readers would have felt the force of the irony here. This is mid-June; by mid-September 1939 all illumination will be doused and the blackout will be in place.[38] And, within the text, prompt on this cue, Mr Streatfield hears what he at first takes to be 'distant music'. His next words are severed. 'The word was cut in two. A zoom severed it. Twelve aeroplanes in perfect formation like a flight of wild duck came overhead. *That* was the music'.

Curiously, Woolf alludes irresistibly back here to the ending of *Orlando*: the wild duck or wild goose, the perfect formation, momentarily naturalize the aeroplanes. But in the ensuing pages, amidst the gossip, we realize that the audience has recognized that ominous zoom-drone music and what it portends: 'Also why leave out the Army, as my husband was saying, if it's history? *And if one spirit animates the whole, what about the aeroplanes?*' (pp. 230—1); 'What we need is a centre. Something to bring us all together. . . . The Brookes have gone to Italy, in spite of everything. Rather rash? . . .*If the worst should come – let's hope it won't – they'd hire an aeroplane, they said*' (p. 231); '*I agree – things look worse than ever on the continent. And what's the channel, come to think of it, if they mean to invade us? The aeroplanes, I didn't like to say it, made one think. . . . No, I thought it much too scrappy*' (p. 232); 'Then when Mr Streatfield said: One spirit animates the whole — *the aeroplanes interrupted*. That's the worst of playing out of doors. . . . Unless of course she meant that very thing' (p. 234).

Unless, of course, she meant that very thing! The section ends 'the gramophone gurgled *Unity — Dispersity*. It gurgled *Un...dis* . . . And ceased'.

The stare upward at the aeroplanes in *Between the Acts* is written in Woolf's diary in the same months as dread of invasion, and invasion by parachutists. The skittishness of the plane in *Mrs Dalloway* has vanished in *Between the Acts*. The twelve planes in perfect formation at the end of *Between the Acts* are machines, though the pattern of their flight mimics that of birds. The sombre untranslatability of the planes here is part of the new meaning of the aeroplanes after the Spanish Civil war. Even as she wrote, Leonard was on fire-watching duties and (15 May 1940) 'Behind that the strain: this morning we discussed suicide if Hitler lands. Jews beaten up. What point in waiting? Better shut the garage doors.' A month later, on almost precisely the first anniversary of that 'mid-June afternoon of 1939', in which *Between the Acts* sets its summoning of the island past, she records Harry West's account of Dunkirk: a survivor's tale in which the safe harbourage of the island still, amazingly, and perhaps only momentarily, holds.

> It pours out — how he hadnt boots off for 3 days, the beach at Dunkirk — the bombers as low as trees — how no English aeroplanes fought. . . . At Dunkirk many men shot themselves as the planes swooped. Harry swam off, a boat neared. Say Chum Can you row? Yes, he said, hauled in, rowed for 5 hours, saw England, landed — didnt know if it were day or night or what town — didnt ask — couldn't write to his mother — so was despatched to his regiment. (20 June 1940)[39]

The jarring within this account flings a further sardonic beam upon the refusal to accord, or to set in hierarchical order, or contain, that marks the writing of *Between the Acts*. Refusing to resolve is here not irresolution, but assertion. In the new world of flight and war the old axes are turned, the old geometries of the island giving way. Woolf writes always as a civilian from *within* the island, even as she records its dislimning. The 'we' of *Between the Acts* is that of the English language, of intertextual play, and mythologized English history, viewed with the sceptical yearning eye of Miss La Trobe. The slow flux of land-shifts described in the book repeatedly reminds the reader that islands are formed, not originary: Mrs Swithin, 'thinking of rhododendron forests in Piccadilly; when the entire continent, not then, she understood, divided by a channel, was all one' (p. 13). Overhead, rupturing the reiteration of island life, go the war planes. Woolf did not live through that war but she recorded a tonic and satiric elegy for the island.

Notes

1 For a thorough account of the history of flight see Charles Harvard Gibbs-Smith, *Aviation: An Historical Survey from its Origins to the End of World War II*, 2nd edn (London: HMSO, 1985)
2 Sigmund Freud, in 'On dreams', added a section on symbolism in the 2nd edn (1911): he there instances airships. *Standard Edition of the Complete Psychological Works of Sigmund Freud*, ed. James Strachey (London: Hogarth Press, 1953), vol. 5, p. 684; lecture 10 of *Introductory Lectures on Psycho-Analysis Standard Edition*, vol. 15, p. 155.
3 *The Diary of Virginia Woolf*, ed. Anne Olivier Bell (London: Hogarth Press, 1982), vol. 4, p. 113. In July 1932 the *Graf Zeppelin* 'took passengers for a circuit tour of Great Britain'.
4 Gertrude Stein, *Picasso* (London: Batsford, 1938) pp. 11, 50.
5 Virginia Woolf, *Between the Acts* (London: Hogarth Press, 1941), p. 231. All further references are to this edition.
6 H. G. Wells, *The War in the Air, Particularly how Mr Bert Smallways Fared* (London: Bell, 1908) pp. 243–4.
7 Naum Gabo, quoted in *St. Ives 1939–64: Twenty-Five Years of Painting, Sculpture and Pottery*, ed. David Brown (London: Tate Gallery, 1985).
8 Harald Penrose, *British Aviation: The Ominous Skies 1935–39* (London: HSMO, 1980), p. 290. Penrose gives no source for this remark. The emphasis on Chamberlain's *flight* to Munich to treat with Hitler in 1938 may seem curious to us, to whom such diplomacy is everyday. His flight, however, marked the entry of the aeroplane as a diplomatic instrument.
9 H. G. Wells, *Twelve Stories and A Dream* (London: Ernest Benn, 1927), p. 5. (First published 1903.)
10 'The argonauts of the air', in *The Plattner Story and Others* (Leipzig: Tauchnitz, 1900‡), pp. 46–7.
11 *The Way the World is Going: Guesses and Forecasts of the Years Ahead* (London: Ernest Benn, 1928), p. 124.
12 Virginia Woolf, *Collected Essays* (London: Hogarth Press, 1966), vol. 4, pp. 167–72.
13 Gibbs-Smith, op. cit., p. 250.
14 James Joyce, *A Portrait of the Artist as a Young Man* (London: Jonathan Cape, 1916), p. 288.
15 W. H. Auden, *The English Auden: Poems, Essays and Dramatic Writings 1927–1939*, ed. Edward Mendelson (London: Faber, 1977), p. 237.
16 ibid., p. 257; John Fuller, *A Reader's Guide to W. H. Auden* (London: Thames & Hudson, 1970), p. 127.
17 *Variorum Edition of the Poems of W. B. Yeats*, ed. Peter Allt and Russell K. Alspach (New York: Macmillan, 1957), pp. 328, 791.

18 *Collected Essays* (London: Hogarth Press, 1966), vol. 4, p. 173.
19 Since writing this essay I have been studying the ways in which the idea of the island has entered a number of scientific discourses, as well as political and literary ones, within the last 150 years. This section of the present essay overlaps briefly with a much longer paper, 'Discourses of the island', forthcoming in a collection of essays on literature and science, edited by Frederick Amrine (Amsterdam: D. Reidel Publishers, 1988).
20 For an excellent discussion of *The Tempest*, and of *Robinson Crusoe* in the context of Caribbean colonization see Peter Hulme, *Colonial Encounters: Europe and the Native Caribbean 1492–1797* (London: Methuen, 1986). *Robinson Crusoe* was one of Virginia Woolf's most admired works. See the discussion of its relation to the inception of *To the Lighthouse* in Juliet Dusinberre, *Alice to the Lighthouse: Children's Books and Radical Experiments in Art* (London: Macmillan, 1987) pp. 276–7, 323.
21 Compare my 'Hume, Stephen, and elegy in *To the Lighthouse*', *Essays in Criticism* (Oxford, 1984).
22 Stephen Kern, *The Culture of Time and Space, 1880–1918* (London: Weidenfeld & Nicolson, 1983), p. 242.
23 *Mrs Dalloway* (London: Hogarth, 1925), p. 90. All further references are to this edition. See, for an enlightening discussion of this passage, Makiko Minow Pinkney, *Virginia Woolf and the Problem of the Subject: Feminine Writing in the Major Novels* (Brighton: Harvester, 1987).
24 *Between the Acts*, p. 30: 'Beyond that was blue, pure blue, black blue; blue that had never filtered down; that had escaped registration'.
25 Gibbs-Smith, op. cit., p. 251.
26 *Diary*, vol. 3, pp. 154–5. Compare my 'The body of the people in Virginia Woolf' in Sue Roe (ed.), *Women Reading Women's Writing* (Brighton: Harvester, 1987) pp. 102–3.
27 *Orlando* (London: Hogarth, 1928) p. 295. All further references are to this edition. Maud Bodkin, *Archetypal Patterns in Poetry: Psychological Studies of Imagination* (Oxford: Oxford University Press, 1934) p. 307, read Shel as a fantasy of masculinity in Orlando's mind: 'it is over his head — the aeroplane having now supplanted the ship — that there springs up the winged wild thing by which the woman finds herself haunted and lured'.
28 *Diary*, vol 4, p. 7.
29 Arthur Eddington, *The Nature of the Physical World* (Cambridge: Cambridge University Press, 1928), p. 274.
30 James Jeans, *The Mysterious Universe* (Cambridge: Cambridge University Press, 1930), pp. 79, 136.
31 *The Letters of Virginia Woolf*, ed. Nigel Nicolson (London: Hogarth Press, 1980), vol. 6, pp. 354, 460.
32 *Diary*, vol. 3, pp. 322–3.
33 *The Years* (London: Hogarth, 1937), pp. 1–2. All further references are to this edition.
34 See for example *Letters*, vol. 6, pp. 413, 419, 421.
35 *ibid.*, p. 402. Caburn was part of the prospect from Rodmell and acted as something of an emotional barometer for her: see, for example, her complaining entry (*Diary*, vol. 3, p. 322) about Leonard Woolf's family which ends: 'It is the most miserable of days, cold and drizzling, the leaves falling; the apples fallen; the flowers sodden; mist hiding Caburn.' Compare also note 28 above.
36 *Letters*, vol. 6, p. 391
37 See, for example, Roger Poole, *The Unknown Virginia Woolf* (Cambridge:

Cambridge University Press, 1978), pp. 216—31; Sallie Sears, 'Theater of war: Virginia Woolf's *Between the Acts*' in Jane Marcus (ed.), *Virginia Woolf: a Feminist Slant* (Lincoln and London: University of Nebraska Press, 1983), pp. 212—35.

38 'At this very moment, half-past three on a June day in 1939' (p. 92); 'sitting here on a June day in 1939' (p. 208). Penrose op. cit., p. 276 points out that 'The thirtieth anniversary of Handley Page Ltd. was on 12th June (1939) — at that time the country was spending almost £2 million a week on aeroplanes.' Living as she did so close to what was then Gatwick aerodrome Woolf could not fail to be aware of the significance of the greatly increased air traffic in the later 1930s and its war menace. When she wrote the novel she was under the flight path of invasion — not now by sea, to be repelled from the island fortress, but by air, with the land below under threat from paratroops and bombs.

39 *Diary*, vol. 5, p. 297.

16

DissemiNation: time, narrative, and the margins of the modern nation[1]

Homi K. Bhabha

(In memory of Paul Moritz Strimpel (1914—87):
Pforzheim — Paris — Zurich — Ahmedabad —
Bombay — Milan — Lugano.)

The time of the nation

The title of my essay — DissemiNation — owes something to the wit and wisdom of Jacques Derrida, but something more to my own experience of migration. I have lived that moment of the scattering of the people that in other times and other places, in the nations of others, becomes a time of gathering. Gatherings of exiles and emigrés and refugees, gathering on the edge of 'foreign' cultures; gathering at the frontiers; gatherings in the ghettos or cafés of city centres; gathering in the half-life, half-light of foreign tongues, or in the uncanny fluency of another's language; gathering the signs of approval and acceptance, degrees, discourses, disciplines; gathering the memories of underdevelopment, of other worlds lived retroactively; gathering the past in a ritual of revival; gathering the present. Also the gathering of the people in the diaspora: indentured, migrant, interned; the gathering of incriminatory statistics, educational performance, legal statutes, immigration status — the genealogy of that lonely figure that John Berger named the seventh man. The gathering of clouds from which the Palestinian poet Mahmoud Darwish asks 'where should the birds fly after the last sky?'

In the midst of these lonely gatherings of the scattered people, their myths and fantasies and experiences, there emerges a historical fact of singular importance. More deliberately than any other general historian, Eric Hobsbawm[2] writes the history of the modern western nation from the perspective of the nation's margin and the migrants' exile. The emergence of the later phase of the modern nation, from the mid-nineteenth century, is also one of the most sustained periods of mass migration within the west, and colonial expansion in the east. The nation fills the void left in the uprooting of communities and kin, and turns that loss into the language of metaphor. Metaphor, as the etymology of the word suggests, transfers the meaning of home and belonging, across the 'middle passage', or the central European steppes, across those distances, and cultural differences, that span the imagined community of the nation-people.

The discourse of nationalism is not my main concern. In some ways it is the historical certainty and settled nature of that term against which I am attempting to write of the western nation as an obscure and ubiquitous form of living the *locality* of culture. This locality is more *around* temporality than *about* historicity: a form of living that is more complex than 'community'; more symbolic than 'society'; more connotative than 'country'; less patriotic than *patrie*; more rhetorical than the reason of state; more mythological than ideology; less homogeneous than hegemony; less centred than the citizen; more collective than 'the subject'; more psychic than civility; more hybrid in the articulation of cultural differences and identifications — gender, race or class — than can be represented in any hierarchical or binary structuring of social antagonism.

In proposing this cultural construction of nationness as a form of social and textual affiliation, I do not wish to deny these categories their specific historicities and particular meanings within different political languages. What I am attempting to formulate in this essay are the complex strategies of cultural identification and discursive address that function in the name of 'the people' or 'the nation' and make them the immanent subjects and objects of a range of social and literary narratives. My emphasis on the temporal dimension in the inscription of these political entities — that are also potent symbolic and affective sources of cultural identity — serves to displace the historicism that has dominated discussions of the nation as a cultural force. The focus on temporality resists the transparent linear equivalence of event and idea that historicism proposes; it provides a perspective on the disjunctive forms of representation that signify a people, a nation, or a national culture. It is neither the sociological solidity of these terms, nor their holistic history that gives them the narrative and psychological force that they have brought to bear on cultural production and projections. It is the mark of the ambivalence of the nation as a narrative strategy — and an apparatus of power — that it produces a continual slippage into analogous, even metonymic, categories, like the people, minorities, or 'cultural difference' that continually overlap in the act of writing the nation. What is displayed in this displacement and repetition of terms is the nation as the measure of the liminality of cultural modernity.

Edward Said aspires to such secular interpretation in his concept of 'wordliness' where 'sensuous particularity as well as historical contingency . . . exist *at the same level of surface particularity* as the textual object itself' (my emphasis).[3] Fredric Jameson invokes something similar in his notion of 'situational consciousness' or national allegory, 'where the telling of the individual story and the individual experience cannot but ultimately involve the whole laborious telling of the collectivity itself'.[4] And Julia Kristeva speaks perhaps too hastily of the pleasures of exile — 'How can one avoid sinking into the mire of common sense, if not by becoming a stranger to one's own country, language, sex and identity?'[5] — without realizing how fully the shadow of the nation falls on the condition of exile — which may partly explain her own later, labile identifications with the images of *other* nations: 'China', 'America'.

The nation as metaphor: *Amor Patria*; *Fatherland*; *Pig Earth*; *Mothertongue*; *Matigari*; *Middlemarch*; *Midnight's Children*; *One Hundred Years of Solitude*; *War and Peace*; *I Promessi Sposi*; *Kanthapura*; *Moby Dick*; *The Magic Mountain*; *Things Fall Apart*.

There must also be a tribe of interpreters of such metaphors — the translators of the dissemination of texts and discourses across cultures — who can perform what Said describes as the act of secular interpretation. 'To take account of this horizontal, secular space of the crowded spectacle of the modern nation . . . implies that no single explanation sending one back immediately to a single origin is adequate. And just as there are no simple dynastic answers, there are no simple discrete formations or social processes'.[6] If, in our travelling theory, we are alive to the *metaphoricity* of the peoples of imagined communities — migrant or metropolitan — then we shall find that the space of the modern nation-people is never simply horizontal. Their metaphoric movement requires a kind of 'doubleness' in writing; a temporality of representation that moves between cultural formations and social processes without a 'centred' causal logic. And such cultural movements disperse the homogeneous, visual time of the horizontal society because 'the present is no longer a mother-form [read mother-tongue or mother-land] around which are gathered and differentiated the future (present) and the past (present) . . . [as] a present of which the past and the future would be but modifications'.[7] The secular language of interpretation then needs to go beyond the presence of the 'look', that Said recommends, if we are to give 'the nonsequential energy of lived historical memory and subjectivity its appropriate narrative authority. We need another time of *writing* that will be able to inscribe the ambivalent and chiasmatic intersections of time and place that constitute the problematic 'modern' experience of the western nation.

How does one write the nation's modernity as the event of the everyday and the advent of the epochal? The language of national belonging comes laden with atavistic apologues, which has led Benedict Anderson to ask: 'But why do nations celebrate their hoariness, not their astonishing youth?'[8] The nation's claim to modernity, as an autonomous or sovereign form of political rationality, is particularly questionable if, with Partha Chatterjee, we adopt the post-colonial perspective:

> Nationalism . . . seeks to represent itself in the image of the Enlightenment and fails to do so. For Enlightenment itself, to assert its sovereignty as the universal ideal, needs its Other; if it could ever actualise itself in the real world as the truly universal, it would in fact destroy itself.[9]

Such ideological ambivalence nicely supports Gellner's paradoxical point that the historical necessity of the idea of the nation conflicts with the contingent and arbitrary signs and symbols that signify the affective life of the national culture. The nation may exemplify modern social cohesion but

Nationalism is not what it seems, and above all not what it seems to itself . . . The cultural shreds and patches used by nationalism are often arbitrary historical inventions. Any old shred would have served as well. But in no way does it follow that the principle of nationalism . . . is itself in the least contingent and accidental.[10]

The problematic boundaries of modernity are enacted in these ambivalent temporalities of the nation-space. The language of culture and community is poised on the fissures of the present becoming the rhetorical figures of a national past. Historians transfixed on the event and origins of the nation never ask, and political theorists possessed of the 'modern' totalities of the nation — 'Homogeneity, literacy and anonymity are the key traits'[11] — never pose, the awkward question of the disjunctive representation of the social, in this double-time of the nation. It is indeed only in the disjunctive time of the nation's modernity — as a knowledge disjunct between political rationality and its impasse, between the shreds and patches of cultural signification and the certainties of a nationalist pedagogy — that questions of nation as narration come to be posed. How do we plot the narrative of the nation that must mediate between the teleology of progress tipping over into the 'timeless' discourse of irrationality? How do we understand that 'homogeneity' of modernity — the people — which, if pushed too far, may assume something resembling the archaic body of the despotic or totalitarian mass? In the midst of progress and modernity, the language of ambivalence reveals a politics 'without duration', as Althusser once provocatively wrote: 'Space without places, time without duration.'[12] To write the story of the nation demands that we articulate that archaic ambivalence that informs modernity. We may begin by questioning that progressive metaphor of modern social cohesion — the many as one — shared by organic theories of the holism of culture and community, and by theorists who treat gender, class, or race as radically 'expressive' social totalities.

Out of many one: nowhere has this founding dictum of the political society of the modern nation — its spatial expression of a unitary people — found a more intriguing image of itself than in those diverse languages of literary criticism that seek to portray the great power of the idea of the nation in the disclosures of its everyday life; in the telling details that emerge as metaphors for national life. I am reminded of Bakhtin's wonderful description of a 'national' vision of emergence in Goethe's Italian Journey, which represents the triumph of the realistic component over the Romantic. Goethe's realist narrative produces a national-historical time that makes visible a specifically Italian day in the detail of its passing time, 'The bells ring, the rosary is said, the maid enters the room with a lighted lamp and says: Felicissima notte! . . . If one were to force a German clockhand on them, they would be at a loss.'[13] For Bakhtin it is Goethe's vision of the microscopic, elementary, perhaps random tolling of everyday life in Italy that reveals the profound history of its locality (Lokalität), the spatialization of historical time, 'a creative humanization of this locality, which transforms a part of terrestrial space into a place of historical life for people'.[14]

The recurrent metaphor of landscape as the inscape of national identity emphasizes the quality of light, the question of social visibility, the power of the eye to naturalize the rhetoric of national affiliation and its forms of collective expression. There is, however, always the distracting presence of another temporality that disturbs the contemporaneity of the national present, as we saw in the national discourses with which I began. Despite Bakhtin's emphasis on the realist vision in the emergence of the nation in Goethe's work, he acknowledges that the origin of the nation's visual *presence* is the effect of a narrative struggle. From the beginning, Bakhtin writes, the realist and Romantic conceptions of time co-exist in Goethe's work, but the ghostly (*Gespenstermässiges*), the terrifying (*Unerfreuliches*), and the unaccountable (*Unzuberechnendes*) are consistently 'surmounted' by the structural aspects of the visualization of time: 'the necessity of the past and the necessity of its place in a line of continuous development . . . finally the aspect of the past being linked to a necessary future'.[15] National time becomes concrete and visible in the chronotope of the local, particular, graphic, from beginning to end. The narrative structure of this *historical* surmounting of the 'ghostly' or the 'double' is seen in the intensification of narrative synchrony as a graphically visible position in space: 'to grasp the most elusive course of pure historical time and fix it through unmediated contemplation'.[16] But what kind of 'present' is this if it is a consistent process of surmounting the ghostly time of repetition? Can this national time-space be as fixed or as immediately visible as Bakhtin claims?

If in Bakhtin's 'surmounting' we hear the echo of another use of that word by Freud in his essay on *The Uncanny*, then we begin to get a sense of the complex time of the national narrative. Freud associates *surmounting* with the repressions of a 'cultural' unconscious; a liminal, uncertain state of cultural belief when the archaic emerges in the midst or margins of modernity as a result of some psychic ambivalence or intellectual uncertainty. The 'double' is the figure most frequently associated with this uncanny process of 'the doubling, dividing and interchanging of the self'.[17] Such 'double-time' cannot be so simply represented as visible or flexible in 'unmediated contemplation'; nor can we accept Bakhtin's repeated attempt to read the national space as achieved only in the *fullness of time*. Such an apprehension of the 'double and split' time of national representation, as I am proposing, leads us to question the homogeneous and horizontal view familiarly associated with it. We are led to ask, provocatively, whether the *emergence* of a national perspective — of an élite or subaltern nature — within a culture of social contestation, can ever articulate its 'representative' authority in that fullness of narrative time, and that visual synchrony of the sign that Bakhtin proposes.

Two brilliant accounts of the emergence of national narratives seem to support my suggestion. They represent the diametrically opposed world views of master and slave which between them account for the major historical and philosophical dialectic of modern times. I am thinking of

John Barrell's[18] splendid analysis of the rhetorical and perspectival status of the 'English gentleman' within the social diversity of the eighteenth-century novel; and of Huston Baker's innovative reading of the 'new *national* modes of sounding, interpreting and speaking the Negro in the Harlem Renaissance'.[19] In his concluding essay Barrell surveys the positions open to 'an equal, wide survey' and demonstrates how the demand for a holistic, representative vision of society could only be represented in a discourse that was *at the same time* obsessively fixed upon, and uncertain of, the boundaries of society, and the margins of the text. For instance, the hypostatized 'common language' which was the language of the gentleman whether he be Observer, Spectator, Rambler, 'Common to all by virtue of the fact that it manifested the peculiarities of none'[20] — was primarily defined through a process of negation — of regionalism, occupation, faculty — so that this centred vision of 'the gentleman' is so to speak 'a condition of empty potential, one who is imagined as being able to comprehend everything, and yet who may give no evidence of having comprehended anything'.[21] A different note of liminality is struck in Baker's description of the 'radical maroonage' that structured the emergence of an insurgent Afro-American expressive culture in its expansive, 'national' phase. Baker's sense that the 'discursive project' of the Harlem Renaissance is modernist is based less on a strictly literary understanding of the term, and more appropriately on the agonistic enunciative conditions within which the Harlem Renaissance shaped its cultural practice. The transgressive, invasive structure of the black 'national' text, which thrives on rhetorical strategies of hybridity, deformation, masking, and inversion, is developed through an extended analogy with the guerilla warfare that became a way of life for the maroon communities of runaway slaves and fugitives who lived dangerously, and insubordinately, 'on the frontiers or margins of *all* American promise, profit and modes of production'. From this liminal, minority position where, as Foucault would say, the relations of discourse are of the nature of warfare, emerges the force of the people of an Afro-American nation, as Baker 'signifies upon' the extended metaphor of maroonage. For warriors read writers or even 'signs':

> these highly adaptable and mobile warriors took maximum advantage of local environments, striking and withdrawing with great rapidity, making extensive use of bushes to catch their adversaries in cross-fire, fighting only when and where they chose, depending on reliable intelligence networks among non-maroons (both slave and white settlers) and often communicating by horns.[22]

Both gentleman and slave, with different cultural means and to very different historical ends, demonstrate that forces of social authority and subalternality may emerge in displaced, even decentred, strategies of signification. This does not prevent them from being representative in a political sense, although it does suggest that positions of authority are themselves part of a process of ambivalent identification. Indeed the exercise of power may be both more politically effective and psychically *affective* because their discursive liminality may provide greater scope for strategic manoeuvre and negotiation. It is precisely in reading between these borderlines of the nation-space that we can see how the 'people' come to be constructed within a range of discourses as a double narrative movement. The people are not simply historical events or parts of a patriotic body politic. They are also a complex rhetorical strategy of social reference where the claim to be representative provokes a crisis within the process of signification and discursive address. We then have a contested cultural territory where the people must be thought in a double-time; the people are the historical 'objects' of a nationalist pedagogy, giving the discourse an authority that is based on the pre-given or constituted historical origin or event; the people are also the 'subjects' of a process of signification that must erase any prior or originary presence of the nation-people to demonstrate the prodigious, living principle of the people as that continual process by which the national life is redeemed and signified as a repeating and reproductive process. The scraps, patches, and rags of daily life must be repeatedly turned into the signs of a national culture, while the very act of the narrative performance interpellates a growing circle of national subjects. In the production of the nation as narration there is a split between the continuist, accumulative temporality of the pedagogical, and the repetitious, recursive strategy of the performative. It is through this process of splitting that the conceptual ambivalence of modern society becomes the site of *writing the nation*.

The space of the people

The tension between the pedagogical and the performative that I have identified in the narrative address of the nation, turns the reference to a 'people' — from whatever political or cultural position it is made — into a problem of knowledge that haunts the symbolic formation of social authority. The people are neither the beginning or the end of the national narrative; they represent the cutting edge between the totalizing powers of the social and the forces that signify the more specific address to contentious, unequal interests and identities within the population. The ambivalent signifying system of the nation-space participates in a more general genesis of ideology in modern societies that Claude Lefort has described so suggestively. For him too it is 'the enigma of language', at once internal and external to the speaking subject, that provides the most apt analogue for imagining the structure of ambivalence that constitutes modern social authority. I shall quote him at length, because his rich ability to represent the *movement of* political power *beyond* the blindness of Ideology or the insight of the Idea, brings him to that liminality of modern society from which I have attempted to derive the narrative of the nation and its people.

In Ideology the representation of the rule is split off from the effective operation of it. . . . The rule is thus extracted from experience of language; it is circumscribed, made fully visible and assumed to govern the conditions of possibility of this experience. . . . The enigma of language — namely that it is both internal and external to the speaking subject, that there is an articulation of the self with others which marks the emergence of the self and which the self does not control — is concealed by the representation of a place 'outside' — language from which it could be generated. . . . We encounter the ambiguity of the representation as soon as the rule is stated; for its very exhibition undermines the power that the rule claims to introduce into practice. *This exorbitant power must, in fact, be shown, and at the same time it must owe nothing to the movement which makes it appear* . . . . *To be true to its image, the rule must be abstracted from any question concerning its origin; thus it goes beyond the operations that it controls. . . . Only the authority of the master allows the contradiction to be concealed, but he is himself an object of representation; presented as possessor of the knowledge of the rule, he allows the contradiction to appear through himself.*

The ideological discourse that we are examining has no safety catch; it is rendered vulnerable by its attempt to make visible the place from which the social relation would be conceivable (both thinkable and creatable) by its inability to define this place without letting its contingency appear, without condemning itself to slide from one position to another, without hereby making apparent the instability of an order that it is intended to raise to the status of essence. . . . [The ideological] task of the implicit generalisation of knowledge and the implicit homogenization of experience could fall apart in the face of the unbearable ordeal of the collapse of certainty, of the vacillation of representations of discourse and as a result of the splitting of the subject.[23]

How do we conceive of the 'splitting' of the national subject? How do we articulate cultural differences within this vacillation of ideology in which the national discourse also participates, sliding ambivalently from one enunciatory position to another? What comes to be represented in that unruly 'time' of national culture, which Bakhtin surmounts in his reading of Goethe, Gellner associates with the rags and patches of everyday life, Said describes as 'the nonsequential energy of lived historical memory and subjectivity' and Lefort re-presents again as the inexorable *movement of signification* that both constitutes the exorbitant image of power and deprives it of the certainty and stability of centre or closure? What might be the cultural and political effects of the liminality of the nation, the margins of modernity, which cannot be signified without the narrative temporalities of splitting, ambivalence, and vacillation?

Deprived of the unmediated visibility of historicism — 'looking to the legitimacy of past generations as supplying cultural autonomy'[24] — the nation turns from being the symbol of modernity into becoming the symptom of an ethnography of the 'contemporary' within culture. Such a shift in perspective emerges from an acknowledgement of the nation's interrupted address, articulated in the tension signifying the people as an *a priori* historical presence, a pedagogical object; and the people constructed in the performance of narrative, its enunciatory 'present' marked in the repetition and pulsation of the national sign. The pedagogical founds its narrative authority in a tradition of the people, described by Poulantzas[25] as a moment of becoming designated by *itself*, encapsulated in a succession of historical moments that represents an eternity produced by self-generation. The performative intervenes in the sovereignty of the nation's *self-generation* by casting a shadow between the people as 'image' and its signification as a differentiating sign of Self, distinct from the Other or the Outside. In place of the polarity of a prefigurative self-generating nation itself and extrinsic Other nations, the performative introduces a temporality of the 'in-between' through the 'gap' or 'emptiness' of the signifier that punctuates linguistic difference. The boundary that marks the nation's selfhood interrupts the self-generating time of national production with a space of representation that threatens binary division with its difference. The barred Nation *It/Self*, alienated from its eternal self-generation, becomes a liminal form of social representation, a space that is *internally* marked by cultural difference and the heterogeneous histories of contending peoples, antagonistic authorities, and tense cultural locations.

This double-writing or dissemi-*nation*, is not simply a theoretical exercise in the internal contradictions of the modern liberal nation. The structure of cultural liminality — *within the nation* — that I have been trying to elaborate would be an essential precondition for a concept such as Raymond Williams' crucial distinction between residual and emergent practices in oppositional cultures which require, he insists, a 'non-metaphysical, non-subjectivist' mode of explanation. Such a space of cultural signification as I have attempted to open up through the intervention of the performative, would meet this important precondition. The liminal figure of the nation-space would ensure that no political ideologies could claim transcendent or metaphysical authority for themselves. This is because the subject of cultural discourse — the agency of a people — is split in the discursive ambivalence that emerges in the contestation of narrative authority between the pedagogical and the performative. This disjunctive temporality of the nation would provide the appropriate time-frame for representing those residual and emergent meanings and practices that Williams locates in the margins of the contemporary experience of society. Their designation depends upon a kind of social ellipsis; their transformational power depends upon their being historically displaced:

> But in certain areas, there will be in certain periods, practices and meanings which are not reached for. There will be areas of practice and meaning which, almost by definition from its own limited character, or in its profound deformation, the dominant culture is unable in any real terms to recognize.[26]

When Edward Said suggests that the question of the nation should be put on the contemporary critical agenda as a hermeneutic of 'worldliness', he is fully aware that such a demand can only now be made from the liminal and ambivalent boundaries that articulate the signs of national culture, as 'zones of control *or* of abandonment, of recollection *and* of forgetting, of force *or* of dependence, of exclusiveness *or* of sharing' (my emphasis).[27]

Counter-narratives of the nation that continually evoke and erase its totalizing boundaries — both actual and conceptual — disturb those ideological manoeuvres through which 'imagined communities' are given essentialist identities. For the political unity of the nation consists in a continual displacement of its irredeemably plural modern space, bounded by different, even hostile nations, into a signifying space that is archaic and mythical, paradoxically representing the nation's modern territoriality, in the patriotic, atavistic temporality of Traditionalism. Quite simply, the difference of space returns as the Sameness of time, turning Territory into Tradition, turning the People into One. The liminal point of this ideological displacement is the turning of the differentiated spatial boundary, the 'outside', into the unified temporal territory of Tradition. Freud's concept of the 'narcissism of minor differences'[28] — reinterpreted for our purposes — provides a way of understanding how easily that boundary that secures the cohesive limits of the western nation may imperceptibly turn into a contentious *internal* liminality that provides a place from which to speak both of, and as, the minority, the exilic, the marginal, and the emergent.

Freud uses the analogy of feuds that prevail between communities with adjoining territories — the Spanish and the Portuguese, for instance — to illustrate the ambivalent identification of love and hate that binds a community together: 'it is always possible to bind together a considerable number of people in love, so long as there are other people left to receive the manifestation of their aggressiveness'.[29] The problem is, of course, that the ambivalent identifications of love and hate occupy the same psychic space; and paranoid projections 'outwards' return to haunt and split the place from which they are made. So long as a firm boundary is maintained between the territories, and the narcissistic wounded is contained, the aggressivity will be projected onto the Other or the Outside. But what if, as I have argued, the people are the articulation of a doubling of the national address, an ambivalent *movement* between the discourses of pedagogy and the performative? What if, as Lefort argues, the subject of modern ideology is split between the iconic image of authority and the movement of the signifier that produces the image, so that the 'sign' of the social is condemned to slide ceaselessly from one position to another? It is in this space of liminality, in the 'unbearable ordeal of the collapse of certainty' that we encounter once again the narcissistic neuroses of the national discourse with which I began. The nation is no longer the sign of modernity under which cultural differences are homogenized in the 'horizontal' view of society. The nation reveals, in its ambivalent and vacillating representation, the ethnography of its own historicity and opens up the possibility of other narratives of the people and their difference.

The people turn *pagan* in that disseminatory act of social narrative that

Lyotard defines, against the Platonic tradition, as the privileged pole of the *narrated*, 'where the one doing the speaking speaks from the place of the referent. As narrator she is narrated as well. And in a way she is already told, and what she herself is *telling* will not undo that somewhere else she is *told*'.[30] This narrative inversion or circulation — which is in the spirit of my splitting of the people — makes untenable any supremacist, or nationalist claims to cultural mastery, for the position of narrative control is neither monocular or monologic. The subject is graspable only in the passage between telling/told, between 'here' and 'somewhere else', and in this double scene the very condition of cultural knowledge is the alienation of the subject. The significance of this narrative splitting of the subject of identification is borne out in Lévi-Strauss' description of the ethnographic act.[31] The ethnographic demands that the observer himself is a part of his observation and this requires that the field of knowledge — the total social fact — must be appropriated from the outside like a thing, but like a thing which comprises within itself the subjective understanding of the indigenous. The transposition of this process into the language of the outsider's grasp — this entry into the area of the symbolic of representation/signification — then makes the social fact 'three dimensional'. For ethnography demands that the subject has to split itself into object and subject in the process of identifying its field of knowledge; the ethnographic object is constituted 'by dint of the subject's capacity for indefinite self-objectification (without ever quite abolishing itself as subject) for projecting outside itself ever-diminishing fragments of itself'.

Once the liminality of the nation-space is established, and its 'difference' is turned from the boundary 'outside' to its finitude 'within', the threat of cultural difference is no longer a problem of 'other' people. It becomes a question of the otherness of the people-as-one. The national subject splits in the ethnographic perspective of culture's contemporaneity and provides both a theoretical position and a narrative authority for marginal voices or minority discourse. They no longer need to address their strategies of opposition to a horizon of 'hegemony' that is envisaged as horizontal and homogeneous. The great contribution of Foucault's last published work is to suggest that people emerge in the modern state as a perpetual movement of 'the marginal integration of individuals'. 'What are we to-day?'[32] Foucault poses this most pertinent ethnographic question to the west itself to reveal the alterity of its political rationality. He suggests that the 'reason of state' in the modern nation must be derived from the heterogeneous and differentiated limits of its territory. The nation cannot be conceived in a state of *equilibrium* between several elements co-ordinated, and maintained by a 'good' law.

> Each state is in permanent competition with other countries, other nations ... so that each state has nothing before it other than an indefinite future of struggles. Politics has now to deal with an irreducible multiplicity of states struggling and competing in a limited history ... the State is its own finality.[33]

What is politically significant is the effect of this finality of the state on the liminality of the representation of the people. The people will no longer be contained in that national discourse of the teleology of progress; the anonymity of individuals; the spatial horizontality of community; the homogeneous time of social narratives; the historicist visibility of modernity, where 'the present of each level [of the social] coincides with the present of all the others, so that the present is an *essential* section which makes the essence *visible*'.[34] The finitude of the nation emphasizes the impossibility of such an expressive totality with its alliance between an immanent, plenitudinous present and the eternal visibility of a past. The liminality of the people — their double inscription as pedagogical objects and performative subjects — demands a 'time' of narrative that is disavowed in the discourse of historicism where narrative is only the agency of the event, or the medium of a naturalistic continuity of Community or Tradition. In describing the marginalistic integration of the individual in the social totality, Foucault provides a useful description of the rationality of the modern nation. Its main characteristic, he writes,

> is neither the constitution of the state, the coldest of cold monsters, nor the rise of bourgeois individualism. I won't even say it is the constant effort to integrate individuals into the political totality. I think that the main characteristic of our political rationality is the fact that this integration of the individuals in a community or in a totality results from a constant correlation between an increasing individualisation and the reinforcement of this totality. From this point of view we can understand why modern political rationality is permitted by the antinomy between law and order.[35]

From *Discipline and Punish* we have learned that the most individuated are those subjects who are placed on the margins of the social, so that the tension between law and order may produce the disciplinary or pastoral society. Having placed the people on the limits of the nation's narrative, I now want to explore forms of cultural identity and political solidarity that emerge from the disjunctive temporalities of the national culture. This is a lesson of history to be learnt from those peoples whose histories of marginality have been most profoundly enmeshed in the antinomies of law and order — the colonized and women.

Of margins and minorities

The difficulty of writing the history of the people as the insurmountable agonism of the living, the incommensurable experiences of struggle and survival in the construction of a national culture, is nowhere better seen than in Frantz Fanon's essay *On National Culture*.[36] I start with it because it is a warning against the intellectual appropriation of the culture of the people (whatever they may be) within a representationalist discourse that may be fixed and reified in the annals of History. Fanon writes against that form of historicism that assumes that there is a moment when the differential temporalities of cultural histories coalesce in an immediately readable present. For my purposes, he focuses on the time of cultural representation, instead of immediately historicizing the event. He explores the space of the nation without immediately identifying it with the historical institution of the state. As my concern here is not with the history of nationalist movements, but only with certain traditions of writing that have attempted to construct narratives of the imaginary of the nation-people, I am indebted to Fanon for liberating a certain, uncertain time of the people. The knowledge of the people depends on the discovery, Fanon says, 'of a much more fundamental substance which itself is continually being renewed', a structure of repetition that is not visible in the translucidity of the people's customs or the obvious objectivities which seem to characterize the people. 'Culture abhors simplification', Fanon writes, as he tries to locate the people in a performative time: 'the fluctuating movement that the people are *just* giving shape to'. The present of the people's history, then, is a practice that destroys the constant principles of the national culture that attempt to hark back to a 'true' national past, which is often represented in the reified forms of realism and stereotype. Such pedagogical knowledges and continuist national narratives miss the 'zone of occult instability where the people dwell' (Fanon's phrase). It is from this *instability* of cultural signification that the national culture comes to be articulated as a dialectic of various temporalities — modern, colonial, postcolonial, 'native' — that cannot be a knowledge that is stabilized in its enunciation: 'it is always contemporaneous with the act of recitation. It is the present act that on each of its occurrences marshalls in the ephemeral temporality inhabiting the space between the "I have heard" and "you will hear"'.[37]

I have heard this narrative movement of the post-colonial people, in their attempts to create a national culture. Its implicit critique of the fixed and stable forms of the nationalist narrative makes it imperative to question those western theories of the horizontal, homogeneous empty time of the nation's narrative. Does the language of culture's 'occult instability' have a relevance outside the situation of anti-colonial struggle? Does the incommensurable act of living — so often dismissed as ethical or empirical — have its own ambivalent narrative, its own history of theory? Can it change the way we identify the symbolic structure of the western nation?

A similar exploration of political time has a salutary feminist history in *Women's Time*.[38] It has rarely been acknowledged that Kristeva's celebrated essay of that title has its conjunctural, cultural history, not simply in psychoanalysis and semiotics, but in a powerful critique and redefinition of the nation as a space for the emergence of feminist political and psychic identifications. The nation as a symbolic denominator is, according to Kristeva, a powerful repository of cultural knowledge that erases the rationalist and progressivist logics of the 'canonical' nation. This symbolic history of the national culture is inscribed in the strange temporality of the future perfect, the effects of

which are not dissimilar to Fanon's occult instability. In such a historical
time, the deeply repressed past initiates a strategy of repetition that
disturbs the sociological totalities within which we recognize the modernity of the national culture — a little too forcibly for, or against, the
reason of state, or the unreason of ideological misrecognition.

The borders of the nation are, Kristeva claims, constantly faced with
a double temporality: the process of identity constituted by historical
sedimentation (the pedagogical); and the loss of identity in the signifying
process of cultural identification (the performative). The time and space
of Kristeva's construction of the nation's finitude is analogous to my
argument that it is from the liminality of the national culture that the
figure of the people emerges in the narrative ambivalence of disjunctive
times and meanings. The concurrent circulation of linear, cursive, and
monumental time, in the same cultural space, constitutes a new historical
temporality that Kristeva identifies with psychoanalytically informed,
feminist strategies of political identification. What is remarkable is her
insistence that the gendered sign can hold such exorbitant historical times
together.

The political effects of Kristeva's multiple, and splitting, women's time
leads to what she calls the 'demassification of difference'. The cultural
moment of Fanon's 'occult instability' signifies the people in a fluctuating
movement *which they are just giving shape to*, so that postcolonial time
questions the teleological traditions of past and present, and the polarized
historicist *sensibility* of the archaic and the modern. These are not simply
attempts to invert the balance of power within an unchanged order of
discourse. Fanon and Kristeva seek to redefine the symbolic process
through which the social imaginary — nation, culture, or community —
become subjects of discourse, and objects of psychic identification. In
attempting to shift, through these differential temporalities, the alignment
of subject and object in the culture of community, they force us to
rethink the relation between the time of meaning and the sign of history
within those languages, political or literary, which designate the people 'as
one'. They challenge us to think the question of community and communication *without* the moment of transcendence; their excessive cultural
temporalities are in contention but their difference cannot be negated or
sublated. How do we understand such forms of social contradiction?

Cultural identification is then poised on the brink of what Kristeva
calls the 'loss of identity' or Fanon describes as a profound cultural
'undecidability'. The people as a form of address emerge from the abyss
of enunciation where the subject splits, the signifier 'fades', the
pedagogical and the performative are agonistically articulated. The
language of national collectivity and cohesiveness is now at stake.
Neither can cultural homogeneity, or the nation's horizontal space be
authoritatively represented within the familiar territory of the *public
sphere*: social causality cannot be adequately understood as a deterministic
or overdetermined effect of a 'statist' centre; nor can the rationality of
political choice be divided between the polar realms of the private and
the public. The narrative of national cohesion can no longer be signified,

in Anderson's words, as a 'sociological solidity'[39] fixed in a 'succession of *plurals*' — hospitals, prisons, remote villages — where the social space is clearly bounded by such repeated objects that represent a naturalistic, national horizon.

Such a pluralism of the national sign, where difference returns as the same, is contested by the signifier's 'loss of identity' that inscribes the narrative of the people in the ambivalent, 'double' writing of the performative and the pedagogical. The iterative temporality that marks the movement of meaning *between* the masterful image of the people and the movement of its sign interrupts the succession of plurals that produce the sociological solidity of the national narrative. The nation's totality is confronted with, and crossed by, a supplementary movement of writing. The heterogeneous structure of Derridean supplementarity in *writing* closely follows the agonistic, ambivalent movement between the pedagogical and performative that informs the nation's narrative address. A supplement, according to one meaning, 'cumulates and accumulates presence. It is thus that art, *techne*, image, representation, convention, etc. come as supplements to nature and are rich with this entire cumulating function' (pedagogical).[40] The *double entendre* of the supplement suggests, however, that 'It intervenes or insinuates itself *in-the-place-of* .... If it represents and makes an image it is by the *anterior* default of a presence ... the supplement is an adjunct, a subaltern instance.... As substitute, it is not simply added to the positivity of a presence, it produces no relief.... Somewhere, something can be filled up *of itself* ... only by allowing itself to be filled through sign and proxy' (performative).[41] It is in this supplementary space of doubling — *not plurality* — where the image is presence and proxy, where the sign supplements and empties nature, that the exorbitant, disjunctive times of Fanon and Kristeva can be turned into the discourses of emergent cultural identities, within a non-pluralistic politics of difference.

This supplementary space of cultural signification that opens up — and holds together — the performative and the pedagogical, provides a narrative structure characteristic of modern political rationality: the marginal integration of individuals in a repetitious movement between the antinomies of law and order. It is from the liminal movement of the culture of the nation — at once opened up and held together — that minority discourse emerges. Its strategy of intervention is similar to what parliamentary procedure recognizes as a supplementary question. It is a question that is supplementary to what is put down on the order paper, but by being 'after' the original, or in 'addition to' it, gives it the advantage of introducing a sense of 'secondariness' or belatedness into the structure of the original. The supplementary strategy suggests that adding 'to' need not 'add up' but may disturb the calculation. As Gasché has succinctly suggested, 'supplements ... are pluses that compensate for a minus in the origin'.[42] The supplementary strategy interrupts the successive seriality of the narrative of plurals and pluralism by radically changing their mode of articulation. In the metaphor of the national community as the 'many as one', the *one* is now both the tendency to totalize the social in a homogenous empty time, and the repetition of that minus in the origin, the less-than-one that intervenes with a metonymic, iterative temporality. One cultural effect of such a metonymic interruption in the representation of the people, is apparent in Julia Kristeva's political writings. If we elide her concepts of women's time and female exile, then she seems to argue that the 'singularity' of woman — her representation as fragmentation and drive — produces a dissidence, and a distanciation, within the symbolic bond itself which demystifies 'the *community* of language as a universal and unifying tool, one which totalises and equalises'.[43] The minority does not simply confront the pedagogical, or powerful master-discourse with a contradictory or negating referent. It does not turn contradiction into a dialectical process. It interrogates its object by initially withholding its objective. Insinuating itself into the terms of reference of the dominant discourse, the supplementary antagonizes the implicit power to generalize, to produce the sociological solidity. The questioning of the supplement is not a repetitive rhetoric of the 'end' of society but a meditation on the disposition of space and time from which the narrative of the nation must *begin*. The power of supplementarity is not the negation of the preconstituted social contradictions of the past or present; its force lies — as we shall see in the discussion of *Handsworth Songs* that follows — in the renegotiation of those times, terms, and traditions through which we turn our uncertain, passing contemporaneity into the signs of history.

Handsworth Songs,[44] is a film made by the Black Audio Collective during the uprisings of 1985, in the Handsworth district of Birmingham, England. Shot in the midst of the uprising, it is haunted by two moments: the arrival of the migrant population in the 1950s, and the emergence of a black British peoples in the diaspora. And the film itself is part of the emergence of a black British cultural politics. Between the moments of arrival and emergence is the incommensurable movement of the present; the filmic time of a continual displacement of narrative; the time of oppression and resistance; the time of the performance of the riots, cut across by the pedagogical knowledges of state institutions, the racism of statistics and documents and newspapers, and then the perplexed living of Handsworth songs, and memories that flash up in a moment of danger.

Two memories repeat incessantly to translate the living perplexity of history, into the time of migration: the arrival of the ship laden with immigrants from the ex-colonies, just stepping off the boat, always just emerging — as in the phantasmatic scenario of Freud's family romance — into the land where the streets are paved with gold. Another image is of the perplexity and power of an emergent peoples, caught in the shot of a dreadlocked rastaman cutting a swathe through a posse of policemen. It is a memory that flashes incessantly through the film: a dangerous repetition in the present of the cinematic frame; the edge of human life that translates what will come next and what has gone before in the writing of History. Listen to the repetition of the time and space of the peoples that I have been trying to create:

In time we will demand the impossible in order to wrestle, from it that which is possible, In time the streets will claim me without apology, In time I will be right to say that there are no stories . . . in the riots only the ghosts of other stories.

The symbolic demand of cultural difference constitutes a history in the midst of the uprising. From the desire of the possible in the impossible, in the historic present of the riots, emerge the ghostly repetition of other stories, other uprisings: Broadwater Farm, Southall, St. Paul's, Bristol. In the ghostly repetition of the black woman of Lozells Rd, Handsworth, who sees the future in the past: There are no stories in the riots, only the ghosts of other stories, she told a local journalist: 'You can see Enoch Powell in 1969, Michael X in 1965'. And from that gathering repetition she builds a history.

From across the film listen to another woman who speaks another historical language. From the archaic world of metaphor, caught in the movement of the people she translates the time of change into the ebb and flow of language's unmastering rhythm: the successive time of instaneity, battening against the straight horizons and the flow of water and words:

I walk with my back to the sea, horizons straight ahead
Wave the sea away and back it comes,
Step and I slip on it.
Crawling in my journey's footsteps
When I stand it fills my bones.

The perplexity of the living must not be understood as some existential, ethical anguish of the empiricism of everyday life in 'the eternal living present', that gives liberal discourse a rich social reference in moral and cultural relativism. Nor must it be too hastily associated with the spontaneous and primordial *presence* of the people in the liberatory discourses of populist ressentiment. In the construction of this discourse of 'living perplexity' that I am attempting to produce we must remember that the space of human life is pushed to its incommensurable extreme; the judgement of living is perplexed; the topos of the narrative is neither the transcendental, pedagogical Idea of history nor the institution of the state, but a strange temporality of the repetition of the one in the other — an oscillating movement in the governing *present* of cultural authority.

Minority discourse sets the act of emergence in the antagonistic *in-between* of image and sign, the accumulative and the adjunct, presence and proxy. It contests genealogies of 'origin' that lead to claims for cultural supremacy and historical priority. Minority discourse acknowledges the status of national culture — and the people — as a contentious, performative space of the perplexity of the living in the midst of the pedagogical representations of the fullness of life. Now there is no reason to believe that such marks of difference — the incommensurable time of the subject of culture — cannot inscribe a 'history' of the people or become the gathering points of political solidarity. They will not,

however, celebrate the monumentality of historicist memory, the sociological solidity or totality of society, or the homogeneity of cultural
experience. The discourse of the minority reveals the insurmountable
ambivalence that structures the *equivocal* movement of historical time.
How does one encounter the past as an anteriority that continually
introduces an otherness or alterity within the present? How does one
then narrate the present as a form of contemporaneity that is always
belated? In what historical time do such configurations of cultural
difference assume forms of cultural and political authority?

Social anonymity and cultural anomie

The narrative of the modern nation can only begin, Benedict Anderson
suggests in *Imagined Communities*, once the notion of the 'arbitrariness of
the sign' fissures the sacral ontology of the medieval world and its overwhelming visual and aural imaginary. By 'separating language from
reality' (Anderson's formulation), the arbitrary signifier enables a national
temporality of the 'meanwhile', a form of 'homogenous empty time'; the
time of cultural modernity that supersedes the prophetic notion of
simultaneity-along-time. The narrative of the 'meanwhile' permits
'transverse, cross-time, marked not by prefiguring and fulfilment, but by
temporal coincidence, and measured by clock and calendar'.[45] Such a
form of temporality produces a symbolic structure of the nation as
'imagined community' which, in keeping with the scale and diversity of
the modern nation, works like the plot of a realist novel. The steady
onward clocking of calendrical time, in Anderson's words, gives the
imagined world of the nation a sociological solidity; it links together
diverse acts and actors on the national stage who are entirely unaware of
each other, except as a function of this synchronicity of time which is not
prefigurative but a form of civil contemporaneity realized in the *fullness*
of time.

Anderson historicizes the emergence of the arbitrary sign of language
— and here he is talking of the process of signification rather than the
progress of narrative — as that which had to come before the narrative
of the modern nation could begin. In decentring the prophetic visibility
and simultaneity of medieval systems of dynastic representation, the
homogeneous and horizontal community of modern society can emerge.
The people-nation, however divided and split, can still assume, in the
function of the social imaginary, a form of democratic 'anonymity'.
However there is a profound ascesis in the sign of the anonymity of the
modern community and the time — *meanwhile* — of its narrative
consciousness, as Anderson explains it. It must be stressed that the
narrative of the imagined community is constructed from two incommensurable temporalities of meaning that threaten its coherence. The
space of the arbitrary sign, its separation of language and reality, enables
Anderson to stress the imaginary or mythical nature of the society of the
nation. However, the differential time of the arbitrary sign is neither
synchronous nor serial. In the separation of language and reality — in the

process of signification — there is no epistemological equivalence of subject and object, no possibility of the mimesis of meaning. The sign temporalizes the iterative difference that circulates within language, of which meaning is made, but cannot be represented thematically within narrative as a homogeneous empty time. Such a temporality is antithetical to the alterity of the sign which, in keeping with my account of the supplementary nature of cultural signification, singularizes and alienates the holism of the imagined community. From that place of the 'meanwhile', where cultural homogeneity and democratic anonymity make their claims on the national community, there emerges a more instantaneous and subaltern voice of the people, a minority discourse that speaks betwixt and between times and places.

Having initially located the imagined community of the nation in the homogeneous time of realist narrative, towards the end of his essay Anderson abandons the 'meanwhile' — his pedagogical temporality of the people. In order to represent the collective voice of the people as a performative discourse of public identification, a process he calls unisonance, Anderson resorts to another time of narrative. Unisonance is 'that special kind of contemporaneous community which language alone suggests',[46] and this patriotic speech-act is not written in the synchronic, novelistic 'meanwhile', but inscribed in a sudden primordiality of meaning that 'looms up *imperceptibly* out of a horizonless past' (my emphasis).[47] This movement of the sign cannot simply be historicized in the emergence of the realist narrative of the novel. It is at this point in the narrative of national time that the unisonant discourse produces its collective identification of the people, not as some transcendent national identity, but in a language of incommensurable doubleness that arises from the ambivalent splitting of the pedagogical and the performative. The people emerge in an uncanny simulacral moment of their 'present' history as 'a ghostly intimation of simultanaeity across homogeneous empty time'. The weight of the words of the national discourse comes from an '*as it were* — Ancestral Englishness'.[48] It is precisely this repetitive *time* of the alienating anterior — rather than origin — that Lévi-Strauss writes of, when, in explaining the 'unconscious unity' of signification, he suggests that 'language can only have arisen all at once. Things cannot have begun to *signify* gradually'.[49] In that sudden timelessness of 'all at once', there is not synchrony but a break, not simultaneity but a spatial disjunction.

The 'meanwhile' is the barred sign of the processual and performative, not a simple present continuous, but the present as succession without synchrony — the iteration of the arbitrary sign of the modern nation-space. In embedding the *meanwhile* of the national narrative, where the people live their plural and autonomous lives within homogeneous empty time, Anderson misses the alienating and iterative time of the sign. He naturalizes the momentary 'suddenness' of the arbitrary sign, its pulsation, by making it part of the historical emergence of the novel, a narrative of synchrony. But the suddenness of the signifier is incessant, instantaneous rather than simultaneous. It introduces a signifying space of repetition rather than a progressive or linear seriality. The 'meanwhile' turns into quite another time, or ambivalent sign, of the national people. If it is the time of the people's anonymity it is also the space of the nation's anomie.

How are we to understand this anteriority of signification as a position of social and cultural knowledge, this time of the 'before' of signification, which will not issue harmoniously into the present like the continuity of tradition — invented or otherwise? It has its own national history in Renan's 'Qu'est ce qu'une nation?' which has been the starting point for a number of the most influential accounts of the modern emergence of the nation — Kamenka, Gellner, Benedict Anderson, Tzvetan Todorov. It is the way in which the pedagogical presence of modernity — the Will to be a nation — introduces into the enunciative present of the nation a differential and iterative time of reinscription that interests me. Renan argues that the non-naturalist principle of the modern nation is represented in the *will* to nationhood — not in the identities of race, language, or territory. It is the will that unifies historical memory and secures present-day consent. The will is, indeed, the articulation of the nation-people:

> A nation's existence is, if you will pardon the metaphor, a daily plebiscite, just as an individual's existence is a perpetual affirmation of life. ... The wish of nations, is all in all, the sole legitimate criteria, the one to which one must always return.[50]

Does the will to nationhood circulate in the same temporality as the desire of the daily plebiscite? Could it be that the iterative plebiscite decentres the totalizing pedagogy of the will? Renan's will is itself the site of a strange forgetting of the history of the nation's past: the violence involved in establishing the nation's writ. It is this forgetting — a minus in the origin — that constitutes the *beginning* of the nation's narrative. It is the syntactical and rhetorical arrangement of this argument that is more illuminating than any frankly historical or ideological reading. Listen to the complexity of this form of forgetting which is the moment in which the national will is articulated: 'yet every French citizen has to have forgotten [*is obliged to have forgotten*] Saint Bartholomew's Night's Massacre, or the massacres that took place in the Midi in the thirteenth century.'[51]

It is through this syntax of forgetting — or being obliged to forget — that the problematic identification of a national people becomes visible. The national subject is produced in that place where the daily plebiscite — the unitary number — circulates in the grand narrative of the will. However, the equivalence of will and plebiscite, the identity of part and whole, past and present, is cut across by the 'obligation to forget', or forgetting to remember. This is again the moment of anteriority of the nation's sign that entirely changes our understanding of the pastness of the past, and the unified present of the will to nationhood. We are in a discursive space similar to that moment of unisonance in Anderson's argument when the homogenous empty time of the nation's 'meanwhile' is cut across by the ghostly simultaneity of a temporality of doubling and repetition. To be obliged to forget — in the construction of the national present — is not a question of historical memory; it is the construction of a discourse on society that *performs* the problematic totalization of the national will. That strange time — forgetting to remember — is a place of 'partial identification' inscribed in the daily plebiscite which represents the performative discourse of the people. Renan's pedagogical return to the will to nationhood is both constituted and confronted by the circulation of numbers in the plebiscite which break down the identity of the will — it is an instance of the supplementary that 'adds to' without 'adding up'. May I remind you of Lefort's suggestive description of the ideological impact of suffrage in the nineteenth century, where the danger of numbers was considered almost more threatening than the mob: 'the idea of number as such is opposed to the idea of the substance of society. Number breaks down unity, destroys identity.'[52] It is the repetition of the national sign as numerical succession rather than synchrony that reveals that strange temporality of disavowal implicit in the national memory. Being obliged to forget becomes the basis for remembering the nation, peopling it anew, imagining the possibility of other contending and liberating forms of cultural identification.

Anderson fails to locate the alienating time of the arbitrary sign in his naturalized, nationalized space of the imagined community. Although he borrows his notion of the homogeneous empty time of the nation's modern narrative from Walter Benjamin, he fails to read that profound ambivalence that Benjamin places deep within the utterance of the narrative of modernity. Here, as the pedagogies of life and will contest the perplexed histories of the living people, their cultures of survival and resistance, Benjamin introduces a non-synchronous, incommensurable gap in the midst of storytelling. From this split in the utterance, from the unbeguiled, belated novelist there emerges an ambivalence in the narration of modern society that repeats, uncounselled and unconsolable, in the midst of plenitude:

> The novelist has isolated himself. The birthplace of the novel is the solitary individual, who is no longer able to express himself by giving examples of his most important concerns, is himself uncounselled and cannot counsel others. To write a novel means to carry the incommensurable to extremes in the representation of human life. In the midst of life's fullness, and through the representation of this fullness, the novel gives evidence of the profound perplexity of the living.[53]

It is from this incommensurability in the midst of the everyday that the nation speaks its disjunctive narrative. It begins, if that's the word, from that anterior space within the arbitrary sign which disturbs the homogenizing myth of cultural anonymity. From the margins of modernity, at the insurmountable extremes of storytelling, we encounter the question of cultural difference as the perplexity of living, and writing, the nation.

Cultural difference

Despite my use of the term 'cultural difference', I am not attempting to unify a body of theory, nor to suggest the mastery of a sovereign form of 'difference'. I am attempting some speculative fieldnotes on that intermittent time, and intersticial space, that emerges as a structure of undecidability at the frontiers of cultural hybridity. My interest lies only in that movement of meaning that occurs in the writing of cultures articulated in difference. I am attempting to discover the uncanny moment of cultural difference that emerges in the process of enunciation:

> Perhaps it is like the over-familiar that constantly eludes one; those familiar transparencies, which, although they conceal nothing in their density, are nevertheless not entirely clear. The enunciative level emerges in its very proximity.[54]

Cultural difference must not be understood as the free play of polarities and pluralities in the homogeneous empty time of the national community. It addresses the jarring of meanings and values generated in-between the variety and diversity associated with cultural plenitude; it represents the process of cultural interpretation formed in the perplexity of living, in the disjunctive, liminal space of national society that I have tried to trace. Cultural difference, as a form of intervention, participates in a supplementary logic of secondariness similar to the strategies of minority discourse. The question of cultural difference faces us with a disposition of knowledges or a distribution of practices that exist beside each other, *Abseits*, in a form of juxtaposition or contradiction that resists the teleology of dialectical sublation. In erasing the harmonious totalities of Culture, cultural difference articulates the difference between representations of social life without surmounting the space of incommensurable meanings and judgements that are produced within the process of transcultural negotiation.

The effect of such secondariness is not merely to change the 'object' of analysis — to focus, for instance, on race rather than gender or native knowledges rather than metropolitan myths; nor to invert the axis of political discrimination by installing the excluded term at the centre. The analytic of cultural difference intervenes to transform the scenario of articulation — not simply to disturb the rationale of discrimination. It changes the position of enunciation and the relations of address within it; not only what is said but from where it is said; not simply the logic of articulation but the *topos* of enunciation. The aim of cultural difference is to re-articulate the sum of knowledge from the perspective of the signifying *singularity* of the 'other' that resists totalization — the repetition that will not return as the same, the minus-in-origin that results in political and discursive strategies where adding-*to* does not add-up but serves to disturb the calculation of power and knowledge, producing other spaces of subaltern signification. The identity of cultural difference cannot, therefore, exist autonomously in relation to an object or a practice 'in-itself', for the identification of the subject of cultural discourse is dialogical or transferential in the style of psychoanalysis. It is constituted through the *locus* of the Other which suggests both that the object of identification is ambivalent, and, more significantly, that the agency of identification is never pure or holistic but always constituted in a process of substitution, displacement or projection.

Cultural difference does not simply represent the contention between oppositional contents or antagonistic traditions of cultural value. Cultural difference introduces into the process of cultural judgement and inter- pretation that sudden shock of the successive, nonsynchronic time of signification, or the interruption of the supplementary question that I elaborated above. The very possibility of cultural contestation, the ability to shift the ground of knowledges, or to engage in the 'war of position', depends not only on the refutation or substitution of concepts. The analytic of cultural difference attempts to engage with the 'anterior' space of the sign that structures the symbolic language of alternative, antagonistic cultural practices. To the extent to which all forms of cultural discourse are subject to the rule of signification, there can be no question of a simple negation or sublation of the contradictory or opposi- tional instance. Cultural difference marks the establishment of new forms of meaning, and strategies of identification, through processes of negotia- tion where no discursive authority can be established without revealing the difference of itself. The signs of cultural difference cannot then be unitary or individual forms of identity because their continual implication in other symbolic systems always leaves them 'incomplete' or open to cultural translation. What I am suggesting as the *uncanny* structure of cultural difference is close to Lévi-Strauss' understanding of 'the unconscious as providing the common and specific character of social facts ... not because it harbours our most secret selves but because ... it enables us to coincide with forms of activity which are both *at once ours and other*'.[55]

Cultural difference is to be found where the 'loss' of meaning enters, as a cutting edge, into the representation of the fullness of the demands of culture. It is not adequate simply to become aware of the semiotic systems that produce the signs of culture and their dissemination. Much more significantly we are faced with the challenge of reading, into the present of a specific cultural performance, the traces of all those diverse disciplinary discourses and institutions of knowledge that constitute the condition and contexts of culture. I use the word 'traces' to suggest a particular kind of discursive transformation that the analytic of cultural difference demands. To enter into the interdisciplinarity of cultural texts — through the anteriority of the arbitrary sign — means that we cannot contextualize the emergent cultural form by explaining it in terms of some pre-given discursive causality or origin. We must always keep open a supplementary space for the articulation of cultural knowledges that are adjacent and adjunct but not necessarily accumulative, teleological, or dialectical. The 'difference' of cultural knowledge that 'adds to' but does not 'add up' is the enemy of the *implicit* generalization of knowledge or the implicit homogenization of experience, to borrow Lefort's phrase.

Interdisciplinarity, as the discursive practice of cultural difference, elaborates a logic of intervention and interpretation that is similar to the supplementary question that I posed above. In keeping with its subaltern, substitutive — rather than synchronic — temporality, the subject of cultural difference is neither pluralistic nor relativistic. The frontiers of cultural difference are always belated or secondary in the sense that their hybridity is never simply a question of the admixture of pre-given identities or essences. Hybridity is the perplexity of the living as it interrupts the representation of the fullness of life; it is an instance of iteration, in the minority discourse, of the time of the arbitrary sign — 'the minus in the origin' — through which all forms of cultural meaning are open to translation because their enunciation resists totalization. Interdisciplinarity is the acknowledgement of the emergent moment of culture produced in the ambivalent movement between the pedagogical and performative address, so that it is never simply the harmonious addition of contents or contexts that augment the positivity of a pre-given disciplinary or symbolic *presence*. In the restless drive for cultural translation, hybrid sites of meaning open up a cleavage in the language of culture which suggests that the similitude of the *symbol* as it plays across cultural sites must not obscure the fact that repetition of the *sign* is, in each specific social practice, both different and differential. It is in this sense that the enunciation of cultural difference emerges *in its proximity*; to traduce Foucault, we must not seek it in the 'visibility' of difference for it will elude us in that enigmatic transparency of writing that conceals nothing in its density but is nevertheless not clear.

Cultural difference emerges from the borderline moment of translation that Benjamin describes as the 'foreignness of languages.'[56] Translation represents only an extreme instance of the figurative fate of writing that repeatedly generates a movement of equivalence between representation and reference, but never gets beyond the equivocation of the sign. The 'foreignness' of language is the nucleus of the untranslatable that goes beyond the transparency of subject matter. The transfer of meaning can never be total between differential systems of meaning, or within them, for 'the language of translation envelops its content like a royal robe with ample folds. . . . [it] signifies a more exalted language than its own and thus remains unsuited to its content, overpowering and alien'.[57] It is too often the slippage of signification that is celebrated, at the expense of this disturbing alienation, or overpowering of content. The erasure of content in the invisible but insistent structure of linguistic difference does not lead us to some general, formal acknowledgement of the function of the sign. The ill fitting robe of language alienates content in the sense that it deprives it of an immediate access to a stable or holistic reference 'outside' itself — in society. It suggests that social conditions are themselves being reinscribed or reconstituted in the very act of enunciation, revealing the instability of any division of meaning into an inside and outside. Content becomes the alien *mise en scène* that reveals the signifying structure of linguistic difference which is never seen for itself, but only glimpsed in the gap or the gaping of the garment. Benjamin's argument can be elaborated for a theory of cultural difference. It is only by engaging with what he calls the 'purer linguistic air' — the anteriority of the sign — that the reality-effect of content can be overpowered which then makes all cultural languages 'foreign' to themselves. And it is from this foreign perspective that it becomes possible to inscribe the specific locality of cultural systems — their incommensurable differences — and through that apprehension of difference, to perform the act of cultural translation. In the act of translation the 'given' content becomes alien and estranged; and that, in its turn, leaves the language of translation *Aufgabe*, always confronted by its double, the untranslatable — alien and foreign.

The foreignness of languages

At this point I must give way to the *vox populi*: to a relatively unspoken tradition of the people of the pagus — colonials, postcolonials, migrants, minorities — wandering peoples who will not be contained within the *Heim* of the national culture and its unisonant discourse, but are themselves the marks of a shifting boundary that alienates the frontiers of the modern nation. They are Marx's reserve army of migrant labour who by speaking the foreignness of language split the patriotic voice of unisonance and become Nietzsche's mobile army of metaphors, metonyms, and anthropomorphisms. They articulate the death-in-life of the idea of the 'imagined community' of the nation; the worn-out metaphors of the resplendent national life now circulate in another narrative of entry permits and passports and work permits that at once preserve and proliferate, bind and breach the human rights of the nation. Across the accumulation of the history of the west there are those people who speak the encrypted discourse of the melancholic and the migrant. Theirs is a voice that opens up a void in some ways similar to what Abraham and Torok describe as a radical *antimetaphoric*: 'the destruction in fantasy, of the very act that makes metaphor possible — the act of putting the original oral void into words, the act of introjection'.[58] The lost object — the national *Heim* — is repeated in the void that at once prefigures and pre-empts the 'unisonant', which makes it *unheimlich*; analogous to the incorporation that becomes the daemonic double of introjection and identification. The object of loss is written across the bodies of the people, as it repeats in the silence that speaks the foreignness of language. A Turkish worker in Germany: in the words of John Berger:

> His migration is like an event in a dream dreamt by another. The migrant's intentionality is permeated by historical necessities of which neither he nor anybody he meets is aware. That is why it is as if his life were dreamt by another. . . . Abandon the metaphor. . . . They watch the gestures made and learn to imitate them . . . the repetition by which gesture is laid upon gesture, precisely but inexorably, the pile of gestures being stacked minute by minute, hour by hour is exhausting. The rate of work allows no time to prepare for the gesture. The body loses its mind in the gesture. How opaque the disguise of

words. . . . He treated the sounds of the unknown language as if they were silence. To break through his silence. He learnt twenty words of the new language. But to his amazement at first, their meaning changed as he spoke them. He asked for coffee. What the words signified to the barman was that he was asking for coffee in a bar where he should not be asking for coffee. He learnt girl. What the word meant when he used it, was that he was a randy dog. Is it possible to see through the opaqueness of the words?[59]

Through the opaqueness of words we confront the historical memory of the western nation which is 'obliged to forget'. Having begun this essay with the nation's need for metaphor, I want to turn now to the desolate silences of the wandering people; to that 'oral void' that emerges when the Turk abandons the metaphor of a *heimlich* national culture: for the Turkish immigrant the final return is mythic, we are told, 'It is the stuff of longing and prayers . . . as imagined it never happens. There is no final return'.[60]

In the repetition of gesture after gesture, the dream dreamt by another, the mythical return, it is not simply the figure of repetition that is *unheimlich*, but the Turk's desire to survive, to name, to fix — which is unnamed by the gesture itself. The gesture continually overlaps and accumulates, without adding up to a knowledge of work or labour. Without the language that bridges knowledge and act, without the objectification of the social process, the Turk leads the life of the double, the automaton. It is not the struggle of master and slave, but in the mechanical reproduction of gestures a mere imitation of life and labour. The opacity of language fails to translate or break through his silence and 'the body loses its mind in the gesture'. The gesture repeats and the body returns now, shrouded not in silence but eerily untranslated in the racist site of its enunciation: to say the word 'girl' is to be a randy dog, to ask for coffee is to encounter the colour bar.

The image of the body returns where there should only be its trace, as sign or letter. The Turk as dog is neither simply hallucination or phobia; it is a more complex form of social fantasy. Its ambivalence cannot be read as some simple racist/sexist projection where the white man's guilt is projected on the black man; his anxiety contained in the body of the white woman whose body screens (in both senses of the word) the racist fantasy. What such a reading leaves out is precisely the axis of identification — the desire of a man (white) for a man (black) — that underwrites that utterance and produces the paranoid 'delusion of reference', the man-dog that confronts the racist language with its own alterity, its foreignness.

The silent Other of gesture and failed speech becomes what Freud calls that 'haphazard member of the herd',[61] the Stranger, whose languageless presence evokes an archaic anxiety and aggressivity by impeding the search for narcissistic love-objects in which the subject can rediscover himself, and upon which the group's *amour propre* is based. If the immigrants' desire to 'imitate' language produces one void in the articulation of the social space — making present the opacity of language, its untranslatable residue — then the racist fantasy, which disavows the ambivalence of its desire, opens up another void in the present. The migrant's silence elicits those racist fantasies of purity and persecution that must always return from the Outside, to estrange the present of the life of the metropolis; to make it strangely familiar. In the process by which the paranoid position finally voids the place from where it speaks, we begin to see another history of the German language.

If the experience of the Turkish *Gastarbeiter* represents the radical incommensurability of translation, Salman Rushdie's *The Satanic Verses* attempts to redefine the boundaries of the western nation, so that the 'foreignness of languages' becomes the inescapable cultural condition for the enunciation of the mother-tongue. In the 'Rosa Diamond' section of *The Satanic Verses* Rushdie seems to suggest that it is only through the process of dissemi*Nation* — of meaning, time, peoples, cultural boundaries and historical traditions — that the radical alterity of the national culture will create new forms of living and writing: 'The trouble with the English is that their history happened overseas, so they don't know what it means'.[62]

S. S. Sisodia the soak — known also as Whisky Sisodia — stutters these words as part of his litany of 'what's wrong with the English'. The spirit of his words fleshes out the argument of this essay. I have suggested that the atavistic national past and its language of archaic belonging marginalizes the present of the 'modernity' of the national culture, rather like suggesting that history happens 'outside' the centre and core. More specifically I have argued that appeals to the national past must also be seen as the anterior space of signification that 'singularizes' the nation's cultural totality. It introduces a form of alterity of address that Rushdie embodies in the double narrative figures of Gibreel Farishta/Saladin Chamcha, or Gibreel Farishta/Sir Henry Diamond, which suggests that the national narrative is the site of an ambivalent identification; a margin of the uncertainty of cultural meaning that may become the space for an agonistic minority position. In the midst of life's fullness, and through the representation of this fullness, the novel gives evidence of the profound perplexity of the living. Gifted with phantom sight, Rosa Diamond, for whom repetition had become a comfort in her antiquity, represents the English *Heim* or homeland. The pageant of a 900 year-old history passes through her frail translucent body and inscribes itself, in a strange splitting of her language, 'the well-worn phrases, *unfinished business, grandstand view*, made her feel solid, unchanging, sempiternal, instead of the creature of cracks and absences she knew herself to be'.[63] Constructed from the well-worn pedagogies and pedigrees of national unity — her vision of the Battle of Hastings is the anchor of her being — and, at the same time, patched and fractured in the incommensurable perplexity of the nation's living, Rosa Diamond's green and pleasant garden is the spot where Gibreel Farishta lands when he falls out from the belly of the Boeing over sodden, southern England.

Gibreel masquerades in the clothes of Rosa's dead husband, Sir Henry

Diamond, ex-colonial landowner, and through this post-colonial mimicry, exacerbates the discursive split between the image of a continuist national history and the 'cracks and absences' that she knew herself to be. What emerges, at one level, is a popular tale of secret, adulterous Argentinian amours, passion in the pampas with Martín de la Cruz. What is more significant and in tension with the exoticism, is the emergence of a hybrid national narrative that turns the nostalgic past into the disruptive 'anterior' and displaces the historical present — opens it up to other histories and incommensurable narrative subjects. The cut or split in enunciation — underlining all acts of utterance — emerges with its iterative temporality to reinscribe the figure of Rosa Diamond in a new and terrifying avatar. Gibreel, the migrant hybrid in masquerade, as Sir Henry Diamond, mimics the collaborative colonial ideologies of patriotism and patriarchy, depriving those narratives of their imperial authority. Gibreel's returning gaze crosses out the synchronous history of England, the essentialist memories of William the Conqueror and the Battle of Hastings. In the middle of an account of her punctual domestic routine with Sir Henry — sherry always at six — Rosa Diamond is over-taken by another time and memory of narration and through the 'grand-stand view' of imperial history you can hear its cracks and absences speak with another voice:

> Then she began without bothering with once upon atime and whether it was all true or false he could see the fierce energy that was going into the telling . . . this memory jumbled rag-bag of material was in fact the very heart of her, her self-portrait. . . . So that it was not possible to distinguish memories from wishes, guilty reconstructions from confessional truths, because even on her deathbed Rosa Diamond did not know how to look her history in the eye.[64]

And what of Gibreel Farishta? Well he is the mote in the eye of history, its blind spot that will not let the nationalist gaze settle centrally. His mimicry of colonial masculinity and mimesis allows the absences of national history to speak in the ambivalent, ragbag narrative. But it is precisely this 'narrative sorcery' that established Gibreel's own re-entry into contemporary England. As the belated post-colonial he marginalizes and singularizes the totality of national culture. He is the history that happened elsewhere, overseas; his postcolonial, migrant presence does not evoke a harmonious patchwork of cultures, but articulates the narrative of cultural difference which can never let the national history look at itself narcissistically in the eye. For the liminality of the western nation is the shadow of its own finitude: the colonial space played out in the imaginative geography of the metropolitan space; the repetition or return of the margin of the postcolonial migrant to alienate the holism of history. The postcolonial space is now 'supplementary' to the metro-politan centre; it stands in a subaltern, adjunct relation that doesn't aggrandise the *presence* of the west but redraws its frontiers in the menac-ing, agonistic boundary of cultural difference that never quite adds up, always less than one nation and double.

From this splitting of time and narrative emerges a strange, empowering knowledge for the migrant that is at once schizoid and subversive. In his guise as the Archangel Gibreel he sees the bleak history of the metropolis: 'the angry present of masks and parodies, stifled and twisted by the insupportable, unrejected burden of its past, staring into the bleakness of its impoverished future'.[65] From Rosa Diamond's decentred narrative 'without bothering with once upon atime' Gibreel becomes — however insanely — the principle of avenging repetition: 'These powerless English! — Did they not think that their history would return to haunt them? — "The native is an oppressed person whose permanent dream is to become the persecutor" (Fanon). . . . He would make this land anew. He was the Archangel, Gibreel — And I'm back'.[66]

If the lesson of Rosa's narrative is that the national memory is always the site of the hybridity of histories and the displacement of narratives, then through Gibreel, the avenging migrant, we learn the ambivalence of cultural difference: it is the articulation *through* incommensurability that structures all narratives of identification, and all acts of cultural translation.

> He was joined to the adversary, their arms locked around one another's bodies, mouth to mouth, head to tail. . . . No more of these England induced ambiguities: those Biblical-satanic confusions . . . Quran 18:50 there it was as plain as the day. . . . How much more practical, down to earth comprehensible. . . . Iblis/Shaitan standing for darkness; Gibreel for the light. . . . O most devilish and slippery of cities. . . . Well then the trouble with the English was their, Their — In a word Gibreel solemnly pronounces, that most naturalised sign of cultural difference. . . . The trouble with the English was their . . . in a word . . . their weather.[67]

The English weather

To end with the English weather is to invoke, at once, the most changeable and immanent signs of national difference. It encourages memories of the 'deep' nation crafted in chalk and limestone; the quilted downs; the moors menaced by the wind; the quiet cathedral towns; that corner of a foreign field that is forever England. The English weather also revives memories of its daemonic double: the heat and dust of India; the dark emptiness of Africa; the tropical chaos that was deemed despotic and ungovernable and therefore worthy of the civilizing mission. These imaginative geographies that spanned countries and empires are changing; those imagined communities that played on the unisonant boundaries of the nation are singing with different voices. If I began with the scattering of the people across countries, I want to end with their gathering in the city. The return of the diasporic; the postcolonial.

Handsworth Songs; Fanon's manichean colonial Algiers; Rushdie's tropicalized London, grotesquely renamed *Ellowen Deeowen* in the migrant's mimicry: it is to the city that the migrants, the minorities, the diasporic come to change the history of the nation. If I have suggested that the people emerge in the finitude of the nation, marking the liminality of cultural identity, producing the double-edged discourse of social territories and temporalities, then in the west, and increasingly elsewhere, it is the city which provides the space in which emergent identifications and new social movements of the people are played out. It is there that, in our time, the perplexity of the living is most acutely experienced.

In the narrative graftings of my essay I have attempted no general theory, only a certain productive tension of the perplexity of language in various locations of living. I have taken the measure of Fanon's occult instability and Kristeva's parallel times into the 'incommensurable narrative' of Benjamin's modern storyteller to suggest no salvation, but a strange cultural survival of the people. For it is by living on the borderline of history and language, on the limits of race and gender, that we are in a position to translate the differences between them into a kind of solidarity. I want to end with a much translated fragment from Walter Benjamin's essay, *The Task of the Translator*. I hope it will now be read from the nation's edge, through the sense of the city, from the periphery of the people, in culture's transnational dissemination:

> Fragments of a vessel in order to be articulated together must follow one another in the smallest details although they need not be *like* one another. In the same way a translation, instead of making itself similar to the meaning of the original, it must lovingly and in detail, form itself according to the manner of meaning of the original, to make them *both* recognisable as the broken fragments of the greater language, just as fragments are the broken parts of a vessel.[68]

Notes

1 In memory of Paul Moritz Strimpel (1914–87): Pforzheim – Paris – Zurich – Ahmedabad – Bombay – Milan – Lugano.
2 I am thinking of Eric Hosbawm's great history of the 'long nineteenth century', especially *The Age of Capital 1848–1875* (London: Weidenfeld & Nicolson, 1975) and *The Age of Empire 1875–1914* (London: Weidenfeld & Nicolson, 1987). See especially some of the suggestive ideas on the nation and migration in the latter volume, ch. 6.
3 E. Said, *The World, The Text and The Critic* (Cambridge, Mass.: Harvard University Press, 1983), p. 39.
4 F. Jameson, 'Third World literature in the era of multinational capitalism', *Social Text*, (Fall 1986).
5 J. Kristeva, 'A new type of intellectual: the dissident', in Toril Moi (ed.), *The Kristeva Reader* (Oxford: Blackwell, 1986), p. 298.
6 E. Said, 'Opponents, audiences, constituencies and community', in Hal Foster (ed.), *Postmodern Culture* (London: Pluto, 1983), p. 145.
7 J. Derrida, *Dissemination*, trans. Barbara Johnson (Chicago: Chicago University Press, 1981), p. 210.
8 B. Anderson, 'Narrating the nation', *The Times Literary Supplement*.
9 P. Chatterjee, *Nationalist Thought and the Colonial World: A Derivative Discourse* (London: Zed, 1986).

10 E. Gellner, *Nations and Nationalism* (Oxford: Basil Blackwell, 1983), p. 56.
11 ibid., p. 38.
12 L. Althusser, *Montesquieu, Rousseau, Marx* (London: Verso, 1972), p. 78.
13 M. Bakhtin, *Speech Genres and Other Late Essays*, ed. C. Emerson and M. Holquist, trans. V. W. McGee (Austin, Texas: University of Texas Press, 1986) p. 31.
14 ibid., p. 34.
15 ibid., p. 36 and *passim*.
16 ibid., pp. 47–9.
17 S. Freud, 'The Uncanny', in *The Standard Edition of the Complete Psychological Works of Sigmund Freud*, ed. J. Strachey (London: Hogarth, 1955), p. 234. See also pp. 236, 247.
18 John Barrell, *English Literature in History, 1730–80* (London: Hutchinson 1983).
19 Houston A. Baker Jr, *Modernism and the Harlem Renaissance* (Chicago: Chicago University Press, 1987), esp. chs. 8–9.
20 Barrell, op. cit., p. 78.
21 ibid., p. 203.
22 Richard Price, *Maroon Societies* quoted in Baker op. cit., p. 77.
23 Claude Lefort, *The Political Forms of Modern Society* (Cambridge: Polity, 1986), pp. 212–14, my emphasis.
24 A. Giddens, *The Nation State and Violence* (Cambridge: Polity, 1985), p. 216.
25 N. Poulantzas, *State, Power, Socialism* (London: Verso, 1980), p. 113.
26 R. Williams, *Problems in Materialism and Culture* (London: Verso, 1980), p. 43. I must thank Prof. David Lloyd of the University of California, Berkeley, for reminding me of Williams' important concept.
27 E. Said, 'Representing the colonized', *Critical Inquiry*, vol. 15, no. 2 (Winter 1989).
28 S. Freud, *Civilisation and Its Discontents*, Standard Edition (London: Hogarth, 1961), p. 114.
29 Freud, op. cit., p. 114.
30 J.-F. Lyotard and J.-L. Thebaud, *Just Gaming*, trans. Wlad Godzich (Manchester: Manchester University Press, 1985), p. 41.
31 C. Lévi-Strauss, *Introduction to the Work of Marcel Mauss*, trans. Felicity Baker (London: Routledge, 1987). Mark Cousins pointed me in the direction of this remarkable text. See his review in *New Formations*, no. 7 (Spring 1989). What follows is an account of Lévi-Strauss' argument to be found in Section 11 of the essay, pp. 21–44.
32 M. Foucault, *Technologies of the Self*, ed. H. Gutman *et al.* (London: Tavistock, 1988).
33 ibid., pp. 151–4. I have abbreviated the argument for my convenience.
34 L. Althusser, *Reading Capital* (London: New Left Books, 1972), pp. 122–32. I have, for convenience, produced a composite quotation from Althusser's various descriptions of the ideological effects of historicism.
35 Foucault, op.cit., pp. 162–3.
36 F. Fanon, *The Wretched of the Earth* (Harmondsworth: Penguin, 1969). My quotations and references come from pp. 174–90.
37 J.-F. Lyotard, *The Postmodern Condition*, trans. Geoff Bennington and Brian Massumi (Manchester: Manchester University Press, 1984), p. 22.
38 Moi, op.cit., pp. 187–213. This passage was written in response to the insistent questioning of Nandini and Praminda in Prof. Tshome Gabriel's seminar on 'syncretic cultures' at the University of California, Los Angeles.

39 Anderson, op.cit., p. 35.
40 J. Derrida, *Of Grammatology*, trans. G. C. Spivak (Baltimore, Md: Johns Hopkins University Press, 1976), pp. 144-5. Quoted in R. Gasché, *The Tain of the Mirror* (Cambridge, Mass.: Harvard University Press, 1986), p. 208.
41 ibid., p. 145.
42 Gasché, op.cit., p. 211.
43 Moi, op.cit., p. 210. I have also referred here to an argument to be found on p. 296.
44 All quotations are from the shooting script of *Handsworth Songs*, generously provided by the Black Audio and Film Collective.
45 Anderson, op. cit., p. 30.
46 ibid., 132.
47 ibid.
48 ibid.
49 Levi-Strauss, op.cit., p. 58.
50 This collection, ch. 2, pp. 19–20.
51 ibid., p. 11.
52 Lefort, op.cit., p. 303.
53 W. Benjamin, 'The storyteller', in *Illuminations.* trans. Harry Zohn (London: Cape, 1970), p. 87.
54 M. Foucault, *The Archaeology of Knowledge*, trans. A. M. Sheridan Smith (London: Tavistock, 1972), p. 111.
55 C. Lévi-Strauss, op.cit., p. 35.
56 Benjamin, op.cit. p. 75.
57 W. Benjamin 'The Task of the Translator', *Illuminations* (London: Cape, 1970), p. 75.
58 N. Abraham and M.Torok, 'Introjection – Incorporation', in S. Lebovici and D. Widlocher (eds), *Psychoanalysis in France* (London: International Universities Press, 1980), p. 10.
59 J. Berger, *A Seventh Man* (Harmondsworth: Penguin, 1975). I have composed this passage from quotations that are scattered through the text.
60 Berger, op.cit., p. 216.
61 S. Freud, *Group Psychology and the Ego*, Standard Edition vol. XVIII (London: Hogarth, 1961), p. 119.
62 S. Rushdie, *The Satanic Verses* (New York: Viking, 1988), p. 337.
63 ibid., p. 130.
64 ibid., p. 145.
65 ibid., p. 320.
66 ibid., p. 353.
67 ibid., p. 354. I have slightly altered the presentation of this passage to fit in with the sequence of my argument.
68 Timothy Bahti and Andrew Benjamin have translated this much-discussed passage for me. What I want to emphasize is a form of the articulation of cultural difference that Paul de Man clarifies in his reading of Walter Benjamin's complex image of amphora.

> [Benjamin] is not saying that the fragments constitute a totality, he says that fragments are fragments, and that they remain essentially fragmentary. They follow each other metonymically, and they never constitute a totality.
> Paul de Man, *The Resistance to Theory*
> (Manchester: Manchester University Press, 1986), p. 91

Index

Aborigines 99, 100, 103; rights
obscured by multiculturalism 104;
Whitman's use of aboriginal names
185–6
Achebe, Chinua 232, 241–4; *Arrow of
God* 241, 243, 245, *No Longer at
Ease* 242; *Things Fall Apart* 242,
243–4
'action at a distance', concept rejected
by Dickens 214–15
Action Française 32, 36, 39
Addison, Joseph 142, 143
aeroplane, as phallic symbol 265;
significance of in Woolf's work
265–9; as symbol of change 282,
287; as symbol of freedom 275–7;
symbolic opposition to island 265,
267, 273, 278–9; as war-machine
282, 287
Africa, significance of in *Bleak House*
214–15, 219
African literature 237–44; eluding
nationalistic definition 232;
European criticism's treatment of
237–9; interpretation of European
influence 238–41
Afro-American literature 244–7
Alberdi, Juan Buatista 86–7
de Alencar, Jose, *O guarani* 80, 81, 82,
86
Allen, Ralph 142, 150
Althusser, Louis 128, 220–1, 294
America, interpretation of in *Uncle
Tom's Cabin* 199–202; westward
expension of 183–4, 185, 193–4
American culture, Whitman's failure to

notice nature of difference in
177–8
American literature, and Leavisian
criticism 260; and sentimentalism
205–7; values of 207
American Revolution, optimistic mood
of 183
Anderson, Benedict 31, 48, 49–50,
52, 55, 75, 84, 100, 103, 293;
Imagined Communities 1, 2, 308–11
Anderson, Perry 100, 252
Anderson, Quentin 178
anti-Semitism, and prehistory 40
aporia (impossibility of interpretation)
227–8
Arac, Jonathan 225, 228
Arendt, Hannah 2
artistic beauty, derived from custom
161
Asturias, Miguel 63; *El Senor Presidente*
57
Auden, W.H. 258, 267, 276, 286;
'Musée des Beaux Arts' 268; 'The
Old Masters' 280–1
Austen, Jane 147, 148
Austin, J.L. 180
Australia: The Daedalus Symposium 104,
107–12
Australia, analyses of 107–9; Labour
government 103, 104; nationalism in
139; post-war immigration 103–4,
108, 111–12; power in 108–9;
relationship with Britain 104
Australian culture, totalizing discourse
of 100, 107, 116
Australian literature, and non-Anglo-

Celtic writing 113–14; relationship with English literature 101–3, 105

Baker, Huston 296–7
Bakhtin, Mikhail 3, 50, 53–5, 60, 294–5, 298
Balibar, Renée 112
Barlow, Joel 187–8
Barrell, John 296
Barres, Maurice 38, 39
Barry, James 158, 159, 174
Barthes, Roland 113, 114
Bello, Andres 84; 'Historical method' 76–7
Benjamin, Walter 52, 55, 311, 314–15
Bentham, Jeremy, *A Fragment of Government* 162
Bernal, Martin 25, 27
Berndt, Catherine and Ronald 106
Bewley, Marius 260
Bill of Rights (1689) 146
Blackstone, Sir William 162, 167–8
Blainey, Geoffrey 107–8
Blake, William 174, 179, 180
Blest Gana, Alberto, *Martin Rivas* 79, 82, 85–6, 88
Bolingbroke, Viscount, *The Idea of a Patriot King* 140–1
Bolivar, Simon 58, 81
Boom novels of Latin America 71–5; and politics 73–4; relation to tradition 72–5, 90–2
Borges, Jorge Luis, 'The wall and the books' 73
Bosch, Juan 74
Boulanvilliers, Comte de 30, 35; *History of the Ancient Government* 26, 27
Brown, John 158, 165
Buckeridge, Bainbridge 154, 155
Burke, Edmund 146–8, 166, 170, 171, 219; *Reflections on the Revolution in France* 146, 171
Burnouf, Emile 32

Caesar, *On the Gallic Wars* 24
Carlyle, Thomas 183; *Past and Present* 150
Carpentier, Alejo 63; *The Kingdom of This World* 72
Carter, David 115–16
Castro, Brian 114–15
Castro, Fidel 71

catalogues in Whitman's style 180, 190–1, 193, 194
Cattaneo, Carlo 25, 27, 28, 29, 34, 40
Cervantes, Miguel, *Don Quixote* 233
character, in Leavisian criticism 252
Chateaubriand, François 82, 84, 254; *The Martyrs* 25–6
Chatterjee, Partha 293
Chaucer, Geoffrey, *The Canterbury Tales* 240
civic discourse, and customary aesthetic 168–70; and revolution 170–1
civic humanism 174
civil Imaginary, in eighteenth-century literature 142–4; operating within society 144
Clark, Leadie M. 177–8, 186
Clark, Manning 107; 'The forerunners' 106
class antagonism, in Leavisian criticism 257–9, 261
climate, effect on national character and art 156–9, 174, 319–20
Cofino Lopez, Manuel 90
Coleridge, Samuel Taylor 170–1
Colley, Linda 145
colonial literature 61–4; *see also* neocolonialism
common speech 53–4
community, bound together by ambivalence 299–300; represented by island 273, 284–6
community of interest, as foundation of nation 18
Comte, Augustus 128, 223
Concise Cambridge History of English Literature, The 234
Conrad, Joseph 6, 61–2, 250–1, 254–6, 260; *Nostromo* 255; *Typhoon* 255–6
conservative view of nation 2
consumerism 198; and feminization of American culture 205–7, 209
Cooper, J. Fenimore 182, 186
Cortazar, Julio 71
counter-revolution 145–7, 149
Coy, Rebecca 184
cultural contagion, between black and white literature 245–7
'cultural cringe' towards English culture 103

cultural difference 304, 312—15, 318;
and ambivalence of nation 199—202,
209—10, 233—9, 259—63; evoked
by postcolonialism 318
cultural studies 3; insight into
nationalism 47
culture, ownership of 100, 114—16
customary aesthetic, applied to
painting 164—5; and beauty 161;
and drama 172—3; and law 162—4;
necessary for representation of
nationhood 173—4
customary law 167—8

Dante, Alighieri, *The Divine Comedy*
233
Davis, Horace 57, 58
Debray, Regis 51—2
Defoe, Daniel 143, 144
Delaruelle, Jacques 115
Derrida, Jacques 4, 130, 291
Detienne, Marcel and Vernant, Jean-
Pierre, *Les ruses de l'intelligence* 228
Dickens, Charles 6, 213; *Bleak House*
213—29; humour in 226—7;
Leavisian criticism of 226; *Dombey
and Son* 225; *Little Dorrit* 220; *The
Pickwick Papers* 218, 227
difference, marking national
superiority 235
discursive formation (Foucault, q.v.)
46—7
Donoso, Jose, *A Personal History of the
Boom* 72
Donovan, Robert Aland 216
Dorfman, Ariel 48
Douglas, Ann, *The Feminization of
American Culture* 205—9
Ducios, Abbé, *Critical History of the
Founding of the French Monarchy* 26,
27—8
Durkheim, Emile 25, 32, 35—40, 223;
preface to the *Année Sociologique*
39—40; *The Division of Social Labour*
39; *The Elementary Forms of the
Religious Life* 36, 40; 'Individualism
and the intellectuals' 37
dynasty, as cause of nation 12—13

Eagleton, Terry 106, 215, 225; *Exiles
and Emigrés* 62; *The Function of
Criticism* 99—100

early tribes, symbolic importance of
23—4
Eliot, George 254
Eliot, T.S. 149; *Four Quartets* 286; 'The
Journey of the Magi' 242; *The Waste
Land* 286
Emerson, Ralph Waldo 178, 184
emigration, theory of in *Uncle Tom's
Cabin* 200, 201
Empires, legacy of 57
Engels, Friedrich 40, 46
English, no longer an English language
6, 48
English Civil War 52
English culture 269—70, 317—18; mid-
twentieth-century 'provincialism' of
261, 262
English reading, limitations of
'universality' 6
Englishness, Leavis's belief in
continuity of 253, 259
Enlightenment, in conflict with
Romanticism 24—5, 26—9, 29—31;
values of 1, 13, 124, 128
epic genre, and novel 50, 56
equality, in Whitman's writing 181—2
ethnography, *see* race
Euripides, *The Bacchae* 246
Europe, monopoly on 'universal
genius' 233—4
European Empire, impossibility of
establishing 8—9
exile, history of nation from viewpoint
of 291; as literary topos 60—4
experience, poststructuralist/Marxist
humanist debate on 214

family, establishment of in bourgeois
society 85; influence of on Leavisian
criticism 258—9; as meeting place of
nature and society 146—7; nuclear
198
Fanon, Frantz 4, 57, 63, 65, 318; *On
National Culture* 302
Faulkner, William 72
feminization, and colonization 208—9;
and growth of American
consumerism 205—7, 209; and idea
of nation 5—6; of men in *Uncle
Tom's Cabin* 203, 204—7, 209;
significance of in *Uncle Tom's Cabin*
205—10

Ferry, Jules 35—6
feudalism, first use of term 26
Fichte, Johann 57, 231
Fiedler, Leslie 75, 78
Fielding, Henry 142—4; *Tom Jones* 142, 143, 147
Flaubert, Gustave 149, 254, 255
forgetting, national necessity for 11, 16, 30—1, 310, 316
formalism, search for transnational narrative 234
Forster, E.M. 61, 258
Foucault, Michel 3, 46, 72, 142, 223, 227, 296, 301—2, 314; *Madness and Civilization* 219—20
Franco-Prussian War 29, 35, 36
Frankish invasions, and kingship 27—8
freedom, in America 197—8, 209—10
French history, Germanist approach to 23—4, 25—31; Romanist interpretation 26—9
French Revolution (1789) 29—30; and development of 'historical' novel 54; and origins of nationalism 140, 144—5, 231
French Revolution (1848) 213
Freud, Sigmund 235, 265, 300, 316; *The Uncanny* 295
Fry, Roger 155, 156, 282
Fuentes, Carlos, *The Death of Artemio Cruz* 72, 91—2
Fuseli, Henry 174
Fustel de Coulanges 25, 27, *The Ancient City* 31—2, 34—5, 38, 39; *Histoire des Institutions* 33, 34

Gallegos, Romulo 74; *Dona Barbara* 80, 81, 86, 88, 89, 90, 91
Galvan, Manuel de Jesus, *Enriquillo* 76, 77, 80—2, 86, 88—9
Garcia Marquez, Gabriel 60, 63, 71; *Autumn of the Patriarch* 57; *One Hundred Years of Solitude* 56, 72
Garis, Robert 225
Gellner, Ernest 23, 31, 32, 293, 298, 310
geography, as foundation of nation 18—19
Germanic invasions and foundations of nationhood 9—12, 23—40
Girard, René 85, 86

Goethe, Johann, *Faust* 233; *Italian Journey* 294
Gomez de Avellaneda, Gertrudis, *Sab* 79—80, 82, 86
Goodwin, Henry 184
Gordimer, Nadine 63
government authority, derivation of 163
Graubard, Stephen 107
Green, H.M., *History of Australian Literature* 105—6
Green, Martin, on F.R. Leavis 259, 261
Greene, Graham 61
Gregory of Tours 34; *History of the Franks* 24
Gross, John 227
Guizot 28, 29

Habermas 142—3; concept of the public sphere 99—100; in modern split between politics and ethics 142—3
Handsworth Songs (film) 306—8
Harlem Renaissance 296—7
Harrison, Martin 115
Hawthorne, Nathaniel 83, 205, 254; *The House of the Seven Gables* 83
Hazlitt, William 53, 146, 149—50, 155—6, 174; 'Patriotism' 136, 145
Hegel, Georg 192
Heine, Heinrich 145
Henkle, Roger, *Comedy and Culture* 227
Henriquez Urena, Pedro, 'Literary currents in Latin America' 74, 90
Herder 139, 231; concept of the *Volk* 53
Hesseltine, Harry 107
heteroglossia (Bakhtin) 50, 54
Hillis Miller, J. 225, 227
historical error, as factor in creation of nation 11
history, as dissolution of community 252—3; interpretation of in *Uncle Tom's Cabin* 199—202; relation to literature 76—9, 84—5
Hoare, Prince 158, 159
Hobsbawm, Eric 49, 50, 219, 291
Hobsbawm, Eric and Ranger, Terence 49
Hoggart, Richard 60
Hollis, C. Carroll 180, 190, 191, 193

Homer, *The Odyssey* 233, 240
Hope, A.D. 105; 'Standards in
  Australian literature' 102—3
Horne, Donald, 'Who rules Australia?'
  108, 110
humour, as *aporia* (impossibility of
  interpretation) 227—8; in *Bleak House*
  226—7

imperialism 45; 233; Dickens's attitude
  to 214
impersonality, in *Bleak House* 216, 217,
  222—4; conferring freedom on
  individual 223—4
inalienable rights 63
incest motif, in Latin-American novel
  86
individual, and changing theories of
  responsibility 219—25; identified
  with island 271; nature of in *Uncle
  Tom's Cabin* 201—2, 204;
  relationship to formation of 'people'
  302; restricted by dictates of nation
  198; rights of 29—30, 144—5; and
  significance of sympathetic heart
  200—1, 204
individual liberty, rise of demands for
  52—3
individual rights, declarations of 132
individuality, ethical dangers of 180
individuals, society composed of 38
industrialization, Whitman's depiction
  of 187—8
information and communication
  55—6
internationalism 1, 45
Ireland 269, 281; treatment of by
  English writers 213
Irish literature, and Leavisian criticism
  258—9
Irving, Washington 182
Isaacs, Jorge, *Maria* 79, 81, 82
island, identification of England with
  269; identification of individual with
  271; myth of fortress-island 266—7,
  270; significance of in Woolf's work
  266,269—73; in *To the Lighthouse*
  272—3

Jacobinism 29, 30—1, 32, 170, 171
Jahn, Jahnheinz, 'Neo-African
  literature' 238—9, 241

James, Henry 62, 147, 149, 236, 254,
  260
Jameson, Frederic 292
Jarrell, Randall 182
Jehlin, Meyra 83, 84
Johnson, Samuel 83, 162—3, 171, 231,
  245
Jose, Nicholas 107, 109—10
Joyce, James 72, 236, 260; *Finnegans
  Wake* 179; *A Portrait of the Artist as a
  Young Man* 268, 280; *Ulysses* 231,
  232

Kant, Immanuel 149; categorical
  imperative 38—9; *Idea for a Universal
  History* 131; *Perpetual Peace* 131
Kaplan, Justin 177, 178
Keats, John 250, 253—4
Kedourie, Elie 57
Kern, Stephen 273
Kettle, Arnold 215—16
Kierkegaard, Soren 180
Kincaid, Robert 225
King, Bruce 53
Kipling, Rudyard 61
Kirkham, E. Bruce 208
knowledge, as purpose of painting
  161—2
Kohler, Erich 234
Kohn, Hans 57, 59
Kramer, Leonie 104, 107, 109
Kristeva, Julia 292; *Women's Time*
  303—6

landscape, as analogy for 'enigma of
  language' 297; as metaphor for
  national identity 295; and writing
  the nation 297
language 10; effect on national
  character and art 156—9; as
  foundation of nation 16—17; as
  'pedigree' of nations 231—2, 245;
  providing continuity in culture
  252—4; resilience of English 286; as
  tool of power 189—90
Latin-American novel 64—6, 71—92;
  of 'Boom' 71—5, 90—2
law, customary 167—8; and customary
  aesthetic 162—4, 167—8; demand for
  new code of 173; natural 128, 146
law codes, as historical sources 24
Lawrence, D.H. 61, 177, 186, 192

Le Carré, John, *The Little Drummer Girl* 215
Leavis, F.R. 100, 250–63; Clark lectures (1967) 262; *The Great Tradition* 149, 254–6, 260; *Revaluation* 254, 256, 257, 258, 262
Leavis, F.R. and Leavis, Q.D., *Dickens the Novelist* 226
Leavis, Q.D. 250, 257–9; Cheltenham lecture 6, 262–3
Leavisian criticism, based on limited historical period 260–3; as intellectual confinement 262–3
Lefort, Claud 297–8, 300, 311
Left, denunciation of 'imperialism' 45
Leggett, William 188
Lehmann-Haupt, Christopher, review of *Mumbo Jumbo* 246–7
Lévi-Strauss, Claude 39–40, 234, 301, 313
Lewis, Gordon 47, 186
liberation theology 66
liberty, classical (Roman) 29–31; modern 29–31
Lincoln, Abraham 199
linear model of western cultural development 235–6
literary criticism, origins of 149; unbalanced by reliance on 'national experience' 213
literary writing, creation of 'civil imaginary' 142–4; and patriotism 141–5
literature, influence on nationalism 48, 138, 149–51; relation to history 76–9, 84–5
local form, as basis of artistic beauty 161, 165–6
Locke, John 145; *Second Treatise of Government* 163
lower social groups, representation of in novel 52
Lowth, Robert 163–4
Lukács, Georg 54–5, 56; *The Historical Novel* 82, 83–4
Lyotard, J.F. 76, 122, 301; *The Postmodern Condition* 123; 'What is postmodernism?' 123

McLuhan, Marshall, *The Mechanical Bride* 198, 209
magical realism 56, 72; in cinema 75

Mahler, Gustav 236
Malinowski, definition of myth 44–5
Mann, Thomas 236
marginal positions, of Afro-Americans 296–7; and re-interpretation of nation 291
marginalization of nation, exploration of 4–6
Mariategui, Carlos José 48–9
Marmol, José, *Amalia* 79, 86, 89
marriage, and establishment of nation 76, 81, 86; and family alliances 86, 88–9
Marti, José 77
Martin, R.B., *The Triumph of Wit* 227
Marx, Karl 32, 40, 46, 315
Marxist humanism, debate with poststructuralism on experience 214
Mattelart, Armand 46
Matthiesson, F.O., *American Renaissance* 178, 190
Matto de Turner, Clorinda, *Aves sin nido* 80, 82, 86
meaning, nature of explored in *Uncle Tom's Cabin* 201
Melville, Hermann 83, 184, 205
metaphor, in nation's transference of community 291; Whitman's avoidance of 191, 193
Meyers, Jeffrey, *Fiction and the Colonial Experience* 61–2
Michelakakis, George 112
migration, and modern nation 291, 315–17
military values, and education 283; praised by Renan (q.v.) 30
Mill, John Stuart 214, 259
Miller, David 225; 'Discipline in different voices' 227
Miller, Perry 83
Milner, Andrew 100, 107
minority discourse, and foreignness of languages 314–18; and post-colonial cultural pluralism 47–8
Mitre, Bartolome 77; *Soledad* 85, 86
modern nation, ambivalence of 293–4
modernism, ambivalence about 'maturity' of Western culture 235–6
Monod, Gabriel 33
Montesquieu, Charles-Louis 158; *Esprit des lois* 128; *Mes Pensées* 125;

Of Politics 124—5; *The Spirit of the Laws* 26
moral consciousness, and establishment of nation 20—1
Morin, Edgar 121
Morris, William 53
motherhood, in American culture 209; in *Bleak House* 214; in *Uncle Tom's Cabin* 202—3, 205—6, 210
multiculturalism 100, 103—4, 108, 109—10; and assimilation 111, 114; as counter-public sphere 114—16; definition of 99; political use of 104, 110—11; turning minority cultures into folklore 112
Murray, Les 110
myth 44—5; 'myths of the nation' 44, 47, 48—9

Nairn, Tom 2, 57; *The Break-up of Britain* 45
narcissism, in attitudes to other races 235
narrative, circularity of 301; derivation of forms 238—9; distancing of in *Bleak House* 225—6; distancing from aerial position 282, 283; of the 'meanwhile' 308—10; and origin of nation 121, 130—2; unisonance of 310; weakened in Leavisian analysis of novel 255
narrative voice, in English prose 146—8
nation, ambivalence of 2—4, 45; as attempt to combat disorder 51—2; attempts to define 5—6, 8—21, 45, 231—2; autonomy relative to other nations 130—1; based on shared experience 19—20; boundaries of 121, 129—30; claims to modernity 293; conservative view of 2; Durkheim's view of 35—40; as fiction/myth 48—9; influence of classical city state 8; instability of concept 232; institution of 121—2; interpretation of as forms of narrative 2—3; as merging of public and private interests 2; and migration 47—8, 60—4, 156—7, 314—16; novelty of 9; origins of 1, 49; as representation of social life 1—2; represented by 'universal' authors 233—4; as result of dynasty

12—13; and sexual difference 5—6, 88—9, 200, 202—9, 258—9; as spiritual principle 18, 19—21; temporality of 3
nation-space, liminality of 299—301
nation-state, as most influential political institution 139; origins of 58—9; *see also* Germanic invasions
national character, and establishment of national taste 169—70; factors influencing 156—9; Pevsner on 156—8; phlegmatic nature of English 155, 156; and place of ornament in art 166—7
national culture, depiction of in painting 154, 156; framed by new code of laws 173; and post-war immigration 156—7
national literature, definition of 99; origins of 234—5; and privileging of national experience 213
national narrative, complexity of time structure 295—6; emergence of 295—7
nationalism, ambivalence of 45; approach of cultural studies 47; and cultural criticism 61; dependence on cultural criteria 235; effect on religion 50—2; and emergent societies 44, 45; and exile 60—4; following separation from European domination 58; and imperialism 138—9; influence on forms of literature 48; and intellectual dependence 59—60; invention of term 139; limiting cyclical theories of art 236, 243; opposed by patriotism 159; relation to state 58; taking over social role of religion 59; and totalitarianism 57
nationalist ideology, employment of language in 231—2
nationhood, influence on marriage 88—9
natural law 128, 146
natural rights 172
nature, abuse of in *Uncle Tom's Cabin* 203, 204
Nazism, use of Tacitus's *Germania* 24
neocolonialism 58—64; in post-war novel 56
New Left Review 213, 214

Nietzsche, Friedrich 221, 235, 314;
   Genealogy of Morals 219
Novalis 231
novel, in America in 1850s 199, 205;
   based on folklore 53; contrasted with
   romance 82–5; elitist nature of in
   Third World 56; as female form of
   literature 82, 83; fixing boundaries of
   nation 49–50; in Leavisian criticism
   254–6, 262–3; and nation-building
   77, 80–1; postmodern 54–6; and
   rise of European nationalism 49–56

Oakeshott, Michael, 'Character of a
   modern European state' 2
Opie, John 158, 159
oral tradition, in African literature 239,
   241
oral and written literature 55
ornament, and national culture 166–7;
   necessity of in painting 158, 165–6
Oxford History of Australian Literature 104

Paine, Thomas 145; *Common Sense* 162
painting, civil humanist theory of
   159–60, 161, 164, 166; and
   depiction of character 155; and
   depiction of national culture 154,
   156; English school of 154–5;
   history as highest genre of 155,
   161–2; as narrative 156; and
   portraiture 155; privatization of 174;
   and representation of form 155–6; as
   representation of general customs
   164–5
Pater, Walter 53–4
patriotism 138; as liberation 145–6;
   and literary writing 141–5, 152;
   meaning of in eighteenth century
   140–5; opposed to nationalism 159;
   Woolf's attitude to 281
pedagogical and performative presence,
   split between 297–9
Penrose, Harald, *British Aviation: The
   Ominous Skies 1935–39* 266–7
people, as marginal integration of
   individuals 301; in narrative address
   of nation 297–302
Pevsner, Nikolaus, *The Englishness of
   English Art* 156
Phillips, A.A. 105; 'The cultural cringe'
   103

philology, comparative 31, 39–40; and
   formation of 'national' literatures 44,
   53; humanist approach 31, 39–40
de Piles, Roger, *Art of Painting* 154
Plato, *The Republic* 89
Poe, Edgar Allan 205
poetry, and development of literary
   criticism 149
politics, and Boom novels 73–4;
   erotics of 76, 85–8, 89, 90; and
   romances 75–6, synonymous with
   style in Whitman's work 178–9; in
   The Waves 280
Poole, Roger 283
Pope, Alexander, *Epilogues to the Satires*
   142
population increase 86–7
populist culture, influence on romances
   90
portraiture, English painters' strength
   in 155
post-colonialism, in Australia 139; and
   effects of immigration 47–8, 156–7;
   and 'nation-centredness' 45, 47,
   61–2; and nature of new nations
   57–60; and nature of responsibility
   63–4; and Rushdie (q.v.) on
   changing uses of English 6, 48,
   316–18
post-structuralism 132, 147; debate
   with Marxist humanism on
   experience 214; and politics 123–4;
   problematics of term 122–3; relation
   to structuralism 123; social and
   historical effects of 123
post-structuralism terms in
   interpretation of nation 3–4
post-war immigration, and national
   culture 156–7
postal politics 124–8; complexity of
   125–6; post coming before politics
   124–5; 'post' taken as postal
   network 124; and secrecy 127
postcolonial novel 139, 151–2
postmodernism 123
Pound, Louise 185
Powell, Enoch 2
prehistory, Romantic interest in 32–3
Pritchett, V.S. 226
professionalism, attitude to in *Bleak
   House* 216–18; politics of in *Bleak
   House* 226–9

public and counter-public sphere
99—100
public virtue, as purpose of painting
159—60, 161, 166

de Quincey, Thomas, *The English Mailcoach* 150—1

race, as foundation of nation 13—16;
see also African literature, Australian literature
radicalism, English 145—6
reader, ideal 251—2, 261
reading, audience for 250; and Leavisian criticism 250—2
realism, changing concepts of 52
Reed, Ishmael 6, 232; *Mumbo Jumbo* 241, 244—7
religion, Durkheim's attitude to 36, 39; as foundation of nation 17—18; modernized by nationalism 50—2, 59; sharing of 10, 11
Renan, Ernest 309—10; *La Monarchie Constitutionelle* 31; *La Réforme Intellectuelle et Morale* 30, 31
republicanism, and education 35—6; Fustel's opposition to 33—4
responsibility, Althusser's views on 220—1; in nineteenth-century business world 218—19; relationship with experience 216—25; and violence in *Bleak House* 221, 223—4
Review of National Literature: Australia 104, 105—7
Reynolds, Sir Joshua 154, 160—74; *Discourses* 161—70, 174; essay on Shakespeare 168, 172—4; essays in *The Idler* 160—1; 'The Ironic Discourse' 171—2
Richards, I.A. 149
Richardson, Samuel 143, 144; *Clarissa* 86
Ricoeur, Paul 46
rights, inalienable 63; individual 29—30, 132, 144—5; natural 172
Roa Bastos, Augusto 63
Roman Empire 9
romances, contrasted with novel 82—5; definition of 82, 83; extent of common ground 79, 80—1; femininity of heroes 88, 89; influence of popular culture 90;

mixture of genres 82—5; predating Boom 75; and rape 91—2
Romanticism, and comparative philology 31—2; compared with sentimentalism 206, 207; concept of 'universal genius' 233; conflict with Enlightenment values 24—5, 26—9, 29—31; and literary depiction of nationalism 44; rejection of 38, 39
Rousseau, Jean-Jacques 52—3, 84, 89, 138, 144, 170; *Emile* 128—9; *Julie* 85; *Project for a Constitution for Corsica* 130—1; *The Social Contract* 129
Rushdie, Salman 6, 48, 63—4; *The Satanic Verses* 317—19; *Shame* 57

Sade, Marquis de 130—1
Said, Edward 3, 25, 27, 44, 60, 100, 138, 234, 292, 299—300
de Sanctis, Francesco 48
Sarmiento, Domingo F. 85, 86
Sartre, Jean-Paul 236
Schaeffle, *Bau und Leben des socialien Körpers* 36—8
Schiller, Herbert 57, 60, 149
scientific theory, Woolf's employment of 280
Scott, Sir Walter 82—4, 148; article on romance 83; *Waverley* 147, 149
Scrutiny 253, 257, 258, 259, 260—1
Sears, Sallie 283
self, relationship with world 184
sentimentalism, validity of in *Uncle Tom's Cabin* 205—7
Seton-Watson, Hugh 47, 57
Shaftesbury, Lord 161, 162
Shakespeare, Reynolds' essay on 172—4
Shakespeare, William, Leavis's attitude to 253; *King Lear* 233; *Richard II* 269—71; *The Tempest* 271
Sieyes, Abbé 144, 231
signification, movement of (Lefort) 297—8; strategies of 296
situational consciousness' (national allegory) 292
slavery, position in *Uncle Tom's Cabin* 205, 207—8; Whitman's attitude to 186—7
Smiles, Samuel 220
Smith, Adam, *The Wealth of Nations* 187—8

social evil, systemic nature of in *Bleak House* 215—17
sociology, basis of in *Bleak House* 223; foundations of 25, 35—40
Sorel, Georges 30, 31; 'The Germanism and historicism of Ernest Ronan' 23
Soyinka, Wole 238, 240; *Blues for a Prodigal* 243
Spengler, Oswald 242, 260
state, relation to nationalism 58
Steele, Sir Richard 142, 143
Stein, Gertrude, *Picasso* 265—6
Stephenson, P.R., 'The foundations of culture in Australia' 101—2, 113
Stowe, Harriet Beecher, *Uncle Tom's Cabin* 199—208
Stowe, Harriet Beecher and Beecher, Catherine, *The American Woman's Home* 208—9
Stravinsky, Igor 236
structuralism, search for transnational narrative 234
Swinton, William, *Rambles Among Words* 190, 195

Tacitus, *Germania* 24, 26—7, 33, 35
Tave, Stuart, *Amiable Humorist* 227
Thackeray, William Makepeace 254
Thierry, Augustin 28, 29, 33; *Considerations on the History of France* 25—6
Third Estate, and Romanist thesis 27—8, 29
Third World, authoritarianism in 57; elitist nature of novel in 56; fiction in 46—7
Thompson, Denys 258
time structures, narrative of the 'meanwhile' 308—10
Todorov, Tzvetan 309
Tompkins, Jane, 'Sentimental power: *Uncle Tom's Cabin* and the politics of literary history' 205—9
transcendentalism, American 184
translation, and Australian native literature 99, 100—1, 106, 111; and cultural difference 314—15
Traubel, Horace 177
Turkish Empire 11, 12
Tutuola, Amos 232, 237, 239—41; *The Palm-Wine Drinkard* 238, 239—40

universality, as accumulation for white perspective 244—5; African approach to 245—7; as applied to African literature 237—9, 244; as critical term 232
unmotivated novels 147

Vaille, Eugene, *Histoire générale des postes françaises* 124—5
Vargas Llosa, Mario 63, 64, 71; *Aunt Julia and the Scriptwriter* 74—5; *Conversation in the Cathedral* 64; *The War at the End of the World* 64—6
Venetian art, English affinity for 157, 165
Vertue and Walpole, *Anecdotes of Painting in England* 155
Veyne, Paul 76
Vico, *First New Science* 26—7
Villaverde, Cirilio, *Cecilia Valdes* 79, 86
violence, and nature of responsibility in *Bleak House* 221, 223—4

Wagner, Richard 236
Wallace-Crabbe, Chris, 'The legend of the legend of the nineties' 107
Ware, Lois 184, 193
Waten, Judah, *Alien Son* 105
Wellek, Rene 250—1
Wells, H.G. 231, 233; 'The argonauts of the air' 267; 'Filmer' 267; 'The present uselessness and danger of aeroplanes' 267; *The War in the Air* 266; *The Way the World is Going* 272
Western domination of world culture 60; *see also* universality
White, Patrick 105, 152
Whitman, Walt 177—95; attitude to England 189; attitude to nature of difference 177—8; avoidance of metaphor 191, 193; change of style in mid-career 192—5; childlike vision 182; claims to democracy 178; conventionality of 184—5; depiction of American spirit 188—9; depiction of himself 191—2; depiction of industrialization 187—8; evocation of senses 181—2; extent of socialism 177, 178; representation of women 180; and slavery debate 186—7; style 178—81; treatment of death 194—5; use of foreign words

in style 185—6, 190; *An American Primer* 178, 185, 189; *Drum Taps* 193—4, 195; *The Eighteenth Presidency* 187; *Leaves of Grass* 178, 179, 185—93 *passim*; *Specimen Days* 193; 'Passage to India' 194; 'Pioneers! O Pioneers!' 193; 'Prayer of Columbus' 194

Williams, Raymond 45, 51, 225, 258, 299; *Politics and Letters* 213—14, 216; *The Country and the City* 263

women, identified with nation 87—8, 91; Whitman's attitude to 180

women's movement, and counter-public sphere 100

Woolf, Virginia 257—8, 265—88; *Between the Acts* 265, 266, 267, 269, 281—8; *Mrs Dalloway* 265, 267, 274—6, 282, 283, 284; *Orlando* 265, 267, 275, 276, 277—8, 282, 286—7; *A Room of One's Own* 277; *Three Guineas* 257—8, 283; *To the Lighthouse* 272—3; *The Voyage Out* 266; *The Waves* 277, 279; *The Years* 265, 267, 281; 'Flying over London' 267; 'The leaning tower' 276

'wordliness', Said's concept of 292

Wordsworth, William 53

work, as alternative to nihilism in *Bleak House* 218

World War One 265—6, 267

World War Two 283—8

Wright, Judith 108

Wright Mills, C. 60

Writing in Multicultural Australia 104, 114

Yeats, W.B. 267, 268; 'An Irish Airman Foresees his Death' 269; 'Reprisals' 269; 'The Second Coming' 242, 243

Young, Robert 123

Ziff, Larzer, *Literary Democracy* 181